Tenth Edition

Contemporary Urban Planning

JOHN M. LEVY

Routledge
Taylor & Francis Group

LONDON AND NEW YORK

First published 2013, 2011, 2009, 2006 by Pearson Education, Inc.

Published 2016 by Routledge
2 Park Square, Milton Park, Abingdon, Oxon OX14 4RN
711 Third Avenue, New York, NY, 10017, USA

Routledge is an imprint of the Taylor & Francis Group, an informa business

ISBN: 9780205851737 (pbk)

Cover Designer: Karen Salzbach

Library of Congress Cataloging-in-Publication Data
Levy, John M.
  Contemporary urban planning / John M. Levy.—10th ed.
    p. cm.
  Includes index.
  ISBN-13: 978-0-205-85173-7
  ISBN-10: 0-205-85173-8
  1. City planning—United States. 2. Urban policy—United States. 3. Urbanization—United States.
4. Sociology, Urban—United States. I. Title.
  HT167.L38 2013
  307.1'2160973—dc23

                                                                    2012000413

Please visit the companion website at www.routledge.com/9780205851737

To Lucie, Rachel, Bernie, Kara, and Christopher

Contents

PART 1 THE BACKGROUND AND DEVELOPMENT OF CONTEMPORARY PLANNING _____

1 An Overview   1
The Need for Planning   1   The Specific Concerns
of Planning   3   Who Are the Planners?   4   Professional
Organizations   5   Satisfactions and Discontents   6
Useful Abilities   7   The Plan of This Book   7   Notes   8

2 The Urbanization of America   9
Urbanization in the Nineteenth Century   9   Urban Trends
in the Twentieth Century   15   Summary   25
Notes   26   Selected Bibliography   26

3 The History of Planning: Part I   27
Colonial America   28   Limited Means and Growing
Problems   30   The Pressure for Reform   31   The Birth of
Modern City Planning   38   The Public Control of Private
Property   40   The Emergence of Regional and State
Planning   44   Grander Visions   47   Summary   51
Notes   52   Selected Bibliography   52

4 The History of Planning: Part II   53
Planning and the Great Depression   53   The Postwar
Period   56   Summary   66   Notes   67   Selected
Bibliography   67

PART 2 THE STRUCTURE AND PRACTICE OF CONTEMPORARY PLANNING _____

5 The Legal Basis of Planning   68
The Constitutional Framework   68   Public Control over
Private Property   70   The Rights of Nonresidents   80

The Fight over Eminent Domain   82   State-Enabling
Legislation   84   The Federal Role   86   Summary   88
Notes   89   Selected Bibliography   90

6   Planning and Politics   91
Why Is Planning Political?   91   Planners and Power   93
The Fragmentation of Power   94   Styles of Planning   98
How Planning Agencies Are Organized   100
Summary   103   Notes   104   Selected Bibliography   104

7   The Social Issues   105
The Social Issues in Planning for Housing   106   Other
Issues   115   Who Does Social Planning?   119
Summary   120   Notes   120   Selected Bibliography   121

8   The Comprehensive Plan   122
The Goals of Comprehensive Planning   122   The
Comprehensive Planning Process   124   How Effective Are
Comprehensive Plans?   132   Summary   133   Notes   133
Selected Bibliography   134

9   The Tools of Land-Use Planning   135
Public Capital Investment   135   Financing Capital
Expenditures   136   Land-Use Controls   140
Making Zoning More Flexible   149   Form-Based
Zoning   160   Other Types of Local Land-Use
Controls   163   Combining Capital Investment and
Land-Use Controls   164   Forces Beyond Local
Control   166   Summary   168   Notes   169
Selected Bibliography   170

PART 3   FIELDS OF PLANNING

10   Urban Design   171
What Is Urban Design?   172   The Urban Design
Process   176   What Is Good Urban Design?   181
Replanning Suburbia: The Neotraditionalists   187
Edge City   193   Visions of the City of the Future   199
Coming to Terms with the Automobile   204
Summary   205   Notes   206   Selected Bibliography   206

11   Urban Renewal and Community Development   208

Urban Renewal   209   Community Development   218
The Housing Question   221   Planning for Housing   223
The Housing Bubble and the Problem of Abandonment   226
Summary   233   Notes   234   Selected Bibliography   235

12   Transportation Planning   236

Recent Trends in Urban Transportation   236   Paying for
Transportation   240   Transportation Planning and Land
Use   241   The Transportation Planning Process   243
Changes in the Federal Role   253   Fine-Tuning
the System   254   The Growing Role of Tolls and
Privatization   255   Smart Highways, Intelligent Vehicles,
and New Machines   257   Summary   259   Notes   261
Selected Bibliography   261

13   Economic Development Planning   262

Historic Roots   263   Perspectives on Local Economic
Development   264   State Economic Development
Efforts   267   Local Economic Development
Programs   269   Summary   278   Notes   278
Selected Bibliography   279

14   Growth Management, Smart Growth, and Sustainable Development   280

The Origins of Growth Management   282   Winners and
Losers in Growth Management   283   A Sampling of
Local Growth Management Programs   285   State-Level
Growth Management   289   Growth Management—Pro
or Con?   294   The Challenge of Smart Growth   295
Planning for Sustainability   298   Summary   303
Notes   304   Selected Bibliography   306

15   Environmental and Energy Planning   307

The Environmental Planning Problem   308
The Question of Global Climate Change   308
Environmental Progress at the National Level   311
A Brief History of National Environmental Policy   314
The Link Between National and Local Environmental
Planning   321   Economic and Political Issues in

Environmental Planning   323   Local Environmental
Planning   327   Energy Planning   331
Summary   338   Notes   339
Selected Bibliography   340

16   Planning for Metropolitan Regions   341
The Political Problem   341   A Brief History of
Metropolitan-Area Planning   343   Minneapolis–St. Paul:
A Tale of Two Cities   347   The Port Authority
of New York and New Jersey   349   The Atlanta Regional
Commission   354   Summary   356   Notes   357
Selected Bibliography   357

PART 4   LARGER QUESTIONS

17   National Planning in the United States   358
Is There National Planning in the United States?   358
The Pattern of Land Settlement   359   Establishing the Rail
Network   361   Water and the West   362   Systematic
Regional Planning   366   The Interstate Highway
System   369   Financing the Suburbs   372
Land Management   375   What's Next?   376
Summary   377   Notes   377   Selected Bibliography   379

18   Planning in Other Nations   380
Planning in Western Europe   380   Planning in Eastern
Europe   408   Planning in Asia   414   Summary   419
Notes   420   Selected Bibliography   422

19   Planning Theory   423
Is Theory Necessary?   423   A Distinction Between Public
and Private Planning   424   The Process of Planning   425
Advocacy Planning: The Question of for Whom   434
Planning from Right and Left   435   Summary   440
Notes   441   Selected Bibliography   442

Index   443

Preface

The term *Planning* is a very general one. There are city and town planners and also corporate planners. The Pentagon employs numerous military planners. The launching of a space shuttle is the culmination of a tremendously complex and sophisticated planning process. And so on.

Planning in its generic meaning, then, is an ubiquitous activity. All types of planning have a conscious effort in common to systematically improve the quality of decision making. The planning discussed in this book is a very small part of the total planning activity in the United States. Specifically, this book focuses on public planning at the substate level, that done by and for cities, counties, towns, and other units of local governments. We will also examine, much more briefly, planning for metropolitan regions, the states, and the question of national planning. One chapter contains a brief survey of planning in other nations.

New to This Edition

This edition of *Contemporary Urban Planning* includes the following new material:

- Updated coverage of the financial crisis and its implications for housing and urban development
- New information on planning for natural catastrophes
- New developments in urban transportation planning, policy and technology
- A discussion on Collaborative Rationality as the next major development in planning theory
- A new section on planning in Asia
- A revised and expanded section on energy planning
- Updated information on environmental policy under the Obama administration
- Coverage on the prospects for high speed inter-city rail transportation

The reader who has sampled other books on planning will notice that this book has some particular emphases, specifically on politics, economics, ideology, law, and the question of winners and losers in particular decisions. These emphases stem from my experience as a working planner. I entered planning in 1969 with a background in economics and journalism but with no specific training in planning. I assumed that if architects planned buildings, then city and town planners planned cities and towns in a similar way; in effect, I thought it was architecture writ large.

It did not take me long to learn that I was wrong. Planning is a highly political activity. It is immersed in politics, and inseparable from the law. The ultimate arbiter of many a planning dispute is the court. And for every case that comes to court, many planning decisions are conditioned by what the participants in the process think would be the decision if the matter did come to court.

Planning decisions often involve large sums of money, both public and private. Even when little public expenditure is involved, planning decisions can deliver large benefits to some and large losses to others. Thus one must understand something of the economic and financial issues at stake.

The study of planning quickly takes one into ideology. Planning issues and controversies inevitably raises questions about the proper role of government and the line between public needs and private rights. What properly is to be a matter of political decision, and what properly should be left to the market? Planners are a fairly idealistic lot and often enter the field to serve the public interest. After immersion in a few public controversies, the beginning planner may wonder whether there *is* such a thing as the public interest, for if there is, there ought to be some general agreement among the public on what it is. But one can spend a long time in some areas of planning without seeing a single instance of this agreement.

I have tried to convey something of the reality of planning practice and of what goes on under the surface of events. I hope that the reader will not find this reality disillusioning, for planning in an open and a democratic society cannot be smooth and simple. Planning as it is—involved in political controversy, tied to legal and economic questions, and connected to issues of ideology—is far more interesting than it would be if it were simply architecture writ large.

The book contains a certain amount of material on history and technology because the issues that planning focuses on are largely ones that political, social, demographic and economic changes bring to the forefront.

The best and most effective planners are those with good peripheral vision—those who not only have mastered the technical side of planning but also understand the relationships between planning issues and the major forces in the society around them. I have endeavored to write a text consistent with that view.

Acknowledgments

It is not possible to thank everyone who assisted in the writing of this book. However, I would like to express gratitude to my former colleagues in the Department of Urban Affairs and Planning at Virginia Tech in Blacksburg, Virginia. Various editions of this book have been reviewed by Ellen Bassett, Mirle Rabinowitz Bussell, Carissa Schively, Sheri Smith, Sujata Shetty, among others, and I am grateful to all of them.

For 10 years before I became an academic, I was employed in various capacities by the Westchester County, New York, Department of Planning, where I had the fine opportunity to learn some of the realities of planning. I am thus indebted to a number of my former colleagues there, in particular Commissioner Peter Q. Eschweiler and Planning Board Chairman the late Dr. William Cassella. When all is said and done, however, the viewpoints expressed here and any mistakes made are my own.

John M. Levy

CHAPTER 1

An Overview

THE NEED FOR PLANNING

Perhaps the first question that has to be answered in a book about planning is simply "why do we need planning?" The need for planning comes down to two words, *interconnectedness* and *complexity.* If there were few of us and the technologies by which we lived were relatively simple, there would be little need for the planning described in this book. We could each go our own way and would gain little from common planning efforts. However, the fact is that we are numerous enough and our technologies complicated enough that this is not the case.

Consider a simple illustration of *interconnectedness,* the use of a few acres of urban land. The amount and character of development on that land will determine the amount of traffic it generates. Developing it with single-family houses will produce a different traffic flow than developing it with apartments, which will generate a different traffic flow than developing it with a neighborhood shopping center. Thus a land development decision is a traffic decision as well. That, potentially, affects everyone in the area. How much of the site is paved, and even what material is used for paving, affects how fast rainwater runs off from the property. Runoff may affect flooding and stream flow conditions miles downstream from the property. The types and quantities of commercial or residential activity on the property may affect air quality, noise levels, water quality, and the visual and social qualities of the area.

Decisions about the residential uses of land will affect housing prices, rents, and vacancies—in short, who lives in the community. Those decisions, in turn, will have effects on the economy of the community and the demands that are placed on the community for educational, social, and other services.

The land-use decisions made by a community shape its very character—what it is like to walk through, what it is like to drive through, what kinds of jobs and businesses exist in it, how well the natural environment survives, and whether the community is an attractive one or an ugly one. In some cases such decisions may directly affect human life and health, for example, whether traffic patterns are safe or hazardous.

Land-use decisions affect the fiscal health of the community. Every property that is developed burdens the community with obligations such as education, police and fire protection, recreational services, and social services. Conversely, every development contributes, directly or indirectly, to municipal revenues through property taxes, sales taxes, or charges and fees. Thus the pattern of land development will affect how heavily the community must tax its residents and the level of public services the community can provide.

The land in question may be privately owned, in which case public control is exercised through a regulatory process. It may be owned publicly, in which case direct public investment will determine its use. But in either case there is a distinct public interest in what happens on the land. It is the fact of interconnectedness that helps justify public planning efforts.

Complexity is the condition that justifies planning as a separate profession and as a separate activity of government. If all of the sorts of relationships suggested were simple, they could be dealt with simply and informally. If the community were tiny, perhaps direct negotiations between private parties would suffice. If the community were somewhat larger, perhaps the relationships could easily be dealt with along with the general flow of municipal business. But the complexity of a modern community renders such simple and direct approaches inadequate.

The complexity of the community also means that many things that in a simpler place could be done privately must be done publicly. In a sparsely populated area water supply and waste disposal could be handled on-site by the individual household. No common decision making would be necessary. In a large metropolitan area, these functions may involve systems that span many communities and involve billions of dollars of capital investment. Comparable comments could be made about transportation, education, public safety, recreation, and the like.

Thus in the thousands of communities in the United States, planning is a formalized and distinct process of government. In relatively small communities, the planning function may be lodged in an unpaid, part-time planning board with the technical work done by a planning consultant. In larger communities, the planning function is generally located within a planning department. Depending on community size, that department may have a staff ranging from one person to several hundred individuals.

In a very small department, the planner (or planners) may be a jack-of-all-trades handling land-use questions one day, capital budgeting another day, and economic development a third day. In a larger agency, there may be considerable specialization of labor. One section of the agency may specialize in zoning issues, another in master planning, a third in planning-related research, another in environmental issues, and so on.

THE SPECIFIC CONCERNS OF PLANNING

What might a community seek to achieve through planning? In a growing community, planners might be concerned with shaping the pattern of growth to achieve a sensible and attractive land-use pattern. That concern means avoiding both oppressively dense development and overly scattered, fragmentary development. It means encouraging a pattern of development that gives residents ready access to recreational, cultural, school, shopping, and other facilities. It means having a street pattern that is convenient to use and through which traffic flows without excessive congestion. It means separating incompatible land uses and activities, for example, high-intensity commercial activity from residential areas. In a modern planned community, it might mean providing a system of pathways so that pedestrian and bicycle traffic is separated from automobile traffic.

The community's planners will also be concerned with the location of public facilities like schools and social service centers, both for the convenience of the people served and for reinforcing the development of a desirable land-use pattern. If the community anticipates or desires significant industrial or commercial development, its planners will be concerned with seeing that sufficient, conveniently located blocks of land are available and that they are served with adequate roads, water, and sewer facilities.

In an older community that is not growing and that does not anticipate growth, planners may be concerned primarily with preserving or improving that which now exists. Thus planners may focus on measures to preserve the quality of the housing stock. In many communities planners will also be concerned with housing cost questions, specifically, how to provide housing for the community's lower-income residents. In many older communities, planners devote much effort to preserving historic buildings and other landmarks. If the community is concerned (as many are) about the health of its downtown, planners may be involved in implementing street improvements and other changes designed to help downtown businesses compete successfully with establishments in outlying areas.

In a community that faces a serious unemployment problem or that sees its property tax base as being inadequate, economic development may be a major task of the planners. Much of their effort may be devoted to creating conditions that encourage existing industry to remain and expand and new firms to locate within the community.

In recent years much planning effort has focused on environmental issues: how to guide and manage development to minimize environmental damage. For example, a planner might be concerned with evaluating the relative environmental merits and financial costs of landfill disposal versus incineration for a municipality's solid wastes and then with helping select the best site.

Planners employed by regional planning organizations may be concerned with improving the regionwide road network, with acquiring or developing land for a regionwide park and open space system, or with improving regionwide sewage disposal and water systems. They will also be concerned with encouraging coordination between the planning efforts of the various municipalities in the region to avoid duplication of capital facilities and interference effects (for example, community A siting its landfill operation at a point where it borders a residential area in community B).

This is far from a complete listing. It is simply meant to give some feeling for the range of planning issues.

WHO ARE THE PLANNERS?

Planners come from a variety of backgrounds. The single most common educational background is formal training in planning, most often a master's degree, either a Master of City Planning (MCP) or a Master of Urban and Regional Planning (MURP). But the field, and particularly larger agencies and consultants, absorbs people with many other backgrounds. Agencies that are large enough to have a separate research operation are likely to hire people with training in economics or statistics. Agencies that do transportation planning are likely to hire people with training in civil engineering and, particularly, transportation engineering. Large agencies often do a substantial amount of data handling and are likely to have on staff a few people with backgrounds in programming and data processing. Agencies that do significant amounts of environmental planning are likely to hire people with backgrounds in biology, chemistry, environmental science, and remote sensing. Planning inevitably involves mapping and spatially organized data, so that geographers and cartographers find their way into the profession. Planning involves many issues of law, particularly in regard to land use and environmental considerations. Thus many attorneys and people with joint training in law and planning have entered the field. In fact, several universities have joint four-year law and planning degree programs.

The majority of planners are employed by government. Of these, the largest share are employed by local governments, that is, by cities, towns, counties, and other substate jurisdictions. Smaller numbers are employed by state governments, by intergovernment organizations like councils of governments (COGs), and by a variety of authorities and special-purpose agencies. Some planners are employed by the federal government, particularly in departments like Housing and Urban Development (HUD), that fund and regulate planning-related activities of local governments. Most planners employed by government are civil servants, but a certain number are political appointees chosen outside the civil service process. Over the years many planners have found their way into municipal administration, where the sort of "big picture" view that planning tends to develop seems to be useful.

A substantial minority of all planners are employed within the private sector. Many work for planning consultants and serve both government and a variety of private clients. A certain number of planners are employed directly by private organizations like land developers and corporations with substantial real property holdings. Some planners work for particular groups that need the planners' skills to make their own case in the public forum. These may be neighborhood or community groups, environmental organizations, and citizens' groups of various types.

PROFESSIONAL ORGANIZATIONS

The most important national organization of planners in the United States is the American Planning Association (APA). In addition to the national organization there are state chapters and many hundreds of local chapters. The national organization publishes two magazines. The *Journal of the American Planning Association (JAPA)*, which comes out quarterly, is the more scholarly of the two. It provides articles on current research and theoretical issues in planning. The APA also publishes *Planning*, which comes out 11 times a year. It is the trade magazine of the profession in the United States. If you want to keep up with what is happening in planning—names, places, programs, controversies, court cases, and the like—it is the best available source. In addition to these two periodicals, the APA, through its Planning Advisory Service (PAS), publishes numerous technical, how-to-do-it reports for the practicing planner.

The work of the planner takes place within a complex legal framework and it is strongly affected by public funding, for one of the biggest, if not the biggest, shapers of the pattern of development is public capital investment. The APA thus lobbies Congress and, at times, state legislatures on a wide variety of matters, some instances of which are discussed later in this book. It is, more than any other organization, the voice of planners in Congress and the state legislatures. Because the law is not only what is passed by legislative bodies but also the precedents established in litigation, the APA takes positions on court cases and from time to time files *amicus curea* (friend of the court) briefs in cases involving land-use controls, environmental regulations, eminent domain, and related matters.

A second national organization is the American Institute of Certified Planners (AICP). This organization certifies planners. The planner who satisfies the organization's professional experience requirements and passes a written exam is certified and can put the letters AICP after his or her name. Some planning jobs require AICP certification, and the certification may carry a certain weight with the user of planning services. For example, a municipality that purchases the services of a planning consultant may be reassured that the consultant is AICP certified.

SATISFACTIONS AND DISCONTENTS

Planning is both anticipatory and reactive. At times planning will be devoted to anticipating and developing responses to problems that have not yet presented themselves. At other times planning will be devoted to responding to problems that are here and demand solutions. In either case, planning is about trying to serve that elusive and controversial—but very important—item known as "the public interest." It can be a profoundly satisfying field when one feels that one has succeeded in making a contribution to the public good. Because much of planning is concerned with the physical environment, the planner can often have the satisfaction of seeing the results of his or her efforts on the ground.

However, the field can also be frustrating, for planners are basically advisors. Sometimes they are heeded and sometimes they are not. And sometimes the planner's brainchild gets more than a little battered during that long trip from drawing board to reality. In general, it is not a good field for someone with a short time horizon or very low frustration tolerance. It is also not a good field for someone who cannot tolerate ambiguity, for many issues that appear black or white at a distance have the dismaying quality of becoming gray as one gets close to them. The field can also present the thoughtful practitioner with ethical ambiguities. For example, both the APA and AICP have professional codes of ethics that enjoin the planner both to serve the public interest and also to render loyal and diligent service to his or her client. Many a planner has wrestled with the question of what to do when, in his or her view, the public interest and client loyalty are at odds with each other.

For someone considering a career in planning, salary is a consideration. Each year the APA does an e-mail survey of its members.[1] For 2010, the median annual salary was $70,000 and the median respondent was 43 years old and had 14 years of planning experience. About 19 percent earned over $100,000. Salaries were highest for planners employed by law firms, development firms, and the federal government. The lowest salaries were for planners employed by smaller nonmetropolitan-area municipalities. For planners with three or less years of experience the median salary was $45,000, suggesting that entry-level salaries were in the $40,000 range. About 70 percent of all respondents were employed by public agencies and about 23 percent were self-employed or employed by consultants.

USEFUL ABILITIES

Of course, the planner needs to have the appropriate knowledge and skill for the particular task at hand, and that can vary considerably from one job to another. One needs different knowledge and skills for doing urban design than, say, for modeling traffic flow. However, some basic abilities are highly important across the whole spectrum of planning.

One basic skill, which is probably not very teachable, is just being able to understand the political environment around oneself. Planning and politics are intimately related, and people who rise in planning generally have political smarts.

Planning is ultimately about persuasion. Good plans that are poorly expressed and poorly presented tend to end up on the shelf under a layer of dust.[2] Therefore the ability to speak well in public—to express an idea cogently and also to respond well to questions and criticism—is extremely important. The planner who cannot do this, if he or she stays in planning, will end up working for the planner who can.

The ability to write well is also extremely important. The planner doesn't need great literary gifts, but it is important to be able to explain things clearly and in a user-friendly way. In both writing and speaking it is important to be able to come in at the right altitude. One doesn't want to write or talk over the audience's heads or befuddle them with technical jargon. But one doesn't want to come in too low and insult their intelligence either. In short, political smarts and good communication skills are important across the entire profession.

THE PLAN OF THIS BOOK

The main body of the book begins with a chapter (Chapter 2) on the history of urbanization of the United States. To a large extent, the history of planning in the United States is a series of responses to problems that have flowed from the process of urbanization. Thus that chapter serves as background for the rest of the book. Chapters 3 and 4 trace the history of planning in the United States in the historical context established by Chapter 2.

Planning is conditioned and limited by the law and takes place within a political process. Ultimately, planning is a political act. In Part 2,

Chapters 5 and 6 establish the legal and political framework in which planning takes place. Chapter 7 lays out some of the main social issues in planning. The concept of the community master plan or comprehensive plan occupies a central place in the development of planning, and the development and implementation of such a plan is often a major task of the planning agency. Chapter 8 presents the comprehensive planning process. Chapter 9 follows with a presentation on the tools of land-use planning to give the reader an understanding of how the community can implement the comprehensive plan.

Part 3 of the book, from Chapter 10, "Urban Design," to Chapter 16, "Planning for Metropolitan Regions," covers a variety of fields in contemporary planning practice. Once the material in Parts 1 and 2 has been assimilated, each chapter in Part 3 will stand on its own.

Part 4 provides a larger view. Chapter 17, "National Planning in the United States," addresses the extent to which we have had de facto national planning.

Chapter 18, "Planning in Other Nations," provides sketches of planning elsewhere with a view to expanding the reader's perspective on U.S. practice—to suggest that the way planning is practiced in the United States is only one of many possible ways, and to highlight the way a society's -basic institutions and ideology shape planning practice.

Chapter 19, "Planning Theory," serves as a wrap-up and expansion of many ideas suggested earlier in the book. It is left to the end so that the reader can approach it with some background and thus put some meat on the bare theoretical and ideological bones.

NOTES

1. See the website of the American Planning Association, www.planning.org
2. For a good presentation on these and related matters, see Michael P. Brooks, *Planning Theory for Practitioners*, Planners Press, American Planning Association, Chicago, 2002, chaps. 12 and 13.

CHAPTER 2

The Urbanization of America

The history of planning in the United States is largely one of response to urbanization and the problems it has brought. To understand that history, it is necessary to have some sense of the main currents of U.S. *urban history*. This chapter will emphasize economic, technological, and demographic trends, for these, over the long term, have far more effect than *discrete* events like elections.

There is something of a break in the trend of U.S. urbanization around the end of the nineteenth century. For convenience, then, we will divide the discussion into two parts: an account of urbanization in the nineteenth century and another from the beginning of the twentieth century to the present.

URBANIZATION IN THE NINETEENTH CENTURY

In the year 1800 the urbanized population of the United States was roughly 300,000, and the total population was 5 million. Thus perhaps 6 percent of the U.S. population lived in urbanized areas. By 1900 the U.S. urbanized population was 30 million, and the total population was 76 million. Approximately 40 percent of the population lived in urbanized areas.[1] From 1800 to 1900 the U.S. population increased by a factor of 15, an annual compounded rate of about 2.4 percent. However, urban populations increased by a factor of 100, an annual compounded rate of about 5 percent. In 1800 the largest city in the United States, New York, had a population of well under 100,000. By 1900 its population was over 3 million.

The Forces Behind Urban Growth

One force behind urban growth was simply national population growth. The U.S. rate of natural increase (births minus deaths) was extremely rapid and was augmented by immigration, particularly after the inauguration of transatlantic steam service in the 1840s. But these facts do not answer the question of why urban growth proceeded so much more rapidly than did total population growth.

Part of the explanation was a side effect of the industrial revolution. As agricultural machinery made farmers more productive, workers were freed to take other employment, much of it in the cities. In 1800 perhaps 85 to 90 percent of the U.S. labor force was engaged in farming. By 1880 that figure was down to about 50 percent.

Another consequence of the industrial revolution was the shift from cottage industries to factory production, creating the need for mass labor forces at specific points. That, in turn, created the need for massed housing nearby. The growth of large-scale manufacturing also brought into being the modern corporation, with a large administrative force concentrated at a single point. Finally, factory production and the enormous increase in consumer goods it created brought into being the department store, which also concentrated a large labor force at a single point.

The growth of large cities was also promoted by the development of low-cost transportation. The coming of railroad and steamboat technology around 1830 gave cities a long reach into their hinterlands to obtain raw materials and agricultural products and also to market the products they produced. In the absence of such transportation, cities would necessarily be small, for the market areas that sustained their commercial and manufacturing sectors would have been small.

The rapid settling of the country and the opening of new lands demanded the creation in short order of a system of cities to perform the commercial and manufacturing processes that the new industrial technology was making possible. Writing in 1899, Adna Weber noted,

> In a new country the rapid growth of cities is both natural and necessary, for no efficient industrial organization of a new settlement is possible without industrial centers to carry on the necessary work of assembling and distributing goods. A Mississippi Valley empire rising suddenly into being without its Chicago and its smaller centers of distribution is almost inconceivable to the nineteenth-century economist. That America is the "land of mushroom cities" is therefore not at all surprising.[2]

Although the four forces noted—population growth, increased agricultural productivity, factory production, and low-cost transportation—are sufficient to explain the rapid growth of urban populations, they do not entirely explain the form of nineteenth-century cities.

Urban Concentration and Density

The distinguishing features of many nineteenth-century cities were concentration and density. As the century progressed, the more gracious and open pattern of the colonial city disappeared. The spaces between buildings vanished, and buildings were built higher. Streets became increasingly congested, and the natural world was replaced by a none-too-attractive human-made world.

Population densities that have never again been seen in the United States were built up in the late nineteenth and very early twentieth centuries. For example, Manhattan island in 1900 had about 2.2 million residents on 22 square miles for an average density of 100,000 people per square mile. In the most densely populated part of the island, the Lower East Side, densities in some wards were several times that high.[3] By 2000, Manhattan's population had fallen to slightly over 1.5 million, a drop of approximately 700,000.

What made nineteenth-century cities so concentrated? Much of the answer lies in the transportation technology of the age. At the opening of the nineteenth century, water transportation was cheap, and land transportation was expensive. The ton-mile cost of transporting freight by canal boat was about one-tenth that of transporting it by horse and wagon. The cost of transporting freight by sailing vessel was still lower than that for canal boat. One effect of these cost differences was to favor the growth of port cities.[4] But another effect was to concentrate economic activity in those areas of the city with direct water access. Since most people got to work by walking, concentration of workplaces inevitably meant concentration of residences as well.

The coming of railroad technology beginning in the 1820s continued the concentrating effect. Over long distances railroad ton-mile rates were a very small fraction of the ton-mile rates for horse and wagon. Thus rail-served sites permitted manufacturers and wholesalers very large cost savings. But achieving these savings meant tremendous concentrations around rail terminals and sidings.

In port cities an ideal industrial location was one between rail lines and docks. The remains of such a configuration can be seen on the Lower West Side of Manhattan today. Old loft buildings once occupied by manufacturers lie immediately to the east of the Hudson shore and up against the former rail lines that connected Manhattan to the rest of the nation.

Today the rail lines are gone, and cargo handling has ceased along the Manhattan waterfront. But in the nineteenth century, the port was busy, and lower Manhattan was a major manufacturing and goods-handling center. Goods could move between Europe and the Midwest through Manhattan and make all but a few hundred yards of the trip entirely by lost-cost modes.

The desirability of rail- and water-served sites made centrally located land very valuable. That feature, in turn, caused the builders of industrial, commercial, and residential structures to use the minimum amount of land for a given amount of structure. Manufacturing and commercial uses were located in multistory loft buildings constructed side to side. For residences the same desire to crowd a maximum amount of structure on a given amount of land led to the tenement, with conditions of crowding that seem appalling by modern standards.

> The residence of the worker in New York City and other large industrial cities in 1850 was frequently the "railroad flat," a walk-up structure that was generally 5 to 7 stories high, 25 feet wide and 75 feet long on a 25 by 100 foot lot. Constructed solidly in rows across entire block faces, these units had four apartments on each floor surrounding a common staircase. The rooms in these apartments were constructed in tandem, with just one room in each apartment provided with a window or two for light and air. No sanitary facilities or water supply were provided for in these structures. The small rear yard contained a multi-seat outhouse and often a well, resulting in deplorable conditions of sanitation and public health.[5]

Thus a population of well over 100 people might be housed on a plot not much more than one-twentieth of an acre in size.

Several other features of emerging nineteenth-century technology also contributed to very dense patterns of development. In contrast to a modern factory, where power to run individual pieces of machinery is supplied electrically, power was generally supplied by a steam engine and transmitted through a system of belts, pulleys, and shafts. The distance that power could be sent in this manner was limited, thus further contributing to the use of compact loft buildings with transmission belts taking power from one floor to another. Shortly after the end of the Civil War, there emerged two other technologies that contributed to higher urban densities: the elevator and steel-frame construction. Together they made the skyscraper economically and structurally possible.

Congestion had more than just aesthetic or psychological consequences. In an age before treatment of water supplies, before modern sewage disposal, and before antibiotics—an age when communicable diseases were the major threat to health—the congestion of the city exacted a huge cost in death and illness. In fact, for much of the nineteenth century, most large cities experienced natural decrease (more deaths than births). They

Tenements on New York's Lower East Side (left) at the end of the nineteenth century. Note the narrow building width and side-by-side construction. The four windows across the building front represent two narrow apartments side by side. Behind them are two more apartments, whose windows open onto the rear yard. Photos like that of the men's sleeping quarters (below) in a New York tenement about 1905 helped put housing conditions at the top of the reformers' agenda.

grew only because of in-migration. The situation was well understood at the time, and decongestion of the city was a major goal of reform-minded citizens and planners.

> Few municipalities have planned intelligently for this rapid urban growth. Buildings have been crowded upon land and people have been crowded within buildings. Urban living has become in many ways inconvenient, unsafe and unhealthful. . . . Transit facilities fail to develop much in advance of demonstrable need, so the population becomes crowded within a limited area. . . . It becomes used to living a life quite divorced from nature. The responsibilities of homeownership are felt only by a few. The sense of citizenship and the sense of moral responsibility for evils suffered by neighbors become weak.
>
> In the interests of both hygiene and public morality, the cottage home is much to be preferred to the tenement dwelling. . . . Tuberculosis is responsible for nearly one-tenth of all deaths in the United States. . . . The tubercule bacillus can live for weeks outside the human body in a sunless, damp room, hall or cellar. The tenement house may thus at once reduce vitality, through absence of sunlight and fresh air, and may provide abundant opportunity for transmission of prevalent and dangerous diseases.[6]

This widely held view helped shape the agenda and direction of the planning profession in the nineteenth and early twentieth centuries.

The Beginnings of Decentralization

Late in the nineteenth century, the first forces for decentralization appeared on the urban scene. These forces have grown in strength to the present time. By the 1880s electric motor and power transmission technology had advanced far enough to make possible the electric streetcar. Faster and cheaper than the horse-drawn trolleys it supplanted, the electric streetcar was a powerful decentralizing force. In a few years the effective radius of the city was doubled. Three miles, a distance the average person can comfortably walk in an hour, had been something of a limit for the population that worked in the urban core. With the streetcar, tendrils of urban growth extended from the city, and the process of suburbanization was begun. In an aptly titled book, *Streetcar Suburbs*, Warner describes how in a few years, the streetcar effectively doubled the radius of Boston and converted the old "walking city" into a modern metropolis.[7] The decentralizing power of rail-based transportation was not lost on the more prophetic writers of the times. In 1902 H. G. Wells wrote,

> Many of our railway-begotten giants are destined to such a process of dissection and diffusion as to amount almost to obliteration. . . . The social history of the middle and later thirds of the nineteenth century . . . has been the history of a gigantic rush of population into the magic radius—for most people—of four miles, to suffer there physical and moral disaster . . . far more appalling than any pestilence that ever swept the world. . . . But new forces . . . may

finally be equal to the complete reduction of all our present congestions. . . . What will be the forces acting upon the prosperous household? The passion for nature. . . . and that craving for a little private imperium are the chief centrifugal inducements. The city will diffuse itself until it has taken many of the characteristics of what is now country. . . . We may call . . . these coming town provinces "urban regions."[8]

Wells was writing about England, but the same forces of national population growth, the growth of manufacturing, and urbanization were operative in the United States.

In common with most nineteenth- and early twentieth-century reformers, Wells viewed the congestion of the city as a profound evil and the coming decentralization as an obviously desirable event. To the nineteenth-century reformer, what we now contemptuously refer to as "urban sprawl" or, sometimes, "suburban sprawl" would have looked like an improvement almost too good to be imagined.

URBAN TRENDS IN THE TWENTIETH CENTURY

Just as nineteenth-century technology proved to be centralizing and to promote very great population densities, twentieth-century technology proved to be exactly the reverse. One decentralizing technology after another appeared on the scene, a process that continues to the present time. For perhaps roughly the first half of the twentieth century, technology favored decentralization within metropolitan areas but did not favor smaller over larger areas. Thus many large metropolitan areas grew rapidly, usually with the major share of growth occurring in their suburban areas.

Figure 2–1 shows the redistribution of population from 1900 to 2010. The figure is based on standard U.S. Bureau of the Census categories. Any point in the nation is located either in a metropolitan or in a nonmetropolitan area. Within metropolitan areas any point is located either in a *central city*, usually a place with a population of 50,000 or more, or in what the U.S. Bureau of the Census refers to as the "part outside" and what is referred to more casually as the *suburbs.* (This terminology has changed slightly for the 2010 census, as explained in the note for Figure 2–1). The distinction between suburb and city is based on jurisdictional lines and thus may not correspond to what you would see on the ground. There may be many areas in the "part outside" that are urban in character; and, conversely, many parts of the central city may have a lower-density, suburban character. Across the century, the U.S. Bureau of the Census has designated new central cities and new metropolitan areas, and existing metropolitan areas have grown as new counties have been added on their peripheries. Thus the picture presented by Figure 2–1 is only a rough abstraction of a very complex situation. Nonetheless, it correctly depicts a massive change.

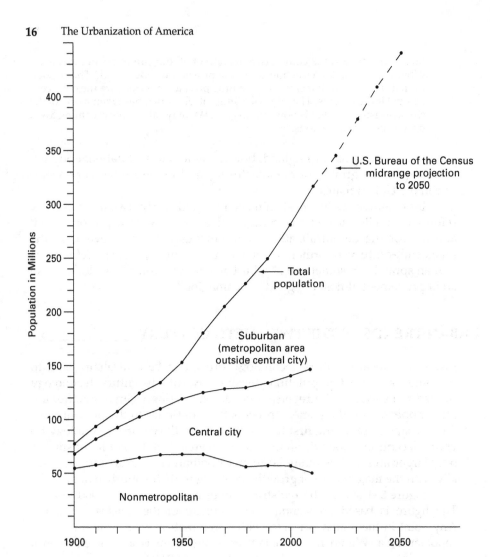

FIGURE 2–1 U.S. population 1900 to 2000 by place of residence, in millions.

Sources: For 1950 and earlier, Donald J. Bogue, *Population Growth in Standard Metropolitan Areas 1900–1950*, Housing and Home Finance Agency, Washington, DC, pp. 11 and 13. For 1960 and subsequent years, the *Statistical Abstract of the United States*, 112th and earlier editions, and direct communication with the Population Division, U.S. Bureau of the Census.

Note: The figures for 1900 through 1940 are estimated for 1950 Standard Metropolitan Statistical Area (SMSA) boundaries. From 1950 on, with each decennial census some SMSAs got larger as additional counties were added to them and some new SMSAs came into being as a function of population growth. Thus the trend lines up through 1940 and those after 1940 were not done on the same basis and are not entirely comparable. For 2010 the Bureau of the Census dropped the term *central city* and substituted *principal city*, distinguishing between *principal cities* in *metropolitan* and *micropolitan* areas, the latter term referring to smaller urbanized places within metropolitan areas. Data from the 2010 census have been adjusted to make them roughly comparable to earlier censuses. The apparent decline in nonmetropolitan population from 2000 to 2010 may be in part an artifact resulting from some areas that were classified as nonmetropolitan in 2000 being reclassified as metropolitan in 2010.

The distinction between suburb and city is based on jurisdictional lines and thus may not correspond to what you would see on the ground. There may be many areas in the "part outside" that are urban in character; and, conversely, many parts of the central city may have a lower-density, suburban character. Across the century, the U.S. Bureau of the Census has designated new central cities and new metropolitan areas, and existing metropolitan areas have grown as new counties have been added on their peripheries. Thus the picture presented by Figure 2–1 is only a rough abstraction of a very complex situation. Nonetheless, it correctly depicts a massive change.

Note how the suburban portion of the total population began to grow very rapidly from the first postwar census (1950) and continued to grow rapidly through the 2010 census. In fact, the suburban population of the United States is now larger than the nonmetropolitan and central-city populations combined.

For population, the big decentralizing force was the automobile. Its speed and flexibility of route and schedule were preconditions for large-scale suburbanization. The first vehicles appeared in the 1890s, but their numbers grew slowly, reaching about 5 million by 1915. About this time, mass production of Henry Ford's Model T began, and the number of autos in the United States increased rapidly, reaching about 25 million by 1930. It is no coincidence that the first great period of suburbanization in the United States began in the 1920s.

The truck bore very much the same relationship to retailing, wholesaling, and light manufacturing as did the automobile to population. It permitted wide-scale decentralization by freeing firms from the necessity of being near rail lines. Retailers could follow their customers, and manufacturers could follow the labor force, with far more freedom than would have been possible a few years earlier. The decentralization of wholesaling followed naturally from the decentralization of retailing, which in turn followed naturally from the decentralization of population.

Other forces also accelerated the process of suburbanization. Improved telephone communications made possible some decentralization of economic activity by reducing the need for face-to-face contact. The development of motion pictures and commercial radio broke the monopoly of central places of entertainment and thus increased the relative attractiveness of outlying residential areas. The invention of the limited-access highway in the 1920s proved also to be decentralizing. The first limited-access divided highway in the United States, and possibly the world, was the Bronx River Parkway in Westchester County, New York, completed in 1926. Parkways were originally envisioned as giving the urban middle class, with its newly acquired automobiles, access to the countryside. Their unanticipated, but more profound, effect was to make it easier to live in suburbia while working in the central city.

Suburbanization proceeded at a moderate pace during the 1920s and then slowed somewhat during the Great Depression of the 1930s.

America's participation in World War II between 1941 and 1945 represented a brief break in the suburbanizing process. Residential construction, other than for war workers, was halted; civilian automobile production was suspended; and gasoline was rationed. When the war ended, the country entered into a sustained suburban housing boom. In the first decade or so after the war, part of the force behind suburbanization came from accumulated demand from the low construction years between 1930 and 1945. But the process continued unabated for many years beyond the period that could be explained by pent-up demand from the 1930s and 1940s.

The Rush to the Suburbs

The forces behind this sustained growth of the suburbs were numerous. Mortgage finance was readily available on attractive terms (see Chapter 17). Employment was high, and incomes were rising rapidly. The nation thus had more wealth to spend on land development, on housing, and on the additional personal transportation that suburbanization required. Automobile ownership rose from 25 million in 1945 to about 40 million in 1950, to 62 million in 1960, 89 million in 1970, 122 million in 1980, and 134 million in 1990. At the end of World War II, there was one automobile for every five Americans. By 1990 there was one automobile for every 1.9 Americans. After 1990, the statistics for the number of automobiles registered in the United States stabilized, but only because so many people switched to vans and sport-utility vehicles (SUVs), which are classified as light trucks rather than automobiles.

Paralleling the increase in automobile ownership was a great expansion of the nation's highway system. Shortly after World War II there began a major surge of highway building by the states, powerfully encouraged by federal subsidies. Practical commuting distances increased, and suburban residence for city workers became much more feasible. Then the National Defense Highway Act of 1956 funded the beginning of the interstate highway system. The suburbanizing effect of the interstate highway system on both population and economic activity was enormous. This matter is discussed in detail in Chapter 17.

Decentralization has also been promoted by improvements in electronic communications. Long-distance direct dialing, common carrier links between computers, closed-circuit television, e-mail, fax, and social networking all reduce the need for face-to-face communication. Having the capacity for interaction at a distance does not cause decentralization, but it permits it if economic or social forces favor it. In many industries like brokerage and insurance, which still maintain a large central-city presence for the highest interaction activities, much "back office" work—like data processing—has moved to the suburbs, to nonmetropolitan America, and overseas. In the first years of this century, much concern has been expressed about the outsourcing to lower-wage nations of all sorts of white-collar work including computer programming, income tax preparation, legal work, call center operations, analysis of X-rays and other medical diagnostic images, and the like. What has made all these outward moves possible is low-cost, instantaneous transmission of words, data, and images. In its way, the microchip may be proving to be as powerful an agent of deconcentration as was the automobile.

The baby boom, a phenomenon that began in the late 1940s, peaked in 1957, and lasted into the mid-1960s, further fueled the suburban housing boom. The increase in births a generation later, the so-called echo of the baby boom, added force to the suburbanizing trend toward the end of the twentieth century. The attraction of the suburbs for couples in the family-formation stage of life is an enormous decentralizing force.

Regional Trends

The period from the end of World War II to the present has also seen major changes in the regional distribution of population as shown in Table 2–1. The movement from "frostbelt" to "sunbelt" has been driven by many forces, some of which are the same as those that powered the movement from city to suburb.

One overriding force has simply been the growth in real per capita income. As people become more affluent, they are able to give more weight to their preferences and less weight to pure economic necessity. That trend has clearly favored warmer climates and places with superior natural amenities. The increase in average life span coupled with a younger retirement age has increased the number of people who receive "mailbox income" (Social Security, pensions, and the like) and are thus free to live where they like. Many of these people have migrated southward. The interstate highway system and electronic communications have made many southern and southwestern locations much more accessible than they previously were. The development of air conditioning made many parts of the South, especially the Deep South, far more attractive than it once was.

One trend the state figures in Table 2–1 do not capture has been the coastward movement of population. By the end of the twentieth century, one-half of the U.S. population lived within 50 miles of a coast. One reason for this is the attractiveness of coastal areas both for scenic and recreational reasons and also, in some cases, more moderate climate. Again, it is affluence and mailbox income that facilitate this trend.

The Age of Central-City Shrinkage

As Figure 2–1 indicates, the decades after World War II saw metropolitan areas grow rapidly in absolute terms and also as a percentage of total population. Within metropolitan areas most growth occurred outside the central cities. However, the picture is a mixed one. Much growth occurred in a number of western central cities. Some of this was genuine urban

TABLE 2–1 Regional Population, 1950–2010 (in thousands)

Region[a]	1950	1970	1990	2000	2010	Percentage Change 2000–2010	Percentage Change 1950–2010
Northeast	39,478	49,061	50,976	53,610	55,411	3.3	40.4
New England	9,314	11,848	13,197	13,983	14,448	3.3	55.1
Mid-Atlantic	30,164	37,213	37,779	39,672	40,963	3.3	35.8
North-central	44,461	56,589	60,225	64,429	67,115	4.5	50.1
East North-central	30,399	40,262	42,414	45,155	46,544	3.0	53.1
West North-central	14,061	16,327	17,811	19,274	20,571	6.7	46.3
South	47,197	62,812	86,916	100,237	115,051	14.8	143.8
South Atlantic	21,182	30,678	44,421	51,769	60,030	16.0	183.4
East South-central	11,477	12,808	15,347	17,023	18,508	8.7	61.3
West South-central	14,538	19,326	27,148	31,445	36,513	16.1	151.2
West	20,190	34,838	54,060	63,198	72,173	14.2	257.5
Mountain	5,075	8,289	14,035	18,172	22,141	21.8	336.2
Pacific	15,115	26,549	40,025	45,026	50,032	11.1	230.2

[a]These regions are standard U.S. Bureau of the Census groupings, as follows: New England: Maine, New Hampshire, Vermont, Massachusetts, Rhode Island, Connecticut; Mid-Atlantic: New York, New Jersey, Pennsylvania; East North-central: Ohio, Indiana, Illinois, Michigan, Wisconsin; West North-central: Minnesota, Iowa, Missouri, North Dakota, South Dakota, Nebraska, Kansas; South Atlantic: Delaware, Maryland, District of Columbia, Virginia, West Virginia, North Carolina, South Carolina, Georgia, Florida; East South-central: Kentucky, Tennessee, Alabama, Mississippi; West South-central: Arkansas, Louisiana, Oklahoma, Texas; Mountain: Montana, Idaho, Wyoming, Colorado, New Mexico, Arizona, Utah, Nevada; Pacific: Washington, Oregon, California, Alaska, Hawaii.

Source: U.S. Bureau of the Census, Census of the Population, 1950, 1970, 1990, 2000, and 2010.

growth. But in many western cities, the city limits extend well beyond the urbanized area. Therefore, much growth that is suburban in character occurs within the city boundaries and appears as part of the central-city total. Then, too, if the city is not surrounded by incorporated municipalities that resist annexation, the city may grow substantially in land area. This was and is the case for many western cities.

In the older and larger cities in the east- and north-central parts of the nation, the general rule was shrinkage. Cities were usually surrounded by other municipalities, so that growth by annexation *was difficult* or impossible. Then, too, high population densities and a preautomobile street pattern made it difficult to compete with the surrounding suburbs for residents and jobs. From 1950 to 2000, the population of Buffalo shrank from 580,000 to 293,000, St. Louis from 857,000 to 348,000, Cleveland from 915,000 to 478,000, Chicago from 3,621,000 to 2,896,000, Boston from 810,000 to 589,000, Pittsburgh from 677,000 to 335,000, and Philadelphia from 2,072,000 to 1,518,000. New York City, an exception, grew slightly, from 7,891,000 to 8,008,000, for reasons discussed subsequently.

The population losses in many older cities were also related to the regional trends noted before. The city in a lagging region is, all other things being equal, more likely to lose population because the market for the goods and services it produces is not growing, nor is there increasing population pressure on it from surrounding areas. Thus for cities like Cleveland or Buffalo, internal forces predisposing to population and job loss were augmented by regional trends. Conversely, sunbelt cities like Fort Myers, Dallas, Houston, or Phoenix grew rapidly, in part because they are situated in growing regions. Central-city population losses were, as one would expect, paralleled by employment losses. Manufacturing jobs continued to move to suburban and exurban locations, drawn by lower land costs, often lower wages, and the availability of large blocks of land that facilitated the building of single-story plants. As suburban populations grew, their buying power necessarily drew both retailers and the wholesalers who serve them out of the city. The growth of the suburban labor force also pulled many business services and headquarters operations out of downtown and into the suburbs, for there is no greater determinant of business location than the availability of labor. Because of the decentralization of employment, there is now much more cross-commuting (commuting from suburb to suburb) than there is commuting from suburb to central city. The day when many suburbs served largely as bedroom communities for the central city is now several decades behind us.

Trends Since 2000

In the first decade of this century the population decline of the nation's largest cities appeared to come to a halt. Of the 50 largest cities in the United States in 2010 only three—Detroit, Chicago, and Cleveland—lost population between 2000 and 2010. All three are in the north-central region of the nation. In the case of the biggest loser, Detroit, the loss of jobs in automobile manufacturing was clearly a major factor.

The nation's biggest city, New York, actually gained almost 400,000 people across the decade. A big factor in New York's demographic turnaround was the nation's high rate of immigration. The outmigration of the native-born population was more than compensated by immigration, both legal and illegal. Perhaps, also, the growth of world trade or, more generally, what we refer to as *globalization* contributed to the city's growth by increasing employment in trade and finance-related activities.[9]

Exactly why the decline in many other large cities stopped is not entirely certain. One factor may have been the changing shape of the U.S. population. With a smaller share of the population in the family formation age the relative push to suburbanization may have been reduced. Immigration, as noted, has been a factor in some cases. We will have more insight when detailed information on age, ethnicity, occupation, and the like becomes available from the 2010 census.

Cities and the Poor

As many central cities lost population and employment in the second half of the twentieth century, their populations also became poorer relative to that of the nation as a whole. In the 1950s, central cities had somewhat less than their proportionate share of the nation's poor. By the 1980s, they had more than twice their proportionate share.

One reason for the urbanization of poverty was simply selective migration. It was, by and large, the city's more prosperous residents who had the income to make the move to the suburbs, often at the same time making the switch from being renters to being homeowners. Another reason was the suburbanization of jobs and thus of income. These factors are closely related. Many firms followed their workers and customers out to the suburbs or beyond. Conversely, many residents of the central city followed their employers out of the central city.

Another factor, and a very important one, was the extremely rapid mechanization of agriculture and the huge increase in agricultural productivity (output per worker) that occurred after World War II. In 1945, the year World War II ended, U.S. farm employment was 10 million, and the U.S. farm population was 25 million. By 1970, farm employment was under 4 million, and total farm population was under 10 million. This decrease occurred despite the fact that the U.S. population had grown from 140 million to 203 million. The agricultural labor force had shrunk by more than half but was able to feed an additional 63 million people and produce a considerable surplus for export. Since 1970, the decline in farm employment and population has continued, but necessarily at a much slower pace.

The effect of this increase in agricultural productivity was to force enormous numbers of farmers off the land and set in motion a great internal migration toward the cities. For the most part, the more prosperous farmers were the ones who could mechanize, acquire more land, and stay in farming. It was the poorer farmers who were rendered surplus and had little choice but to head for the cities. A displaced rural and small-town population, much of it without nonagricultural job skills and often with little formal education, poured into many of the nation's central cities during the 1950s, 1960s, and early 1970s. Unfortunately, this was the very time that the central cities were losing large amounts of manufacturing and goods-handling work, the kind of employment that might have sustained many of these rural-to-urban migrants. Thus in some ways the situation for these internal migrants was more difficult than that which had faced the wave of European immigrants who had arrived in the late nineteenth and early twentieth century. Though social services were not nearly as good at the turn of the century as they were five decades later, the European immigrants of that earlier time were arriving when urban labor markets were expanding and before automation and other modern technologies were decimating the demand for relatively low-skilled manual labor.

Today we take it for granted that in the older and more run-down sections of most central cities, the population will be largely black or other minority. This situation, too, results largely from the mechanization of agriculture. In, say, 1940, most U.S. blacks lived in the states of the old Confederacy and were a largely rural and small-town population. The mechanization of agriculture and the concurrent increases in agricultural productivity hit black farmers especially hard because they were often the poorest of the poor. Many were tenant farmers or sharecroppers rather than owners of the land that they farmed. If the farmer who owned the land could cut costs by replacing manual labor with machinery, the tenant farmers had no choice but to move.[10] And that move, more often than not, was to the central cities. Thus to the problems that any large, rapid rural-to-urban migration would create were added a host of other problems relating to racial discrimination, the legacy of three centuries of slavery, and some decades of Jim Crow.[11]

Few if any nations have been able to deal well with mass rural to urban migration, but the great migration just described is now several decades behind us and progress has been made. Many of the children and grandchildren of those who migrated to the cities now have the skills to function in a modern economy, and many are now firmly ensconced in the middle class. In a general sort of way it may be that the stabilizing of urban populations and the revival of many urban areas is partly due to the resolution of much of the trauma of the great migration. Fragmentary evidence suggests that the income gap between central cities and suburban areas is narrowing, but a definitive statement on that will have to await the analysis of income data from the 2010 census.

The Boomburg Phenomenon

Robert Lang and Jennifer Lefurgy have popularized the term *boomburg*, which they define as a city of 100,000 or more whose population has grown at double-digit rates for each of the last three decades, and that is not the central city of a metropolitan area.[12] They list 54 such cities from Anaheim, California, to Westminster, Colorado. The largest of the group, Mesa, Arizona, had a population of over 400,000 in 2002. Most of the cities they list are in the West and Southwest. That is partly because a great deal of recent U.S. population growth has been there, but also because they specify that to be included in the category, the place in question must be incorporated as a city. They note that there are many Boomburg-like places in other parts of the country, for example, the Washington, DC, metropolitan area, that are not on the list, only because they are not incorporated as cities.

The typical boomburg is within a metropolitan area and may account for much of the total growth of that area. It has the ingredients that we think of as constituting a city—a large population, considerable employment, a substantial amount of retailing and entertainment activity, and the like. It may also contain a considerable diversity of population as measured along lines of race, ethnicity, national origin, and economic status.

But boomburgs do not seem very urban as we usually think of that term. You might go to a boomburg to live or to work, but you would be unlikely to go there to see the sights. As Lang and Lefurgy note, Mesa, Arizona, has a population that is bigger than that of Minneapolis or Atlanta, and yet how many Americans who do not live in the Southwest have ever heard of it?

The typical boomburg is very much a creature of the automobile. One telling statistic quoted by Lang and Lefurgy is that their entire set of 54 boomburgs—containing over 10 million people and some millions of jobs—have fewer tall buildings, defined as over 115 feet, than do just two small, more traditional cities, Alexandria and Arlington in the DC metro area, which have a combined population of not much over 300,000 people.

> Some boomburgs contain substantial amounts of office space: Scottsdale, Arizona and Plano, Texas have dozens of office buildings and millions of square feet of floor space—mostly upper end space at that. Yet together these two communities have only four high rise office buildings. Welcome to the boomburgs, where low-slung office cubes line the freeways.[13]

They also note the absence of downtowns in many boomburgs.

> There are plenty of boomburgs—even big ones—in which pedestrian-oriented areas are only several blocks or even one block. The so-called downtowns of cities such as North Las Vegas and Chandler [Arizona] are quite literally one block.[14]

Until very recently the boomburg was a major, perhaps the major, emerging form in the United States. That is no longer so. In fact, many boomburgs and boomburg-like places are in serious economic trouble. In fast-growing places much employment—construction, real estate, finance—comes from the fact of growth itself. When growth stops, the blow to the job market is more severe than in a slower-growing area. Then, too, in places that have experienced rapid growth and perhaps also a bubble in real estate prices many property owners owe more on their properties than the properties are worth. These "underwater" properties increase the rate of foreclosure and abandonment, a matter discussed in more detail in Chapter 11. In early 2011 it was reported that the biggest percentage increase in people whose incomes were under the federal poverty line was in the Sarasota–Bradenton Metropolitan Statistical Area (MSA) on the Gulf Coast of Florida, a place that has many boomburg characteristics.[15]

When construction activity comes back to more normal levels, will boomburg growth continue, or will the recent financial crisis and real estate price collapse have marked a permanent break in the U.S. pattern of development? That remains to be seen. Apart from issues connected to real estate prices, financing, and tax treatment, the fate of the boomburgs may also be significantly influenced by petroleum prices and developments in automotive technology, for the boomburgs are one of the most heavily automobile dependent forms of development.

SUMMARY

The forces that produced a hundredfold increase in urban population in the United States between 1800 and 1900 included national population growth, increased agricultural productivity, the growth of factory production, and the development of low-cost modes of transportation. The nature of nineteenth-century transportation contributed to an extremely dense pattern of urban development.

In the late nineteenth century, the first signs of suburbanization became visible as the electric streetcar began expanding the old "walking city." In the twentieth century, automotive transportation, electronic communications, and increased income promoted massive suburbanization of population and economic activity, which continue to the present time.

We noted the slowdown of central-city population growth in the decades after World War II and the declines in the population of many of the largest cities, particularly inland industrial cities such as Cleveland and St. Louis. But at the same time that central-city growth slowed, the total population of metropolitan areas continued to grow rapidly.

In the post–World War II period, central cities have grown poorer relative both to the suburbs and to nonmetropolitan areas. The selective outmigration of more prosperous households and the loss of employment to suburbs, nonmetropolitan areas, and overseas competitors have contributed to this trend. Another factor was the migration to the cities of a large, generally poor population pushed off the land by the rapid mechanization of agriculture in the decades after World War II.

We noted that from 2000 to 2010 the population shrinkage in larger central cities slowed considerably and that one factor behind this may be the changing age structure of the U.S. population. We also noted the rapid growth of the boomburgs in recent years and its abrupt cessation with the financial crisis of 2008 and the subsequent recession.

NOTES

1. For urban data going back many decades, see *Historical Statistics of the United States*, U.S. Bureau of the Census, Department of Commerce, Washington, DC.
2. Adna Weber, *The Growth of Cities in the Nineteenth Century*, The Macmillan Company, New York, 1899. Reprinted by Cornell University Press, Ithaca, NY, 1963, p. 20.
3. Ibid., p. 460.
4. For discussion of the relationship between transportation costs and the growth of cities in the late eighteenth and early nineteenth centuries, see Alan Pred, *City Systems in Advanced Economies*, John Wiley, New York, 1977.
5. Frank S. So et al., eds., *The Practice of Local Government Planning*, International City Managers Association, Washington, DC, 1979, p. 27.
6. James Ford, "Residential and Industrial Decentralization," in *City Planning*, 2nd ed., John Nolen, ed., D. Appleton & Co., New York, 1929, pp. 334 and 335. The first edition was printed in 1916, and the article appears to have been written between 1910 and 1916.
7. Sam Bass Warner, *Streetcar Suburbs: A Process of Growth in Boston*, Atheneum, New York, 1968.
8. H. G. Wells, *Anticipation: The Reaction of Mechanical and Scientific Progress on Human Life and Thought*, Harper & Row, London, 1902, quoted in *Post Industrial America: Metropolitan Decline and Inter-Regional Job Shifts*, George Sternlieb and James W. Hughes, eds., Rutgers University Center for Urban Policy Research, New Brunswick, NJ, 1975, p. 176.
9. The term is in very widespread use but does not have a precise, commonly agreed upon definition. In a general way it refers to the increasing interrelationship and interdependence among nations due to, but not entirely limited to, the increase in world trade as a percentage of total world output, increasing travel and migration between nations, the increasing importance of multinational corporations, the increasing international flows of capital and increasing interaction between capital markets in different nations, and the increasing amount of communication of all sorts across national boundaries.
10. For a vivid description of the impact of mechanization on black tenant farmers in the production of cotton in the immediate post–World War II period, see Nicholas Lemann, *The Promised Land: The Great Black Migration and How It Changed America*, Alfred A. Knopf, New York, 1991, pp. 5–6.
11. For an exposition of the view that much of our present problem with poverty, family breakup, and crime in central cities results from lack of job opportunities, see the work of William J. Wilson, most recently *When Work Disappears*, Alfred A. Knopf, New York, 1997. For a somewhat different perspective, see Robert D. Waldinger, *Still the Promised City?*, Harvard University Press, Cambridge, MA, 1996.
12. Robert E. Lang and Jennifer B. Lefurgy, *Boomburgs: The Rise of America's Accidental Cities*, Brookings Institution Press, Washington, DC, 2007.
13. Ibid., p. 14.
14. Ibid., p. 15.
15. "Et in Arcadia ego," *The Economist*, January 29, 2011, p. 27.

SELECTED BIBLIOGRAPHY

CALLOW, ALEXANDER B., *American Urban History*, Oxford University Press, 1973.

GLAAB, CHARLES N., and BROWN, THEODORE A., *A History of Urban America*, The Macmillan Company, New York, 1973.

MCKELVEY, BLAKE, *The Urbanization of America*, Rutgers University Press, New Brunswick, NJ, 1963.

WEBER, ADNA, *The Growth of Cities in the Nineteenth Century*, first printed in 1899, reprinted by Cornell University Press, Ithaca, NY, 1967.

CHAPTER 3

The History
of Planning: Part I

The history of city and town planning, in its full sense, goes back many centuries. The logical and orderly arrangement of streets and public spaces in Roman towns, for instance, indicates the existence of a high level of city planning before the birth of Christ. However, since the focus of this book is present-day planning, we do not present a full history of the subject. This chapter begins with a note on the prerevolutionary period in the United States and proceeds through the first great age of suburbanization, the 1920s. The next chapter picks up the story from the start of the Great Depression and carries it through to the present.

The focus of this chapter, as of the book as a whole, is on events in the United States. However, the chapter does contain some discussion of planning in Europe as well, for the development of planning in the United States was and is closely tied to events across the ocean. In fact, today the American planner who observes the practice of planning in Europe—whether by visiting new towns in Scandinavia, France, or the Netherlands; by observing the preservation of historic districts in any one of a number of countries; or simply by observing the sensitivity and wisdom with which the Swiss have treated a beautiful but potentially fragile natural heritage—will realize that there is still much that we can learn from the Europeans.

Up to now, planning in the United States and in Europe has had much more influence on other parts of the world than the rest of the world has had on Europe and the United States. For example, some thousands of Third World students have studied planning in the United States and Europe, whereas there has been little if any flow of students in the opposite direction. But that unbalanced flow of influence may change in the decades

to come. At present there is a tremendous amount of modern urban planning activity in the Third World, particularly in those nations that have
experienced the most rapid economic growth. This includes much work
in existing cities, the planning of numerous new towns, the planning of
modern public transportation systems, and the planning of highways to
accommodate the very rapid increase in automobile ownership now taking place. Inevitably, we in the West will begin learning from non-Western
experience, both from successes and from failures.

COLONIAL AMERICA

Prior to the American Revolution, municipalities had strong powers to
control the use of land and thus shape their own form. These powers
came out of a European tradition that treated the town or village as an
independent corporation, which might own, control, or dispose of most of
the land within its boundaries. Many U.S. communities started as grants
to individuals or groups, which then, by virtue of the grant, had the
power to dispose of land within their borders. Communities had broad
powers to control economic activities within their borders. For example,
municipal governments frequently had the power to decide whether an
individual was to be allowed to practice a particular trade or business.
Thus colonial towns had formidable powers to shape their patterns of
development. They also faced weaker growth pressures than was later to
be the case.

Today one can see the results of prerevolutionary town planning in
many communities where subsequent growth pressures were not so overwhelming as to sweep away all traces of earlier times.[1] Prerevolutionary
planning survives well in parts of New England away from major
metropolitan areas, including much of New Hampshire and Vermont as
well as parts of Maine, western Massachusetts, and parts of Connecticut
and Rhode Island. The urban pattern that characterizes such towns—the
town square, the reasonable amounts of space between buildings, the
simple rectangular street pattern—are all legacies of the town planning
of the period. The regular pattern of development and the open areas in
Savannah are also an example of prerevolutionary town planning. The
land for the city was a grant to a single individual, James Oglethorpe, who
as grantee had the power to plan and to impose an orderly and a gracious
pattern on subsequent development.

The Revolution changed much of this. A certain amount of disorder
was one price to be paid for political and personal freedom—a small price
for what was gained, but still a price. Quite obviously, the Revolution
ended the practice of creating municipalities through the mechanism of

James Oglethorpe's 1733 plan for Savannah (top left) and the gracious and open results from an 1855 drawing (top right). William Penn's 1682 plan for Philadelphia is shown at bottom. In both plans, note the symmetry, the differentiation between primary and secondary streets, and the provision of public open space.

royal grants to individuals. More important, it placed the bulk of political power in the hands of the states, and it made substate units of government "creatures of the state," possessing only those powers granted them by the states. Municipal powers to control the use and disposition of land were thus greatly diminished. The Constitution contains numerous safeguards for the rights of private property. (See, for example, the quotation from the Fifth Amendment in Chapter 5.) The protection of private property rights limits the capacity of a municipality to control development on privately owned land. Finally, the Revolution ushered in a very different set of attitudes, which weakened the influence of hierarchy, social status, and authority; strengthened the claims of individualism; and enhanced the prestige of entrepreneurial activity. That general change in consciousness favored a more freewheeling and less orderly process of development.[2]

LIMITED MEANS AND GROWING PROBLEMS

The reductions in the powers of municipalities occasioned by the Revolution preceded by only a very few decades the emergence of the enormous growth pressures discussed in Chapter 2. Many municipalities grew rapidly, with little public control over the pattern of growth. In most cases municipal planning was in the hands of the commercial elite of the city.[3] Planning thus often focused on the commercial heart of the city and ignored residential areas, particularly the poorer ones. Often, planning was concentrated on steps to facilitate the commercial and industrial growth of the city, such as inducing a railroad to extend a branch line to the city or improving the docks and the waterfront. Street patterns were often laid out to facilitate land subdivision and speculation.

The rectangular "gridiron" pattern became commonplace for exactly these reasons. It was easy to lay out, and it facilitated subdivision and speculation. More imaginative plans and plans adapted to particular terrain and topographic features were relatively rare. As land values rose with the growth of urban populations, pressures on remaining open space increased. Few municipalities were willing to accept the costs of acquiring land to protect it from development. Rapid growth, a strong regard for the sanctity of private property, the lure of quick profits from land development and speculation, and a feeling that promoting commercial growth was the number-one function of municipal government were dominant motifs of the early-nineteenth-century urban scene.

There were a few exceptions to the picture just presented. For example, L'Enfant's plan for Washington, DC, was a unified vision of how street pattern, public spaces, and structures should form a grand design. And the motivation behind it was essentially civic, not commercial. In

Savannah, Georgia, Oglethorpe's original plan continued to guide the development of the city into the mid-nineteenth century. A number of the public squares shown in the figure on page 29 still remain. But more often than not, the forces of growth ran rampant over the prerevolutionary plans. For example, William Penn's plan for Philadelphia, formulated in the 1680s, called for a system of broad streets, public open spaces, and setbacks around individual structures. But the growth pressures that began in the late eighteenth century simply overwhelmed the plan. The side yard setbacks disappeared as houses were built wall to wall in block-long rows. Alleys were cut through blocks and then filled with row housing. Many public open spaces disappeared into commercial or residential use. There was no shortage of gracious and attractive city plans in eighteenth-century America, but most of them, like Philadelphia's, did not survive the growth pressures of the nineteenth century. By and large, Calvin Coolidge's famous aphorism, "the business of America is business," though uttered a century later, described early-nineteenth-century urban America quite well.

THE PRESSURE FOR REFORM

As urban populations and the density of urban development increased, pressures for reform mounted. U.S. planning history and tradition to a large extent mirror concern with the problems arising from urban growth. Over the years these problems have included sanitation and public health, the disappearance of urban open space, housing quality and overcrowding, the ugliness and grimness of the nineteenth-century industrial city, traffic congestion, and the problem of providing urban populations with adequate mobility. In recent years planning effort has also been directed to problems of urban unemployment, to urban fiscal problems, to a variety of issues that might be lumped under the heading of social justice, and to issues of environmental preservation and quality, among others.

Sanitary Reform

In the mid-nineteenth century, sanitary conditions in most cities were appalling by modern standards. Human wastes were generally disposed of on-site in a backyard septic tank or cesspool—a situation that is a major menace to public health at high densities. The menace was compounded because most water for household use came from wells and streams. Thus contamination of drinking water sources was common. In an age before antibiotics and vaccinations, waterborne diseases like cholera and typhoid fever were major killers. So, too, were insect-borne diseases like malaria, yellow fever, and typhus. The mechanics of disease transmission were not known in the mid-1800s, for the relationship between bacteria and disease was still undiscovered. However, it was understood that large amounts of decaying material or stagnant water bred disease, perhaps because of "vapors" given off by putrefying materials.

Sewers, where they existed, served not to carry away organic wastes but to carry off storm water and prevent flooding. Very often they were constructed large enough for a worker to go inside to make repairs. Water flow was too slow and too intermittent to carry off wastes, and so sewers themselves often became "elongated cesspools."[4]

About 1840 a simple but very important invention that promised to be the agent of reform was made in England. This was the "water carriage" sewer. The insight behind the invention was remarkably simple. If a sewer pipe was made with a relatively small diameter, a cross section like an egg sliced through the long way, and provided with a sufficient source of water, it would essentially be self-cleansing. The water velocity would be sufficient to carry off animal carcasses, fecal matter, and so on. Household wastes, instead of being dumped in on-site cesspools, could be piped into a common sewer and transported for miles before being released. The prospect for improvement in public health was enormous.

But building a water carriage sewer system for a city required planning on a major scale. Since the system was operated by gravity, the topography of the city had to be taken into account in the layout of streets. Because the system depended on a necessary volume of flow, streets had to be built with crowns to divert rainwater into sewers. Deciding where to install sewer lines meant that data on population distribution and health conditions were needed. The "sanitary survey" of the late nineteenth century—a mapping of houses, cases of contagious disease, and presence of outhouses and cesspools and the like—was perhaps the first systematic data collection and mapping effort to be seen in many cities. The amount of planning required to provide sewers to a city did not constitute comprehensive planning. But it did require that at least one aspect of the city be considered as a whole.

Planning for adequate waste disposal was only a part of the larger goal of a generally healthful environment. It was understood that dark, damp, crowded places were associated with higher rates of disease and death. Thus a more complete planning effort would include provision of open space, consideration of sunlight and ventilation, and some contractual arrangements (see Chapter 9) to prevent excessive density of development. In densely developed urban areas, little could be done about these latter considerations. Providing sewers was largely a matter of fitting a system to an existing pattern of development. However, in developing new areas, a more comprehensive approach could be taken.

Sanitation and Integrated Design.   Frederick Law Olmsted, probably the outstanding U.S. planner/urban designer of the second half of the nineteenth century, designed a number of new communities in which all these elements were part of an integrated design. The design was carefully keyed to the contour of the land for adequate drainage of both sewage and storm water. The location of swampy areas, brooks, streams, and other physical features was taken into account for health as well as aesthetic reasons. For example, it was known that malaria, which was widespread in the United States in the mid-nineteenth century, was somehow associated with swampy and poorly drained areas. Thus design that was sensitive to drainage patterns could minimize its incidence. The location of open spaces and plantings was also considered for their effects on the adequacy of light and ventilation. In Olmsted's mind, planning was largely to be judged by the extent to which it reduced disease. Sunlight, good air circulation, and an adequate amount of vegetation were, in his view, the most effective preventives of disease.

Urban Open Space

The interest in sanitation dovetailed with another preoccupation of nineteenth-century planners, the provision of urban parkland. In an analogy that was used at the time, just as good ventilation would make a house a healthier house, so too would parkland serve to ventilate a city. Many splendid examples of municipal park design date from the mid-nineteenth century. New York's Central Park, designed by Frederick Law Olmsted and Calvin Vaux in 1857, furnished inspiration for parks in many other cities. The park covers a rectangle in Manhattan roughly two-and-one-half miles long by one-half mile wide. Bordered on all sides by dense urban development, it provides the Manhattanite with a beautifully landscaped piece of countryside in town. Across the East River in Brooklyn is a much less well-known but equally fine piece of Olmsted's design work, Prospect Park, with a splendid system of meadows, wooded areas, connecting paths, and two artificial lakes. In the case of both parks, as was true for the parks of many other cities, had these areas not been acquired for public use, they would have soon been covered with a dense carpet of development. Other examples of Olmsted's work in park design can be seen in Buffalo, Chicago, Montreal, Detroit, Boston, Bridgeport, Rochester, Knoxville, and Louisville.

Housing Reform

A major item on the agenda of nineteenth-century urban reformers was the condition of housing for the urban poor.[5] The issue of housing for those who do not have enough income to obtain adequate housing on the private

Riverside, a Chicago suburb, was planned by Frederick Law Olmsted and Calvin Vaux shortly after the Civil War. The curvilinear street pattern, close attention to fitting the street pattern to the topography, preservation of green areas, and separation of through traffic from local traffic are all commonly used design techniques today.

market has been on the planning agenda ever since. In the nineteenth century, housing reform largely took the form of pressing for legislation that mandated minimum standards for housing quality.

In New York City the first legislation regulating tenement construction was passed in 1867, and other legislation followed at intervals thereafter. The city's 1901 Tenement House Act is considered a landmark in this tradition. It cut lot coverage back to 70 percent and required a separate bathroom for each apartment, courtyards (for light and ventilation) whose width was determined by building height, and improved fire safety measures. It also set up a Tenement House Commission, with a staff of inspectors and enforcement powers. By 1920 at least 40 other cities had enacted building codes backed by some enforcement machinery.[6]

Although much was accomplished through housing regulation, we must also note what was not done. Housing reform in the United States took a conservative direction. The more far-reaching housing policies that had been adopted in some European countries were rejected here, much to the disappointment of the more radical reformers. In Europe much public money was invested in building housing for workers of modest means.

Municipal governments often played the roles of landowner, developer, and financier. Local and national governments took the view that it was a responsibility of government to provide adequate housing at acceptable cost. The sort of policy that appealed to the more radical U.S. housing reformers was exemplified by the city of Ulm, Germany. The city acquired 1,400 acres of suburban land, planned the area, built housing, and sold it at cost to working-class families. The city also subsidized the building of cooperative apartments along with related community facilities.[7] But the view that prevailed in the United States was that housing is to be provided by the market and that the most government should do is to regulate the market. Government was not to be a landowner, a developer, or a source of housing capital. Even Lawrence Veiller, the moving force behind the 1901 Tenement House Act, believed that only local government should concern itself with housing and that such concern should be limited to regulatory matters and general planning issues such as street layout. He opposed the idea that public monies should be spent on housing.

The United States subsequently did move toward public housing and housing subsidies (see Chapter 4) but, in contrast to Great Britain, Germany, France, the Netherlands, and other European nations, has never gone very far in that direction. The great majority of Americans live in housing that has been built for profit by the private market. Whether the United States would have been wise to follow the European approach is arguable. But, regardless of its merits or demerits, the European approach looked too much like socialism to be accepted in the United States.

The Tradition of Municipal Improvement

Another part of the planning tradition that emerged in the second half of the nineteenth century might loosely be called municipal improvement. Its origins are generally traced to the founding of an improvement society in Stockbridge, Massachusetts, in 1853.[8] The civic improvement movement grew rapidly, at first largely in New England and then nationally. In 1900 the National League of Improvement Associations was founded, to be supplanted two years later by the American League for Civic Improvement. The agenda for the hundreds of civic improvement organizations included diverse items like tree plantings, antibillboard campaigns, paving of streets and sidewalks, provision of drinking fountains and public baths, provision of parks and recreational facilities, and numerous other public matters. The movement initiated a tradition of public concern with planning issues that was receptive to municipal and regional planning, and it continues in force to the present.

The Municipal Art Movement

Toward the end of the nineteenth century, there formed an interest in municipal aesthetics that is generally referred to as municipal or civic art.

A fusion of art, architecture, and planning, it attempted to transcend the mere utilitarianism of the late-nineteenth-century city and to make it a place of beauty as well. Though later criticized for attending to the cosmetic aspects of urban life rather than the most pressing problems, the movement had a strong component of idealism.

> The darkness rolls away, and the buildings that have been shadows stand forth distinctly in the grey air. The tall facades glow as the sun rises; their windows shine as topaz; their pennants of steam, tugging flutteringly from high chimneys, are changed to silvery plumes. Whatever was dingy, coarse, and ugly, is either transformed or hidden in shadow. The streets, bathed in the fresh morning light, fairly sparkle, their pavements from upper windows appearing smooth and clean. There seems to be a new city for the work of a new day. . . . There are born a new dream and a new hope. And of such is the impulse to civic art.

Distinguishing between "civic art" and "art" in its usual meaning, the same writer stated,

> It is municipal first of all. If men seek it they seek it not for art's sake, but for the city's; they are first citizens and then, in their own way, artists jealous of the city's looks because they are citizens. . . . they so band themselves together and so commission sculptors, painters, artists, and landscape designers for the glorifying of civic art—not just because it is art, but because it is civic.[9]

The results of the movement are still visible all over America in the form of arches, fountains, statues, and other works of urban design and decoration. Much of the inspiration came from Europe—St. Paul's and the Thames embankment in London, the Arc de Triomphe in Paris, and other public areas in European cities. The motivation to catch up with the Europeans stemmed in part from the economic growth of nineteenth-century America, for it was wealth and leisure that gave us the feeling that we could afford that which was not purely functional.

The City Beautiful Movement

The City Beautiful movement brought together the ideas of municipal art, civic improvement, and landscape design. The event that is generally considered to mark the beginning of the movement is the 1893 Columbian Exposition in Chicago. Intended to celebrate the four-hundredth anniversary of the discovery of America, though it opened a year later, it had been the object of a major competition between a number of cities.

Designed by Daniel Burnham, the most prominent architect and urban designer of the day, and Frederick Law Olmsted (the designer of Central Park), the fairgrounds presented the visitor with a carefully integrated combination of landscaped areas, promenades, exposition halls, and other buildings. By the time the exposition closed, some 26 million people had seen it. The exposition opened the nation's eyes to what planner, architect, and landscape architect, working in concert, could do.

> In this "White City" of almost 700 acres Chicagoans and millions of visitors, accustomed to urban ugliness, saw for the first time a splendid example of civic design and beauty in the classic pattern and on a grand scale, and they liked it. Indeed it marked the beginning in this country of orderly arrangement of extensive buildings and grounds.[10]

One effect of the exposition was to set off a wave of a particular type of planning activity in American cities. Plans coming out of the City Beautiful movement tended to focus on those things over which municipal government had clear control—streets, municipal art, public buildings, and public spaces. The results can be seen today in dozens of cities, particularly in civic centers, municipal buildings, and the like. Probably the best-known example of City Beautiful planning is the Mall and its immediate surroundings in Washington, DC.

Two examples of the fruits of the municipal art–City a century later. Above, Grand Army Plaza in Brooklyn, New York, and, below, the Pulitzer Fountain at Fifty-Ninth Street and Fifth Avenue in Manhattan.

The design was presented in the 1902 Report of the Senate Park Commission, more commonly known as the McMillan Commission after the senator who chaired it.[11] Its carefully designed vistas, the symmetry and axial layout (i.e., the Washington Monument placed at one end of the reflecting pool and the Lincoln Memorial at the other end), the formality, the classicism, and the scale and magnificence of the whole conception are hallmarks of the City Beautiful–era design. The City Beautiful movement obviously has close links to the municipal art movement, and to argue about whether a particular turn-of-the-century city hall and adjacent public spaces are products of one movement rather than the other is unimportant. Perhaps what distinguishes the two movements is more a matter of scale than intent. The municipal art movement tended to focus on particular points in the city: an arch, a plaza, a traffic circle, a fountain. The City Beautiful movement sought to create or remake a part of the city: a civic center, a boulevard, a parkway.

THE BIRTH OF MODERN CITY PLANNING

The single most important offshoot of the City Beautiful movement, as far the development of an American planning tradition is concerned, was the *Plan of Chicago*. Interest in citywide planning, particularly within the business community, had been growing since the exposition. In 1906 the Merchants Club, essentially a chamber of commerce, commissioned Daniel Burnham to develop a plan. The work of planning was funded by the Commercial Club, another business organization, with $85,000, and the finished plan was presented to the city as a gift in 1909. The plan was remarkable for its scope. It laid out a system of radial and circumferential highways, some extending as far as 60 miles from the city center. Thus in its transportation elements it was a regional as well as a city plan. It laid out an integrated public transportation system and suggested the unification of rail freight terminals. Chicago's Union Station is one outgrowth of the plan. Extensive plans for street widening and overpasses at critical points were made. A system of parks and wildlife preserves both within and proximate to the city was also suggested.

In a remarkable act of foresight, the plan's sponsors appreciated that the political and public relations side of planning was just as important as the technical side and set about fostering the public will to accomplish the plan. The original plan was a lavishly printed and expensive document that could have only a limited circulation. To make the concept of the plan known to the populace at large, a summary version was printed with private funds and given to every property owner in the city and to every renter who paid more than $25 per month.

Shortly thereafter a version of the plan was done as a textbook and widely used in the eighth grade of the city schools. Not only did this reach many students as they were about to leave school—for many students ended their education with primary school at that time—but the plan also found its way into many households by this route. The plan was also promoted by means of illustrated lectures, a popular form of entertainment in that preelectronic age, and also by a short motion picture, *A Tale of One City.*

The city responded with the creation of a Planning Commission charged with the responsibility for carrying out the plan. As a strategy, the planners decided that one concrete accomplishment was needed to demonstrate that the plan was not simply an idle dream. The particular project chosen was to carry Twelfth Street across the railroad yards south of the Loop on a viaduct and thus facilitate the flow of traffic within the city's downtown. When this was accomplished, skepticism about the practicality of the plan was greatly reduced, and one project after another was funded by bond issues. By 1931 close to $300 million had been raised by bond issues and special assessments to finance various elements of the plan.

The Columbian Fountain at the 1893 Columbian Exposition in Chicago.

The double decked Wacker Drive and several large bridges were major improvements along the main stem of the Chicago River.... The South Branch of the Chicago River was straightened, and harbor facilities were enlarged in the downtown area and at Lake Calumet. The famous Navy Pier was built far out into Lake Michigan. Now land was slowly built up as the Lake was pushed back and over 20 miles of lake-front park and beaches resulted.... And within these lake-front parks notable museums and other institutions were developed, much as Burnham and his associates had suggested. The outlying forest preserves were vastly extended until by 1933 they included 32,400 acres.[12]

By its very impressiveness, both as a document and as a real accomplishment, the Plan of Chicago defined for a long time the planner's and perhaps also the informed citizen's view of what a plan should be. In particular, a plan should be comprehensive, and it should have a relatively long time horizon. The plan should be effectuated largely through public capital investment on publicly owned land. Support by the citizenry would be essential to provide the political will for making the necessary investment.

Some modern concepts of planning were absent from the Plan of Chicago. Among these were a concern with social issues, the notion of frequent plan revision and updating, and the view that the public should participate in the making of the plan rather than just receive and approve it as a finished document. The plan has sometimes been criticized for its emphasis on land and structures and its slighting of social issues. But judging the plan by the standards of a later day is not entirely fair. As a product of its time, it is a remarkable accomplishment.

THE PUBLIC CONTROL OF PRIVATE PROPERTY _____

The reader may have noticed that all the elements discussed in connection with the Plan of Chicago essentially pertained to public land, whether it was actually in public ownership at the time or was to be acquired at some later time. This focus on public-owned land was not accidental, for at the turn of the century, the public had little control over the uses to which privately owned land might be put.

One important part of the history of planning has been the evolution of public control over privately owned land. Beginning in the very late nineteenth century, a series of laws and court cases began to establish the right of local government to control the use of land that it did not own. The capacity of government to zone land for different uses was fairly well established by 1920 or so, though the definitive Supreme Court decision did not come until a few years later. The zoning process is one in which a municipal government can exercise control over the density with which land is developed, the types of uses permitted, and the physical configuration (heights of buildings, setbacks from property lines, etc.) of development. Typically, the community is divided into a number of zones displayed on a zoning map, and the permitted uses, densities, and design for each zone are specified in the zoning ordinance. The zoning process, as well as some related types of land-use controls, are described in detail in Chapter 9.

The Rush to Zone

The 1920s saw zoning ordinances appear across the nation with remarkable speed. The causes are not difficult to see. The legal precedents had been or were being established, and a very complex but legally defensible zoning ordinance enacted in New York City in 1916 gave some notion of what might be done. Automobile ownership was climbing at roughly 2 million vehicles per year. Within built-up areas, congestion, particularly in commercial districts, was mounting. Beyond that, widespread automobile ownership was promoting a vast wave of suburbanization. One way to control congestion in commercial areas and prevent the invasion of residential areas by commercial development was through zoning. To many communities, both in older areas and on the suburbanizing fringe, the power to zone looked like the best way to protect what was desirable in the status quo against the vagaries of rapid economic and social change. Perhaps a single-family neighborhood was threatened with invasion by filling stations, used car lots, and hamburger stands. Zoning it so that only single-family houses could be built seemed like an effective and costless way to protect it from the undesirable side effects of progress.

Then, as now, zoning was not only a tool of planning and a technique for shaping the future, but also a device for defense of an existing order. And though no court would accept this as a legitimate purpose of zoning, the act of zoning might raise property values. Zone a pasture on the edge of town for manufacturing, and dreams of a prosperous retirement would glimmer in the eyes of the farmer who owned it. In fact, overzoning for commerce and industry was one of the hallmarks of the early age of zoning. For—aside from the pleas of expectant property owners—what municipality did not need more jobs and more tax dollars?

As we shall see, most planners regard zoning as only one aspect of planning and, particularly, as only one tool for implementing the master plan. In the early 1920s, zoning often preceded planning and, in the minds of many, became almost synonymous with planning (a confusion that is much less common but not unheard of today). That view is not terribly surprising. A new technique with apparently substantial power to alter events had appeared on the scene, and it would take awhile before its limits and its potential for abuse would become evident.

In 1921 it was estimated that there were 48 municipalities, with a combined population of 11 million, that had zoning. By 1923 the figures had risen to 218 municipalities and 22 million people.[13] The move toward zoning was further accelerated in 1924 when the U.S. Department of

Commerce, headed by Herbert Hoover, came out with a model state zoning enabling act. Drafted by Edward M. Bassett, the attorney who had drawn up New York City's zoning ordinance a few years earlier, the Standard Enabling Act encouraged many states to adopt their own enabling acts. These acts, which specifically authorized local zoning laws, encouraged many more municipalities to enact zoning laws because the acts reassured them that their new laws would be able to withstand court challenge.

The Growth of Community Master Planning

Although the single most important trend in planning in the 1920s was the spread and acceptance of land-use controls, other events were occurring as well. In city after city, planning was institutionalized with the establishment of a planning commission. In some cases commissions had paid staffs that did the actual plan-making. More frequently, plans and zoning ordinances were drawn up by planning consultants. Roughly two dozen planning consultant firms were active in the United States in the 1920s.

Community plans of the period typically covered the following:[14]

> Land use (often considered synonymous with zoning)
> Street pattern
> Transit
> Rail (and where appropriate, water) transportation
> Public recreation
> Civic art

The goals of these plans typically included a number of items. One was an orderly and attractive pattern of land use. Related to this was avoiding the juxtaposition of incompatible land uses, for example, a factory in a residential area. Another goal was achieving a well-functioning system for both private and public transportation. Still another was to achieve an adequate system of parks and recreational areas. Goals of municipal beautification and attractive design for public spaces, for example, the area around the city hall, were common. Safeguarding property values and making the community attractive for business were very common general motivations behind the more specific goals already noted. The imprint of the City Beautiful movement and the Plan of Chicago are clear.

By modern standards these plans were less than complete. They neglected housing, except in the sense that zoning specified what housing types were permissible in the various zones. They generally neglected to plan for public capital investments, which in the view of most contemporary planners are often more powerful shapers of land use than are land-use controls. Citizen participation as we know it today was still beyond the horizon. Then, too, many planners of the time thought of the plan as something to be laid down once and then followed, much as an architect's drawings are to be followed as the building is erected.

A more modern view, as we shall see, is that the plan is to be periodically monitored and revised as events take development in directions not anticipated in the plan or as community goals change.

But these limitations having been noted, it must be said that the typical plan for the 1920s was a major step forward in comprehensiveness from

Master plan for Radburn, New Jersey, done in the 1920s, at left. At lower right is a detail for a court showing the separation of vehicular from pedestrian traffic. The housefronts face the walkway on the periphery of the block with vehicular access from the center roadway at the rear of the houses. That general plan has since been used in many planned communities. At lower left is an internal pathway for pedestrian use.

the focus on public places and public spaces that had dominated the City Beautiful movement of a decade or two earlier. It covered the entire municipality, and it addressed a number of matters of municipality-wide concern.

As is the case today, most planning took place in established places where the planner worked within the constraints inherited from earlier periods. But a certain number of planners did have the ultimate design opportunity, the chance to plan a community *de novo*. Mariemont near Cincinnati; Palos Verdes in California; Longview, Washington; Chicopee, Massachusetts; Kingsport, Tennessee; Venice, Florida; and Radburn, New Jersey, are among the new communities planned in this period. Some, like Mariemont, were essentially residential and very often ended as expensive residences for the upper-middle class. Others, like Chicopee, were developed as industrial towns and contained places of employment and residences for the working class as well. Some were completed in the 1920s, and some were stopped short of full development by events beyond the planners' control.

For example, Radburn, New Jersey, billed as a suburb "for the motor age," was roughly half-built when the Great Depression began. It was never completed and today stands surrounded by conventional post–World War II suburban development. But the part that was completed is, in the eyes of many, a fine residential area. Planners and students of urban design still make field trips to Radburn. Large blocks of internal open space, a system of internal pathways, and a street pattern that keeps the automobile from intruding make it a very attractive living environment. House prices are high, vacancies are low, waiting lists are long, and many residents seem to take special pride in being Radburnites. By that ultimate arbiter, the marketplace, it is a very successful community. In general, many of the communities planned in the 1920s have stood the test of time quite well. When the planners had a clean slate, they often did very well. The more difficult feat was, and still is, to do well in an existing community, where the planner is stuck with the decisions (and mistakes) of the past and must confront a sea of special interests and local politics.

THE EMERGENCE OF REGIONAL AND STATE PLANNING _____

The 1920s also saw a growing interest in planning for an entire urban region, an idea that had been foreshadowed by the Burnham Plan of Chicago. Suburbanization and the emergence of widespread automobile ownership rapidly made city boundaries obsolete as the functional city—the economic and social city—often sprawled across dozens of political jurisdictions.

Perhaps the most comprehensive regional plan was one drawn up for the New York City region. The area then contained a population of 10 million, since grown to over 18 million. The plan covered 5,528 square miles, of which only 300 were New York City itself. The remainder consisted of nearby counties in New York State, Fairfield County in Connecticut, and about 2,000 square miles in adjacent parts of New Jersey.

The plan was drawn up by a nonprofit, nongovernment group, the Committee on a Regional Plan, which later metamorphosed into the Regional Plan Association (RPA), a group that exists to the present time. Funding for the plan, roughly $500,000, was provided by a philanthropy, the Russell Sage foundation.[15] The committee had no political power or status whatsoever. Thus whatever influence it had came purely from the force of its ideas and whatever public and political support those ideas could garner. Yet over the years the plan has had considerable effect on the physical shape of the region. Not only did it help guide the development of the New York region, but also it served as a model for many other metropolitan-area planning efforts in decades to come.

The first task of the planners was simply to define the region. The criteria they used, which are still hard to improve upon, were described in this way: (1) "they [the region's boundaries] embraced an area within which the population can and does travel in a reasonable time from home to place of work"; (2) "they included the large outlying recreational areas within easy reach of the metropolitan center"; (3) "they followed the boundaries of cities and counties at the periphery"; and (4) "they had regard to the physical characteristics, such as watersheds and waterways."[16]

The transportation sections covered highway, rail, water, and, perhaps surprisingly for the period, air transportation. The highway portions envisioned a complex of radial and circumferential routes, many of which have since been built. In a few cases, routes that were envisioned originally as rail routes have subsequently been built as highways. By modern standards the plan was perhaps overly focused on physical features and capital investment and underemphasized some social and economic issues. But it was still a remarkable document in that it provided a unified vision of a three-state region containing hundreds of separate municipalities.

Regional plans appeared in numerous other parts of the country during the 1920s. John Nolen, a prominent planner and landscape architect, in 1929 listed about 15.[17] Many, like the plan for the New York region, were entirely private ventures. For example, the Tri-State District plan for the Philadelphia area (parts of Pennsylvania, New Jersey, and Delaware) was paid for by private subscription. Others, such as that done by the Boston Metropolitan Planning Commission, an official organization created by legislative act, were publicly funded. In several cases large counties engaged in regional planning even though the planning took place within a single political jurisdiction. On the East Coast, Westchester County, New York, with an area of about 450 square miles, engaged in extensive regional planning activity through the mechanism of the county parks commission. The results of that effort are visible today in the form of parkways and a splendid county park system of some 15,000 acres. On the West Coast, the largest county effort was that of Los Angeles County, with an area of about 4,000 square miles. Unlike the other regional plans of the era, it included a county zoning plan, believed to be the first in the United States.

Transportation plans done for the New York Regional Plan in the 1920s. A large part of what was planned has subsequently been built, though some of the transit links have been built as highways. The highway map (left) covers about 10,000 square miles, and the transit map (below) about 2,500 square miles.

In all cases other than counties, regional planning efforts had to be carried out in the face of the fact that there is no appropriate political entity corresponding to an urban region. Thus there is inevitably a question of where the political power to carry out the plan will be found. Intergovernment agreements may create some political basis for carrying out the plan. In some cases public authorities, which have some of the powers of government, have been created. Perhaps the best known of these is the Port Authority of New York and New Jersey, which has built or operated bridges, tunnels, port facilities, bus terminals, and airports and which has played a substantial role in shaping the New York region. But as a generality, the weakness in regional planning efforts was and is the mismatch between the nature of the tasks and the fragmentation of the underlying political structure. In the 1960s Robert Wood wrote a book on the New York region, with its complex of city, town, village, and county governments as well as numerous school districts, sewer districts, and other quasi-government organizations.[18] The book's title, *1400 Governments,* states in a phrase the essence of the problem.

The 1920s also saw the beginnings of state planning efforts. Statewide planning is bedeviled by a problem that is somewhat the opposite of the regional planning problem. The region is a natural unit that lacks an appropriate political structure. The state is the opposite, a political structure whose boundaries do not define a "natural" planning unit. Most states have boundaries that do not conform to any geographic, economic, or social reality. For example, New York State, which was the first state to attempt a statewide planning effort, extends from Montauk Point on Long Island, roughly due south of Rhode Island, to the shores of Lake Erie. The residents have little in the way of common interests other than that they are subject to the same state government. The state of Colorado has a natural break where the Rockies rise up out of the Great Plains. The eastern part, in a topographic and an economic sense, is part of the Great Plains. But the western part of the state, in an economic and a topographic sense, is part of the Rockies. The state's rectangular borders bear no relationship to these realities. Comparable comments can be made for most states. Yet despite these problems, a number of states have made substantial strides in statewide planning, particularly with regard to environmental and growth management issues, as will be seen in subsequent chapters.

GRANDER VISIONS

The history of planning so far recounted is a largely pragmatic one, that of a profession seeking to solve problems within the existing urban framework. But there has also been within the profession a minority with much grander ambitions—one that seeks not simply improvement of the

existing pattern but also a major restructuring of the form of human settlement. Although the issues change, the tension between those who see
planning as an activity that optimizes development under the existing
rules and those who hold a more radical view, who see the proper role of
planning as rewriting the rules, is one of the central themes of planning
history.[19]

Perhaps the most influential of all reformers and visionaries was
the Englishman Ebenezer Howard. A court stenographer by profession,
Howard conceived a vision of the city of the future and of a system of
such cities. He set it forth in a short and very simply written book, *Garden
Cities of Tomorrow*, published in 1902.[20] Howard observed the congestion
and pollution of late-nineteenth-century London and concluded that
hope for the future lay in diverting population growth to new urban
centers. People moved from the countryside to the congestion of the city
for compelling economic and social reasons, but they paid a great price.
The solution was to create new towns ("garden cities"), which would
offer the economic and social advantages of the city combined with
the tranquillity, healthful environment, and closeness to nature of the
countryside.

Howard proposed the following general design. The total development would have an area of about 6,000 acres (there are 640 acres in
a square mile). The urbanized area itself would have an area of about
1,000 acres and be laid out in a circle about 1½ miles in diameter. A garden and a grouping of public buildings would constitute the core and
would be accessible by radial boulevards. The core would be ringed by
residential areas divided into neighborhoods by the boulevards. The
residential ring would, in turn, be ringed by commercial and industrial
establishments. The commercial and industrial ring would be enclosed
in a circular rail spur, which would connect the city to other garden cities and to the central city of the region. Around the urban area would
be agricultural and institutional uses. The dimensions of the city would
be such that any resident would be within a few minutes' walk of both
the city core and the places of work on the periphery. Yet he or she
would live in an area from which industrial uses and heavy traffic were
excluded.

The city, by virtue of quick rail access, would have close economic
links to other cities, but it would have enough economic activity within
its boundaries so that the great majority of its residents would not have to
commute. Total population in the city would be about 30,000, and there
might be another 2,000 or so people in the 5,000 acres surrounding the city.
In the words of Lewis Mumford, perhaps the best-known U.S. writer on
architecture and urbanization, the garden city as conceived by Howard
was more than just a bucolic retreat.

[It should] . . . be large enough to sustain a varied industrial, commercial, and social life. It should not be solely an industrial hive, solely an overgrown market, or solely a dormitory; instead, all these and many other functions, including rural ones, should be contained in a new kind of urbanization to which he applied the slightly misleading name of garden city. Howard had no thought of a return to the "simple life" or to a more primitive economy; on the contrary, he was seeking higher levels of both production and living. He believed that a city should be big enough to achieve social cooperation of a complex kind based on the necessary division of labor, but not so big as to frustrate these functions—as the big city tended to do even when viewed solely as an economic unit.[21]

Howard perceived that no matter how well designed and well balanced the garden city might be, it could not exist in isolation. He envisioned a system of cities, all at a modest scale, as shown schematically in the accompanying illustrations. As Mumford characterized Howard's view,

a city, no matter how well balanced, can never be completely self-contained. He pointed out that in a group of garden cities united by rapid transportation each would have facilities and resources that would supplement those of the others; so grouped, these "social cities" would in fact be the functional equivalent of the congested metropolis.[22]

Howard, as did many other nineteenth-century reformers and planners, saw the fragmented private ownership of land as an impediment to good urban form because each property owner would be motivated to develop his or her land as intensely as possible and with no regard to its effect on the rest of the community. Thus one feature of his plan was common ownership of land, with profits from land development reverting to the municipal treasury.

The plan is a remarkable mixture of vision and practicality. Howard was a doer and an organizer as well as a visionary. In 1903 a company he organized purchased a site of 3,818 acres 35 miles from the center of London and proceeded to build the Garden City of Letchworth. Writing about it in 1945, F. J. Osborn stated,

For Letchworth was, and remains, a faithful fulfillment of Howard's essential ideas. It has today a wide range of prosperous industries, it is a town of homes and gardens with ample spaces and a spirited community life, virtually all its people find employment locally, it is girdled by an inviolate agricultural belt, and the principles of single ownership, limited profit, and the earmarking of any surplus revenue for the benefit of the town have been fully maintained.[23]

A second planned community in the greater London area, Welwyn Garden City, was begun by Howard in 1919 with quite successful results.

Ultimately, Howard's work influenced urban development in dozens if not hundreds of communities from Radburn in the United States to

Chandigarh in India. Radburn is very much an outgrowth of the garden city movement, as are Columbia, Maryland, and Reston, Virginia. In western Europe numerous new communities were built after World War II to deal with a desperate shortage of housing resulting from the low rates of construction during the Great Depression and the destruction of housing during the war. These communities, too, are an outgrowth or extension of Howard's garden city vision.

In the last two decades of the twentieth century, neotraditional design, also referred to as the new urbanism, became one of the most

GARDEN CITY AND RURAL BELT

The plan for the entire 6,000 acres is shown at the upper left. Note the radial routes dividing the city into sectors and the circumferential rail line. One sector is shown at the lower left. Note the Grand Avenue and school. At the lower right is a schematic illustration of the system of garden cities. Replace the intermunicipal railway with a modern beltway and the garden cities with suburban subcenters like Tyson's Corner, Virginia, and the design looks relatively modern.

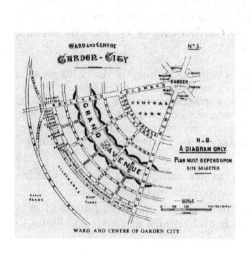

WARD AND CENTRE OF GARDEN CITY

CORRECT PRINCIPLE OF A CITY'S GROWTH

discussed trends in planning and urban design in the United States (see Chapter 10). It clearly draws much of its inspiration from Howard's work, as its proponents readily acknowledge. In recent years there has been a spate of new town planning in a number of Third World countries. There, too, Howard's garden city concept has had an influence, albeit with some modern twists that Howard could not have anticipated. For example, the new town of Putrajaya—located near Kuala Lumpur, Malaysia, in an area that the Malaysian government is seeking to develop as an information technology (IT) oriented development center—bills itself as "the country's first intelligent garden city."[24] Both its own design and its relationship to the larger city of Kuala Lumpur suggest a Howardian influence.

SUMMARY

This chapter covered the history of planning in the United States from the colonial period to the end of the 1920s and the onset of the Great Depression. The Constitution makes no direct mention of substate units of government. Thus municipalities became "creatures of the state," exercising only those powers granted them by the states. The Constitution also expanded the rights of individuals with regard to property rights and due process. The combined effect was to reduce greatly the power of municipalities to control the use and development of land within their boundaries. Early-nineteenth-century urban growth thus often occurred with a minimum of planning and public control. The crowding, ugliness, and haphazard development of many nineteenth-century cities gave birth to a series of reform movements, which shape to the present day much of the agenda of planning in the United States.

Among the movements discussed were sanitary reform, the movement to secure urban open space, the movement for housing reform, the municipal improvement movement, the municipal art movement, and the City Beautiful movement. The Columbian Exposition of 1893 is often considered to mark the birth of the City Beautiful movement. The 1909 Plan of Chicago marked the beginning of the age of modern city planning and shaped the ideas of planners, politicians, and citizens about what a comprehensive plan should be and how it should be implemented.

The tradition of public control of the use of privately owned land evolved slowly, in part because of constitutional questions involved in the "taking" issue. However, roughly by the time of World War I, the right of local governments to exercise substantial control over the use of private property was reasonably well established. Post–World War I suburbanization, facilitated by a rapid expansion in automobile ownership, propelled hundreds of communities into zoning and master planning. The same period also saw the beginnings of regional planning as the automobile dispersed jobs and residences, creating vast urban regions.

NOTES

1. For a detailed account of prerevolutionary planning, see John W. Reps, *The Making of Urban America*, Princeton University Press, Princeton, NJ, 1965.
2. For an exposition of this change, see Gordon S. Wood, *The Radicalism of the American Revolution*, Vintage Books, Random House, New York, 1991.
3. For a discussion of urban government in the United States during the nineteenth century, see Charles N. Glabb and A. Theodore Brown, *A History of Urban America*, 2nd ed., Macmillan Publishing Company, New York, 1976.
4. See John A. Peterson, "The Impact of Sanitary Reform upon American Urban Planning," in *Introduction to Planning History in the United States*, Donald A. Krueckeberg, ed., Rutgers University Center for Urban Policy Research, New Brunswick, NJ, 1983, pp. 13–39.
5. For an example of reformist literature on urban housing and living conditions in the nineteenth century, see Jacob Riis, *How the Other Half Lives: Studies Among the Tenements of New York*, Dover, NY, 1971. First published by Scribner & Sons, New York, 1890.
6. Blake McKelvey, *The Urbanization of America*, Rutgers University Press, New Brunswick, NJ, 1963, p. 120.
7. Mel Scott, *American City Planning Since 1890*, University of California Press, Berkeley, 1971, p. 131.
8. For an account of the civic improvement movement, see John A. Peterson, "The City Beautiful Movement: Forgotten Origins and Lost Meanings," in Krueckeberg, *Planning History*.
9. Charles Mulford Robinson, *Modern Civic Art or The City Made Beautiful*, 4th ed., G. P. Putnam's Sons, New York and London, 1917, p. 1. First edition published in 1903.
10. Robert L. Wrigley Jr., "The Plan of Chicago," in Krueckeberg, *Planning History, p. 58.*
11. Jon A. Peterson, "The Nation's First Comprehensive City Plan: A Political Analysis of the McMillan Plan for Washington, D.C.,"
Journal of the American Planning Association, vol. 251, no. 2, June 1985, pp. 134–150.
12. Ibid., p. 70.
13. Scott, *American City Planning*, p. 194.
14. Ibid., p. 228.
15. Ibid., p. 261.
16. *Regional Plan of New York and Its Environs,* vol. 1, Committee on the Regional Plan of New York and Its Environs, William F. Fell Co., Printers, Philadelphia, 1929, p. 133.
17. For a contemporary description of regional planning efforts in the 1920s, see John Nolen, "Regional Planning," in *City Planning,* 2nd ed., John Nolen, ed., D. Appleton & Co., New York, 1929, pp. 472–495.
18. Robert C. Wood, *1400 Governments: The Political Economy of the New York Metropolitan Region,* Harvard University Press, Cambridge, MA, 1961. By *quasi-government* is meant a public body having some of the powers of government. For example, a school district has the power to collect taxes and to issue tax-exempt bonds.
19. See William H. Wilson, "Moles and Skylarks," in Krueckeberg, *Planning History,* pp. 88–121. Reprinted from William H. Wilson, *Coming of Age: Urban America 1915–1945,* John Wiley, New York, 1974.
20. Ebenezer Howard, *Tomorrow: A Peaceful Path to Real Reform* in 1898; republished with revisions as *Garden Cities of Tomorrow* in 1902; reissued by MIT Press, Cambridge, MA, 1970.
21. Lewis Mumford, "The Ideal Form of the Modern City," in *The Lewis Mumford Reader,* Donald L. Miller, ed., Random House, New York, 1986, p. 166.
22. Ibid., p. 169.
23. Howard, *Tomorrow,* p. 13.
24. The easiest way to get an idea of the development is to Google Putrajaya and also Cyberjaya, another new town being developed in proximity to Kuala Lumpur. They are in an area that the government of Malaysia has designated as an information technology (IT) corridor as part of the national economic development strategy.

SELECTED BIBLIOGRAPHY

See Selected Bibliography, Chapter 4.

CHAPTER 4

The History of Planning: Part II

This chapter covers the eight-decade period from the beginning of the Great Depression to the present time. The Depression years stand as an isolated decade sandwiched between the prosperous 1920s and the beginning of World War II. The period from the end of the war to the present is very different. Although marked by enormous social, political, and technological changes, it is a more or less continuous period. The 1930s was a period in which capitalism functioned very poorly and in which the enemy abroad, fascism, was on the political right. In the postwar period, capitalism in the United States, by and large, functioned well, and the enemy abroad, communism, was on the political left. Our former enemies had been defeated and were now our allies. Our former ally was now our mortal enemy. Then, in a series of remarkable events beginning in 1989, the Soviet empire in Eastern Europe and then the Soviet Union itself broke up, and the Cold War appeared to be over. These events will affect the background against which planning issues are decided well into the twenty-first century.

One theme of this book is that one cannot understand the history of planning by itself. One must see planning in a historic and an ideological context. This brief contrast between the 1930s and the postwar era is included to remind the reader to view the last eight decades of planning history against a changing ideological background.

PLANNING AND THE GREAT DEPRESSION

The 1930s was a peculiar time in the history of planning. It awakened great optimism about planning, and indeed, several new areas of planning were opened up. Yet on balance, for those who had great hopes for planning, this time was something of a disappointment. To those planners who would wish to see the scope of planning greatly enlarged—and this does not include all planners—the Depression years still have the bitter-sweet taste of a tantalizing opportunity nearly grasped. What happened?

The country began to slide into depression with the stock market crash of 1929, and economic conditions gradually worsened for the next several years. By the time President Franklin D. Roosevelt was inaugurated in March 1933, the unemployment rate was in the 25 percent range, and the cash value of goods and services produced had fallen by almost half since 1929. The fact that the free enterprise system was clearly malfunctioning and was unable to connect idle workers with idle machinery created an intellectual climate that favored planning in a way that the prosperous 1920s had not.

Planning is an ambiguous term. It may include everything from the most minor control over land use in a small town to Soviet-style centralized economic planning. But political moods and movements can be intellectually fuzzy. In general, the economic distress and disillusion of the Great Depression tended to favor more *planning*, whatever that word might mean.

Relatively little consensus existed about what ought to be planned or by what principles. Within the Roosevelt administration there was a wide ideological spectrum. Roosevelt himself was not a radical. He was a pragmatist who would adjust and tune the system as required but who had no agenda for large-scale restructuring. Some in his administration, such as the secretary of the interior, Harold Ickes, were relatively conservative. Others, like Rexford Tugwell and Henry Wallace, who were well to Roosevelt's left, favored major change and a major shift of economic power from private to public hands.

Apart from the administration there was a Congress that, although much more willing to experiment than it had been in better times, was hardly radical. Finally, there was the Supreme Court, then a relatively conservative body that in modern terms might be described as "strict constructionist."[1] The Court turned out to be a major limitation on the amount of social and economic experimentation in which the national government might engage.

A number of planning initiatives began during the Great Depression.[2] Some persist to the present, whereas others have sunk without leaving much trace.[3] One initiative that lasted was the federal funding of local and state planning efforts. Federal funding was provided for planning staffs, both as a job-creation measure and as a commitment to planning. Numerous communities used federal funds to build and staff planning departments, to develop maps and databases, and to formulate plans, including many community master plans. In the slow-growing, fiscally strained environment of the 1930s, many plans simply sat on the shelf. But the federal funding did help build the size and technical competence of the profession.

Federal funding and increased state interest in planning accelerated a trend that had begun in the late 1920s, namely, the creation of state planning agencies. By 1936 every state except one had a state planning board.

The focus of these boards varied greatly. In many, particularly those in which agriculture was a dominant part of the economy, the focus was on conservation and farmland preservation. In others the primary focus was on urban issues, including housing quality, sewage treatment, water pollution, the provision of adequate recreational facilities, public finance, and urban governance. Much of the work of state planning agencies focused simply on finding the facts, whether that meant mapping areas of soil erosion in a rural area or studying public finance and the structure of government in a metropolitan area.

The federal government moved into the provision of low-cost housing, an area in which it has remained in one way or another ever since. The motivation was twofold. First was the obvious goal of improving the housing of the poor. The second goal was expansion of construction as a way of stimulating the economy. At first the federal government built public housing directly. Then a Supreme Court decision forced a change in the program, and the federal government switched to providing financial support, both capital and operating, for local public housing authorities. There are today somewhat over 1 million units of public housing in the United States and several million units of privately owned but publicly subsidized units. That public presence in the housing market had its origins in the Great Depression.

In the mid-1930s, the Resettlement Administration embarked on a program of new town-building. The program lost favor with Congress after a time and was discontinued in 1938. However, three new communities, Greenbelt, Maryland; Green Hills, Ohio; and Greendale, Wisconsin, were constructed.

The housing initiative of the federal government that had the most far-reaching effects was not one that fell in the realm of planning but rather in the realm of finance. That was the provision of mortgage insurance by the Federal Housing Administration (FHA) noted briefly in Chapter 2 and discussed in more detail in Chapter 17. Few, if any, acts of the federal government have had more effect on the pattern of settlement than FHA mortgage insurance.

The conceptual basis for Urban Renewal was also a Depression-era development. Economists and others within the federal government foresaw the difficulty that central cities would have in competing with suburban areas for development capital, largely because of differences in site-acquisition costs (see Chapter 11). The solution proposed was the City Realty Corporation, an organization that would use federal subsidy monies plus the power of eminent domain to produce marketable development sites at below cost.[4] World War II swept the City Realty Corporation off the national agenda, but the idea, under a different name, became one of the bases of the Housing Act of 1949, which established Urban Renewal.

Still another Depression-era initiative was the first planning for what was to become the interstate highway system. World War II shelved the idea for a time, but it reappeared as the National Defense Highway Act of 1956. This initiated the building of the interstate highway system, the largest single construction project in U.S. history.

The Depression also saw the creation of the National Resources Planning Board (NRPB) under the leadership of Rexford Tugwell, a member of FDR's so-called *brain trust*. Though the board never fulfilled the dreams of those who favored the major move to the left, it did do a certain amount of useful work. One contribution was the support of local and state planning efforts. Another was the making of an inventory of natural resources on a national scale. In the conflicting political currents of the time, noted earlier, the board did not make much of a mark on the nation and in 1943 was dissolved by Congress. The war and national preoccupation with war-related matters was one cause of its demise. Another cause was that any organization that seeks to plan on a broad canvas will naturally step on toes and make enemies.

Whether the NRPB's dissolution is a cause for sorrow or rejoicing is largely a matter of ideology. From the left its dissolution looks like a major missed opportunity. From the right its dissolution looks like a slaying of the socialist monster in its crib before it could grow to maturity and do any damage.

Finally, the Depression era saw the start of a number of regional planning efforts, the best known of which was the Tennessee Valley Authority (TVA). Established in 1933 to provide a combined approach to flood control, power generation, and natural resource conservation, the TVA was planned on a major scale. Dams that served for flood control also produced power, which facilitated rural electrification and brought industry into the valley. The creation of lakes behind dams naturally led the agency into recreation planning. Among those who favored a much larger role for government, the TVA occasioned much enthusiasm as a prototype for what large-scale regional planning could accomplish.

Other regional initiatives included the New England Regional Commmission, the Colorado River Basin Compact, and the Pacific Northwest Regional Planning Commission. The latter two ultimately resulted in the construction of the Boulder, Bonneville, and Grand Coulee dams.

THE POSTWAR PERIOD

World War II provided a sharp break with the Depression and Depression-era issues. The conversion to a war economy quickly ended the unemployment of the 1930s, and political and military events abroad shifted the nation's political focus from internal to external. From the end of the war to this writing, the country has followed a generally successful economic course. It is true that there have been several recessions, the most severe of which is the one that began in 2008, and several brief inflationary episodes, but on the whole, the U.S. economy has flourished. There was thus much less willingness, at least until the present, to contemplate radical changes than there had been during the Depression. Perhaps this unwillingness was just a matter of heeding that bit of folk wisdom, "If it ain't broke, don't fix it." Then, too, the success of capitalist economies in Western Europe, Japan, and North America contrasted with the poor performance of centrally planned economies in the Soviet Union and Eastern Europe and militated against major moves toward national planning.

Postwar planning initiatives thus took place in a relatively conservative framework. Where possible, they involved a heavy reliance on private initiative and private capital. Typically, the major planning initiatives also involved a combination of federal, state, and local effort. A share of the funding and some legislative guidelines were provided by the federal government, but much of the initiative, detailed planning, and implementation came from state and local governments. As discussed in Chapter 18, planning in many European nations in the 1980s and 1990s came to resemble the American model much more than it had in the early postwar period, partly for some of the same ideological reasons and partly for economic reasons.

The Expansion of Municipal Planning

The postwar period saw a large expansion of planning activity at the city, town, and country levels. The causes of this expansion were numerous. The prosperity of the postwar period gave municipal governments more funds to spend on planning. The satisfaction of private wants with the growth of the postwar economy naturally turned people's attention to public needs. It is easier to be concerned about the quality of one's community when one is well fed, well housed, and financially secure than when one is not. Postwar suburbanization, as it had after World War I, stimulated planning activity in thousands of suburban cities and towns by thrusting on them the problems of growth. The difference was that this time there was no Depression to cut short the suburbanization process. The growth of local planning activity was also powerfully stimulated by the federal government. Federal grants, Urban Renewal, and other programs discussed in this chapter stimulated the expansion of planning agencies. Beyond that, federal funds were made available to local agencies for general planning purposes under section 701 of the Housing Act of 1954 and subsequent legislation.

Urban Renewal

The first major initiative to appear after the war was Urban Renewal or, as it was called in its early days, Urban Redevelopment. The difficulties that cities faced in competing with suburban areas for investment capital had been perceived during the later years of the Depression. In the Housing Act of 1949, Congress set up the mechanism by which cities might be enabled to compete more effectively with outlying areas. At the time, the biggest need of the cities appeared to be for investment in housing, both to clear away many acres of slum housing and also to alleviate severe housing shortages resulting from low rates of construction during the Great Depression and World War II. Thus Urban Renewal started as a slum clearance and housing program. It soon added a major commercial thrust as well. By the time the program was ended in 1973, some $13 billion of federal funds had been expended. Several billions more were spent on projects that were in the pipeline at that time and were subsequently completed. Adjusted for inflation, expenditures on Urban Renewal probably totaled in the range of $100 billion in today's dollars. A great deal had been accomplished, but there were also very high human costs in the form of neighborhood disruption and the forced relocation of hundreds of thousands of households. The program is discussed in detail in Chapter 11.

The Age of Highway Planning

Another major theme of the postwar period was highway planning and highway building. The period after the war witnessed an enormous amount of suburbanization accompanied by massive increases in automobile ownership, as noted in Chapter 2. Coincident with the suburbanization of population was the suburbanization of economic activity. As a consequence of the changing distribution of economic activity, there was also a significant increase in the importance of truck transportation relative to rail transportation in the carriage of both intra- and intermetropolitan freight. Because of these pressures, one metropolitan region after another moved into large-scale highway planning. The first and possibly best known of these was the Chicago Area Transportation Study (CATS).

The postwar period also saw the building of the interstate highway system, which, measured in physical terms, is the largest engineering project in the history of the nation. The idea, as noted, is of Depression-era vintage, but work did not begin until after the passage of the National Defense Highway Act of 1956. Most of the system was constructed in the 1960s and 1970s. By the end of the 1980s, only a few links remained to be completed. The system, about 40,000 miles in length, has been a major force in reshaping the nation, largely, one suspects, in ways unanticipated by its planners. The transportation planning process is described in Chapter 12, and the interstate highway system is discussed in more detail in Chapter 17.

Environmental Planning

Environmental planning, a term that would have been virtually unrecognizable 50 years ago, emerged as a field at the end of the 1960s. Its emergence can be traced to two separate background forces. First, with the growth of population and prosperity, humanity had acquired more ability to damage the environment. More people, more kilowatt-hours of electricity generated, more vehicle miles driven, more acres covered with paving and structures—all meant that the natural environment was at greater risk. Second, and more important according to some, were changes in what we produced and the way we produced it. Around 1940 there began a revolution in the types of materials we produced and used. Up to that time most of our materials were naturally occurring substances, though often processed and modified in some way. Since then we have increasingly relied on substances that have never before existed, that often have some degree of toxicity, and for which natural pathways of degradation do not exist. For example, in a very influential book, *Silent Spring,* Rachel Carson argued that DDT (a compound that had been known for some decades but came into use only about the time of World War II) was entering the food chain, with all sorts of dire consequences both to the ecosystem in general and to humans—who eat fairly high up on the food chain—in particular.[5] Barry Commoner in *The Closing Circle* (a title whose ominous ring fits the tone of the book well) cited a long list of changes in products and processes with adverse environmental consequences; for example, pesticides, chemical rather than natural fertilizers, and the increasing use of plastics like polyethylene for which natural degradative pathways do not exist.[6]

By the end of the 1960s, mounting concern with the effect of our impact on the environment resulted in the passage of the National Environmental Policy Act (NEPA), and the creation of the Environmental Protection Agency (EPA). The act also required the filing of an environmental impact statement (EIS) for a project involving substantial amounts of federal funding, a stipulation that more than any other single event brought the field of environmental planning into being. Simply complying with the requirement that an EIS accompany a request for federal funding created employment for large numbers of environmental planners. In the following years many states passed laws analogous to NEPA, often referred to as "little NEPA" acts. Congress passed numerous other pieces of environmental legislation such as the Clean Air Act and the Toxic Substances Control Act. In each case, the studies and planning required to comply with the requirements of the law expanded the field of environmental planning. Increasing consciousness of environmental issues has also prompted agencies doing traditional land-use planning to consider environmental aspects that a few years ago were often ignored in the planning process. The subject is pursued further in Chapter 15.

A subfield of environmental planning, energy planning, abruptly came into being in 1973 following the Arab–Israeli War. The oil embargo that followed the war very quickly caused a quadrupling of crude oil prices and a 50 percent increase in the cost of gasoline. In the next two decades, interest in energy planning waxed and waned with the rise and fall of oil prices. At this writing, interest in the field is very strong. For reasons discussed in Chapter 15, a great many people are convinced that the long-term price trend is upward. To concern about future energy prices have been added growing concerns about the role of fossil fuel burning in climate change as the scientific consensus on that question has strengthened. As a result, concern about restraining fossil fuel consumption is widespread throughout the planning profession, and energy planning is one of the field's big growth areas.

Growth Control and Growth Management

In the 1960s growth control and growth management emerged as a distinct area of planning and also as an area of legal and moral controversy. Two separate trends in the postwar period combined to create this field. The first was the growth of population and the movement of population from central cities into suburban and exurban areas. Many communities felt themselves threatened by growth and thus saw a need to develop a means to prevent growth entirely or to limit and control it. The second factor was the growing environmental consciousness of the 1960s. Concern with the natural environment in general easily translated into concern with the natural environment of a particular city or town or county and furnished motivation and rationale for local growth-control efforts. One movement of the 1960s, spawned by global environmental concerns, was zero population growth (ZPG), whose slogan for would-be parents was "stop at two."[7] Concern with population control at the global or national level spilled over into concern with growth control at the local level even though the logical connection between them is minimal at best.

The growth-control movement raised legal and moral issues that have not been easy to resolve. In fact, there is now a substantial record of litigation pertaining to the subject. One question at issue is exactly what rights communities have to exclude potential residents. The subject is pursued in Chapter 5.

The Growth of Statewide Planning

Beginning in the late 1960s, the nation began to witness an increase in statewide planning efforts. This development was closely related to growing concern over environmental issues. In general, state planning efforts do not supersede local planning efforts but rather add another layer of control. State planning may address a variety of environmental or growth management goals that, because they transcend municipal boundary lines, cannot be adequately handled at the local level. A number of state planning processes are described in Chapter 14.

Economic Development Planning

In the period immediately after World War II, it was generally thought that the economic function of government was simply to ensure that the national economy functioned well. Specifically, the main problem was to employ suitable fiscal and monetary policies to maintain a high level of employment and a reasonable degree of cyclical stability. To the extent that there was poverty stemming from unemployment, the way out was thought to be economic growth in order to bring more people into the workforce and exert upward pressure on wages.

After a time, however, it became apparent that prosperous as the nation was, there were parts of the country in which poverty and unemployment were rampant. The first geographic area so recognized was the Appalachian region, sandwiched between the much more prosperous East Coast and the then thriving Midwest. The terms *pockets of poverty* and *structural unemployment* came into use.

At the beginning of the 1960s, the federal government began to fund local economic development programs through a series of agencies and programs discussed in Chapter 14. Briefly, its intention was to promote by means of planning and subsidies the flow of capital into distressed areas. Initially, most of the federal effort regarding structural unemployment had a rural and small-town focus, for in the early 1960s that was where the problem was most acute. Gradually, with the urbanization of poverty discussed in Chapter 2, the focus of these efforts became more urban.

For reasons of political ideology, the Reagan administration was opposed to such programs. The federal government largely withdrew from the field during the 1980s and has never returned to it in a major way. However, the states and thousands of local governments still pour much effort and billions of dollars into economic development. The structural unemployment issue is one of the prime motivations for such efforts. The other major motivation is property tax relief. This motive was greatly strengthened in 1978 by the passage of Proposition 13 in California, which greatly limited the ability of local governments to increase property taxes and which was followed by similar actions in a number of other states. For municipal governments trapped between citizen resistance to taxation on the one hand and rising costs of providing services on the other, expansion of the tax base through economic development often seems like the best way out. If anything, interplace economic competition has grown more intense since the 1980s, and economic development planning is a major area of planning.

Planning for Smart Growth

In the mid-1990s, Maryland invented the term *smart growth* to describe its antisprawl state development plan. Within a few years, the term became one of the most, if not the most, commonly used planning terms in the United States. Closely allied with older ideas about growth management, smart growth was touted as the latest and most important answer to the problem of sprawl. With the U.S. population growing at somewhat more than 3 million people per year, and with most of that growth going into suburban areas, traffic congestion and other problems associated with sprawl were becoming daily more important to the public and to the planners who serve that public. Sprawl and smart growth are discussed in Chapter 14.

Planning and Public Safety

The need for safety was an important force behind the evolution of cities, for the city was a more defensible place than an isolated settlement in the countryside. Several centuries ago, technology began to change that picture. When the cannon first appeared in Europe in the late fifteenth century, city walls began to lose their protective value. In the twentieth century, the invention of the airplane converted cities from places of safety into huge targets, as World War II made unmistakably clear. In the early years after World War II, the existence of the Soviet Union armed with nuclear weapons made U.S. cities look like a major military liability. Many thought that the more densely urbanized we were, the more we invited nuclear attack and also the less able we would be to survive such an attack.

Urban planners and federal officials began to discuss the question of whether promoting a more scattered pattern of development would be in the national interest.[8] However, this line of thought never gathered enough adherents to have a major effect on the U.S. pattern of development, though it may have affected the location of some defense facilities and the commercial and residential development associated with them. One reason that the United States did not adopt a policy of intentional dispersion was that very large numbers of people in this country believed that nuclear war between the United States and the Soviet Union simply would not occur. The key acronym was MAD (Mutual Assured Destruction), and the key assumption was that the leadership of the Soviet Union, though reprehensible in many ways, was cautious and sane. As the Cold War waned and détente grew, concern with the security implications of the pattern of development gradually evaporated. In looking back, it is clear that those who placed their faith in MAD were correct.

The events of September 11, 2001, placed the relationship between the pattern of settlement and safety back on the planners' agenda. No terrorist attack could approach the destructiveness of a nuclear exchange, but on the other hand, such an attack had happened, and the destruction it caused was still massive. Unlike the leadership of the Soviet Union, the leadership of al Qaeda was not cautious, and to most Americans, it also did not seem to be entirely sane. It was instantly clear to Americans that terrorism was not something that happened just in the Middle East or Sri Lanka or Kashmir. From 9/11 forward, Americans would have to contend with the possibility of terrorism at home.

Security concerns showed up in a variety of small ways in building design, site design, and the way that buildings and public spaces operated. Shatterproof glass and stronger construction appeared in some new, larger structures. Barriers that make it impossible to bring a motor vehicle close to a building have become commonplace in some urban areas. The new landscaping for the Washington Monument left the basic appearance of the monument site unaltered but surrounded the monument at some distance with walkways that have low walls sufficient to stop a truck from getting close to the monument.

How much effect the threat of terrorism will have on urban form in the long term will largely depend on whether there are further terrorist acts in the United States. If Americans feel relatively safe from terrorism, the long-term effects of 9/11 on U.S. cities will be small. If fear of terrorism does measurably affect urban form, the overall effect is likely to be a dispersing one. Measures to keep traffic and parked vehicles away from buildings and, generally, to achieve safety through distance will necessarily be easier to implement and less costly in low-density environs. Such measures will be hardest to implement in densely built-up areas like lower Manhattan or downtown Chicago.

Planning for Natural Disasters

The possibility of natural disaster has figured in planning for a very long time, but interest in the subject has grown considerably in recent years. The real (inflation adjusted) costs of natural disasters have been at least doubling per decade, in large part because increasing numbers of people live and work in areas prone to natural disaster, particularly coastal areas and, most notably in California, areas prone to forest fire. Attention was especially focused on planning for natural disaster by Hurricane Katrina in 2005, both because of the size of the disaster and the realization of how unprepared we were to deal with it. The earthquake and tsunami that hit Japan in 2011 did the United States no direct harm but emphasized again that even a country as economically and technologically advanced as we are can still suffer huge losses of life and property from natural disaster.

Planning for natural disaster is difficult. Though the possibility of the event can be anticipated—the Japanese were no strangers to earthquake and tsunami—the exact timing, place, and scope of the event cannot be anticipated. Adequate planning and response more often than not must be multijurisdictional, so coordination between municipalities, states, regional agencies, and the federal government may be required. And, as we have seen with Hurricane Katrina and other natural disasters, the costs for both preparation and repair may be huge. Deciding what to do in preparation for the possibility, dealing with the event when it happens, and then deciding how, and in some cases whether, to rebuild afterward all can pose big problems. One writer on the subject, Robert Verchick , suggests three basic rules for doing adequate planning for natural disasters:

- Go green.
- Be fair.
- Be safe.[9]

The first point, go green, means working *with* nature, rather than *against* it, to minimize the extent of possible disasters. For example, in the case of a low-lying coastal area—like the Gulf Coast—that is prone to storm surge, one step would be to preserve or rebuild the wetlands that absorb wave energy and reduce the force of the surge. In an area prone to forest fires, it might mean using forestry practices that preserve stands of old-growth trees since such areas are relatively less likely to burn or tend to burn more slowly.

The second item, be fair, refers to the fact that, in the aggregate, some groups of people suffer much more from natural disasters, both during and for a long time afterward, than others and that good planning must take this into account. This point is discussed further in Chapter 7.

The third point, be safe, expresses Verchick's view that safety considerations in disaster planning sometimes get pushed aside by other matters like financial interest. For example, preventing development in flood plains contributes to safety but may be opposed by property owners and others for financial reasons. He suggests that the emphasis be on safety.

The complexity of planning for natural disaster can be enormous. Consider some of the questions that might have been or still might be considered for New Orleans and vicinity after Katrina.

A comprehensive planning approach for New Orleans might start with some very basic hydrologic considerations. What, if anything, is to be done about the Mississippi Delta? If nothing is done, a combination of subsidence and the washing away of soil in the Delta will render the city more and more flood prone and raise very serious questions about its long-term prospects. Multibillion-dollar engineering projects to change the hydrodynamics of the Delta are one option. Improving the system of levees, but not attempting to change the overall hydrodynamics of the Delta, is another option. The choice of whether to write off part of the city and let it revert to a more natural state or to try to reconstruct the entire city are both options, in part depending on the previous choices. The economic effect on the entire region around New Orleans of major changes in the size of the city need to be considered. Much of the agricultural output of the American Midwest passes through the Mississippi on its way to other parts of America and the rest of the world. So what happens to the Port of New Orleans has ramifications far beyond New Orleans or the state of Louisiana.

Those are just a few basic physical questions about the New Orleans area. A still larger effort would integrate planning for the New Orleans area with that for the larger Gulf Coast region. Beyond physical design there are a host of social planning questions, particularly for the populations displaced by Katrina. Some of these are discussed in Chapter 7.

Not that much of the grand-scale comprehensive planning suggested earlier has been done post-Katrina. To reinforce a point made at various places in this book, planning and politics cannot be separated and, politically, such an effort was just not in the cards. Whether it will be someday remains to be seen. Chapter 17 might give the reader a few thoughts on what such planning might look like.

Planning for an Age of Reurbanization

Among many planners there is a strong feeling that an age of reurbanization, whatever form it might take, is or will soon be upon us. As one speaker at the 2011 American Planning Association (APA) convention said, "We tried sprawl and it didn't work"; this seemed to express the feeling of many of the participants.

Is an age of reurbanization soon to be upon us? A bit of history follows. Looking back, it is clear that in the years following World War II a great many forces favored suburbanization and sprawl. The two terms are not synonymous but there is some overlap. Growing prosperity made widespread automobile ownership possible and new highways, largely funded with federal money, made it relatively easy to get to work from dispersed locations. Provisions in the federal tax code and changes in mortgage financing facilitated mass homeownership (see Chapter 17). The birthrate was considerably higher than it is today so that young children made up a much larger percentage of the population. In 1957, the peak year of the baby boom, there were 4.3 million births in the United States for a population of 172 million. In 2010 there were 4.1 million births for a population of 308 million. The age at which both men and women first married was about half a decade younger than it is today. Men's labor force participation rates were not much different from what they are at present, but women's rates were very much lower. That favored the lifestyle of dad goes to work and mom stays home in the tract house in the suburbs with the kids. Personal income was much more evenly distributed than it is today, and large numbers of blue-collar workers in manufacturing, construction, and transportation among other fields earned enough, very often in unionized jobs, to manage a suburban house. No one worried that the big V8 under the hood of the family car was contributing mightily to the greenhouse effect because no one—except a few scientists who understood the basic physics of it and thought it might be of theoretical interest—had ever heard of it. There wasn't much anxiety about fuel costs, either. For a number of years after World War II the United States was a net exporter of crude oil.

Take that basic picture, admittedly simplified and idealized, turn it around 180 degrees, and the forces behind suburbanization and sprawl look much weaker. For example, large numbers of single people in their twenties should mean less demand for a *Leave It to Beaver* life setting and more demand for something more urban and sophisticated. Exactly what form reurbanization might take—perhaps a rebirth of central cities, or intensified development in suburban centers, or small nodes of development with many urban characteristics—remains to be seen. In any case, it is not hard to see why many planners think we may be on the cusp of a major turn in the pattern of development and why, at a convention of planners, terms like *walkability, nodes, density,* and *transit* are frequently heard. This subject will come up repeatedly in the chapters that follow.

SUMMARY

This chapter noted the increased interest in planning during the Great Depression, in part as a result of the poor performance of American capitalism during this period. Though the hopes of those such as Rexford Tugwell, who favored a major swing toward national planning, were disappointed, some planning initiatives that lasted well into the postwar period did have their origins in the 1930s.

Urban Renewal and the interstate highway system were conceived during the Great Depression, though not enacted into law and funded until after the war. Federal subsidization of housing and federal financial support of local planning efforts began during the Great Depression. Statewide planning, seen to a limited extent in the 1920s, became widespread during the Great Depression. World War II quickly ended the unemployment of the Depression years and shifted the nation's political focus from internal to international affairs.

The political climate of the postwar period was very different from that of the Great Depression, and there was little support for national planning. In fact, the National Resources Planning Board was abolished during World War II and was never reconstituted. Nonetheless, there was a major expansion of planning activity, in large measure fueled by federal grants and pushed forward by national legislation. Among new or expanded activities were Urban Renewal, highway planning (including planning for the interstate highway system), environmental planning, community development, planning for growth management, and local economic development planning. In recent years, the question of *smart growth* has come to the fore as increasing numbers of people become concerned about the issue of sprawl driven by continuing population growth.

Among the forces behind the increase in planning activity were the growth in population and wealth, the rapid suburbanization and increased automobile ownership that followed World War II, the weakened competitive position of many central cities vis-á-vis the suburbs, and increasing concern with the effects of human activity on the natural environment.

NOTES

1. Meaning a relatively literal interpretation of the Constitution based on the "original intent" of its authors and relatively little willingness to define new individual rights or new obligations of government that are not clearly implied by the wording of the Constitution. The reader who wants to pursue the debate over whether the Constitution should be interpreted strictly or flexibly might see Robert Bork, *The Tempting of America: The Political Seduction of the Law*, Free Press, New York, 1990.

2. For a general account of the New Deal, see William E. Leuchtenburg, *Franklin Delano Roosevelt and the New Deal*, Harper & Row, New York, 1963; or Arthur M. Schlesinger, *The Coming of the New Deal*, Houghton Mifflin, Boston, 1958.

3. For a general account of Depression-era planning initiatives, see Mel Scott, *American City Planning Since 1890*, University of California Press, Berkeley, 1965, Chap. 5.

4. Guy Geer and Alvin Hansen, "Urban Redevelopment and Housing," a pamphlet published by the National Planning Association, 1941. For additional references to Urban Renewal, see Chapter 11.

5. Rachel Carson, *Silent Spring*, Houghton Mifflin, Boston, 1962. (Note: DDT was subsequently banned in the United States but is in use in parts of the Third World.)

6. Barry Commoner, *The Closing Circle*, Alfred A. Knopf, New York, 1971.

7. For a statement of the ZPG view, which was widely read and quoted at the time, see Paul Ehrlich, *The Population Bomb*, Ballantine Books, New York, 1971.

8. Michael Quinn Dudley, "Sprawl as Strategy: Planners Face the Bomb," *Journal of Planning Education and Research*, vol. 21, no. 1, Fall 2001, pp. 52–63.

9. Verchick, Robert R. M., *Facing Catastrophe: Environmental Action for a Post Katrina World*, Harvard University Press, 2010, Chap. 1.

SELECTED BIBLIOGRAPHY

HALL, PETER, *Cities of Tomorrow*, Blackwell, London, updated edition, 1996.

KRUECKEBERG, DONALD, A., ED., *Introduction to Planning History in the United States*, Rutgers University Center for Urban Policy Research, New Brunswick, NJ, 1983.

REPS, JOHN W., *The Making of Urban America*, Princeton University Press, Princeton, NJ, 1965.

SCOTT, MEL, *American City Planning Since 1890*, University of California Press, Berkeley, 1965.

Note: For references to particular fields of planning mentioned in this chapter, see the Selected Bibliography for the chapter that treats that field in detail.

CHAPTER 5

The Legal Basis of Planning

Planning, as discussed in this book, is an activity of government. It involves the exercise of powers vested in the government and the expenditure of public funds. It is limited by, among other things, the limitations of the powers of government. In this chapter we describe the legal framework and the legal limitations within which local and state governments act. In Chapter 6 we turn to the political framework.

THE CONSTITUTIONAL FRAMEWORK

The Constitution, although it has much to say about which powers and responsibilities are assigned to the federal government and which powers and responsibilities are delegated to state governments, is silent on the issue of how the powers of government are to be divided between state and substate units of government. In fact, a literal reading of the Constitution gives no indication that there are to be substate units of government at all: Words like *city, town, township, village, parish,* or *county* are totally absent. (The word *district* is mentioned, though its meaning is not entirely clear.)

As a result, it was understood from very early in the history of the United States that substate units of government derive all of their powers from the state or, in a phrase that came into use some years later, are "creatures of the state." This understanding, which was articulated in a strict manner by Judge John F. Dillon in 1868, has become known as Dillon's rule.[1]

Briefly, the rule is that a substate unit of government has only those powers expressly granted to it by the state, or those powers that are directly and un- arguably implied by those powers expressly granted it by the state.

In the years after the Dillon decision, a number of states modified their constitutions with *home rule* provisions or passed *home rule* legislation. In these states, substate governments have any power that is not forbidden them by the state and not in conflict with the state constitution or other state legislation. Thus all states can be classified as either Dillon rule states or as home rule states.[2] The central point, however, is that regardless of whether the state is a Dillon rule state or a home rule state, the powers of substate governments come from the state. This is equally the case under the only-those-powers-directly-permitted Dillon's rule form or under the those-powers-not-forbidden home rule form.

Obviously a state government cannot assign to a substate govern- ment powers that it itself does not have. But of those that it has, some will be assigned to substate units of government. In general, the structure of local governments and the powers and responsibilities of local govern- ments are specified in charters, state enabling laws, and state constitutions.

Powers and Limitations

Just as state governments grant powers to local governments, they also can and do impose obligations on them. Local governments are also guided and limited in their actions by rights guaranteed individuals by the U.S. Constitution or by state constitutions. When there is disagreement over issues of individual rights or the extent of government power, the ultimate arbiter is the court system. Local planning efforts are thus limited by what the courts will allow or what local officials, property owners, and other concerned parties believe the courts might allow were the issue at hand put to a legal test. In many cases, local planning efforts are also influenced by what the courts require local governments to do.

Early planning efforts such as the Plan of Chicago often took place in the absence of any specific planning framework. In the Chicago case, the plan was formulated by a group that had no legal mandate or authority and that, in essence, delivered the plan as a gift to the city. The plan was implemented by the city through exercise of the normal powers of govern- ment. Specifically, the city used its powers to levy taxes and to issue bonds to raise funds, which were used to finance projects called for in the plan. The power of the city to enter into contracts was used to acquire proper- ties in voluntary transactions. Where that did not avail, the city's powers of eminent domain were used to acquire property through condemnation.

The power of *eminent domain* is important and deserves a brief expla- nation. The phrase means that government has the right to take property for public purposes. The building of roads, for example, generally involves the taking of private property for the right of way. When government takes property, it must compensate the owner for the value of what is taken. If agreement cannot be reached between government and property owner, the matter goes to court. After hearing expert testimony, the court then determines the value of the loss imposed on the property owner by the act of taking. That value, the condemnation award, must then be paid to the property owner by the government. The eminent domain process is an example of the exercise of government power subject to limitation by the constitutional rights of individuals. Specifically, the taking clause of the Fifth Amendment states, "nor shall private property be taken for public use, without just compensation"—hence the necessity for the condemnation award. The Fourteenth Amendment states that no person shall be deprived of "life, liberty, *or property* without due process of law"—hence the requirement for a judicial procedure should voluntary agreement not be reached. The Fourth Amendment guarantees "the right of the people to be secure in their persons, houses, papers and effects against *unreasonable* searches and seizures." Thus the taking of property for a trivial purpose would not be sustainable in court.

PUBLIC CONTROL OVER PRIVATE PROPERTY

Public control over the use of private property is a very different matter from the public taking (with "just compensation") of private property. The evolution, over several decades, of the right of government to exercise some control over the use of privately owned property is one of the central stories in the history of modern planning. Were local governments unable to exercise control over the use of privately owned land, the practice of planning in the United States would be vastly different and more limited.

Public control of the use of private property involves the imposition of uncompensated losses on property owners. This point requires a word of explanation. Consider someone who owns a building lot in a downtown area. Market forces such as the demand for office space and the cost of construction create a situation in which the most profitable use for the site is a 12-story office building. If the municipality, however, limits the height of structures on the site to 6 stories, the difference in profit between the 12- and the 6-story building is a loss imposed on the owner of the site. This principle is true whether the owner would develop the site, sell the site to another party who would develop it, or lease the site to someone else who would build on it. In the first case the owner would take the loss directly in the form of reduced operating profits. In the latter two cases the loss would be manifest as a lower selling price or lower rental fee for the site.

The land-use control technique that has evolved over the years, zoning (see Chapter 9 for details), does exactly what is alluded to: It limits the uses to which land can be put. If the most profitable use is not among the permitted uses, a loss is necessarily imposed on the owner. However, no compensation need be paid to the owner, nor is a judicial procedure required for the community to exercise control and thereby impose the loss. The community's zoning law stands unless the property owner brings a successful lawsuit against the community. This capacity to obtain the benefits of limiting an owner's use of his or her property without having to pay compensation clearly accounts for the popularity of zoning. The community obtains partial rights of ownership—some control over the use of the property—without having to go to the expense of becoming an owner. Note that this is very different from taking with compensation under *eminent domain*. In that case, the municipality does become the owner of the property.

Given the apparent conflict between such community powers and constitutional guarantees regarding property rights—most particularly the requirement for just compensation in the taking clause of the Fifth Amendment—it is not surprising that it took many years and many court cases to establish the zoning rights of communities. Even today the legal structure of zoning is still evolving, and many an attorney earns his or her living in zoning-related litigation and negotiation. Some on the political right view all zoning as fundamentally illegitimate because it represents an uncompensated taking and hence a violation of constitutionally guaranteed property rights.[3]

The legitimacy of zoning rests on the legal concept of the *police power.* That perhaps misleading term refers to the right of the community to regulate the activities of private parties to protect the interests of the public. Very often a phrase like *health, safety, and public welfare* will be used to indicate the range of public interests that may be safeguarded through exercise of the police power. Thus a law that limited the height of buildings so that they not cast the street below into a permanent shadow might be justified as an exercise in the police power. So, too, might a law that prevented certain industrial or commercial operations in a residential neighborhood. So, too, might laws that prevented property owners from developing their lands so intensely that undue congestion resulted in nearby streets.

The rights of the community under the concept of the police power and the rights of the property owner under constitutional and other safeguards push in opposite directions. Exactly where the equilibrium point is located is a matter to be decided by the courts. The question of how much and for what purposes government can take some of the value of privately owned property, as in the building height example, is generally referred to as the taking issue and is the subject of a very large literature.[4] The question of what regulatory actions do or do not constitute a taking is crucial because if it is determined that a taking has occurred, then the Fifth Amendment of the Constitution requires that payment be made to the property owner. If no taking has been made, then no compensation is required.

The process by which municipalities acquired some control over the use of private land began in the late nineteenth century. It typically started with the passage of legislation that limited the use of, and hence took some of the value of, privately owned property. The legislation was then appealed in court by the property owner because of the loss it imposed. Very often the loser of the first trial appealed to a higher court. Through this process of litigation and appeal, the extent and the limitations of the public power to control private land use has been and continues to be defined.

A very early case in this long history was *Mugler v. Kansas* in 1887. The U.S. Supreme Court sustained a Kansas prohibition law that forced the closing of a brewery without compensation. The owners of the brewery argued that compensation was due, but the Court held that a loss imposed through exercise of the police power to protect the health or safety of the community required no compensation. Note the distinction between police power and eminent domain here. Had the brewery been taken under eminent domain, compensation clearly would have been required. In 1899 a bill passed by Congress limited the heights of buildings in residential sections of Washington, DC, to 90 feet, and heights of buildings on some of the widest streets to 130 feet. Light, air, and traffic congestion in the streets were the considerations behind the ordinance. In 1904 the Massachusetts legislature passed somewhat similar legislation for Boston. Structures in the business district were limited to 125 feet, and structures elsewhere to 80 feet.

In 1909 the city of Los Angeles carried the idea of public control over the private use of land further by dividing the city into a number of commercial districts plus a residential district. In the latter, commercial uses were permitted only as exceptions. In what became a landmark case, the city compelled a brickyard in a residential area to cease operations. The item of public welfare being protected was the interest of residents in having an environment not subject to undue noise, dust, and traffic. The owner sued the city, a series of appeals followed, and the case ultimately went to the U.S. Supreme Court. In *Hadacheck v. Sebastian* the Court sustained the city. Though this was, literally, a nuisance abatement rather than a zoning case, the effect of the decision was clearly a strengthening of municipal rights under the police power.[5]

The city that enacted what might be considered the first modern zoning ordinance—though it left much to be desired by present standards—was New York. In the early twentieth century, lower Manhattan was growing rapidly as a commercial center. Steel-frame construction and the elevator were making it practical to build to unprecedented heights of 40, 50, or even 60 stories. The horizontal expansion of the business district was limited by the fact that Manhattan is an island. In fact, at the latitude of Wall Street— then, as now, the center of the financial district—one can walk across the island from the East River to the Hudson River in perhaps 15 minutes. To add to the congestion, the city was in the process of building a subway system, which permitted employers in the business district to reach far out into the other boroughs for their labor forces. Thus the same rapid transit that permitted central residential densities to fall was, paradoxically, permitting increased employment densities downtown.

With downtown space at a premium, builders tended to cover the entire lot and to build without any setbacks. The result was a building shaped like a child's building block set on end. Such buildings darkened the streets below and cast shadows several blocks long. By being allowed to build straight up from the property line, builders could accidentally or otherwise impose major losses on adjacent property owners by casting the facing wall of an adjacent structure in a perpetual shadow.

At the same time that concern over skyscraper development was growing, merchants in the fashionable Fifth Avenue retailing area were concerned that the invasion by manufacturing firms displaced from lower

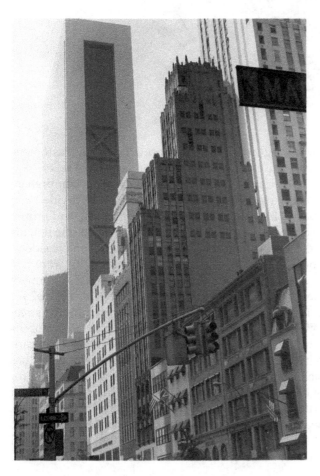

The stepped-back configuration of the old-style office building in the foreground shows the effect of New York's 1916 zoning law. The modern structure at the rear rises without distinct setbacks but has a gradual taper in its lower floors and does not cover the entire lot.

Midtown Manhattan zoning districts as designated in the 1916 plan. The numbers are building height limits expressed as multiples of street width.

Manhattan would lower the tone of the area and drive away customers. They thus put pressure on the city government for some sort of relief.

Prompted by these concerns, the city in 1916 enacted a comprehensive zoning ordinance covering all five boroughs. The city was divided into three districts on the basis of land use: residential, commercial, and mixed. Overlaid on these use districts were five height districts, where the heights were expressed as multiples of street widths, ratios justified on considerations of congestion and sunlight. Also overlying the entire city were five districts that specified ground coverage requirements such as minimum lot sizes. Beyond that, the ordinance also specified a building "envelope" for skyscrapers, which mandated that there had to be setbacks from the street at higher levels. The stepped-back design that can be seen today in dozens of Manhattan office buildings comes from this ordinance and has been caricatured by some as a modern ziggurat (from a Babylonian temple built as a series of stepped-back terraces). But regardless of the aesthetic merits (or lack thereof) of many of these stepped-back structures, they were a major improvement over structures that rose straight up from the lot lines.[6]

The ordinance was designed by an attorney, Edward M. Bassett, who is generally regarded as the father of zoning in the United States. Bassett designed it in such a way as to ground every facet in some matter of public health, safety, or welfare. Thus he produced an ordinance that proved invulnerable to the inevitable court challenges. Again, the fact that the provisions of the ordinance rested on the police power further established the principle that compensation need not be paid for any loss of property value that the zoning might impose. This point is critical, for if compensation had to be paid, public control of land use would be more expensive, far more cumbersome, and far less widespread than is now the case. A theoretical argument can be made that there are some disadvantages to the fact that municipalities can essentially treat the zoning power as a free good, but we reserve this more modern view for Chapter 9.

In 1926 any lingering doubts about the constitutionality of zoning were relieved when a zoning case finally reached the U.S. Supreme Court. In the case of *The Village of Euclid v. Ambler Realty Co.*, the Court sustained a village zoning ordinance that prevented Ambler Realty from building a commercial structure in a residential zone.[7] The point that a municipality could impose an uncompensated loss upon a property owner through the mechanism of land-use controls was now firmly established. In effect, the court had ruled that such a loss need not constitute a taking of property, for a taking of property would require compensation as in the taking clause of the Fifth Amendment quoted earlier. The term *Euclidean Zoning*, named for the town of Euclid, is now used to refer to conventional zoning ordinances rather than to some of the more modern and flexible types discussed in Chapter 9.

In the years after 1926, backed by the *Euclid* decision, state and local courts supported and expanded the power of municipal governments to zone and otherwise regulate the use of privately owned land, and zoning became almost universal in urban and suburban areas. With one minor exception, the Supreme Court did not hear another zoning case for half a century.

In 1978, litigation over New York City's landmark preservation reached the court as *Penn Central Transportation Company v. New York City.*[8] The company, which owned Grand Central Station, had sought to build a skyscraper atop the station, but it was blocked because the city Landmarks Preservation Committee had designated the station as a historic site. The company argued that the loss it sustained by being denied permission to build over the station was so severe that it constituted a taking. The company won in the lower court, was reversed in New York State's appellate court, and then appealed to the U.S. Supreme Court. In a split decision the Supreme Court rejected the plaintiff's appeal and sustained the city. Most planners were very pleased with the decision because it seemed to expand the scope of the zoning power. It made it clear that the behavior of a private property owner could be constrained for purely aesthetic reasons. It also made it clear that such control could be applied to a single structure or parcel rather than just to an entire district. In the years since the *Penn Central* decision, the U.S. Supreme Court has ruled in a number of land-use cases. These cases are summarized in the box beginning on page 78.

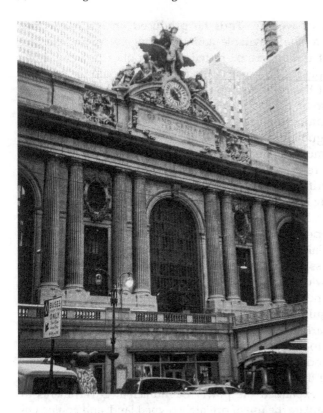

The 42nd Street facade of Grand Central Station, part of what was saved by the *Penn Central* decision.

Beginning about the end of the 1980s, something of a property rights counterattack began, and this event bears explanation. The question of whether—and if so, how much—government should be able to regulate the use of private property has an ideological dimension. Those on the political right will generally take the view that government's ability to regulate should be sharply limited, for the relative sanctity of the rights of private property is a fundamental part of the right-wing political position. By contrast, those on the political left are far more likely to place less value of the rights of private property and thus to favor greater public regulation. As the United States moved to the right politically toward the end of the twentieth century, what came to be called the *property rights* movement became more powerful.

A number of states have passed laws that required "takings impact analyses" before the implementing of environmental regulations.[9] These laws are too new to tell whether they will have a major effect. To the extent that they do, it will presumably be to reduce the ability of the states to control, without compensation, the uses to which environmentally sensitive land may be put—or, perhaps, to assert that land is environmentally sensitive. Bills to require governments to pay compensation for losses imposed by regulation have been proposed in approximately two dozen state legis-latures, but so far only one bill has passed. That one, in Mississippi, applied only to forest land. Nationally, takings bills have been introduced in both House and Senate, but none have become law.

The movement to define as takings all reductions in property values caused by regulations has made most progress in Oregon. In November 2000, the voters passed Measure 7. This referendum, backed by a property rights organization called Oregonians in Action, required governments to "compensate landowners for loss of value resulting from govern-ment actions that restrict or curtail the use of their property." Opponents argued that converting almost any restriction on land use into a taking would impose a huge financial burden on both the state and the local gov-ernments.[10] The state estimated the total cost of the measure at $4.5 billion annually, with about two-thirds of that falling on local governments and the remainder on the state government. They argued that because of this burden, the ability of governments to protect beaches, impose urban growth boundaries, and even enforce zoning laws would be greatly reduced. The opponents also took the position that although advocates of the measure couched their arguments in terms of fairness—government should pay for what it takes—the measure was actually a huge blow to government's ability to protect the public interest in land development and represented a type of initiative that Oregon voters had turned back several times before. One opponent of the measure, an attorney for the League of Oregon Cities, stated that "you have stripped the government of a fundamental power to regulate." Opponents of the measure made a procedurally based argument that the measure was impermissibly broad in that it affected, in a single action, a very wide variety of government powers. In 2002, to the relief of many planners and environmentalists, the court accepted the plaintiff's argument and struck down Measure 7. The planners' relief, however, was short-lived. On November 2, 2004, the voters of Oregon approved Measure 37, which essentially repeated the substance of Measure 7 but was more narrowly drawn to be able to resist challenge in court. The key passage in Measure 37 is

> If a public entity enacts or enforces a new land-use regulation or enforces a land-use regulation enacted prior to the effective date of this amendment [to prior state legislation, ORS Chapter 197] that restricts the use of private real property or any interest therein and has the effect of reducing the fair market values of the property, or any interest therein, then the owner of the property shall be paid just compensation.[11]

The measure does exclude from compensation regulations pertaining to public health, compliance with building codes, and some other matters. But it potentially makes almost any other kind of regulation that imposes a loss on a property owner a taking and thus subject to compensation. Further, the measure is retroactive to the time that the property owner acquired the property. Thus for example, if some years ago after you had bought a piece of land it was rezoned from, say, single-family housing at two units to the acre to single-family housing at one unit per acre, you might have a potential claim against the municipality that did the rezoning.

Not surprisingly, Measure 37 has been the subject of litigation. On February 21, 2006, in *Mac Pherson v. DAS* the Oregon Supreme Court found for the plaintiff and sustained the measure, an obvious setback for the planners. But then, in November 2007 the voters of Oregon passed Proposition 49, which repealed some of what the planners had considered to be the more onerous aspects of Proposition 37. Again, the boundary between the rights of property owners on the one hand and the rights of government on the other to limit the use of private property without compensation had shifted with the changing political scene.

As might be expected, a wide array of environmental organizations are intensely opposed to takings bills. The American Planning Association (APA) is also strongly opposed and has mounted a serious lobbying effort. Should such requirements become commonplace, they could exert an enormously inhibiting effect on regulatory agencies at all levels of government. Fears of incurring huge bills for compensation would make agencies extremely cautious and prompt them to err on the side of underregulation. They might also, as the APA has claimed, enrich attorneys and consultants by producing an explosion of litigation over whether or not a reduction in value sufficient to require compensation had occurred.

THE SUPREME COURT AND THE TAKING ISSUE

From *Euclid v. Ambler* in 1926 until the 1980s the U.S. Supreme Court heard only one significant case involving land-use controls: the *Penn Central* case discussed earlier in this chapter. Then, beginning in 1987 the Court heard six cases all concerned with the taking issue.

In *Nollan v. California Coastal Commission* (1987) the court prevented the commission from requiring Nollan to provide public beach access as a condition of enlarging his house on the grounds that there was no "essential nexus" (connection) between house enlargement and beach access.

In *Lucas v. South Carolina Coastal Council* (1992) the court ruled in favor of the plaintiff, Lucas. The state had blocked any further development on the seaward side of a setback line. That prevented Lucas from developing on two beachfront building lots. The court ruled the state's action a taking and ordered it to provide Lucas with $1.6 million in damages.

In *Dolan v. City of Tigard* (1994) the court again ruled in favor of the plaintiffs, preventing the municipality from requiring that the plaintiffs dedicate land for public purposes in return for a variance that would permit enlargement of their store's parking lot. As in *Nollan*, the court's position was that there was not a sufficient nexus to justify the municipality's demand.

In *Palazzolo v. Rhode Island* (2001) the court again found for the plaintiff. Here, the court blocked the state from preventing Palazzolo from filling in coastal wetland to build a 74-unit housing development. The court found for the plaintiff on the grounds of reasonable "investment backed" expectations despite the fact that the regulations against such development were in place at the time that Palazzolo bought the property.

The five justices finding for Palazzolo were Rehnquist, O'Conner, Kennedy, Scalia, and Thomas, all appointed by Republican presidents. The four voting against him were Ginsburg, Breyer, Souter, and Stevens, all appointed by Democratic presidents. In fact, the lineup was exactly the same as in the *Bush v. Gore* decision of 2000. Again, the link between planning and ideology seems evident.

Planners were not happy with any of these decisions, for by expanding the definition of what constituted a taking they all limited the public power to effect the use of privately owned land. In the next two cases they got some relief. In *Tahoe-Sierra Preservation Council et. al. v. Tahoe Regional Planning Agency et al.* (2002) the question was whether a 32-month development moratorium on development to allow for the making of a regional plan constituted a taking (which would require compensation to the plaintiff). The court rejected the plaintiff's "time is money" argument, taking the position that when the moratorium was up the owners could then recoup the value of their investments. Had the decision gone the other way, just taking the time to go through a thorough planning process might expose a municipality to considerable financial risk. The moratorium had been imposed in the early 1980s; the case was decided two decades later. The wheels of justice can grind slowly.

In *Stop the Beach Renourishment v. Florida Department of Environmental Protection et al.* (2010) the U.S. Supreme Court ruled for the defendants in a decision that very much pleased the planners. In the case that came up through the Florida Court of Appeals and then the Florida Supreme Court, a group of beachfront property owners sued to stop the state from replenishing beachfront that had eroded in front of their houses. That sounds counterintuitive, but their suit had a certain logic to it. If the state replenished the beach that had eroded in front of their homes any newly created beach beyond the old high-water mark would now be state property and that, they claimed, might block their access to or view of the ocean. The U.S. Supreme Court upheld the Florida Supreme Court (which had overruled the Florida Court of Appeals) and denied the homeowners' claims. Had the homeowners won it would have called into question the state's right to restore many miles of beachfront without having to pay compensation, a very serious matter in a state with as much beachfront as Florida. More generally it pushed the ever-changing boundary between public and private rights a bit in the public direction.

THE RIGHTS OF NONRESIDENTS

At one time it was assumed that the only parties who had the legal standing to bring suit against a municipality's zoning ordinance were property owners, for it was their property whose value might be reduced by the ordinance. But since the early 1960s it has been understood and acknowledged by the courts that there are instances where nonresidents and people who do not own property within a municipality may have legal standing to bring suit against a municipality's land-use controls.

Generally such suits have been brought against suburban communities over the matter of land-use controls that, in the view of the plaintiffs, unnecessarily restrict the types of development permitted (hence the term *restrictive zoning*). Typically, the ordinance under attack is a zoning ordinance that limits development in a part, or in some cases all or virtually all, of the municipality to single-family houses on large lots.

Many suits have been brought by minority organizations or their advocates, sometimes in conjunction with builders or developers. Very often the legal basis has been the equal protection clause of the Fourteenth Amendment to the U.S. Constitution. This is the last clause in the last sentence of section I and reads:

> nor deny to any person within its jurisdiction the equal protection of the laws.

The argument is that if the law makes it almost impossible for people to live in a municipality by preventing the construction of housing that they can afford, the law is hardly offering them equal protection. It was also argued that because the average income of blacks is well below the average income of the entire U.S. population, the burden of such zoning laws falls with special force upon blacks and is thus discriminatory.

There have been other arguments as well. One is that if a municipality uses its zoning power to drastically reduce the amount of housing that can be built within its borders, that zoning decision drives up housing prices in other municipalities by displacing to them some housing demand that it would otherwise have satisfied itself. That, in turn, suggests that parties outside of the municipality may have a stake in that municipality's land-use policies.

One of the earliest decisions to accept the latter argument was handed down by the Supreme Court of Pennsylvania in 1965.

> It is not difficult to envision the tremendous hardship, as well as chaotic conditions, which could result if all the townships in this area decided to deny to a growing population sites for residential development within the means of at least a significant segment of the population.[12]

Probably the best-known case involving the rights of outsiders is that of *Southern Burlington NAACP v. Mt. Laurel (NJ)*. In 1975 the Supreme Court of New Jersey found that the town's zoning ordinance excluded entire classes of people including minorities and was invalid under the New Jersey Constitution. It ordered the town to prepare a new ordinance.[13]

In 1983 a group of cases, generally referred to as *Mt. Laurel II*, pushed the first decision further. It imposed an obligation on communities to take positive steps, not just eliminate exclusionary zoning ordinances, to provide housing opportunities for low- and moderate-income residents. The wording of the decision made clear that the range of such steps might be quite broad, including not only rezoning large blocks of land but also eliminating any ordinances that might stand in the way of low- and moderate-income housing—for example, subdivision controls on street widths or buffering requirements—and might also include preferential tax treatment or subsidization for low- and moderate-income housing. The decision also suggested that setting aside some units in more expensive development for low- and moderate-income residents might be required (see inclusionary zoning in Chapter 9).

Alarm among many suburban communities was considerable. In 1985 the New Jersey legislature passed a bill that established a state Council on Affordable Housing. If the council approved the municipality's plan, the municipality would then be immunized against a *Mt. Laurel*–type lawsuit. And, indeed, being able to provide this type of immunity was widely understood to be one of the purposes of the law. The law essentially provided that the council, working with the municipality, would set numerical targets. The municipality could meet those targets both by means of the units constructed within its own borders and by means of a Regional Contribution Agreement (RCA) under which a payment of $20,000 per unit would be given to another community to help it build the remaining units for which the first community was obligated.

In 1986, in a case generally referred to as *Mt. Laurel III*, a builder brought suit but the state's Supreme Court held the law to be constitutional. In the years that followed, a number of units were built under the *Mt. Laurel* arrangements.

The RCA process by which a municipality could deal with its affordable-housing requirements seemed fine to some people but displeased others greatly. What you think of the RCA approach may depend on how you define the problem. If you think the problem is how to achieve social and economic integration, you are likely to view the approach negatively. On the other hand, if you think the main problem is how to get low- and moderate-income housing built somewhere, you may view the approach favorably.

In any case, those who took the former position gradually gained ascendancy in New Jersey, and in 2008 the state adopted the Affordable Housing Reform Bill, which abolished the RCA system, imposed direct affordable-housing requirements on municipalities, and provided some funding for implementation.[14] In commenting on the bill when then Governor Corzine signed it into law on June 17, 2008, one of the bill's sponsors, State Senator Dana L. Redd, stated:

> This isn't just an issue of reducing overcrowding in our cities; it's also about making sure that growth is fair and balanced. Towns that are able to sustain growth, should make sure that they are willing to welcome new residents from all walks of life. Household income is not an indicator of a family's worth, and it's time a number of our higher income, suburban municipalities took notice of that fact.

The timing of the bill was not fortuitous. In the fall of 2008 the financial crisis ensued and the U.S. economy contracted sharply, which was devastating for state and local government finances. Shrinking economic activity cut the yield on sales and income taxes, while foreclosures, housing abandonment, and reduced property values cut the yield on property taxes. At the same time, nothing happened to reduce the necessary level of state and local expenditures. That left little, if any, money available to implement the new law. Then, too, the question of low- and moderate-income housing was dwarfed by larger housing issues, as discussed in Chapter 11. How the Affordable Housing Reform Bill will work out and whether the long-running *Mt. Laurel* story is over remain to be seen.

THE FIGHT OVER EMINENT DOMAIN

It has long been accepted that government can take property, with just compensation, for public purposes. If governments could not do this, a single intransigent property owner could permanently block the building of a road, the assemblage of land for a park, the building of a school, and the like. But within this overall understanding there is much room for what the term *public purpose* means.

The Urban Renewal program (see Chapter 11), which got under way shortly after passage of the Housing Act of 1949, used eminent domain in a new way. Local governments would take private property to assemble blocks of land for projects and then, when site development work had been done, sell or lease the land to developers, who then built housing or commercial buildings. This meant that eminent domain was used to transfer property from one private party to another private party, rather than from private party to government. The private-party-to-private-party transfer occasioned much resentment. In time a property owner went to court to prevent an urban renewal agency from taking his or her property for this purpose. The case was appealed to the U.S. Supreme Court, and in 1954 in *Berman v. Parker* the court found against the plaintiff. That is, the process was constitutional.

That decision seemed to settle the matter, but resentment simmered. Half a century later in 2005, in *Kelo v. New London* [Connecticut], the issue came to the Supreme Court again, and again the Court found against the plaintiff. In effect, the Court affirmed *Berman v. Parker*. But this time the decision unleashed a torrent of anger against the eminent domain process and its real or imagined abuses.

In the year after the *Kelo* decision, all 44 state legislatures that met in that year (not every state legislature meets every year) took up eminent domain bills. Of the 44 legislatures, 28 passed bills restricting the use of eminent domain.[15] There was considerable variation among the bills, but the most common feature was language that restricted the rights of state and local governments to take private property if it was to be transferred to another private party. Generally, there were a few exceptions to this so that private property could be transferred to a common carrier, which would include, for example, railroads and pipelines, and to utility companies. But the sort of transfers done in urban renewal and community development programs were banned. Many of the states specifically banned private-party-to-private-party transfers for "economic development" purposes, effectively saying the same thing in different terms.

To some degree, how you feel about this legislative overruling of *Kelo* will be a matter of your overall political stance. If you basically trust government and if private property rights are not that sacrosanct to you, you are likely to feel that the *Kelo* decision was right and the state legislatures made a mistake. If you feel the reverse on those two matters, then you are likely to be pleased to see the state legislatures, in effect, reverse *Kelo*. In short, the more to the left you are politically, the more likely you are to be happy with *Kelo*, and the more to the right you are, the more likely you are to be happy to see it cancelled out. Beyond the ideological, there was resentment against the whole process of eminent domain because of instances in which government agencies treated property owners in a high-handed manner or in which the private-party-to-private-party transfer process was abused. The potential for a sweetheart deal in which a politically well-connected developer profits unduly from such a transfer is very real.

In addition to the bills passed by state legislatures, there were in 2006 a number of referenda intended to restrict the use of eminent domain. Of these, nine passed, often by large majorities, and two failed. One of those that passed, Arizona 207, also carried language that drastically expanded the definition of a regulatory taking. Basically, the referendum stated that if a restriction on the use to which property could be put reduced the value of that property after the owner had purchased it, the owner was entitled to compensation. There were a few exceptions, such as for matters of public health and safety.

The restrictions on the use of eminent domain and the expansion of the definition of regulatory taking are separate issues, and you could argue that if they were to be put up for referendum, they ought to be separate, for that would give the voters maximum freedom of choice. But in fact they were bundled together so the voter could vote for them only as a pair. Whether the regulatory taking definition would have passed had it been separate is an open question. As a matter of political strategy, those who favored it were shrewd in getting the two items bundled together, for their cause clearly benefited from a groundswell of anger against the perceived abuses of eminent domain.

One might wonder where things stand, given that the Supreme Court upheld *Kelo*, but legislation and referenda blocked that which *Kelo* had allowed. The answer is quite straightforward. All the Supreme Court said is that private-party-to-private-party transfers via eminent domain cannot be blocked on constitutional grounds. But when a state chooses to ban them, then they cannot be done in that state.

What is the planner's stake in all of this? Regardless of what one feels about the rightness or wrongness of the state bans on private-party-to-private-party transfers, it is clear that states and local governments have lost one important tool for a variety of community and economic development purposes. Urban Renewal, as described in Chapter 11, would have been a very different, and probably much smaller, program had such transfers not been possible.

How the part of Arizona 207 that pertains to regulatory taking will play out in practice is not yet clear, for inevitably there will be a court case, the loser will appeal, and that entire process will take a while.

STATE-ENABLING LEGISLATION

Another change in the legal framework of planning since the days of the Plan of Chicago has been the passage of state legislation that defines in broad terms the local planning function. Legislation varies greatly from state to state. In most cases, legislation merely permits localities to engage in particular planning activities. But in other cases, the legislation requires that communities perform certain planning acts. Note, incidentally, that state-enabling legislation also defines municipal obligations and powers with regard to taxation, borrowing, the judicial system, the provision of police protection, and many other matters.

As an example of state-enabling legislation with regard to planning, consider the state of Virginia.[16] Legislation requires that all cities, towns, and counties establish a planning commission and adopt a master plan. The intent of the state's local planning legislation is given as follows:

> To encourage local governments to improve public health, safety, convenience and welfare of its citizens and to plan for the future development of communities to the end that transportation systems be carefully planned; that new community centers be developed with adequate highway, utility, health, educational and recreational facilities; that the needs of agriculture, industry and business be recognized in future growth; that residential areas be provided with healthy surroundings for family life; and that the growth of the community be consonant with efficient and economical use of public funds.

Having laid out the general reasons for requiring communities to plan, the law then goes on to state,

> The governing body of every county and municipality shall by resolution or ordinance create a local planning commission. . . . In accomplishing the objectives . . . such planning commissions shall serve primarily in an advisory capacity to the governing bodies.

The law requires that each city, county, or town draw up a master plan, and then, in a general way, suggests the areas the plan is to cover:

> The local commission shall prepare and recommend a comprehensive plan for the physical development of the territory within its jurisdiction. Every governing body in this state shall adopt a comprehensive plan by July one, nineteen hundred eighty.

Note the requirement for adoption as well as for plan preparation. The reason for this wording is that plans themselves are not laws. They become law and acquire force when the legislative body of a community passes a resolution stating that the attached document (the plan) is adopted as the master plan of the municipality.

The legislation stipulates that the plan and accompanying maps, plats,[17] and so on "may include, but need to be limited to" the following:

1. The designation of areas for various types of public and private development and use, such as different kinds of residential, business, industrial, agricultural, conservation, recreation, public service, flood plain and drainage, and other areas
2. The designation of a system of transportation facilities, such as streets, roads, highways, parkways, railways, bridges, viaducts, waterways, airports, ports, terminals, and other like facilities
3. The designation of a system of community service facilities, such as parks, forests, schools, playgrounds, public buildings and institutions, hospitals,

community centers, waterworks, sewage disposal or waste disposal areas, and the like

4. The designation of historical areas and areas for urban renewal and other treatment

5. An official map, a capital improvements program, a subdivision ordinance (this term is explained in Chapter 9), and a zoning ordinance and zoning district maps

Where state laws or state constitutions permit municipalities to engage in certain acts of planning, it could be said that they are merely granting permission for municipalities to do that which is implicit under the concept of the police power. There is some truth in this. However, planning-enabling acts and zoning-enabling acts are useful in that they encourage municipalities to plan, define the scope of planning, and furnish legal support for the municipality should its plans be challenged in court. As noted, many planning-enabling acts go beyond simply permitting communities to plan and *require* them to plan. These laws thus establish a minimum planning effort that every community must make.

The Legal Link to State Planning

As noted in Chapter 4, many states engage in some statewide planning. Such planning efforts generally impose legal requirements on local governments to ensure that they act in conformity with state plans or planning requirements. For example, if a state engages in planning designed to preserve wetlands, it may require that local governments not grant permits for development in or near wetlands until certain types of studies have been made or hearings conducted. These requirements prevent local governments from permitting actions that contravene the intent of state plans. Since local governments are "creatures of the state," it is clearly within the power of the state to bind local governments so that they act in conformity with state-established guidelines.

THE FEDERAL ROLE

One way the federal government exerts an influence on local planning practice is through legal requirements, such as those discussed in connection with air quality in Chapter 16. However, the largest influence is through the giving of grants and the requirements that the federal government attaches to the receipt of those grants.

In 2008 federal grants to state and local governments totaled $495 billion, or roughly $1,600 for every person in the United States, and accounted for approximately one-fourth of total state and local government expenditures. With this flow of funds necessarily comes considerable oversight and control. This massive flow of funds has not always been a part of the U.S. political picture. In 1960 federal aid to state and local governments was about

$7 billion.[18] After adjusting that figure for inflation, there was a ninefold increase in federal aid between 1960 and 2007. Adjusting that figure for population growth yields a real per capita increase of about 5.4 times.

Why this pattern of transfers evolved can be explained in various ways. Sometimes it is said that the federal government can raise monies more easily than state and local governments because it has "the best revenue sources." This is largely a reference to the personal income tax, which over the years has proven to be highly income elastic.[19] A more general explanation is simply that state and local governments are restrained in their taxing behavior by fear of losing residents and economic activity to other jurisdictions that tax more lightly. The federal government is not nearly so restrained in this regard.

Another explanation, which places its emphasis on political behavior rather than economic rationality, is offered by the Public Choice theorists. They attribute much of the expansion of the federal government's role in local and state affairs to the vote-seeking competition between politicians to deliver revenues raised elsewhere to their own constituents.[20]

These intergovernmental grants give the federal government enormous influence over localities, both directly and also indirectly through the states. Making certain types of behavior a prerequisite for receiving grants is one way. For example, the federal government has no literal power to compel a community to adopt certain procedures to include citizens in its planning processes. However, if the implementation of the plans, or even the formulating of the plans, will be done partly with federal funds, the federal government can achieve the effect of requirement simply by making citizen participation a requirement for the receipt of federal funds. And in fact, planning at the city, town, and county levels is heavily conditioned by such federal requirements.

Very often the federal government does not even need to monitor the behavior of the recipient government to achieve compliance. The reason is simple: If the local government violates a federal funding requirement, it is likely to face a lawsuit from some individual or group seeking to block its use of federal funds on the grounds that it has violated a condition of receiving such funds. For example, failure to include low- and moderate-income citizens in the decision-making process for community development planning is likely to bring such a suit from a low-income or minority advocacy group. Failure to heed guidelines attached to a federal grant for construction of a wastewater treatment plant might bring a suit from an environmental organization. Thus, many of the guidelines attached to grants are self-enforcing.

Another way to influence local behavior is simply by providing funds for the purpose. When Congress wanted to encourage states and localities to do water-quality planning, it provided grants for doing so. Many localities that did water-quality planning in the late 1970s and early 1980s did not want to do it enough to use their own funds. However, they were happy to do it with federal funds from section 208 of the Clean Water Act of 1977.

Mandated Responsibilities

The federal government also influences local and state planning activities by direct requirements, or "mandates." For example, the Clean Air Act amendments of 1970 require the EPA to establish certain air-quality standards. To meet these standards, states are required to produce state implementation plans (SIPs). Although the states have great latitude in the precise manner in which these air-quality standards are to be met, the federal legislation does force them to plan and also establishes minimum targets (levels of air quality) for which to plan. The legislation also specifies in general ways the items that state plans must contain. For example, the state plan must contain provisions for reviewing plans for construction of facilities that might produce sufficient emissions to prevent achievement of federally mandated air-quality standards. Thus plans for a solid-waste incinerator that might push levels of air pollutants above federally mandated standards would have to be reviewed. Should a state government fail to make such a review or make the review in an inadequate manner, it might open itself up to legal action by an environmental group or other concerned parties.

The situation just described represents a particular style of regulation that is commonly used by federal and state governments. The regulating body does not tell the regulated party what to do in detail. Rather, the regulated party is told what must be achieved but is left with wide discretion concerning how to do so. Perhaps the best-known example of this regulatory style is seen in the rules pertaining to automobile fuel economy. Average mileage standards, Corporate Average Fuel Economy (CAFE), for the total fleet produced by a manufacturer were established, and fines for exceeding this standard were set. But carmakers were told nothing about what technologies to use in achieving these goals.

One advantage of this approach is that overall goals are formulated at a high level, where decision makers have an overview of "the big picture." But technical decisions are made by those who are closer to the problem and thus better informed about details. As a practical matter this style is also likely to be much more acceptable in a political system like that of the United States—one in which power is widely distributed and in which there are strong local governments and a tradition of resistance to excessive central authority.

SUMMARY

Planning occurs within a framework of state legislation, for the municipality as a "creature of the state" has only those powers granted it by the state. It also bears those responsibilities imposed on it by the state. The capacity of a municipality to implement plans is also circumscribed by constitutionally guaranteed individual rights.

Zoning, the best known of land-use control devices, is an exercise of the "police power." The contradictions, real or apparent, between the zoning process and constitutional guarantees relative to property and to due process go far to explain why the process of establishing the rights of municipalities to zone took several decades. Even today, the zoning power is still evolving through a process of legislation, litigation, and judicial decision.

Planning-enabling legislation defines the powers of municipalities with regard to planning and, in many cases, also defines the obligations of the community with regard to planning. For example, it may require that the community have a comprehensive plan and that the plan include certain elements.

The federal government exerts a large influence over the local planning process. In some cases it does so by laws and regulations. More often, it does so through requirements attached to funding or simply through the pattern of federal grants. The predominant flow of funds is downward: from the federal government to state and local governments, and from state governments to local governments.

NOTES

1. John F. Dillon, *Commentaries on the Law of Municipal Corporations*, 5th ed., Little, Brown & Co., Boston, 1911, vol. 1, sec. 237. It can be argued that the "creature of the state" concept is not quite so literally true as it once was. Since World War II there has been a trend for the powers and obligations of local governments to be defined in state constitutions rather than in laws or charters. If one takes the view that the state constitution comes from the people and creates both the state government and the local governments, one could argue that the state and local governments exist in parallel and are thus coequal.

2. Jesse L. Richardson Jr., Meghan Zimmerman Gough, and Robert Puentes, *Is Home Rule the Answer? Clarifying the Influence of Dillon's Rule on Growth Management*, The Brookings Institution, Washington, DC, 2003.

3. As an example of the antizoning position, both for legal and for other reasons, see Jack C. Harris and William Douglas Moore, "Debunking the Mythology of Zoning," *Real Estate Review*, vol. 13, no. 4, Winter 1984, pp. 94–97.

4. For an account of the legal issues involved in taking, see Daniel R. Mandelker, *Land Use Law*, The Michie Co., Charlottesville, VA, 1982.

5. For a history of the evolution of zoning, see Mel Scott, *American City Planning Since 1890*, University of California Press, Berkeley, 1971, chaps. 2 and 3.

6. See Charles F. Flory, "Shaping the Skyscrapers of Manhattan," *Real Estate Review*, vol. 13, no. 2, Summer 1983, pp. 48–53.

7. 272 U.S., 365 (1926).

8. Jerome S. Kayden, "Celebrating How the Supreme Court's Preservation of Grand Central Terminal Helped Preserve Planning Nationwide," *Planning*, June 2003, pp. 20–23.

9. John Tibbetts, "Everybody's Taking the Fifth," *Planning*, January 1995, pp. 4–10.

10. R. Gregory Nokes, "Opponents Call Measure 7 Threat to Land, McCall Legacy: Critics Step Up Their Attack on the 'Takings' Proposal, Which a New Poll Indicates Has Solid Support," *The Oregonian*, November 2, 2000, p. A7. See also Charles E. Begs, "Court Hears Argument on Property Compensation Measure," Associated Press Newswire, September 10, 2001.

11. For the complete text of Measure 37, go to www.sos.state.or.us/elections/nov22004/guide/meas/m37_text.html.

12. *National Land and Investment Company v. Kohn*, 215, A. 2d 597 (Pa. 1965).

13. For a brief account of the collective effect of these decisions, see Wendy U. Larsen, "The Failure to Legislate: Mt. Laurel II," *Urban Land*, April 1983, pp. 34–35. For *Mt. Laurel III*, see Harold A. McDougal, "From Litigation to Legislation in Exclusionary Zoning Law," *Harvard Civil Rights Civil Liberties Law Review*, vol. 22, 1987, pp. 623–663.

14. www.nj.gov/governor/news/news/2008/approved/20080717.html.

15. See the website of the National Conference of State Legislatures at www.ncsl.org/programs/natres/emindomainleg06.htm.
16. Code of Virginia, 1950 (as amended), Title 15.1, chap. 11.
17. A plat is a map or diagram showing a parcel of land divided into building lots.
18. By "local governments" is meant all municipal and county governments and also school and other districts.
19. The term *elastic* in this usage means that percentage increases in tax revenues exceed percentage increases in income.
20. For a very quick, readable summary of the Public Choice view, see "The Public Choice Revolution," James Gwartney and Richard Wagner, *The Intercollegiate Review*, Spring 1988, pp. 17–26. For more extensive treatments, see other works by these two authors as well as works by Gordon Tullock and James Buchanan.

SELECTED BIBLIOGRAPHY

Buck, Peter L., ed., *Modern Land Use Control*, The Practicing Law Institute, New York, 1978.

Burns, James M., Peltason, J. W., and Cronin, Thomas E., *Government by the People*, 6th ed., Prentice Hall, Upper Saddle River, NJ, 1996.

Mandelker, Daniel R., *Land Use Law*, The Michie Co., Charlottesville, VA, 1982.

Stuart Meck, Paul Wack, and Michelle J. Zimet, "Zoning and Subdivision Regulations," in *The Practice of Local Government Planning*, 3rd ed., International City Management Association, Washington, DC, 2000, pp. 343–374.

CHAPTER 6

Planning and Politics

WHY IS PLANNING POLITICAL? _____

For several reasons, planning generally takes place in a highly politicized environment.

1. Planning often involves matters in which people have large emotional stakes—for example, the character of a neighborhood or the quality of a school district. A planning decision that you do not like may intrude itself into your life every day because its fruits are located where you live or work. The often very emotional suburban resistance to subsidized housing is largely a matter of residents' fears about the effect it will have on the local school system. The residents may be right or wrong, but either way it is easy to understand why they become passionate about what they think will affect the happiness and safety of their children. (In Chapter 7, see the box on pages 107–110 about the city of Yonkers.) Vociferous citizens' opposition was the major force that ended Urban Renewal (see Chapter 12). Few actions of government can arouse more emotion than a program that might force the citizen to give up an apartment or relocate his or her business to make way for what one writer called "the federal bulldozer."

2. Planning decisions are visible. They involve buildings, roads, parkland, properties—entities that citizens see and know about. Planning mistakes, like architectural mistakes, are hard to hide.

3. Like all functions of local government, the planning process is close at hand. It is easier for the citizen to affect the actions of a town board or a city council than the actions of a state legislature or of Congress. That feeling of potential effectiveness encourages participation.

4. Citizens correctly assume that they know something about planning without having studied it formally. Planning involves land use, traffic, the character of the community, and other items with which they are familiar. Therefore, citizens tend not to defer to planners.

5. Planning involves decisions with large financial consequences. Mr. X owns 100 acres of farmland on the urban fringe. Land values in the area are rising, and it is clear that the land will soon pass from agricultural to a more intensive use. If municipal sewer and water lines are extended along the road fronting the property, the land will be suitable for garden apartment development at 12 units per acre, making it worth, say, $100,000 per acre. On the other hand, if the land is not served with utilities, development there will be limited to single-family houses on 1-acre lots, and land will be worth $10,000 per acre. Mr. X now has a $9 million interest in whether the municipal master plan shows sewer and water lines down a particular road. Variations on this theme could easily be posed in terms of zoning, street widening, community development, construction of public buildings, flood-control measures, and the like.

Even those who own no property other than the house they live in may feel, quite correctly, that they have a substantial financial stake in planning decisions. For many people, their biggest single source of net worth is not in bank accounts or stock certificates but in home equity (what the home would bring when sold minus what is owed on it). Planning decisions that affect house values may thus assume major importance to homeowners.

6. There can be a strong link between planning questions and property taxes. The property tax is one of the financial mainstays of local government as well as of public education. Planning decisions that affect what is built within a community affect the community's tax base. That affects the property taxes that community residents must pay. And these taxes are hardly a trivial sum. In 2010 total property tax collections in the United States were approximately $470 billion, or a little over $1,500 per capita. Concern over property tax levels has been very great for many years. Witness Proposition 13 in California and comparable property tax limits in a number of other states.

PLANNERS AND POWER

Planners are basically advisors. Alone, the planner does not have the power to do many of the things that cause change within the community: to commit public funds, to enact laws, to enter into contracts, or to exercise the power of eminent domain. Where the planner does have some legal powers, perhaps in connection with land-use controls, as discussed in Chapter 9, they are powers granted by the legislative body and removable by that same body. The planner's influence on events, then, stems from the capacity to articulate viewpoints and develop consensus and coalitions among those who do wield significant power.

A plan is a vision of the future. A planner moves events to the extent that he or she can cause that vision to be shared. In the early years of planning—as noted in connection with the Plan of Chicago—the view was that the plan came solely, or almost solely, from the head of the planner. It was then his or her task to sell that vision to the public and to the political establishment of the community. This is exactly what was done with great success in the Chicago case by Burnham and his associates.

A more modern view is that good plans spring from the community itself. In this view the planner's proper role is to facilitate the planning process and to aid it with his or her own expertise, rather than to deliver the plan full blown. Several points can be made in favor of the modern approach. First, it avoids elitism. The planner has particular skills that the average citizen does not have, but that capacity does not make the planner wiser in general. Second, there is no way that the planner, or any other single individual or group, can have a complete and an accurate view of the interests of the citizenry as a whole. Only the individual can really know his or her own needs and preferences. If that is true, only by taking the citizenry into the planning process at an early stage can their interests be fully represented. Last, it can be argued that a plan formed with substantial community input is more likely to be carried out than a plan of equal quality that has simply been drawn up directly by professionals. The very act of participating in the planning process informs the citizen about the details of the plan. Giving time and energy to the process of planning builds the citizens' commitment to the plan. What was "their plan" now becomes "our plan." But there are also some counterarguments. We will come to these shortly.

Planners now view involvement with politics very differently than they did a few decades ago. In the 1920s and 1930s, it was common to try to isolate the planning process from politics—to keep planning "above" politics. A common political arrangement was to have the planner report solely to a "nonpolitical" planning board. In time it was realized that since the political sphere was where decisions were made, isolating the planner from politics rendered him or her much less effective. Then, too, it came to be realized that the term *nonpolitical* is misleading. If one appoints a group of prominent citizens as a lay board, one has, in fact, made a political decision. A group of nonprominent citizens might give the planners a very different set of instructions. No one is really nonpolitical, for everyone has interests and values, and that is the substance of which politics is made.

The notion of the planning function as one that should be nonpolitical is related to the urban political reform movement of the late nineteenth and early twentieth century.[1] Political power was wrested from the old machines like New York's Tammany Hall and vested in civil servants; so-called reform administrations; and in some cities, professional, nonpartisan managers. The city manager form of government, in which the elected mayor has a largely ceremonial role and the real administrative responsibility and authority are vested in a city manager hired by the legislative body, comes from the reform movement.

In the reform view, politics was a seamy and often corrupt process, and the more that planning could be kept out of it, the better. A more modern view would be that the reform movement was in some measure a victory of the upper-middle class over machines, which often represented, albeit with some of the gravy skimmed off the top, the working class and newly arrived immigrants. In short, reform was not the elimination of politics so much as a transfer of political power.

THE FRAGMENTATION OF POWER

The environment in which the planner operates is characterized by a diffusion of political, economic, and legal power. This condition is probably true for any planner anywhere, but it is particularly true in the United States. Political power in the United States is fragmented in several ways. First, it is distributed among different levels of government. State and local governments are much stronger in relation to the national government than is the case in most of the other democratic states of the Western world such as France or Great Britain. In general state and local governments raise much more of their own revenues than do their counterparts in other democracies. Financial responsibility and political autonomy are related. The relatively greater autonomy of state and local governments in the United States goes back to the Constitution, which, as its writers intended, sharply limits the power of the federal government. Resistance to central authority is an old American political tradition.

Political power is also fragmented through the so-called separation of powers among the executive, legislative, and judicial branches. That separation goes back to the founding of the country and the intent of the drafters of the Constitution to restrain government by structuring it so that the power of each branch would counterbalance the powers of the other branches. Planning as a government activity is clearly a function of the executive branch. However, implementing virtually any plan requires funding. Both the levying of taxes and the appropriation of funds are legislative functions. The powers of both the executive and the legislative branches are, of course, constrained by the judicial branch. That branch, at the federal level, is nominated by the executive branch and confirmed by the legislative branch.

In addition to being fragmented along the executive-judicial-legislative line, local government may also be fragmented in an administrative sense. A metropolitan area that constitutes a single economic and social entity may be divided into dozens or even hundreds of political jurisdictions. In addition to governments, there may be a variety of districts that have some governmental powers and responsibilities. School districts, for example, generally have the power to tax and sometimes have the power of eminent domain. In many states the school-board members are elected directly by the residents of the district, and those members, in turn, choose the district's superintendent. The administrative structure that runs the schools thus exists in parallel to the structure of local government but is not a part of that government. Yet both structures tax the same population, both may make land-use decisions, and both may issue debt and make capital investments. Similar comments can be made with regard to water, sewer, transportation, and other authorities.

The United States has a strong tradition of respect for property rights. Conflict over the exact location of the boundary between the rights of the public and the rights of property owners is inevitable. The determination of the boundary is ultimately made in the courts, that is, by the judicial branch. We also note that the courts are often the guardians of individual rights and in this role may require certain actions by the other branches of government. Court-mandated school integration is perhaps the best-known example, but there are many others. For example, how the courts interpret the language of the Americans with Disabilities Act (ADA) of 1992 determines exactly what steps municipalities must take and what expenditures they must make for individuals with disabilities.

Power in the nongovernmental sphere is also widely distributed. The citizens in their role as voters are the ultimate power. But groups of individuals also constitute power blocs. The citizen as a homeowner is part of a very powerful bloc, as any planner working in a community with a large percentage of owner-occupied housing units quickly learns. In many communities the citizen as a member of a labor union is part of a powerful bloc. The citizen as a member of an environmental group such as the Sierra Club or a local conservation group is a member of another bloc. Those who own substantial amounts of property, whether vacant land or structures, constitute still another source of power. So, too, are the community's employers.

There is a very strong relationship among land-use planning, capital investment, and construction activity. Thus the construction industry—both management and labor—is often a major participant in planning decisions and in planning controversies.

Not only do citizens participate in the planning process both as individuals and as members of groups, but there is also a certain amount of *citizen participation* organized by the planners themselves. This is done partly to involve the public in planning questions, as noted before, but also because it is often a legal requirement. Much federal funding for highways, water and sewer systems, local economic development projects, and the like requires evidence of organized citizen participation before monies can be disbursed. Such requirements are not readily evaded. In fact, they are self-enforcing because the planners and municipal officials know that if the requirements are not met, the project may well be stopped by a procedurally based lawsuit that claims that the federal citizens' participation requirements were not met.

Most planners, on balance, look favorably on citizen participation, but it can have its frustrations. The planner who takes a comprehensive view of the city or town may be very frustrated by citizens who are tremendously concerned with what happens in their immediate vicinity but relatively unconcerned about the "big picture." It is the experience of most planners that citizens participate very readily on issues close to their homes but that it is usually very difficult to get them involved in larger-scale questions like regional planning. In a sense, the citizen's perspective is often like perspective in drawing: Objects that are close to the viewer appear much larger than objects of the same size that are farther away. Then, too, even if you as a planner are strongly committed to citizen participation you may feel very frustrated when your professional judgment, perhaps backed by many hours spent studying a particular situation, is rejected because it conflicts with citizens' (or politicians') casual opinions. Of course, this is the same frustration that the economist, the policy analyst, or any other expert experiences when giving advice in a political situation.

It is a basic fact of political life that it is easier to mobilize people in opposition than it is to mobilize them in support. Thus often there are groups that have the power to stop things from happening, but no group that has the power to make things happen. Citizen opposition has shot down many a planner's brainchild. In the sense that any citizen has the opportunity to make his or her voice heard, citizen participation is democratic. But it is not always as representative as one might at first think. Citizens' groups and movements are self-selected and may represent a very small percentage of the population, but local governments often respond to the pressure of vocal and determined minorities. The idealistic young planner who sees his or her ideas about, for example, affordable housing stomped to death by prosperous homeowners at a public meeting may come away from the experience wiser, sadder, and harboring mixed feelings about the benefits of "power to the people."

The person who had the most effect upon the physical form of the New York metropolitan area is, without doubt, Robert Moses.[2] Moses, whose career started early in the twentieth century, well before the age of citizen participation, was brilliant, forceful, extremely adept at political manipulation, and sure that he was right. In his early adulthood, at least, he was also idealistic. He was, in large measure, responsible for the building of highways and bridges, the building of parks, the construction of all sorts of community facilities, and the destruction of large amounts of housing and many small businesses to make way for his projects. He had little interest in what the public wanted, but rather in what he thought was needed. He was both widely admired and widely detested. It is hard to evaluate his overall effect on the New York region because it is hard to say what the region would be like if he had not lived. All one can say with any degree of certainty is that it would be quite different.

Nineteenth-century Paris had its own Robert Moses—named Baron Haussmann. He, too, was possessed of an iron certainty, great ability, and great forcefulness. If you go to the center of Paris, the part that most tourists see, it is likely to strike you as a splendid piece of urban design and a wonderful place to spend some time. Of course, if you had been one of the many thousands of poor nineteenth-century Parisians rendered homeless as Haussmann razed whole neighborhoods to make way for his vision (see the photograph on page 172), you might have had a very different view of the man. In any case, he would not have concerned himself with your opinion, and probably not with your welfare either.

But regardless of how the planner may feel about citizen participation, and in the writer's experience most planners have some ambivalence on the subject, it is here to stay. The days when people used "you can't fight city hall" as an expression about accepting the inevitable are long gone. A population that is better educated, more affluent, less deferential to authority, and possibly more generally suspicious of "the establishment" than it was decades ago is not going to sit passively on the sidelines. The day of the Moseses and Haussmanns is long gone.

The planner usually finds little within the community on which there is unanimous agreement. Majority positions can often be found, and compromises can be reached. But it is rare when all parties can agree on precisely what constitutes the public interest. When propositions are stated as generalities, they often elicit more agreement than when they are stated as specific proposals. For example, we all favor enhanced environmental quality. But raise the issue of shutting down a particular facility, and you quickly find that one person's environmental protection is another person's unemployment. Planning, like politics, is in large measure the art of compromise.

STYLES OF PLANNING

We have suggested that the planner works in an environment of widely distributed power, conflicting interests, and less than total agreement. How, then, are planners to conduct themselves? Styles of planning vary among individuals and also among places. Few planners will fit exactly into any one of the types that follow but rather will display different amounts of the several pure types in their professional roles.

1. *The planner as neutral public servant.* In this role, planners take a politically neutral stance and fall back on their professional expertise, which they will use to tell the community how best to do what it wishes to do. They will not, in general, try to tell the community what it ought to do. The advice and technical work they present to the community, subject to law and personal and professional ethics, will largely be confined to "how to" and "what if" and not "should" or "should not."

2. *The planner as builder of community consensus.* This is essentially a political view of the planner. It became more popular in the postwar period as it grew very clear to most planners that the older view of the planner as nonpolitical public servant was at great variance from the way that planning questions actually are resolved.[3]

In this view, planning cannot be separated from politics. Politics is the art of taking divergent views and divergent interests and bringing them into sufficient harmony to permit action to be taken. The role of the politician, then, is that of broker between various interests.[4] Since no plans can be implemented without political will and political action, the planner, too, must be very close to, or perhaps a part of, the political process. The advocate of this view, for example, would hold that the older notion of having the planner report solely to a supposedly nonpartisan lay planning board is a prescription for impotence: It is better to make the planner an integral part of the bureaucracy or the political structure where the decisions are made. How much planners can move the community in their own direction varies. The planner who is visibly at great odds with the main values and desires of the community often becomes an unemployed planner.

3. *The planner as entrepreneur.* This is not a role that planners originally envisaged for themselves but one in which many find themselves. When the planners run an agency that is particularly task-oriented, they very often become entrepreneurs. For example, in Urban Renewal programs, public funds were used to clear and prepare sites, which were then sold or leased for development by private capital. The planner who ran an Urban Renewal agency had to market sites, find developers, and negotiate contracts. Local economic development programs have as their primary goal increasing private investment in the community. Thus the economic development planner is necessarily drawn into an entrepreneurial role involving marketing, negotiation, and financing.

4. *The planner as advocate.* In this role the planner acts as a representative for certain groups or certain positions and chooses to advance particular interests. The concept of advocacy planning, which developed in the early 1960s, sprang from the view that there are groups in society that lack the political and economic strength to advance their own interests adequately. Thus they need to be specially represented in the planning process. Specifically, advocacy planning cut its teeth on the issue of exclusionary zoning (see Chapters 9 and 19). Advocacy planners, the best known of whom was the late Paul Davidoff, took the position that suburban zoning laws locked out the poor and minority-group members and then set about to change such laws by means of persuasion and, more important, litigation.[5] The advocacy planner, like the attorney, does not generally claim to represent the majority but rather the interests of a particular client. Those interests may or may not coincide with interests of the majority of the community or, for that matter, of the nation.

In general, advocacy planners who represent less prosperous subgroups of the population have at least some element of a radical political perspective. It is the view that society exploits, mistreats, or otherwise abuses some of its citizens that is likely to propel one into an advocacy role. If, on the other hand, one sees society as generally fair and just, one is not likely to see much need for advocacy planning.

The notion of advocacy may also be used in a slightly different sense. Rather than serve as the advocate of a particular group in society, the planner may advocate a particular cause or program, such as parks, mass transit, highways, or environmental preservation. The planner who represents a cause may have a somewhat easier time of making a claim to serving the public interest as a whole than does the planner who represents a particular group. But even here, if one picks almost any goal, it will generally turn out that accomplishing it creates some gainers and some losers.

5. *The planner as agent of radical change.* This is a view held by only a few practicing planners. Planners who hold a full-blown radical perspective are likely to find the day-to-day work of planning in most organizations frustrating and painful because they will have to cooperate on a daily basis with a system for which they have little respect. Among planning academicians there are a fair number, though definitely a minority, who take a neo-Marxian or critical theory position and see the promotion of radical political and economic change as a proper long-term goal for planning. This subject is discussed further in Chapter 19.

HOW PLANNING AGENCIES ARE ORGANIZED _____

Planning agencies vary greatly in size and purpose. What follows is typical but far from universal. As noted, the old idea of a planning agency's being outside and "above" politics has been almost universally abandoned. The modern planning agency is a part of the executive branch of the municipal government. Its head, like the commissioners of other departments, reports to the chief elected official or, if there is a manager form of government, to the city or town manager. Very commonly, the planning director or commissioner is a political appointee nominated by the chief elected official and confirmed by the legislative body, just as the head of a federal department is nominated by the president subject to confirmation by the Senate. The commissioner is often required to have specific qualifications such as a master's degree in planning or membership in the American Institute of Certified Planners (a certification based on education, experience, and passing an examination). As an appointed official, the commissioner or director can be dismissed at the will of the chief elected official. In that sense, as in many other ways, the ultimate power to plan is vested in elected officials and, therefore, in the body politic of the community.

Beneath the commissioner is a staff, who often have civil service status. In this case a position such as assistant planner, associate planner, planner, and so forth has defined requirements such as degrees and education. The newly hired individual typically goes through a provisional period of six months or a year and, if judged satisfactory, then receives a permanent appointment. Because of the difference between a political and a civil service appointment, the staff often have a good deal more permanency than the commissioner has.

In addition to reporting to the chief elected official, the head of the planning agency may also report to a lay planning board, typically made up of citizens who have been nominated by the chief executive officer and confirmed by the legislative body. Its members serve with no or, at most, token pay. The purpose of the board is to provide some citizen input to and oversight for the planning agency. Such boards vary greatly: Some are merely rubber stamps; others may be very active and forceful. Some boards see their role as essentially supervisory, whereas others may use their own status within the municipality to advance the program of the planning agency. A board whose members are articulate and energetic can make a major contribution to building public support for planning.

The planning agency may also report directly to the community's legislative body. Often, the municipality's charter or bylaws will specify subjects on which the agency will report. For example, the charter might specify that the agency will deliver an annual report evaluating the various items proposed in the municipality's capital budget.

If the agency is of moderate or larger size, there are likely to be several sections that handle different aspects of the planning task. For example, there may be a group that handles comprehensive or long-range planning. There may be another group that handles land-use control issues and performs such functions as zoning and subdivision reviews (see Chapter 9). Still another group may review matters related to the capital budget such as investment in water and sewer facilities, roads, municipal facilities, and the like. In some agencies there will be a research section that makes population forecasts and revenue estimates and, generally, tries to provide a solid quantitative and factual basis for the actions of the rest of the agency. Other sections might deal with environmental or transportation issues. In the 1970s, when community development funds began to flow from the Department of Housing and Urban Development, many planning agencies set up sections to handle the disbursement of these funds. For example, a county agency might have had a community development section that reviewed the plans of and funded the community development activities of subcounty units of government or private groups. From time to time, other planning-related functions of government may be lodged in planning agencies. For example, economic development organizations have been lodged in many planning agencies.

Combined departments are common. Many planning agencies have been merged with community development departments. Which agency is the dog and which agency is the tail depends upon the priorities of the municipality. Another arrangement is the combined Planning and Public Works Department. The argument for the merger is that both deal with different elements of the same process, namely, land development. The head of one such combined agency told the author that such an arrangement enlarges the perspective of all parties. The planners become more aware of the engineering and cost realities. The engineers become more aware of the larger picture and begin to think about what to do as well as how to do it.

In small municipalities there may be only one or two planners, who function as jacks-of-all-trades without the specialization of labor just described. In fact, in many municipalities there is no full-time planner. Rather, there is a planning board of lay members, and the technical work of planning is performed either by consultants or sometimes by personnel of a higher-level planning agency. For example, a county or multicounty agency might provide technical support to towns within its area.

Planning Consultants

There are numerous planning consulting firms in the United States, and a substantial minority of all planners are employed by consultants. In general, municipalities with larger planning staffs use consultants primarily for specialized tasks such as environmental studies, traffic studies, planning for specialized facilities such as solid waste disposal sites, or major urban design work. For municipalities with small or no professional planning staffs, consultants are likely to be retained for basic planning tasks such as the drawing up of master plans and zoning ordinances. In fact, a very substantial percentage of all master plans and zoning ordinances in the United States have been done by planning consultants.

Having work done by a consultant rather than in-house has both advantages and disadvantages. One advantage may be the consultant's specialized knowledge and breadth of experience. A disadvantage may be that the consultant does not know the municipality very well and so may miss things that someone familiar with the municipality would see. Consultant–community relationships vary. The consultant may proceed as expeditiously as possible—for time is money—and provide the town with a "cookie-cutter" plan or zoning ordinance that draws heavily on work the consultant has done elsewhere and that may not suit this particular municipality well. In other cases the relationship is a long-term one; the consultant comes to know the municipality, its political establishment, and its citizens very well, and, in effect, serves as the municipality's planning department.

Reaching Out to the Public

Because planning is a collective activity and because no agency will be very successful without a broad political base, planning agencies generally have a number of links to the community through various advisory or lay groups. These links may be formal or entirely casual. One approach is the advisory panel: A group of citizens interested in a particular issue, say, environmental quality, maintain a liaison with the planning agency. The agency solicits information and advice from the group on planning decisions that have significant environmental impact. Citizens interested in housing might constitute another group with which the agency has frequent contact. In a college town in which I lived, there are citizens' groups concerned with sidewalks, bicycle paths, and urban design, and the planning agency has frequent contact with all of them. Such groups often furnish support for planning department initiatives, as well as useful data and ideas. But even when the citizens and the planners disagree, it is generally better to communicate on a continuing basis than simply to meet occasionally in an adversarial situation. Differences that can often be negotiated through informal contacts may solidify beyond compromise if they first surface in a public environment and people take stands from which it is later awkward or embarrassing to retreat. As discussed in Chapter 8, planning agencies also make extensive use of public meetings and presentations when developing plans. Meetings are useful in building support, in helping the agency understand and be responsive to citizens' preferences and concerns, and in meeting legal requirements for citizens' participation.

Beyond all these approaches, most planning agencies reach out to the community through a variety of informal means. The planning director or staff members speaks before the Rotary Club, the League of Women Voters, the Chamber of Commerce, and other groups. Many agencies send out press releases and otherwise seek media coverage so that people know what the agency is doing and why. Modern computer and communications technology is rapidly expanding the range of real-time public participation in the planning process. A few of these new techniques are sketched out in Chapter 8.

But one way or another, outreach is essential. The agency that does not build a base of popular support within the community is not likely to accomplish very much. For reasons noted earlier, this is truer now than it was some decades ago.

SUMMARY

Planning takes place in a highly political environment because (1) planning often involves issues in which citizens have a large emotional stake; (2) the results of planning decisions are often highly visible; (3) planning questions are more accessible to citizens than those handled at the state or national level; (4) citizens feel they have insight into planning questions and are not overly deferential to planners' expertise; (5) planning decisions often have large financial effects on property owners; and (6) planning decisions may have significant effects on property tax rates.

Planners exercise little or no power directly but rather affect events to the extent that they affect the political processes of the community. In the last several decades, the idea of planning as a nonpolitical process has given way to a more realistic view of the planner as one of a number of participants in the political process. The older view of the planner as presenting a finished plan to the community has now been supplanted by the view that planning is a community process, that the planner facilitates and supports with technical expertise.

Depending on the community and the personality and ideology of the planner(s), a variety of planning styles can be identified: (1) the planner as neutral public servant, (2) the planner as builder of community consensus, (3) the planner as entrepreneur, (4) the planner as advocate, and (5) the planner as agent of radical change.

NOTES

1. For a discussion of the reform tradition in urban politics, see Blake McKelvey, *The Urbanization of America*, Rutgers University Press, New Brunswick, NJ, 1963, particularly chaps. 6 and 7. See also Edward C. Banfield, *City Politics*, Harvard University Press, Cambridge, MA, 1963. For more recent references to work on the reform movement, see John M. Levy, *Urban America: Processes and Problems*, Prentice Hall, Upper Saddle River, NJ, 2000, chap. 5.
2. Robert A. Caro, *The Power Broker*, Random House, New York, 1974.
3. One early work that examined the disparity between a purely rational and technical approach and the way decisions are actually reached is Martin Meyerson and Edward C. Banfield, *Politics, Planning and the Public Interest*, The Free Press, Glencoe, IL, 1955. A shorter presentation of some of the same arguments can be found in Edward C. Banfield, "Ends and Means in Planning," *International Social Science Journal*, vol. 11, no. 3, 1959. The article is reprinted in Andreas Faludi, *A Reader in Planning Theory*, Pergamon Press, New York, 1973. Another article in this connection is Norman Beckman, "The Planner as Bureaucrat," *Journal of the American Institute of Planners*, vol. 30, November 1964, also reprinted in Faludi, *Planning Theory*. See also Alan Altshuler, *The City Planning Process: A Political Analysis*, Cornell University Press, Ithaca, NY, 1965; Herbert J. Gans, *People and Plans*, Basic Books, New York, 1968; and Anthony J. Catanese, *Planners and Local Politics*, Sage Publications, Beverly Hills, CA, 1974.
4. A number of planners have become quite interested in mediation techniques in this regard. See, for example, Lawrence Susskind, "Mediating Public Disputes," *Negotiation Journal*, January 1985, pp. 19–22.
5. Paul Davidoff, "Advocacy and Pluralism in Planning," *Journal of the American Institute of Planners* (now the *APA Journal*), vol. 31, 1965. See also Paul Davidoff and Thomas A. Reiner, "A Choice Theory of Planning," *Journal of the American Institute of Planners*, vol. 28, May 1962. Both are reprinted in Faludi, *Planning Theory*.

SELECTED BIBLIOGRAPHY

Banfield, Edward C., *City Politics*, Harvard University Press, Cambridge, MA, 1963.

Brooks, Michael P., *Planning Theory for Practitioners*, Planners Press, American Planning Association, Chicago, 2002.

Catanese, Anthony James, *Planners and Local Politics*, Sage Publications, Beverly Hills, CA, 1974.

Catanese, Anthony James, *The Politics of Planning and Development*, Sage Publications, Beverly Hills, CA, 1984.

Forester, John, *The Deliberative Practitioner*, MIT Press, Cambridge, MA, 1999.

Friedmann, John, *Planning in the Public Domain: From Knowledge to Action*. Princeton University Press, Princeton, NJ, 1987.

Goldberger, Paul, *Up from Zero: Politics, Architecture and the Rebuilding of New York*, Random House, New York, 2004.

Harrigan, John J., *Political Change and the Metropolis*, Little, Brown & Co., Boston, 1985.

Hoch, Charles, *What Planners Do: Power, Politics, Persuasion*. American Planning Association, Chicago, 1994.

Jacobs, Allan, *Making City Planning Work*, American Society of Planning Officials, Chicago, 1978.

Lucy, William, *Close to Power: Setting Priorities with Elected Officials*, American Planning Association, Chicago, 1988.

Meyerson, Martin, and Banfield, Edward C., *Politics, Planning and the Public Interest*, The Free Press, Glencoe, IL, 1955.

Nelson, Arthur C., and Lang, Robert E., *The New Politics of Planning: How States and Local Governments are Coming to Common Ground on Reshaping America's Built Environment*, Urban Land Institute, Washington, DC, 2009.

CHAPTER 7

The Social Issues

The two professions from which modern urban planning sprang are architecture and landscape architecture, both of which are concerned largely with physical design. In earlier years planners often tended to emphasize design and physical issues over social issues, as the discussion of the Plan for Chicago indicated. But planners have long recognized that what at first glance appear to be simply matters of design can have powerful social implications.

In the 1960s and 1970s, dissatisfaction within the profession reached major proportions over what many saw as an underemphasis on social issues, and many planners began to define themselves as "social planners" and to speak of a subfield of "social planning." This change within the profession had a number of roots.

The Civil Rights movement of the late 1950s and early 1960s focused attention on issues of justice and fairness. Many planners felt that they could not simply be neutral civil servants doing the bidding of "the establishment" if they did not approve of its goals and policies. The wave of riots and arson that hit U.S. cities from Newark to Watts in Los Angeles in the mid-1960s revealed a deep well of dissatisfaction and distress among minority populations and added to the perception that we as a society must be doing something wrong. Shortly thereafter, the Vietnam War split a generation of Americans. Those who felt that the war was wrong tended to carry that perception over into many domestic issues. If the establishment was wrong in Vietnam, they felt, it was wrong also at home.

Another reason for the change in focus was that many projects that appeared to be well planned in physical terms did not work out well when considered in a broader view. Urban Renewal, discussed in Chapter 11, was one such case. So, too, was public housing. The Pruitt-Igoe public housing project in St. Louis was a large project built according to what were then considered good design practices. The project won a design award from the American Institute of Architects (AIA). Socially, however, it was a failure, with high rates of crime, vandalism, illegitimacy, and so on. Ultimately, the city, unable to deal with the multiple social problems of Pruitt-Igoe, demolished the buildings and cleared the site.[1] Clearly, physical design does not solve people's psychological, family, economic, legal, drug, alcohol, and other problems. A project, however well done from an architectural and site design perspective, that isolated large numbers of people with serious problems in a small area simply set the stage for disaster. In general, high-rise construction has worked out very badly in public housing and a number of other projects like Cabrini Green in Chicago have been torn down since Pruitt-Igoe. On the other hand, many high-rise condominiums and cooperative apartments have worked out very well, as indicated by the premium prices that they command.

THE SOCIAL ISSUES IN PLANNING FOR HOUSING _____

Housing is probably the area in which physical planning decisions have their greatest social effects. Land-use controls and decisions about capital facilities like water and sewer lines affect how much housing and what type of housing will be built. That decision affects rents and house prices, and thus who will live in the community. Through the mechanism of cost, one pattern of housing may favor racial integration whereas another will favor racial segregation. Because where children live determines where they go to school, housing policy can turn out to be educational policy as well (see the box on pages 107–110). Where one lives can determine one's access to recreation, to social services, and, perhaps most important, to employment. Policies and economic forces that separate the housing that low-income workers can afford from the jobs for which they are qualified can produce unemployment. Prolonged unemployment can lead to family breakup, with links to welfare dependency, alcoholism, crime, and other social pathologies. It has been persuasively argued that the formation of the "urban underclass" is, in part, due to prolonged, large-scale unemployment in urban areas.[2] Thus decisions about housing policy effect what many regard as one of America's most pressing social problems.

Even if we forget matters of race, class, and poverty entirely, decisions about housing can have powerful effects on how people live. Suppose the land-use controls in a suburban town permit the building of only single-family houses on half-acre or larger lots. By limiting what can be built to a single, expensive type of structure, the town has made some very personal decisions for its residents. Many of the children who are raised in the town will not be able to afford to live there as young adults. When a couple is divorced, the partner who does not get the house may have to leave town because there is no housing that he or she can afford. A couple with a grown retarded child who cannot live alone but could function well in a group home may be very affected by whether or not the town permits large, old, single-family houses to be converted into group homes. Many communities have experienced bitter fights over whether or not to permit group homes.

A couple who would like an elderly parent to live with them will be concerned about whether or not the town's zoning law permits accessory, or so-called mother-in-law, apartments to be attached to or constructed adjacent to single-family houses. There are vastly more single-parent families in the United States today than there were a few decades ago. Among two-parent households, there is now a much higher percentage in which both parents work outside the home. Land-use controls that permitted homes, workplaces, and child-care facilities to be close together would simplify the lives of many families. In some communities expanding the variety of housing types to accommodate the increasing number of smaller households would be useful.

THE YONKERS HOUSING CASE

Yonkers is an old city of 199,000 located in Westchester County, New York. On the west the city is bounded by the Hudson River and on the south by the Bronx, one of the five boroughs of New York City. To its north and east the city borders prosperous suburban areas of Westchester County.[3] In 1980, the city contained 27 public housing projects, 26 of which were built in its southwest corner. In some ways this location made sense. As the oldest and most densely developed part of the city, the southwest corner contained the largest share of old, substandard multifamily housing. Building the public housing there thus cleared many of these obsolete units.[4] The southwest corner of the city is also the part of the city with the best access to public transportation (bus, commuter rail, and the New York City subway system). Thus a family that could not afford a car could live there and still have reasonably good mobility for such purposes as getting to work. The southwest corner was also the part of the city in which much of the city's poor were living at the time the public housing was built.

But these respectable planning considerations were not the only reason public housing was concentrated there. Another consideration was *political feasibility*. This bland term meant that the predominantly white population of the rest of the city opposed public housing in their neighborhoods because they disliked or feared the poor black population that would occupy it. The city's politicians, administrators, and planners, as well as the officials of the federal government's Department of Housing and Urban Development (HUD), which funded the housing, bowed to that opposition by ruling out sites that failed the political feasibility test.

In 1980 the Justice Department, subsequently joined by the National Association for the Advancement of Colored People (NAACP), brought suit against the city and against HUD, alleging that the siting of the housing had created a condition of de facto school segregation. This violated the principles of school integration established in *Brown v. Board of Education*, a landmark case decided by the Supreme Court in 1954.[5] In 1985 Judge Leonard B. Sand of the Southern District Court in New York found both the city and HUD guilty. That decision was sustained on appeal by the U.S. Supreme Court of Appeals for the Second Circuit in 1987. In June 1988 the U.S. Supreme Court refused to hear an appeal by the City of Yonkers. At the end of its legal road and under threats by Judge Sand of massive fines, the city in a consent decree agreed to a plan for the building of public housing in other neighborhoods.

In spite of the disapproval of the city by Judge Sand and much of the press, many Yonkers residents did not feel guilty about their defiance of the court. Many felt that they knew all they had to know about street crime and school problems. Rightly or wrongly, they were not about to be educated on the subject by judges, sociologists, planners, or editorial writers.

Defiant city residents were sustained in their view that they were morally right, even if legally wrong, because Yonkers had substantially more than its proportionate share of Westchester County's public housing. By an unfortunate coincidence, Judge Sand had a weekend home in Pound Ridge, an upper-income Westchester town whose population was almost entirely white. Pound Ridge could never be accused of mislocating its public housing because it did not have any at all. To dramatize what they felt was the judge's hypocritical position, Yonkers residents took to driving up to Pound Ridge to picket the judge's house.

There followed more than a decade of political maneuvering, at least one mayoral election that turned almost entirely on the housing question, and one lawsuit that went all the way up to the U.S. Supreme Court. Then the city began to implement the court order. About 200 units of low-income housing were built on seven different sites. These units are not true public housing because they are not owned and operated by the city. Rather, they are publicly assisted housing. They were built with private capital and are owned privately. However, there is a very heavy public subsidy behind them and strict income limits on who may rent them. Typically built in groups of four, the units were designed to blend in with the surrounding single-family housing. According to the Municipal Housing Authority of Yonkers, which operates the units, the new housing has been well accepted by neighborhood residents.

At the same time that the scattered-site housing was built, a number of other publicly assisted housing projects were built in older, less affluent neighborhoods in the southwest corner of the city—the city's traditional location for public housing.

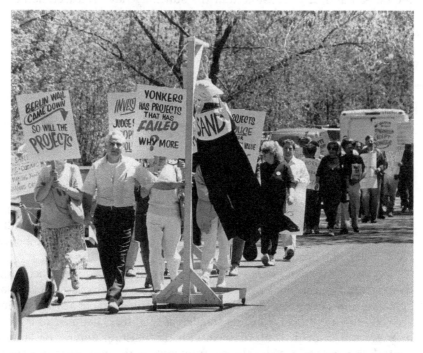

Yonkers residents protesting the proposed construction of public housing. The figure hanging in effigy is Judge Sand. (Mark Vergari, Gannett Suburban Newspapers)

In 2007 the legal story finally came to an end with the signing of an agreement between the city and the original plaintiffs. In return for the plaintiffs' dropping the suit, the city agreed to continue for the long term to provide subsidy money for the 200 units and some other units as well, and to permit completion of some scattered-site housing then "in the pipeline."

At present, housing construction in the city is slow, as it is nationally. When the housing market improves, it is the city's expectation that additional publicly assisted housing will continue to be built within its borders, primarily in the southwest part of the city. Subsidy money will come partly from private sources, partly from New York State, and partly from Westchester County's Housing Implementation Fund, which issues bonds as general obligations (see Chapter 9) of the county to support low- and moderate-income housing.

Looking back, what did the suit achieve? The one unarguable accomplishment was the building of the 200 or so scattered-site units. Clearly, that would not have happened without the suit. On the other hand, it is possible that the suit may have reduced somewhat the amount of other publicly assisted housing built during the two-decade interval between the suit's filing and its final settlement simply because all of the contention and political turbulence frightened away some private capital. What effect the suit may have had on public attitudes toward the questions it raised and decisions about publicly assisted housing in other municipalities is a matter of speculation.

The Special Case of Private Communities

Perhaps the most important recent trend in housing construction in the United States is the remarkably rapid growth of private communities. By the end of the 1990s it was estimated that there were more than 40 million Americans living in over 200,000 private communities.[6] Those numbers are considerably higher today.

A *private community* is one in which residence requires becoming a member of a community association, paying fees to that association, and agreeing to abide by its rules. Private communities almost always begin as areas within a political subdivision such as a county. Planned as a whole, they are not built in conformance with the existing zoning or land-use controls but rather are developed pursuant to rezoning, the issuance of variances, or an overall site-plan review process. Essentially, the developer's architectural or planning consulting firm becomes the planner and the municipal planning agency, and the legislative body that it advises becomes the judge or arbiter of the plan. Often private communities are said to be "master-planned" in that there is a single plan for the entire community. This is a somewhat different usage of the term *master plan*, which ordinarily means the plan for an entire city, county, or other civil division. In the great majority of cases, private communities are built in suburbia or outside metropolitan areas entirely, for that is where large blocks of undeveloped land are to be had. Private communities within established urban areas are much rarer.

In some cases private communities ultimately incorporate as separate political entities. For example, Reston, Virginia, began as just described but is now incorporated as the town of Reston within Fairfax County.

Many of the first private communities were retirement communities, often with explicit age restrictions. For example, rules might stipulate that at least one member of a household be at least 55 years old and that no permanent member of the household be younger than 18 years old. More recently, however, large numbers of private communities have developed for working-age populations as well.

Many private communities are open in the sense that anyone can enter them and move about freely within them, though many community facilities such as pools and parks are open only to residents and guests. But an increasing number are now "gated," with entrance denied to all except residents and guests. In 2001 it was estimated that approximately 4 million U.S. households lived in gated communities.[7] That number has undoubtedly grown considerably since then.

For the developer, the private community has a marketing advantage because the buyer is getting not just a house but a complete package. That package may include physical security, often a community of somewhat similar and like-minded people, community recreational facilities, and the benefits of an integrated design. For example, many private communities have extensive systems of bicycle and pedestrian paths. These are easily integrated into a *de nouveau* design but are usually difficult to "retrofit" into an existing urban or suburban pattern. The complete package, or parts of the package, can be fine-tuned toward particular segments of the market. Sometimes the fine-tuning can be carried quite far. In Ladera Ranch, a large planned community in Orange County, California, there is a subdivision called "Covenant Hills" with homes done in a traditional style and with a Christian school for the subdivision's children. There is another subdivision, "Terramor," for households that the developers referred to as "cultural creatives." There the housing is more contemporary and it has, instead, a Montessori school.[8]

Private communities have been very popular, but they also have their critics. The key word of those who decry the trend is *balkanization*. Critics ask what happens to the sense of a larger community as more and more people opt for separate communities. Edward Blakely, a professor of planning at the University of California, Berkeley, argues,

> It has been over three decades since this nation legally outlawed all forms of public discrimination—in housing, education, public transportation, and public accommodations. Yet, today, we are seeing a new form of discrimination—the gated, walled, private community. I call it the "forting up phenomenon."[9]

He then adds,

> Economic segregation is scarcely new. . . . But the gated communities go farther in several respects. They create physical barriers to access. And they privatize community space, not merely individual space. . . . When offices and retail complexes are placed within the walls, the new developments create a private world. . . . This fragmentation undermines the very concept of *civitas*—organized community life.

If large numbers of the more prosperous withdraw to the enclave of the private community, one might ask what the condition will be of the remainder of the population that does not have the resources to make such a move. What will happen to the quality of public services and civic life in older urban places? Blakely puts it differently when he asks, "Do we really want to give up on the American dream of racial and class integration?" But the underlying argument is the same.

This view that the private community and particularly the gated community are fundamentally balkanizing and destroy a more widespread sense of community is held by many.[10] It fits into a larger view that higher-status and higher-income people are increasingly separating themselves from the larger culture.[11]

Green Valley, Nevada, is a private community built by the American Nevada Corporation in 1978. By 1992 it had grown to a population of 34,000 on 8,400 acres and was projected to reach more than 60,000 early in this century. Writing from a critical stance, David Guterson says,

> No class warfare here, no burning city. Green Valley beckons the American middle class like a fabulous and eternal dream. In the wake of our contemporary trembling and discontent, its pilgrims have sought out a corporate castle where in exchange for false security they pay with personal freedoms; where the corporation that does the job of walling others out also walls residents in.[12]

How might the proponent of the private community respond to these charges? One response is simply that private communities clearly are giving many people what they want. Their success in the market leaves no doubt about that. If we believe in maximizing consumer choice in clothing and automobiles, why not in communities as well?[13] What the residents of new communities want is not something reprehensible, but simply what they see as a good life for themselves and their families. If one big motivation for moving to a private community is concern for the well-being and safety of one's family, just what is so terrible about that?

To Blakely's comment on class and race integration, the would-be resident of the private community might note that we now have a large amount of class and race segregation in most metropolitan areas. It is not as though private communities were destroying some Eden of integration. He or she might also note that integration may happen most easily and naturally among people who are somewhat similar in terms of income and class, as is the situation in many private communities.

This writer does not mean to pass judgment on the private community phenomenon but only to note the arguments. Clearly, this pattern of development has social implications that far transcend the matter of physical design.

The Problem of Homelessness

In the 1980s and 1990s, most observers of the urban scene agreed that the number of homeless people was increasing. More recently, higher levels of unemployment and the wave of foreclosures following the 2008 financial crisis have undoubtedly pushed homelessness higher. Planners are certainly not the only professionals to be concerned with this problem. Social workers, mental health professionals, the police, and attorneys have much more direct contact with the problem than do planners. But the problem of homelessness does have a planning dimension.

The number of homeless people is not known with any degree of accuracy, for they are a hard group to count and to define. Those who have looked at the question attribute the homeless problem to several overlapping causes.[14] A certain number of homeless people are so because of mental illness. The number of people with mental illness on the street has been increased by the deinstitutionalization of mental patients in recent years. That occurred partly because of what is generally referred to as the "patient's rights" movement, which took the position that no patient should be held against his or her will unless that patient constituted a threat to himself or herself or to other people. But note that causality can run both ways. If someone's mental health is already shaky, the stress of being homeless may push that person into clinical mental illness. A certain percentage of the homeless population is so because of involvement with drugs or alcohol. Obviously, there is an overlap with the first category. We also note that the stress of being homeless may push someone in the direction of drugs or alcohol.

In addition, there are those who are homeless for economic reasons. Thus unemployment or family breakup can contribute to homelessness. Writers of a conservative bent have tended to stress the character and behavior of homeless individuals. Writers on the other side of the political spectrum tend to emphasize poverty and housing costs.

The planner may be able to make some contribution to easing the problem of homelessness via his or her involvement with housing policy. Municipal housing policy affects the entire housing stock, and that includes the low-cost end of housing, whose availability is directly related to the problem of homelessness. William Tucker, among other writers, has argued that municipal housing policy has accidentally contributed to homelessness by drying up the supply of cheap housing.[15]

Urban Renewal (see Chapter 11) demolished a great deal of low-rent, low-quality housing. The goal was to eliminate low-quality housing, but doing that inevitably shrank the supply of low-cost housing at the same time. At the very bottom of the rental market, Single Room Occupancy (SRO) hotels and flophouses have been particular targets of neighborhood and business district improvement programs. However, if the most that someone can afford to pay for housing is a few dollars a night, then eliminating the SRO or the flophouse renders that person homeless. Note that the SRO that is torn down in one place cannot generally be replaced with one elsewhere, since most zoning codes will not permit their construction. Then, too, the SRO is likely to be an old structure that has depreciated to a fraction of its replacement cost. Thus a new structure to serve the same purpose would not be feasible financially, even if it were legal. William Tucker, cited earlier, argues that rent controls also produce homelessness. He argues that by driving down vacancy rates, they make low-cost housing unavailable. If you need a cheap apartment, the fact that some people are now living in such, thanks to rent control, does you little good if the vacancy rate hovers near zero.[16]

Assuming that there is some truth in the preceding line of argument, what is the planner to do? Part of the planner's role, as suggested elsewhere in this book, is to take a big picture view and to make plain the connections, like those previously discussed, to the rest of the body politic. But the planner who sees the problem in the terms just suggested is in a difficult situation. Homeless people do not constitute a powerful political constituency, whereas businesspeople and permanent residents do. Then, too, it is easy to be sympathetic both with homeless individuals and also with those who wish homeless people to be anywhere but here. One can feel sympathy for the homeless person who stations himself or herself in the shopkeeper's doorway and also feel sympathy for the shopkeeper, who does not want this individual to drive away his or her customers. The planner can advocate housing policies that do not reduce the supply of housing at the low end. He or she can push for some expansion of low-cost housing through more flexible zoning—for example, by permitting accessory apartments or apartments over stores. Such units may or may not house the homeless directly, but they will ease the pressure on the remaining low-cost housing stock. For those of the homeless population who for reasons of mental health cannot function on their own, the planner can advocate flexibility in zoning and housing codes so as to make it easier to build group homes and other forms of congregate housing.

OTHER ISSUES

The Social Side of Planning for Catastrophe

One might think that planning for catastrophe would be one case where there is a unitary public interest. After all, floodwaters can't tell a rich person from a poor person. But it turns out that in initial vulnerability, safety and security immediately after the event, and in the longer-term restoration and rebuilding phase, natural catastrophes do hit different categories of people very differently.

Consider the flooding of New Orleans by Hurricane Katrina in 2005. By and large it was poorer people who lived in the lower-lying parts of the city and were thus most vulnerable to the initial event. Most of the evacuation from the city was by car, which obviously favored people who had enough income to own a car. People with adequate savings did much better in the aftermath than people who lived paycheck to paycheck or were dependent on public assistance. Just as poor people are more vulnerable, so too are older people. If nothing else, they are likely to have less strength, energy, and good health with which to tolerate stress, cold or extreme heat, exhaustion, anxiety, interruption of access to medical care, and the like.

Reconstruction after the event may create a very different sort of community than was there before the event and may leave us some social issues to ponder. Robert Verchick, mentioned in Chapter 4, gives this example. When Hurricane Katrina hit the Gulf Coast east of New Orleans it swept away large numbers of houses close to the shoreline. Many of these houses were relatively low-cost "stickbuilt" (wood-frame) houses on concrete slabs, a type of construction that is easily swept away. After the storm, in some areas there ensued a speculative boom in all this suddenly vacant land followed by the construction of much more substantial and more storm-resistant buildings. Some of these were commercial and some residential—for example, high-rise condominiums, many of which were essentially vacation homes for affluent people. The original community was gone and there was no way it could be reconstituted in the new housing.

In a way there was a dim resemblance to what sometimes happened in Urban Renewal (see Chapter 11), with nature accomplishing in a few hours what the clearance phase of Urban Renewal did over many months. One policy question is whether our best choice is to go with the market forces, the scenario just described, or whether to try to restore something of the original community. If the choice is the latter, then specifically what do we do? Simply rebuilding the area as it was with the knowledge that it might be washed away again does not necessarily seem like a good choice. Deciding what to do, and how to pay for it, is not simple.

More generally, social planning for natural disasters might include planning for the temporary or not-so-temporary housing of people displaced by the event. That might involve planning for sites, utilities, and the provision of services. Planning for evacuation should go beyond just making sure there is adequate road capacity, but also include arranging to accommodate those who can't manage on their own.

Bigger questions include that of the return of displaced population versus long-term resettlement, and how much to invest in physical reconstruction versus how much to spend on services to the effected population. If, as is likely to be the case, there are trade-offs between restoration of the precatastrophe community and way of life and economic development, how do we weight those contradictory goals? All of these matters are questions not only for planners, but also for the body politic of the municipality and, beyond that, the state or states as well as the nation as a whole.

The Social Side of Economic Development

Economic development is another area in which issues of physical planning quickly reveal a social side. Assume that a community needs jobs and new tax revenues but is handicapped by a shortage of sites suitable for commercial development. It could use its power of eminent domain to take some land, carry out the necessary site preparation, and then market the land for commercial use (as noted in Chapter 5, this strategy, once very widely used, is now not legal in a number of states). But the land now contains housing, whose residents will be forced to move. Should the community do so anyway? Will a functioning neighborhood be destroyed, and if so, are the new jobs and new tax revenues worth it? If it is to be done, what arrangements will be made to rehouse the displaced population? Or will the population that now lives there simply be given notice, a modest moving allowance, and then left to its own devices?

Often the promotion of the local economy involves giving subsidies or tax breaks to firms to encourage them to locate in the community instead of elsewhere. In that case, public funds are being given indirectly to entrepreneurs, investors, and stockholders, who may be a good deal wealthier than the average taxpayer. Should we be troubled by this treatment?

Some planners are very comfortable with this approach: That is the way the game is played in this capitalist society, and by and large, the system works better than other alternatives. Others, such as Norman Krumholz, a former planning director of the City of Cleveland, are outraged by it.[17] Regardless of what position one takes on the point, it clearly contains serious questions of social philosophy.

Transportation Planning

Transportation planning has many social implications. As noted in Chapter 11, much of the conflict over Urban Renewal had to do with the taking of land for urban expressways, actions that necessarily displace people and that change or destroy the basic fabric of neighborhoods. How a region's transportation system is structured and how transportation is priced affect people's access to work, to public services, and to a whole range of activities.

Environmental Policy

Environmental decisions can have major social consequences. If an environmentally fragile area is the last site in town that might accommodate some low- and moderate-income housing, there is a serious question of values to be addressed. As noted in Chapter 15, one person's environmental protection may be another person's unemployment. Again, what looks like a physical question rapidly reveals a social side.

The Question of Environmental Justice

In recent years there has been considerable interest among planners in *environmental justice* and the related issue, *environmental racism*. The central question is whether the poor and minorities bear a disproportionate share of the burden of environmental problems and, if so, why? Numerous studies have been done on the subject, and books and articles have been written about it. Some planning schools offer courses in environmental justice. The Environmental Protection Agency (EPA) has become involved in environmental justice both in administration and also in funding research. The department's statement on the subject begins as follow:

> Environmental Justice is the fair treatment and meaningful involvement of all people regardless of race, color, national origin, or income with respect to the development, implementation, and enforcement of environmental laws, regulations, and policies. Fair treatment means that no group of people, including a racial, ethnic, or a socioeconomic group, should bear a disproportionate share of the negative environmental consequences resulting from industrial, municipal, and commercial operations or the execution of federal, state, local, and tribal programs and policies.[18]

Determining the facts of the matter may be difficult. Assume that a municipal landfill or incinerator is surrounded by low-cost housing occupied largely by minority-group members. Is that the result of intentional discrimination in choosing the site of the facility? Did it occur because, in the politics of making the location decision, the residents of the area had less political clout and, in effect, lost the game of "hot potato"? Or is the explanation more innocent—that the facility, its location chosen in a fair and reasonable way, reduced property values, and so over the years the area filled with residents whose low incomes limited their choice in the housing market? Answering those questions may require considerable digging into the history of the site and its surroundings.

Gender Issues

In the 1990s it was asserted that planning decisions might have a sexual-identity element. In 1997 a group called Gays and Lesbians in Planning (GALIP) was formed as a division of the American Planning Association (APA) to represent the interests of gays and lesbians.[19] One item that GALIP members mentioned was the recognition of and planning for districts that, either commercially or residentially, are oriented to gays and lesbians. Within the planning profession, reaction to the formation of GALIP was mixed. Some took an "it's-about-time" view. Others argued that planning is about serving a general public interest and that the assertion of a separate gay and lesbian interest is divisive. How big a set of gay and lesbian issues can be identified and developed remains to be seen.

Feminism and Planning

A number of planning educators who define themselves as feminists have argued that there are feminist perspectives on planning and a set of feminist issues that should be, and often are not, addressed in planning. For example, a number of feminist planners have suggested that the way many suburbs were planned seemed more to suit the interests of men than women. The argument first surfaced in a major way in the 1960s with *The Feminine Mystique*, which, among many other points, argued that a house in a suburban subdivision where there are nothing but similar houses, even though it might be a nice house equipped with all the best furnishings and appliances, is really something of a prison for the woman who stays home all day with the children, and that this isolation contributes to boredom and depression.[20] In fact the author, Betty Friedan, referred to the matter as "the problem that has no name." Whether that argument has lost some importance in the intervening years, as labor force participation rates for mothers of young children have risen and as the percentage of the adult female population living in households with children has declined, is an open question. More generally, feminists have suggested that in the past, planning (like almost all other professions) was male dominated, that most of its literature was written by men, and that most of its historic figures were male.[21] This naturally tended to "privilege" male over female interests. Feminists suggest that a city or a metropolitan area laid out by women rather than men might be a very different place.[22]

Planning and Aging

The leading edge of the baby boom (roughly 1947–1965) is now reaching retirement age. Middle-range projections by the Bureau of the Census show the total U.S. population increasing by about 26 percent from 2010 to 2035 but the 65 and over population growing by 80 to 90 percent. That huge age wave from the baby boom will push a whole range of social planning questions to the forefront. A more numerous retirement age population will control a larger share of the nation's income and accumulated wealth, and will constitute a larger percentage of the nation's voters.

The place where the changed demographic structure will probably have its biggest effect on planning practice is in housing and land use. Seniors, who live largely in one- and two-person households, have very different housing needs and housing preferences than other age groups. They also have different needs for health, recreation, and public services. Transportation planning (see Chapter 12) will be affected. Public transportation in the United States now, with the exception of commuter rail and metro service, is largely used by the less prosperous—those who do not own automobiles. A large number of affluent seniors who cannot or do not want to drive could put a very different spin on that.

Social Planning for Whom?

The social issues noted in this chapter reinforce a basic theme of this book, which is that almost all but very minor planning decisions impose gains and losses. Planners who define themselves as social planners often feel that they should attempt to tip society's scales toward the less fortunate (or tip them so they favor the fortunate a bit less). But many other planners take the position that their task is to serve the majority of the community or to serve a general public interest so far as they can identify it. These planners might also argue that a single community cannot do much about broad equity issues such as the distribution of income. Therefore, such matters are necessarily left to higher levels of government, where the means are more commensurate with the size of the problem.

WHO DOES SOCIAL PLANNING?

If one asks practicing planners whether there is a separate field of "social planning" one will get answers ranging from "Of course" to "What is it?" If a planner is doing something that is directly devoted to a social end, say, administering community development funds for a day care or an adult literacy program, clearly that planner is engaged in "social planning." The great majority of planners, however, do not spend most of their time on explicit social planning. But almost any decision that involves how sizable blocks of land will be used or how sizable sums of public money will be spent has social implications. In that sense, any planner who is conscientious and competent is engaged in social planning.

SUMMARY

All planning decisions of significant size have social implications. For many planners and planning agencies, social issues present themselves most strongly in the realm of housing. This chapter presents some of the older housing issues such as how much variety of housing type is permitted, as well as the implications of the extremely rapid growth of private communities, both the open and the gated variety. It also notes some social issues in connection with economic development and environmental planning. Whether or not one recognizes a separate field of social planning, it is clear that the social side of what at first might appear to be purely physical or design questions should not be ignored.

NOTES

1. A graphic and an entertaining account of the Pruitt-Igoe fiasco can be found in Tom Wolfe, *From Bauhaus to Our House*, Farrar, Straus and Giroux, New York, 1981.
2. See William J. Wilson, *The Truly Disadvantaged*, University of Chicago Press, Chicago, 1987.
3. The county, population of about 870,000, contains a total of 43 municipalities, of which Yonkers is the largest.
4. Whether clearing substandard units is always desirable is arguable because it may have the effect of tightening the market and thus driving up rents. However, the removal of substandard units was standard Urban Renewal doctrine when Yonkers public housing was built.
5. In this decision the Supreme Court rejected the previous "separate but equal" doctrine and ruled that segregation itself, regardless of whether or not the facilities were otherwise equal, was unacceptable. For the reader interested in the Yonkers case, the best source is the *New York Times Index*, for the *Times* has covered the case regularly since Judge Sand's 1985 decision.
6. Clifford J. Treese, ed., *Community Associations Factbook*, Community Associations Institute, Alexandria, VA, 1993 and 1999. Further information on private communities can be found on the website of the Community Associations Institute, www.caionline.org.
7. Bureau of the Census, American Housing Survey, 2001.
8. Bill Bishop, *The Big Sort*, Houghton Mifflin, New York, 2008, p. 212.
9. Edward Blakely, "Viewpoint," *Planning*, January 1994, p. 46.
10. See, for example, David Dillon, "Fortress America," *Planning*, June 1994, pp. 8–12.
11. Christopher Lasch, *The Revolt of the Elites and the Betrayal of Democracy*, W. W. Norton, New York, 1995.
12. David Guterson, "No Place Like Home," *Harper's Magazine*, November 1992, pp. 55–61.
13. The idea that a greater number of communities would maximize consumer choice (the citizen is regarded as a consumer of public services) and move the market for public services toward the economists' model of the perfect market goes by the name of the *Tiebout hypothesis*, after the economist Charles Tiebout. A presentation of the idea can be found in Ronald C. Fisher, *State and Local Public Finance*, 2nd ed., Richard D. Irwin Co., Chicago, 1996, chap. 5. The hypothesis was originally propounded in an article by Tiebout, "A Pure Theory of Local Expenditures," *Journal of Political Economy*, October 1956, p. 422.
14. For a good general account of the problem, see Christopher Jencks, *The Homeless*, Harvard University Press, Cambridge, MA, 1994. For a summary of various estimates of the US. homeless population through the late 1980s, see Karin Ringheim, *At Risk of Homelessness*, Praeger, New York, 1990.
15. William Tucker, "How Housing Regulations Cause Homelessness," *The Public Interest*, Winter 1991, pp. 78–88.
16. For a brief discussion of the economics of rent control and references to the literature, see John M. Levy, *Essential Microeconomics for Public Policy Analysis*, Praeger, New York, 1995, chaps. 3 and 10.

17. Pierre Clavel, *The Progressive City: Planning and Participation,* 1969–1984, Rutgers University Press, New Brunswick, NJ, 1987, chap. 3.
18. EPA press release, June 22, 2004. This release and much other information are available on an EPA website, www.epa.gov/compliance/environmental justice/.
19. Karen Finucan, "Gay Today," *Planning,* February 2000, pp. 12–16. GALIP's website is www.geocities.com/capitolhill/lobby/7016/galip.htm.
20. Betty Friedan, *The Feminine Mystique,* W.W. Norton, New York, 1963.
21. At present, enrollments in U.S. planning schools are about equally divided between men and women so that however much male dominance there is in the field, this should be reduced as more women rise to senior positions.
22. For a sampling of arguments and references to the feminist planning literature, see Susan S. Fainstein and Lisa J. Servon, eds., *Gender and Planning,* Rutgers University Press, 2004; and Barbara Rahder and Carol Altilia, "Where Is Feminism in Planning Going: Appropriation or Transformation" *Planning Theory,* vol 3., no. 2, 2004, pp. 107–116.

SELECTED BIBLIOGRAPHY

ANDERSON, WAYNE R, FRIEDEN, BERNARD J., and MURPHY, MICHAEL J., EDS., *Managing Human Services,* International City Management Association, Washington, DC, 1997.

BOLAN, RICHARD S., "Social Planning and Policy Development," in *The Practice of Local Government Planning,* International City Management Association, Washington, DC, 1979.

CLAVEL, PIERRE, *The Progressive City: Planning and Participation, 1969–1984,* Rutgers University Press, New Brunswick, N], 1987.

HOWFE, ELIZABETH, "Social Aspects of Physical Planning," in *The Practice of Local Government Planning,* 2nd ed., International City Management Association, Washington, DC, 1988.

CHAPTER 8

The Comprehensive Plan

In the planning literature, one sees the terms *comprehensive plan, general plan,* and *master plan* used synonymously. At present, the term *comprehensive plan* is in most common use and will be used here for all three. It refers to the most basic plan prepared to guide the development of the community. One characteristic of the comprehensive plan is that physically, it covers the entire community. Another defining characteristic is that it is long term. Comprehensive plans typically have time horizons in the range of 20 years. Recall from Chapter 5 that having a plan may be optional or may be required by the state.

THE GOALS OF COMPREHENSIVE PLANNING _____

Since municipalities differ, the following list of goals will not be complete, nor will every item necessarily apply to every community. Because the goals overlap, another writer might list them differently yet cover the same ground. Note that all the following goals, with the possible exception of the last, readily fit within the rubric of the phrase *health, safety, and public welfare,* cited earlier in connection with the police power.

1. *Health.* Achieving a pattern of land use that protects the public health is a well-established planning goal. One aspect might be prohibiting densities of development that threaten to overload water or sewer facilities. In areas that do not have public water and sewer facilities, it may mean spacing houses far enough apart to prevent leakage from septic tanks from contaminating well water. It may involve separating industrial or commercial activities that produce health hazards from residential areas. It may mean banning certain types of industrial operations from the community entirely.

2. *Public safety.*   This goal may manifest itself in numerous ways. It might mean requiring sufficient road width in new subdivisions to ensure that ambulances and fire equipment have adequate access in emergencies. Many communities have flood plain zoning to keep people from building in flood-prone areas. At the neighborhood level it might mean planning for a street geometry that permits children to walk from home to school without crossing a major thoroughfare. In a high-crime area it might mean laying out patterns of buildings and spaces that provide fewer sites where muggings and robberies can be committed unobserved.[1]

3. *Circulation.*   Providing the community with adequate circulation is an almost universal goal of comprehensive planning. This means a system of streets and perhaps also parking facilities that make possible an orderly, efficient, and rapid flow of vehicular and pedestrian traffic. In a municipality in which there is serious flood or storm hazard planning the circulation system might include planning for rapid evacuation, perhaps by planning the system so that inbound lanes can quickly be converted to outbound lanes. In many communities it also means providing for adequate public transportation. Planning for transportation and planning for land use are intimately connected, as is discussed in detail in Chapter 12.

4. *Provision of services and facilities.*   An important part of most comprehensive planning efforts is determining the location of facilities such as parks, recreation areas, schools, social services, hospitals, and the like. In addition to planning for facilities, it is also important to plan for a pattern of land use that facilitates the provision of public services like police and fire protection, water, and sewers. For example, the pattern of land use will affect the feasibility and cost of providing public water and sewer facilities. The location of housing relative to the location of schools will determine whether children can walk or must be bused to school.

5. *Fiscal health.*   There is a relationship between the pattern of development and the fiscal situation of the community. Any development will impose some costs on the community (fire protection, police protection, traffic, education, etc.). Similarly, virtually any development will generate some revenues for the municipality (property taxes, sales taxes, user charges, and other fees of one sort or another). Some uses will yield surpluses, and others deficits. Generally speaking, it is not very difficult to predict which uses will do which. In fact, a fairly substantial literature exists on this very point.[2] Many communities will plan for a pattern of land use that will hold down property taxes. But there are limits here. Does the community have the right to practice "fiscal zoning"—using its land-use controls to keep out types of housing or economic activity that are likely to cost the community more for additional services than they yield in additional revenue? How much can a community limit the building of multifamily and small-lot single-family housing to control costs? The courts have not spoken with total unanimity on this matter, and many an attorney has earned a comfortable living litigating such points.

6. *Economic goals.* In thousands of communities, economic growth or maintenance of the existing level of economic activity is an important goal. There is a link here with the fiscal goal, but there may be other motivations as well, most notably providing employment for community residents. Thus a community may seek to develop a pattern of land use that provides for commercial and industrial sites, provides good access to such sites, and facilitates supplying utilities to such sites. Other steps that a municipality may take to stimulate its own economic development are discussed in Chapter 13.

7. *Environmental protection.* This goal is an old one but, as noted in Chapter 15, has become much more common since the 1960s. It might involve restrictions on building in wetlands, steep slopes, or other ecologically valuable or fragile lands. It might involve preservation of open space, ordinances to control discharges into water bodies, prohibition or limitations on commercial or industrial activities that would degrade air quality, and so on. In recent years, many municipalities have also come to see a need to do what they can to reduce total greenhouse gas emissions, an attitude exemplified by the phrase "think globally, act locally."

8. *Redistributive goals.* Some planners of the political left would argue that a goal of planning should be to distribute downward both wealth and influence in the political process.[3] In a limited number of communities, planners have been able to bend the planning process in that direction. For an account of a few such instances, see the book by Pierre Clavel cited in Chapter 7.

THE COMPREHENSIVE PLANNING PROCESS

We noted in Chapter 6 that over the last several decades, the comprehensive planning process has changed from one in which a small group handed down a plan to one in which the making of the plan is a participatory process open to the citizens of the community. This section describes a participatory plan-making process. The process will vary from one community to the next, but we can identify some common elements.

1. *A research phase.*   One cannot plan very much if one does not have a sense of the present state of events and their probable future direction. Thus many comprehensive planning efforts began with a data-gathering and forecasting phase.

2. *Clarification of community goals and objectives.*   At some point, preferably early in the process, there has to be some agreement about what the plan is intended to achieve. This is not to say that agreement will ever be total.

3. *A period of plan formulation.*

4. *A period of plan implementation.*

5. *A period of review and revision.*

Though presented as a sequence, these items necessarily overlap. Insights gained in the research phase will reveal problems that affect the goals the community will formulate. But selecting goals will affect what things a community should know about itself. Thus the research and the goal-formation processes tend to proceed simultaneously. Research regarding population trends might lead to formulating the goal of acquiring an additional 500 acres of parkland. That, however, suggests another research question: Is the community able to pay for it? Steps 1 and 2 inevitably become intertwined.

Plan formulation tends to modify goals by making plain the real implications of generalized goals. A community might set a goal of "an adequate supply of housing at affordable prices." It is hard to be against such a goal: Few will come out publicly in favor of an inadequate supply of housing at exorbitant prices. But when the community looks at the matter in detail, it may not like what the goal implies. Getting prices down to affordable levels may mean building smaller housing units at higher densities than present residents want. Perhaps getting prices down will also necessitate a major increase in housing supply, with attendant increases in traffic congestion and overcrowding in the schools. Perhaps an increase in the supply of lower-cost housing will impose costs that push up property tax rates. At this point the community may go back and rethink its goal.

In the following sections we discuss the five steps in detail.

Planning Research

Most planning agencies, particularly those large enough to have a research staff, do considerable research. One common type of study is the "population forecast." One cannot plan without having an idea of for how many people one is planning. It is also important to know something about the likely age structure of the population. One hundred people over the age of 65 make very different demands on the community than do 100 elementary school students.

There are various approaches to forecasting population. A common technique is the "cohort survival" method. In this, the present population is mathematically "aged" into the future. In other words, each age and sex group, or "cohort," of the population is advanced through time and its numbers adjusted for expected mortality.[4] Adjustments are made for net migration (moves in minus moves out) and births. The advantage of the technique is that it presents a detailed picture of the structure of the population rather than just an estimate of the total number of people. The mathematics is relatively simple, but getting good results is another matter. At the city, county, or town level, the big differences in growth rates between places are largely due to differences in net migration. Predicting net migration accurately is difficult. At the present it is much more an art than a science.

Then, too, the interaction between plans and forecasts can muddy the waters.[5] For example, in many suburban areas, housing stock is the factor that limits population growth. One might estimate net migration on the basis of past performance, but how does one factor into these estimates the effect on population of land-use control ordinances that will be enacted next year and that may be affected by this year's forecasts? In the ideal planning situation, the making of plans and the making of forecasts should be related. Such coordination is not easy to achieve.

Another basic study is the "land-use inventory."[6] Such a study begins with a mapping of existing land uses (residential, industrial, commercial, educational, recreational, etc.). It also characterizes undeveloped land in terms of suitability for different uses. The common practice is to prepare a series of maps that show land characteristics such as topography, flood plains, areas of well or poorly drained soil, and so on. In many cases the land-use study also contains information on land ownership, generally distinguishing among public, private, and institutional holdings at a minimum. The study might also identify major private or major institutional holders. The study may also identify some infrastructure characteristics, particularly water and sewer service. It may also identify some legal characteristics such as zoning categories, though these are less permanent than most of the other items mentioned.

In recent years the traditional paper map for the recording of the results of land-use studies has been supplemented by electronic mapping systems generally referred to as Geographic Information Systems (GISs). In a GIS, data are stored in digital form. For example, to store a contour line in the system, a technician moves a digitizer along the contour line of a topographic map, and the path of the digitizer is converted to digital form and stored in the computer's memory. Information such as assessed values, zoning categories, census data, and the like can also be entered as numbers or letters. The electronic database can then quickly be used to produce a variety of maps, calculations, tabulations, and so on. The map that might take a draftsperson days to draw can often be produced by a GIS in a few minutes.

At the regional scale, GISs now make use of data from satellite cameras. Images, from both within and outside the visible light spectrum, come from the satellite camera in digital form and are then "imported" into the GIS database. Among the material that can be mapped from such digital information are vegetation, topography, hydrology, land use, temperature, and some geologic features. The level of precision is not usually sufficient for small parcels, but it may be quite adequate for work at a large scale and costs only a fraction of what it would cost if obtained by conventional methods.

Beyond these two most common studies are a host of others that may or may not be done, depending on needs and resources. If economic development is an issue, an economic study may be done. The degree of sophistication may vary from a simple listing of present employers to a highly sophisticated econometric model built by a consultant.[7]

Almost all comprehensive plans contain a circulation element. Thus studies of traffic flow characteristics along the existing transportation network are likely to be done early in the master-planning process. Some general estimates of future traffic flows based on projections of future population and employment are also likely to be made at an early stage. There is a strong interaction between transportation planning and land-use planning. The amount of development in an area is a major determinant of the number of trips that will be made to and from the area. On the other hand, the accessibility of the area will in large measure determine how much development takes place there. Thus land-use and transportation planning should go hand in hand.

Studies related to infrastructure are common. Water supply and the provision of sewer service are key elements in shaping the pattern of development in growing areas. Studies may be done to determine potential areas for sewers and areas that are amenable to the development of public water supply systems. In areas where public water and sewer supply are not feasible, studies may be devoted to ground water supply and quality.

Soil characteristics may come in for serious study at this point. If an area is not to have sewers, for whatever reason, the amount of development that can occur may be limited by the capacity of the soil to absorb safely household wastes from septic tanks. This capacity will vary greatly with soil types. A sandy, well-drained soil may safely permit building several houses per acre. On the other hand, soil with a great deal of clay or bedrock lying close to the surface may require an acre or two of land per house for safe disposal of household waste. Soil characteristics such as shrinkage and swelling as the water content of the soil changes will affect the types of buildings that can be constructed. The capacity of the soil to absorb water will affect flooding potential, an important characteristic in considering the type and intensity of development appropriate for the area.

Many communities will do recreation studies as part of a master plan, looking at population, recreational preferences, existing facilities, and so forth. In general, such studies will inventory the present supply of facilities and services. Future needs may be estimated by applying standards (so many acres of parkland per 1,000 of population, for example) to the municipality's projected population, and by surveys that determine citizen preferences. The gap between the existing situation and the estimated need is used to establish preliminary planning goals.

In recent years, planning at the comprehensive stage has taken on an increasingly fiscal cast. Many municipalities have found themselves under strong fiscal pressures, the sources of which are various. In many central cities and some small communities, expenses have risen while the tax base has stagnated. In other cases tax bases have grown substantially, but municipalities have still faced very strong resistance to tax increases, as exemplified by California's Proposition 13 noted in Chapter 4.

Fiscal studies generally involve analyzing trends and making forecasts of expenditures, revenues, and tax rates. Studies may also be done to estimate capital needs and capital costs. The purpose of a fiscal study is to permit the community to match the other elements of the plan to the financial resources that it is likely to have. In fact, it is very difficult to say whether a plan is realistic without some knowledge of its financial underpinning.

Formulating Community Goals

Ideally, goals should be formulated with a knowledge of the essential facts of the situation, a knowledge of the limitations under which the municipality operates, and a realistic view of the options open to the community. Developing such knowledge is the ultimate purpose of the research component just described. The purpose of the goal-setting process is to formulate a limited number of goals that do not contradict each other and that have enough public and political support behind them to give them a reasonable chance of actually coming to pass.

The planning agency's role in this process might be providing a forum for discussion (organizing meetings, obtaining media coverage, setting up advisory committees), providing facts and laying out options, and synthesizing and articulating the results of the discussions and deliberations. The process of setting goals should be an open one in that citizens and groups who have a stake in the outcome of the planning process are not excluded. This consideration is not just a matter of fairness or a legal requirement, but also one of practicality. Those who have had a hand in shaping a plan are more likely to support it than those who have not.

Formulating the Plan

When the baseline studies have been done and agreement has been reached on goals, the work of formulating the plan can begin. In larger communities the plan is generally drawn up by the municipality's planning agency. In smaller communities it is common for the plan to be drawn up by a planning consultant and submitted to the community for approval.

The first step in plan formulation is generally to lay out a variety of options. For example, assume that one goal is to reduce traffic congestion in the central business district. Options might include widening or straightening the main street, constructing a bypass, building a parking structure to reduce on-street parking, converting from a two-way to a one-way street system, or some combination of these.

When all the reasonable options have been listed, it is time to begin considering their respective costs and merits. This process is sometimes referred to as "impact analysis." One item to be considered is cost and what the costs would imply for the municipal tax rate and debt structure. That study might look not only at direct costs of the options, but also at indirect considerations such as estimated effects on sales tax receipts and property values. Another item would be the number of households and businesses affected by the taking of property and the disturbance of traffic flow during construction. The planners would also examine the relative degree of improvement in traffic flow that might be expected from each option. Aesthetic and urban design issues would also be examined. When the impact assessments have been made, the preferred option can be selected. Note that it is often a good idea to bring affected parties such as property owners, residents, and businesspersons into the impact assessment and option-choosing process. First, they are likely to make useful contributions. Equally important, no plan can be implemented without political consent. It is better to resolve differences early around a conference table than later in the courts or the press.

The combined cost must also be ascertained to know whether it is manageable. If it is not, choices among goals must be made.

Implementing the Plan

As noted earlier, the two most powerful tools for carrying out the physical side of the plan are capital investments as called for in the capital budget and land-use controls. Capital investments in roads, public facilities, and utilities create the basic conditions that permit development, which land-use controls then shape and channel. Ideally, capital investments and land-use controls should be consistent with one another and with the comprehensive plan. If coordination is lacking, the results are likely to be disappointing. For example, if capital investments create powerful pressures for development in areas that the comprehensive plan shows as developing at low density, the stage has been set for litigation, controversy, and frustration.

Review and Updating

Almost inevitably, community development will not unfold quite as envisioned in the master plan. Planning is anything but an exact science. Then, too, the pattern of development is shaped by all sorts of forces that are beyond community control and in many cases beyond prediction. Thus after a short time the community may not be quite where the plan would have it, and so some replanning will be necessary. Just as a navigator takes frequent bearings and replots the course accordingly, the community checks its situation periodically and adjusts its plans. But the analogy is not entirely accurate. In the case of the navigator, the destination remains the same. In the case of the municipality, the goals themselves may change as realities both inside and outside the municipality change.

For the plan to be effective over a long term, periodic review is essential. Ideally, the review applies to all the major plan elements. First, it applies to the database. Population, revenues, expenditures, housing stock, employment, and so on inevitably will not evolve exactly as predicted. Large disparities may show up fairly quickly. Consider, for example, cost projections for capital expenditures. A major component of the cost of capital expenditures is the cost of borrowing money. But predicting interest rates accurately over the long term lies somewhere between extremely difficult and impossible.

Beyond updating the database on which the plan rests, it is also necessary to update goals and strategies. Ideally, the municipal government will have a commitment to updating the plan at regular intervals. If this cannot be done, the plan loses its relationship to reality. If government personnel and citizens perceive the plan as a static and increasingly irrelevant document, it soon loses its political force. The act of updating it keeps it relevant and keeps the body politic committed to it. It also institutionalizes planning as an activity within the community.

Maintaining community interest in the planning process is one of the most important tasks of any planning agency. Thus public relations is a major aspect of successful planning. The planning director's speech to the Rotary Club, the appearance in a high school civics class, and the periodic newspaper article on what the city or town or county is planning for solid-waste disposal or parklands or economic development or housing or downtown business district revitalization are all part of that effort. In one southern town, planning agency staff have appeared in first- and second-grade classrooms and run six- and seven-year-old children through a simple experience in laying out a neighborhood. That strategy may not pay off for a quarter of a century, but, then, planning is a long-term process.

The Technology of Citizen Participation

In years gone by the main venue for participation was the public meeting, and the methods for communicating about the plan were limited. The public could be shown maps, artists' renderings, and models of subdivisions or other proposed developments. The main instrument for citizen expression of opinion was the raised hand followed by the spoken comment, perhaps supplemented by a letter to the planning board or the editor of the local paper. Those modes are still important, but technology is expanding the process very rapidly.

Text messaging and social media have expanded communication tremendously so the citizen who can't be present physically or isn't happy about speaking in front of a group can still make his or her opinion felt. Mobile devices can let the citizen participate while he or she is riding the bus or sitting on a park bench. Some places have used virtual worlds and gaming to bring citizens into the process. For example, role-playing might let citizens explore different personal situations, perhaps regarding housing or employment. Geographic databases like Google Maps make it easier for citizens to communicate their locations or locations that they are concerned about. Apps that allow a citizen with a handheld communications device to select a site and then see what that site would look like if developed as planned offer the citizen what has been termed "augmented reality." Computer graphics software that continuously changes the image of a planned area gives the user the visual effect of walking through it. Access to interactive databases may permit the citizen to simulate the effects of different options—for example, how the municipalities' total greenhouse gas emissions will change if bus service is provided over a particular route or if more or less dense housing patterns are developed or how different zoning requirements will affect property tax rates. Touch screen tables may permit a citizen to move elements of a plan and see how different physical layouts play out in terms of factors such as traffic flow. As with all types of modeling, the results are only as good as the data that go into the model and the model builder's understanding of how the variables in the model interact. So nothing is guaranteed. But such interactive processes draw the citizen into the planning process, open up the range of possibilities, and potentially permit more thoroughgoing communication about plans. At present, the technology is changing rapidly and there is great variety in what is being done in various municipalities.

HOW EFFECTIVE ARE COMPREHENSIVE PLANS? _____

To a great degree the effectiveness of the plan depends upon the degree of commitment by the municipal government and the citizens to the plan. If the municipal government and the citizens are committed to the goals of the plan, then the power of government to raise money, to spend money, and to use the municipality's powers to control land use can be used to move toward the vision embodied in the plan. This is the situation in many municipalities. But in other municipalities, commitment to the plan may be less solid. The plan may exist on paper, but little will be done to make it come to pass. In the extreme, the plan may just be a *pro forma* document that exists because the state requires every municipality to have an adopted comprehensive plan or because having a plan is a requirement for state or federal grant programs in which the municipality is interested.

Some municipalities are in a stronger position to stick to a plan than are others. A prosperous municipality that has an adequate tax base will have both the funds to make the public investments that support the plan and also the ability to reject development that clearly contravenes the plan. A poor municipality may find that it simply does not have the fiscal capacity to make the investments required to implement the plan. A combination of a weak tax base and high unemployment may put it in the position of being unable to turn away any proposed development, even if that development contravenes the intentions of the plan.

Where there is little growth to be channeled and directed, the plan may be relatively ineffectual. At the other extreme, if economic forces beyond the control of the municipality are making the plan grow at a very rapid rate, it may be very hard for the planners and the municipal government to stay ahead of the game and stick to the comprehensive plan. The crisis of the day will crowd out everything else.

Unpredictable events may have a big effect on whether the vision in the plan comes to pass. For example, a county develops a comprehensive plan and sticks to it for a while. At this point a major investor acquires a large block of land and draws up a design for a planned community (see Chapter 7). The plan looks good to the municipality in terms of land use and economic and fiscal impact. But it requires rezoning of a substantial part of the county and thus scrapping major parts of the comprehensive plan. In short order, the plan is subjected to a major rewrite. Comparable scenarios could readily be suggested for other major commercial development or large facilities constructed by higher levels of government. Prediction is basic to any long-term plan, and life is unpredictable.

Some populations are fundamentally more supportive of planning than are others. In the writer's observation, college towns often are quite supportive of planning. Their educated and economically comfortable, albeit not rich, populations seem to be comfortable with it and often take a big interest in it.

The overall political stance of the population is very important. As suggested in Chapter 5, where the boundary between the rights of private property and the rights of the public, considered as a whole, should lie is an ideological question, or to put it another way, a right–left question. So the overall political complexion of the population will have an effect on how much or how little the body politic thinks it ought to plan.

In brief, then, the plan reflects the community from which it springs. There is as much variation in plans and in their effectiveness as there is among places themselves. In Chapter 19 we discuss some alternative approaches to the comprehensive planning approach and the pros and cons thereof.

SUMMARY

The comprehensive plan covers the entire municipality and has a long time horizon, typically 20 years or so. The goals of a municipality's comprehensive planning process might include issues of health, public safety, circulation, provision of services and facilities, fiscal health, economic development, environmental protection, and, perhaps, some redistributive goals.

The comprehensive planning process can be divided into these five major stages:

1. Research
2. Clarification of goals and objectives
3. Plan formulation
4. Plan implementation
5. Review and revision

Though shown as separate steps, there is much overlap between them because what is learned in one step may cause the community to modify what was established in a preceding step. For example, the detailed work of plan formulation, by revealing the true costs of pursuing a particular goal, may cause the community to reconsider its goals. We also noted that periodic review of problems and progress and subsequent updating of the plan are essential if the plan is to continue to affect the development of the community. Active participation by the citizens in the planning process is an essential element. The chapter ends with a brief statement on possibilities from citizen participation that are being opened up by recent advances in computer technology.

NOTES

1. For a discussion of the relationship between design and safety from crime, see Oscar Newman, *Defensible Space*, The MacMillan Company, New York, 1972.

2. See, for example, George Sternlieb et al., *Housing Development and Municipal Costs*, Rutgers University Center for Urban Policy Research, New Brunswick, NJ,

1973; or Robert W. Burchell and David Listokin, *The New Practitioners Fiscal Impact Handbook,* Rutgers University Center for Urban Policy Research, New Brunswick, NJ, 1985.

3. Norman Krumholz, "A Retrospective on Equity Planning: Cleveland, 1969–79," with comments, *APA Journal,* vol. 48, no. 2, Spring 1982, pp. 163–184.

4. For an introductory account of this technique and comparison with other techniques, see F. Stuart Chapin and Edward J. Kaiser, *Urban Land Use Planning,* 3rd ed., University of Illinois Press, Urbana, 1979, chap. 6.

5. The terms *forecast* and *projection* are often used interchangeably, but to demographers there is a distinction. The former implies the analyst's best estimate of what will happen. The latter is simply a math-ematical exercise showing what the population will be if certain rates of birth, death, inmigration, and outmigration are obtained. A forecast can be proven right or wrong by future events. But a projection, if the mathematics is done correctly, cannot be said to be wrong.

6. See Edward J. Kaiser, David R. Godschalk, and F. Stuart Chapin, Jr., *Urban Land Use Planning,* 4th ed., University of Illinois Press, Urbana, 1995.

7. For an account of different types of community economic studies, see John M. Levy, *Urban and Metropolitan Economics,* McGraw-Hill Book Co., New York, 1985, chap. 4. See also Thomas S. Lyons and Roger E. Hamlin, *Creating an Economic Development Action Plan,* Praeger, Westport, CT, 2001.

SELECTED BIBLIOGRAPHY

ANDERSON, LARZ T., *Guidelines for Preparing Urban Plans,* American Planning Association, Chicago, 1995.

ANDERSON, LARZ T., *Planning the Built Environment,* American Planning Association, Chicago, 2000.

BRANCH, MELVILLE C., *Continuous City Planning,* John Wiley, New York, 1981.

HOCH, CHARLES J., DALTON, LINDA C., AND SO, FRANK S., EDS., *The Practice of Local Government Planning,* International City Management Association, Washington, DC, 2000.

KAISER, EDWARD J., GODSCHALK, DAVID R., AND CHAPIN, F. STUART, *Urban Land Use Planning,* 4th ed., University of Illinois Press, Urbana, 1995.

KENT, T. J., *The Urban General Plan,* Chandler, San Francisco, 1964.

CHAPTER 9

The Tools of
Land-Use Planning

The comprehensive plan, as described in the preceding chapter, largely pertains to the pattern of land use. In this chapter we discuss the tools available to the municipality to effectuate its land-use plans. Essentially there are two broad categories of direct actions by which a municipality can shape its land-use pattern. These are (1) public capital investments and (2) land-use controls. Some land-use decisions, often very important ones, are determined by higher levels of government and other large players that are not a part of the municipal body politic. These decisions are discussed at the end of this chapter.

PUBLIC CAPITAL INVESTMENT

Though we devote more space in this chapter to land-use controls, in the long term, public capital investment is the more powerful shaper of the pattern of development. Public capital investment creates very powerful economic forces that shape development and, unlike land-use controls, public capital investments such as roads or bridges or water mains are there to stay for many decades.

Accessibility is the most important determinant of land value. Retailers want to locate where they are accessible to the maximum number of potential customers and also where they will be seen by the maximum number of potential customers. The builders of office buildings want to place the buildings where they are most accessible to potential employees and visitors. Manufacturers want easy access for workers and suppliers, and easy access to customers. Office operations need access to workers and to individuals and other firms with which they do business.

The most accessible sites will thus command the highest prices. And builders, seeking to make the most efficient use of an expensive resource (land), will develop most intensely on the most expensive land. Public expenditures on roads and highways, as well as other investments that determine accessibility, have a powerful effect on the pattern of land development. In a densely developed urban area, investment in mass transportation is a powerful shaper of land values and hence the pattern of development. In a place such as Washington, DC, where the Metro system is an important part of the total transportation picture, the building of a new stop may create hundreds of millions in land values. In a congested area the building of a parking structure may have a powerful effect on land values and the amount of development by rendering that location more accessible.

Public investment in water and sewer lines is another major shaper of the pattern of development. Without public water and sewer service, residential development is generally limited to single-family houses on fairly large lots. Commercial development is also comparably restrained. Thus the extension of water and sewer lines can produce great changes in the intensity of development.

Public investment in facilities such as schools and universities, airports, and harbor facilities can also be major shapers of the land-use pattern. Public acquisition of parkland can also shape the land-use pattern, because permanently rendering some land undevelopable channels the flow of development.

FINANCING CAPITAL EXPENDITURES

Capital expenditures are generally financed with bonds. A bond is basically a promise to make repayments to the buyer on a regular, prearranged basis. Generally, interest payments are made once or twice a year, and the principal is repaid on the bond's maturity date. Between the time that a bond is issued and its maturity date, the bond's market value will vary, but the periodic interest payments (dividends) and the final payment at maturity are fixed from the beginning.[1]

One reason for using bonds is that capital expenditures often involve large sums of money and they are often "lump," meaning that they come along in an irregular manner. Thus financing them out of the municipality's or state's operating budget would lead to big swings in expenditures from year to year. Another reason is that capital expenditures generally deliver their benefits over a period of decades. Thus asking current taxpayers to pay for a project up front would be asking them to fund something from which they may receive only a small share of the total benefits.[2]

In contrast to capital expenditures, the ordinary operations of state and local governments are funded with current revenues rather than bonds. In fact, states and local governments are generally prohibited from borrowing to pay for short-term expenses.[3] The prohibitions may be in state constitutions or in state-enabling legislation that specifies the rules under which local governments operate. This prohibition makes a good deal of sense, for politicians might otherwise be tempted to borrow long term to pay for recurrent expenses to keep down tax rates. But that ultimately can put the state or municipality in an untenable financial position. In the nineteenth century a number of state bankruptcies came about in just this manner, and that is how the prohibitions came into being.

The Capital Budget

Most local governments maintain a separate capital budget and capital improvements plan (CIP). In fact, in many states, local governments are required to maintain a capital improvements plan, often with a time horizon of five years or so.[4] The CIP lays out the expected sequence of investments and thus gives the municipal government a rough schedule of when and in what amounts it will have to issue bonds and also a rough indicator of how much it will have to spend on debt service (payments of interest and principal) each year. Adopting the capital budget is the prerogative of the municipality's legislative body. Generally, the budget that the legislature passes, with or without modification, is proposed by the municipality's executive branch. Because capital expenditures have such a powerful effect on how the municipality develops, it is very important for the planning agency to have a hand in the preparation of the capital budget and the CIP.

Types of Bonds

Two main types of bonds are issued to finance public capital investment. For a task such as financing a new municipal building, the most common practice is to issue a general obligation (GO) bond. Such a bond is guaranteed by the "full faith and credit" of the municipal government, meaning that if the municipal government fails to make interest or principal payments on time, a court may require the municipal government to use any resources that it has to repay the bondholders. Because such bonds are a direct obligation on the municipal government, they are issued under strict limits. In many states, a municipality's total outstanding general obligation debt may not exceed a certain percentage of its property tax base.[5] For example, in Virginia, state law limits a municipality's outstanding general obligation debt to 10 percent of its real property tax base. A referendum is required in a number of states before local or state government can issue general obligation bonds. Municipal governments are also prohibited from using bonds to pay for operating expenses because the temptation to shift the burden of present operations to future taxpayers would be a very strong one.

Note that in two regards just noted, state and local governments operate under very different rules than does the federal government. First, the federal government does not maintain separate capital and operating budgets and does not make a sharp distinction between capital and operating expenditures. Second, the federal government does not operate under a balanced budget requirement. The Congress does impose a limit on the size of the national debt, but when the debt bumps up against the debt limit, Congress can raise the limit, and this has happened many times.

Revenue Bonds

If the capital expenditure in question can be expected to deliver a reasonably predictable stream of revenue, then it can be financed with revenue bonds. These bonds are generally not obligations of the municipal or state government. Rather, they are backed by a claim on the revenues that the facility is expected to generate. Thus toll roads, parking structures, water and sewage treatment plants, airports, stadiums, and other such revenue generating facilities can be financed by these bonds. Facilities that do not generate revenues directly cannot be financed with revenue bonds. Given a choice, municipal governments prefer revenue bonds because such bonds are not an obligation of government and therefore are not subject to debt limits and do not require referenda. What they generally do require is the opinion of a bond-rating agency such as Standard and Poor or Moody's that there will be adequate revenues to pay off the bonds. Otherwise, the bonds will not be marketable.

Grants

As noted in Chapter 5, local government expenditures, both capital and operating, are heavily conditioned by grants from higher levels of government, and some reasons why this system has developed are discussed there. There is a very large flow of federal grants to the states and a much smaller flow of grants that bypasses the states and goes directly to local governments and some districts, especially school districts. There is also a very large flow of grant money from the states down to local governments and districts.[6] Grants come in a number of types, the most common being the closed-end matching grant, in which up to some limit the donor will match the expenditures of the recipient government. The Interstate Highway System and many sewage treatment plants were built with 90 percent federal money and 10 percent local money. Many other road projects have been done with a 50–50 federal–local match. Grants may have a very large effect on local capital expenditures both because they may be the difference between possible and impossible and also because they change the system of prices that the local government faces. For example, a local government might want to acquire some parkland, but not badly enough to pay the full price. If it can buy the land for 50 cents on the dollar because the state or federal government is picking up the other 50 cents, then it may decide to make the purchase.[7]

Capital Investment Financing and the 2008 Recession

The previous text describes the situation with financing capital expenditures as it has been until recently, but there may be some changes in the wind. In the last several years a great many state and local government budgets have come under serious pressure for a variety of reasons and many face very large deficits. The situation that may well be the most serious and which has received the most attention is that of California, where the 2011 deficit was estimated to be in the $25 to $26 billion range, about $700 per capita. There is also growing default risk at the substate level. The near default of Harrisburg, Pennsylvania in 2010 and the default of Jefferson County, Alabama in 2011 may be straws in the wind.

One problem is that many states and some municipal governments have very large unfunded pension obligations. Ideally, pension funds are fully funded. That is, sufficient funds are put away each year to meet the future pension obligations that were incurred in that year. Calculating how much should be put away to fund future pensions depends on what assumptions are made about future interest rates and stock prices, because the assets in the pension fund are primarily bonds and stocks. Falling interest rates and declining stock values have made many pension funds far from fully funded. Apart from that, many state and local governments have purposely made very rosy assumptions about future returns to be able to justify smaller fund contributions. Given that politicians stand for two- or four-year terms but pension obligations stretch out over decades, the temptation to stint on this year's contributions is understandable. Unfunded pension liabilities threaten a huge drain on budgets for the years to come as well as the need for increased contributions to pension funds in the short term.

State budgets have also been pushed into deficit as states' revenues from personal income taxes, sales taxes, and corporate income taxes declined in the 2008 recession. Federal aid to state governments increased in 2009 with the economic stimulus package, but the stimulus was not renewed. By the 2011 fiscal year the political pressure to cut the large federal deficit forced large cuts in many grant programs, a situation that is expected to persist for at least several years. When state budgets become tight, local governments feel the pressure because a substantial share of local government funds come from the states. Then, too, at this time local government revenues from sales taxes and property taxes, as well as miscellaneous business taxes, have declined. Raising taxes to meet deficits is difficult for state and local governments for two distinct reasons. One is the present antitax political climate of the United States. The second is that state and local governments are in competition with other state and local governments for investment and jobs. Raising taxes if competing jurisdictions do not presents a real economic risk.

Extreme fiscal pressure on state and municipal governments may gradually produce some modification of the traditional prohibitions against borrowing long term to fund operating expenses. That is beginning to happen in fact if not in name—witness, for example, Chicago's selling off its future rights to tolls on the Dan Ryan Expressway as noted in Chapter 12, leaseback arrangements, and the selling of the rights to other state and local revenue sources.

GO bonds are, in principle, a first-rank obligation of state and local governments. So, too, are those revenue bonds which have governmental guarantees (some do and some do not). But how matters would play out if a state or local government faced a choice between defaulting on its debts, failing to make pension payments to retired employees, or failing to provide essential public services is not known. Court decisions would play a central role, but exactly how they would rule is far from certain. The last time there were a significant number of defaults on state and local debt was during the Great Depression (1930s), so there is little recent precedent by which to judge.

LAND-USE CONTROLS

Although land-use controls are not as powerful a shaper of land use as is public capital investment, they are still extremely important. Their development and implementation constitute a major share of the work effort of most planning agencies. In the minds of many citizens, land-use controls are almost synonymous with planning.

In this section we discuss subdivision controls, zoning, and several miscellaneous types of land-use controls.

Subdivision Regulations

Subdivision regulations are an old form of land-use control, going back to the early nineteenth century and before. Their enforcement is an exercise of the police power by the municipality within the framework of the powers granted it by the state.[8] Subdivision regulations control the manner in which blocks of land over a certain size may be converted into building lots. Before building lots can be sold or the owner can make improvements, the municipality must approve a plat (map) of the property. The ordinance will require at a minimum that the map show streets, lot lines, and easements (rights of way) for utilities. It also will stipulate what improvements must be made before building lots can be sold or before building permits may be granted. Thus the community is able to compel the property owner to construct internal streets that link up in a satisfactory manner to the municipality's street system and meet its standards for width, safety, and quality of construction. Similarly, it can compel the developer of the property to provide sewer, water, and drainage facilities that meet the community's standards. Subdivision requirements frequently also stipulate that certain land dedications (or payments in lieu of such dedications) be made to the community by the developer for schools, recreation, or community facilities. Many subdivision regulations require that the design of the subdivision be compatible with the municipal master plan and zoning ordinance, thus reinforcing the implementation of these documents. In general, subdivision regulations apply to residential development, but in some communities they also govern some commercial and industrial development.

Though less well-known than zoning laws, subdivision regulations give communities substantial power to ensure that new residential development meets community standards and fits in with community development plans. Like zoning laws, subdivision regulations are subject to litigation and various forms of political pressure. Like the power to zone, the power to regulate subdivisions can be abused. For example, some communities, seeking to screen out less affluent people or less expensive housing that will carry a lower assessment and therefore pay less in property taxes, have enacted subdivision regulations that impose unnecessarily high costs on builders, thus blocking the construction of moderately priced housing.

Zoning Ordinances

The best-known form of land-use control is the zoning ordinance.[9] This is generally prepared by the community's planners or planning consultant. The document acquires its legal force when the community's legislative body passes a measure adopting it. Generally speaking, there are two parts to the zoning ordinance. The first part is a map that divides the community into a number of zones. The map is sufficiently detailed so that it is possible to tell in which zone(s) any given parcel of land lies. Most commonly, all of the community is zoned. However, there are some cases, particularly nonurban counties, in which part of a community is zoned and part is not. The second part is the text, which specifies in considerable detail what may be constructed in each zone and to what uses structures may be put. The box on pages 143–145 shows some of the details for one zoning classification in Fairfax County, Virginia.

Among the items generally specified by the ordinance are the following:

1. *Site layout requirements.* These may include, among other things, minimum lot area, frontage and depth, minimum setbacks (minimum distance from structure to front, side, or rear lot line), maximum percentage of site that may be covered by structure, placement of driveways or curb cuts, parking requirements, screening requirements, and limits on the size or placement of signs.

2. *Requirements for structure characteristics.* These may include maximum height of structure, maximum number of stories, and maximum floor area of structure. The last is often cast in terms of floor area ratio (FAR), which indicates a maximum permissible ratio of floor area to site area.

3. *Uses to which structures may be put.*   In a residential zone the ordinance might specify that dwellings may be occupied only by single families and then proceed to define what constitutes a family. The ordinance might also enumerate certain nonresidential uses permitted in the zone such as churches, funeral homes, and professional offices. In commercial zones the ordinance will generally specify which uses are permitted and which are not. For example, in a manufacturing zone the ordinance might specify that sheet metal fabrication operations are permitted but that rendering operations are forbidden.

4. *Procedural matters.*   The ordinance will specify how it is to be determined whether building plans are in conformity to the zoning ordinance. (A common arrangement is that the building inspector shall make such determination and must deny a building permit application if the plans are not.) The ordinance will generally also specify an appeals procedure by which an applicant can apply for relief. In many communities the initial appeal authority is vested in a special body generally referred to as the Zoning Board of Appeals. If not, the review process is often assigned to the planning board or to the municipal legislative body.

The Popularity of Zoning.
Zoning has been, since shortly after its inception, by far the most common means by which communities have sought to control land use. What accounts for its popularity? The answer is quite simple. Zoning has considerable power to achieve goals that the community favors, and it is almost free. Unless a "taking" has occurred (see Chapter 5), no compensation need be paid to property owners for reductions in property values caused by limitations imposed by the zoning ordinance on the type or intensity of use permitted. In effect, the municipality gets one of the rights of ownership, namely the right to exercise some control over the use to which the property will be put, without having to purchase it.[10] The only costs to the municipality are administrative and legal expenses.

In principle, the same effects could be achieved by exercise of the power of eminent domain or by contract between municipality and property owner. But either of those courses would necessitate major expenditures by the municipality.

In fact, contracts between governments and property owners have been used to affect land use. Generally, the contract is referred to as an easement. This is an agreement by the property owner to forgo some right(s)—for example, that of subdividing the property or developing it in some way—in return for a payment. For example, Suffolk County, New York, has made widespread use of easement purchases to maintain land on eastern Long Island in agricultural use. Such a device can be highly effective, for the purchase of an easement provides an ironclad guarantee to the community in the form of an enforceable contract that property will not be used in a manner proscribed by the easement. In other places a similar effect has been obtained through special tax treatment. Where farmland preservation is a goal, land that is kept in agricultural use is taxed very lightly compared with the tax that must be paid on it when it is placed in some other use.

Easements and special tax treatment are used in most states, but, unlike zoning, their application is quite spotty. The explanation for this difference is cost.

The Effectiveness of Zoning.   How effective is zoning in shaping land use? There is tremendous variation among communities, ranging from almost totally ineffective to highly effective. Zoning may be quite effective in a growing area where the land-use pattern is not yet fully determined. Here zoning can shape the urban pattern by blocking or limiting growth in some areas and thus, in effect, diverting it to other areas. Often in prosperous developed areas in which there is substantial pressure for change in land use, zoning may be effective in preventing or moderating that change. For example, a prosperous inner suburb might successfully resist the transformation of single-family neighborhoods to multifamily neighborhoods even though the economics of the local housing market favor such a change.

On the other hand, zoning may be relatively ineffective in older urban areas where the land-use pattern is essentially established and where growth forces are not very powerful. Zoning, by itself, cannot address the redevelopment problem, for controls cannot compel anyone to invest in an area. Zoning may also be relatively weak if the community is so eager for investment that it readily adjusts its zoning to suit developers' preferences. Zoning may also be weak or absent in semirural or rural areas where the residents do not see much need for it.

THE INGREDIENTS OF A ZONING ORDINANCE

This material is reproduced from a Fairfax County, Virginia, zoning ordinance. Note that it specifies permitted uses, site geometry, ground coverage, and building height and bulk.

Commercial District Regulations
Part 5 4-500 C-5 Neighborhood Retail Commercial District

4-501 Purpose and Intent The C-5 District is established to provide locations for convenience shopping facilities in which those retail commercial uses shall predominate that have a neighborhood-oriented market of approximately 5000 persons, and which supply necessities that usually require frequent purchasing and with a minimum of consumer travel. Typical uses to be found in the Neighborhood Retail Commercial District include a food supermarket, drugstore, personal service establishments, small specialty shops, and a limited number of small professional offices.

Areas zoned for the C-5 District should be located so that their distributional pattern throughout the County reflects their neighborhood orientation. They should be designed to be an integral, homogeneous component of the neighborhoods they serve, oriented to pedestrian traffic as well as vehicular. The district should not be located in close proximity to other retail commercial uses.

Because of the nature and location of the Neighborhood Retail Commercial District, they should be encouraged to develop in compact centers under a unified design that is architecturally compatible with the neighborhood in which they are located. Further, such districts should not be so large or broad in scope of services as to attract substantial trade from outside the neighborhood. Generally, the ultimate size of a C-5 District in a given location in the County should not exceed an aggregate gross floor area of 100,000 square feet or an aggregate site size of (10) acres.

4–502 Permitted Uses

1. Accessory uses as permitted by Article 10.
2. Business service and supply service establishments.
3. Churches, chapels, temples, synagogues and other such places of worship.
4. Drive-in banks, limited by the provisions of Sect. 505 below.
5. Eating establishments.
6. Fast food restaurants, limited by the provisions of Sect. 505 below.
7. Financial institutions.
8. Offices.
9. Personal service establishments.
10. Private schools of general education, private schools of special education.
11. Public uses.
12. Quick-service food stores, limited by the provisions of Sect. 505 below.
13. Repair service establishments.
14. Retail sales establishments.
15. Telecommunication exchanges.

4–506 Lot Size Requirements

1. Minimum lot area: 40,000 sq. ft.
2. Minimum lot width: 200 feet
3. The minimum lot size requirements may be waived by the Board in accordance with provisions of Sect. 9–610.

4–507 Bulk Regulations

1. Maximum building height: 40 feet
2. Minimum yard requirements
   A. Front yard: Controlled by a 45° angle of bulk plane, but not less than 40 feet
   B. Side yard: No Requirement
   C. Rear yard: 20 feet
3. Maximum floor area ratio: 0.50
4. Refer to Sect. 13–108 for provisions that may qualify the minimum yard requirements set forth above.

4–508 Open Space 20% of the gross area shall be landscaped open space
4–509 Additional Regulations

1. Refer to Article 2, General Regulations, for provisions which may qualify or supplement the regulations presented above.
2. Refer to Article 11 for off-street parking, loading and private street requirements.
3. Refer to Article 12 for regulations on signs.
4. Refer to Article 13 for landscaping and screening requirements.

One key to effective zoning is synchronization between land-use controls and public capital investment. It is possible for a community's land-use and capital investment policies to be at odds with one another and for each to undermine and frustrate the intent of the other. For example, a capital investment program might generate forces for a type or intensity of development that is proscribed by the zoning. In this case either the capital investment has been partly wasted, or economic pressures will force changes in the zoning. Conversely, if the zoning permits levels of development that are not supported by necessary road and utility investment, nothing is likely to happen. The community will then have the pleasure of watching its industrial or office zone grow weeds year after year.

The Limitations of Zoning.   Zoning is limited by both economic and legal forces. If the value of land in a use permitted by zoning is very much lower than the value of that land in a use that is forbidden but for which a market exists, property owners have strong motivation to try to change the zoning. They may expend substantial funds on litigation, or they may devote substantial effort to building a coalition of forces to lobby for zoning change. If the community is hungry for jobs and additions to its tax base, potential investors may indicate to the community that if it does not show flexibility, their capital will be invested in some other community, one that can recognize a good thing when it sees it.

To illustrate, consider a prototypical suburban scenario. Mr. X owns 100 acres of vacant land, which has been in his family for generations. He rents the land to a local farmer for enough money to cover his property taxes. The land in its present low-density residential zoning category has a market value of $10,000 per acre. A major real estate developer perceives that were development of condominiums at medium density possible, the land would be worth $50,000 an acre. She approaches Mr. X and offers to buy an option. Specifically, for $10,000 Mr. X gives the developer the right to buy the property for $12,000 an acre at any time during the next two years. If the developer chooses not to exercise her option, Mr. X still keeps the $10,000.

Having purchased the option, the developer now tries to change the zoning. If her attorney tells her that the municipality's zoning of the property is on weak legal ground, she may approach the municipality, indicate to it why its position is weak, and suggest that compromise is in everyone's best interest. The municipality's legal position may be weak for any number of reasons. Comparable parcels in other areas of the municipality may be zoned for more intensive development. Hence a charge of inconsistency (of treating equals unequally) may be leveled against the municipality in court. Perhaps the zoning of the property is not in keeping with the municipality's master plan. If so, the developer can argue that the zoning is capricious and inconsistent. Perhaps the developer can show that on the basis of utilities, access, and other considerations, the property could sustain far more development than the zoning permits. In this case she can argue that the present zoning cannot be justified on the grounds of the police power.

Hearing all this and after due consultation with their planning consultant and attorney, the municipal officials might well decide that compromise is indeed in order. In that case they may recommend to the municipality's legislative body that it amend the zoning ordinance. If the community is adamant and the developer is sure the legal situation favors her, she might bring suit and begin to fight it out in court. The issue might be settled in court or, seeing the tide of legal battle flowing against it, the municipality might decide to compromise.

Alternatively, the developer can take a less confrontational tack. She can engage a local planning consultant to design a condominium development for the site. The consultant comes up with a proposal nicely presented with attractive drawings and a model. Then the consultant performs a set of calculations referred to as a "fiscal impact analysis," which shows that for every additional dollar the project will cost the community for services, its property taxes and other contributions to the municipal treasury will amount to two dollars. (See the box on property taxes on pages 148–149.) The developer's proposal does not fail to note how many dollars of retail sales within the community will be made from condominium residents, a point that will not be lost on the municipality's business community. The report will also note how many years of on-site construction labor the project will require, a point that should bring in a few more allies, particularly if construction employment has been soft recently.

At this point the report is presented to the town government with appropriate newspaper and other publicity. When public hearings are held, the developer or her spokespeople adopt a posture of reasonableness and conciliation. If there are aspects of the plan to which the citizens object, she will listen attentively and endeavor to find mutually satisfactory compromises. For example, if residents worry that the development will send too many children to the local schools, she may offer to build more studio and one-bedroom units and fewer two- and three-bedroom units, thus bringing in more childless couples and fewer large families. The relationship between unit size, household size, and number of school-age children has been studied often and can be predicted fairly well. Thus this sort of "architectural birth control" can often be practiced quite effectively.

The developer will also structure the proposal to give herself room to be reasonable. If she would be satisfied with building six units to the acre, the initial plan may call for eight units to the acre. This strategy leaves her something that can be given up after suitable protest but without causing her real pain.

The developer may or may not obtain a zoning change in this manner. Any planner who has spent some time working in the suburbs has seen such situations go both ways. The point, however, is that the party desiring the zoning change has numerous avenues open.

Note that if the developer is successful in obtaining the rezoning, she has, in effect, made a very large sum of money even before construction begins. She has obtained land worth $50,000 an acre for the price of $12,000 an acre plus the cost of the option. In fact, were she to forget about the project and simply to sell the rezoned land to another developer, she would make a very large profit.[11]

Because of the large sums of money at stake in some land-use decisions, the practice of zoning is not immune from bribery and corruption. An FBI sting operation in Fresno, California, resulted in eight convictions, with the longest sentence being 30 months, in connection with exchange of bribes and campaign contributions for favorable zoning decisions.[12]

The playing of zoning games is hardly limited to those on the private side of the fence. Municipalities often zone substantial amounts of land in economically unrealistic categories. This practice suits the municipal interest quite well, for it gives the municipality a bargaining position that it would not have were the land zoned realistically in the first instance.

In the late 1970s the town of Harrison, New York, became the home of Texaco's corporate headquarters. The headquarters imposed few costs on the town yet provided a substantial property tax payment, clearly a very desirable situation from the town's perspective. How did this arrangement happen? The site was 100 acres or so of land zoned for single-family houses on two-acre lots. As it happened, the site was in a developing commercial area and was close to the intersection of two interstate highways. It clearly had potential for much more valuable use than low-density single-family housing. The fact that a zoning change was needed for economically realistic development put the town in a strong negotiating position. First, the town was able to turn away any development proposal it did not like. In addition, the need for a rezoning gave the town the power to insist on site features, like below-ground parking and deep setbacks, which the corporation might not otherwise have chosen to provide.

PROPERTY TAXES AND ZONING

Zoning cannot be fully understood without some understanding of property taxes. Property tax collections by local governments and school districts were $470 billion in 2010 and account for approximately three-fourths of all local tax collections. Given the size of that number, few significant zoning decisions are made without considering the property tax implications. Here, very briefly, is how property taxes are levied. The municipality maintains a ledger (either on paper or electronically), referred to as the property tax roll. Each property in the municipality appears on this roll. Generally speaking, the roll will have one column for "land" and another column for "improvements," the latter essentially meaning structures. In each column is recorded the assessed value of the land or structure. The value, determined by the municipality's assessor, presents his or her estimate of what the property would bring if sold in an "arm's length" transaction.[13] Some municipalities have "full value assessment." Others use "fractional assessment." Where fractional assessment is used, all properties should be assessed at the same fraction of market value.[14] The municipality and other taxing jurisdictions each have a property tax rate that is applied to the assessed value of the property to determine how much tax is owed. For example, if the tax rate is $2.50 per 100 of assessed value and the property is assessed at $50,000, the tax owed is $50,000 × 2.50/100 = $1,250.

For the municipality as a whole, the equation is tax base × tax rate = tax yield. Tax base in this equation is the sum of all of the assessed values on land and improvements subject to tax.[15]

If a given development will bring in more in taxes than it will cost in additional municipal expenses, either (1) the same level of municipal services can be maintained for a lower tax rate or (2) a higher level of services can be maintained at the same tax rate. If the costs of servicing the new development exceed the tax revenues that it will yield at the current tax rate, those relationships are reversed.

Though this discussion is cast in terms of a municipal tax rate, there may actually be several property taxes within a given community. For example, properties in a town located within a county and having an independent school district may be subject to a town tax, a county tax, and a school tax. In some suburban areas, where the structure and responsibilities of government are not as large as in a city and where a large percentage of all households have school-age children, the school tax constitutes the majority share of the total tax burden.

The property tax has been subject to a barrage of criticisms over the years. However, it remains in universal use. For one thing it is easy to administer and enforce. The assessor assesses, and the Receiver of Taxes sends the bill. If the property owner fails to pay the bill, the municipality can foreclose the property and sell it at auction to recover the back taxes. It is probably the hardest tax to evade. An individual or business may be able to conceal some income, but no one has yet figured out how to hide a house or a factory.

The physical immobility of land and structures is also an important reason why local governments place major reliance on the property tax relative to other taxes. Where jurisdictions are small, the heavy use of income, sales, or business taxes can readily chase economic activity and wealthy residents out of town. Thus the property tax is the safest tax, and perhaps the only tax, upon which a local government can place very much weight.

Similar comments might be made with regard to residential development. If a rezoning is necessary to permit the building of multifamily housing, the municipality might say no to a low-income housing proposal but yes to a structurally similar development intended for small affluent families—a form of discrimination that few if any courts would sustain were it written into the zoning ordinance.

MAKING ZONING MORE FLEXIBLE

Zoning is a crude instrument. It prescribes what cannot be done, but it cannot make anything happen. Its very rigidity may lead to less than optimal results. For example, assume a zoning district permits a certain amount of development on a given-sized lot within a given zone. If some lots are developed to the full amount permitted but other lots remain vacant or are developed to only part of the permitted intensity of use, the district may function quite well. On the other hand, if every lot is developed to full intensity, the congestion, traffic, and noise may be overwhelming. Yet a municipality can hardly tell a property owner not to develop as much as the owner of an adjacent plot simply because the other property owner was first. Such a position would carry little weight in court.

"Zoning saturation" studies have frequently shown that if a municipality were developed to the full extent that the zoning allowed, its population would be several times the present level. The population of New York City, the most densely developed city in the United States, has ranged between 7 and 8 million in recent decades. Some time ago a saturation study showed that if built up to the full extent the law allowed, the city could have a population of some 30 million. A saturation study of Yonkers, New York, with a population of about 200,000 on 20 square miles, showed that the city could, if fully developed as the law permitted, have a population of about 600,000. This would make it the most densely populated city in the United States. In neither case is there any chance of such development occurring.

The disparity between actual and theoretical development does raise questions about the precision of zoning. Clearly, zoning is not the determinant of the structure of a city in fine detail if there is that much space between the overcoat of zoning and the body of development.

Zoning is vulnerable to the criticism that it severely limits the freedom of the architect and site designer and may thus lower the quality of urban design. Rules promulgated to cover substantial blocks of land are likely to be suboptimal with regard to particular sites or parcels.

Zoning has also been criticized for producing a sterile environment through an excessive separation of uses. The most influential criticism of this sort was delivered in the 1960s by Jane Jacobs.[6] She argued that by excessive separation of uses—residents here, stores there, and so on—planners produce urban environments that are sterile and sometimes dangerous as well. They are sterile because of lack of variety of uses and building types, she argued, and dangerous because the single-use street is deserted for some part of the day and thus is an inducement to crime.

One area of which Jacobs spoke very highly is Manhattan's Greenwich Village. This is an old area, characterized by small and frequently irregularly shaped blocks and a great mix of uses. Most buildings are not very high, typically four to six stories. The same block will often contain a fine-grained mix of residential and nonresidential uses. In fact, many buildings have stores, restaurants, coffeehouses, and the like on the ground level with apartments above. The area has a lively street life, which lasts into the late hours of the night, and it is generally considered a desirable neighborhood in which to live. Jacobs argued that the sort of diversity, charm, and activity that characterize the West Village is often blocked by the rigidities of zoning and planners' excessive concern with separation of uses. She argued that the area owed much of its charm to the fact that it had developed before the advent of zoning (zoning is not retroactive). Though Jacobs is not a planner herself, her criticism made many planners rethink the intent and effects of zoning on neighborhoods. In fact, Jacobs's criticisms of zoning, which were radical in the 1960s, are now part of the standard wisdom of planning. Her ideas about the desirability of a fine-grained mixture of uses are central to the *new urbanism* discussed in Chapter 10.

In April 1996 *The New York Times* reported a case in which areas of New York thrived only because they were able to escape the rigidities of the city's zoning law, partly because budget problems restricted the number of building inspectors available to enforce the rules. In the 1970s, alarmed at its rapid loss of manufacturing jobs, New York City limited the use of many thousands of acres so as to permit almost nothing but manufacturing. These acres included many blocks, particularly in lower Manhattan, of old manufacturing loft buildings that could no longer compete as locations for manufacturing. However, these buildings had another potential. *The New York Times* noted the following:

> The lofts and warehouses of SoHo and Tribeca, where rents were cheap and huge open [internal] spaces were available, proved to be ideal for the hip hybridization of computer technology, art and residence that the city now crows triumphantly about as Silicon Alley.
>   This transformation was possible only because the zoning regulations were not enforced.[17]

In an effort to make zoning a finer instrument, a variety of techniques have evolved in recent years. These, in general, are designed to make land-use controls more flexible and more negotiable. The basic idea is that increasing flexibility allows the parties to land-use negotiations to bargain and thus realize what economists refer to as "the gains of trade."

Let us say that the land developer would like to do something that is prohibited under the letter of the zoning law. On the other hand, the municipality might like the developer to do something that he or she is not legally required to do. Why not have an ordinance so structured that some bargaining is possible? Presumably we need not fear that the municipality will lose out. If, on balance, the trade is not in the municipal interest, the municipality will not consent. A number of newer techniques follow.

Bonus or Incentive Zoning

Many communities will allow increased residential densities if developers include some units earmarked for low- and moderate-income tenants. For example, the law might stipulate eight units to the acre in a particular zone but permit an increase to ten units if 15 percent of the units are reserved for low- and moderate-income tenants. The developer gets the scale economies of denser development, and the community moves a bit closer to meeting its low- and moderate-income housing goals.

The two Greenwich Village streets shown here, though photographed in 2004, are very much as they were at the time that Jane Jacobs wrote. In the top photo, there is an off-Broadway theater on the left and a restaurant on the right with a small apartment house in between and apartments over both commercial uses. Access is overwhelmingly pedestrian, for the street that serves the neighborhood is narrower than would be permitted in even the smallest modern suburban subdivision. In the lower photo, note the mix of structure types and the stores under the apartments.

Many cities have made comparable arrangements with regard to office development. The zoning ordinance might stipulate a certain height limitation but permit additional height or stories if the developer will provide certain amenities at ground level—for example, a plaza in front of the entrance to the building, a direct entrance to a subway station, or a "vest-pocket" park or sitting area.

Transfer of Development Rights

The intent of transfer of development rights (TDR) is to concentrate development in areas where it is wanted and to restrict it in areas where it is not. To do so, a sending and a receiving area are designated. Property owners in the sending areas who do not develop their properties to the full extent permitted by the law may sell their unused rights to property owners in receiving areas. The technique might be used to preserve open space, to limit development in an ecologically fragile area, or to achieve historic preservation goals, among others.[18]

One might ask, "Can this not be done with conventional zoning simply by permitting high densities in some areas and low densities in other areas?" In a literal sense, the answer is yes. However, in a practical sense, the answer may be no. Assume that the intent of the community master plan is to keep development very sparse in a particular area. If the community simply zones that way, say, a minimum lot size of 10 acres for a single-family house, it may have imposed large losses on property owners. Even if it can win in court, the municipality has created a constituency opposed to the plan. On the other hand, if it gives the property owners salable development rights, both their motivation and grounds for suit are eliminated. If the municipality wishes to preserve old buildings in a historic zone, one way to do it is to let the property owners there have salable development rights. When they sell their development rights to property owners in an area where the municipality wants growth (the receiving area), they will no longer want to tear down their old buildings, for having sold their rights, they can no longer redevelop at higher densities.

Won't the property owners in receiving areas object to, in effect, having to buy off owners in sending areas? Not necessarily, for if purchasing development rights is not profitable, receiving area property owners will not purchase them. Presumably a market in development rights will develop, the price moving to a position high enough to motivate owners in the sending area to sell yet low enough to make purchase profitable for property owners in the receiving area.

For the municipality, the technique, like zoning itself, is essentially costless. The payments to some property owners come not from the municipality's taxpayers but from other property owners. Whether the municipality's taxpayers may ultimately pick up some of those costs in the form of higher rents and higher prices is another issue.

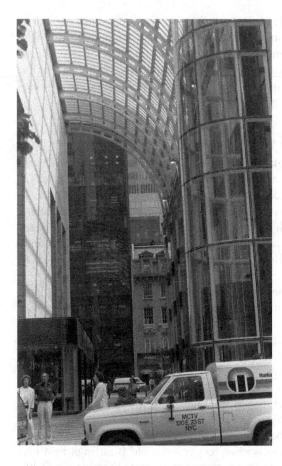

A glass-roofed arcade connects two parallel streets at the AT&T headquarters building in Manhattan. Some willingness to deviate from the rigidities of traditional Euclidean zoning is usually necessary to achieve an interesting and unusual result like this.

This technique was the object of some controversy in its first years in part because it appeared that it might be susceptible to some abuse. After all, if the owners of land in "rocky promontory" or "trackless swamp" were given salable rights, that would be a windfall, and yet a developer elsewhere might still be willing to pay for them. However, despite initial doubts, the technique is proving itself. For a particularly successful example, see the box below. For a study of the conditions under which TDR seems to work best, see Rick Pruetz and Noah Standridge.[19]

THE HIGH LINE AND TDR

One unusual and important project in which TDR played a key role is in the construction of New York City's High Line, a 1½-mile-long elevated linear park in Manhattan.[20]

The story begins in the mid-1930s. At that time an elevated railroad line, approximately 30 feet above ground level, running mid-block between 10th and 11th Avenues in Manhattan, was completed. The line went between buildings, sometimes over one-story buildings, and in a few cases, through buildings. It replaced a ground-level rail line and separated steam-powered freight trains from pedestrian and automotive traffic at ground level. Thus in its day it was a major traffic improvement. At the time, the Chelsea district through which the High Line ran contained considerable manufacturing and warehousing activity. Slightly to the west, the docks along the Hudson River were in active use for the handling of ocean freight. The line thus served an important commercial purpose.

In time, the economics of the area changed. Manufacturing and warehousing activity declined and the docks on the Hudson lost their shipping business to other ports that had the space to handle containerized freight. The High Line carried less and less freight. In 1980 the line carried its last shipment, three carloads of frozen turkeys.

The question then became what to do with the High Line. For about 20 years it was simply a rusting eyesore that served no purpose, depressed the value of nearby properties, and looked like a prime candidate for demolition. In fact, it was spared from demolition only because of uncertainty over who was responsible for its demolition.

In 1999 a citizens' group called Friends of the High Line formed the idea of getting the High Line converted into an above-street-level walking path, or urban linear park. In 2002 the newly elected administration of Mayor Michael Bloomberg endorsed the idea and brought the city's planning department into the process. One key problem was land ownership. For the project to proceed, the city had to become the owner of the land under the High Line. Buying the land or condemning it and paying the condemnation award would be a complex and expensive proposition. The problem was solved through the use of transfer of development rights. The property owners in question were given development rights that they could sell to property owners along 10th and 11th Avenues. The city thus obtained ownership without direct outlay or the necessity for condemnation. At that time the Manhattan market for both residential and commercial real estate was strong and so the property owners who received the development rights found a ready market for them. Note that in this case the sending and receiving areas are very close, about half a block, or roughly 100 yards, apart.

Funding for building the High Line comes from the city, federal grants, and private sources. The High Line has proven to be extremely popular, and somewhat comparable projects are under consideration

At top left, the High Line right-of-way before work began. At right, the High Line shortly after its opening to the public in June 2009. Note how it passes through the adjacent building. Bottom left, the building is a new hotel supported on columns and underneath which the High Line passes.

in Chicago, Philadelphia, Jersey City, and St. Louis. The additional pedestrian traffic it has brought to the area and the transferred development rights have sparked a building boom on 10th and 11th Avenues.

Inclusionary Zoning   *like our complet*

In inclusionary zoning, developers who build more than a specified number of units must include a certain percentage of units for low- and moderate-income households.[21] It differs from the incentive or bonus approach in that the inclusion of low- and moderate-income units is not discretionary. It is the same, however, in that it shifts some of the costs of housing such households to the developer. He or she, in turn, is likely to shift at least some of that cost to the other buyers or renters.

Planned Unit Development

Planned unit development (PUD) has been widely used in the last several decades, and its popularity is still growing. PUD techniques vary, but a prototypical ordinance might work like this: The entire community is zoned in a conventional (Euclidean) manner. However, the law provides that a property owner with a minimum number of acres, say, 20, has the option of applying to develop his or her holdings as a PUD. In this case the property is subject to a different set of controls. The density permitted may or may not be the same as that stipulated by the conventional ordinance, and the uses permitted may or may not be the same. The entire site plan will be reviewed as a single entity under a review process specified by the PUD ordinance.

Some PUDs are entirely residential, and some are entirely commercial. In many cases, however, PUDs contain a greater mix of uses than would be permitted under conventional ordinance. Many PUDs that are predominantly residential contain some retailing. Numerous PUDs contain a mix of residential and commercial uses. Because the entire site plan is reviewed at one time, the benefits of mixing uses can often be had without risking some of the disadvantages. For the urban designer, PUDs can offer vastly more room for creative and innovative design than can be had working under a conventional ordinance.

One problem with many business areas, both downtown and suburban, is that they become almost deserted in the evening. Mixing residential uses with commercial uses tends to make the area more active in the evenings and on weekends. The mixed-use concept can make both commercial and residential areas more interesting and less sterile. Essentially, the PUD technique places some power to control land use in the hands of a review board or other group, which looks at that particular site design. It allows a degree of innovation and flexibility that cannot be obtained under an ordinance that must fit all cases.

But, like all other techniques, PUD has its disadvantages and its critics. Fort Collins, Colorado, stopped using PUDs in the late 1990s for two reasons. One reason was opposition from adjacent property owners. The property owner who bordered a PUD knew in general what would be in the PUD but didn't know specifically what land use would border his or her own property. That uncertainty made property owners uneasy and created an anti-PUD constituency. Municipal officials were also concerned that the development of a large number of PUDs, even if each were well designed, would make it harder to produce a unified plan for the area as a whole.

Cluster Zoning

Cluster zoning is another technique intended to free the site designer from the rigidity of conventional, Euclidean zoning while still letting the community retain control of the overall effects of the development. Cluster ordinances, which generally apply to residential development, permit the building of houses on smaller lots, provided that the space thus saved is used for community purposes. For example, the zoning ordinance might specify a minimum lot size of one-half acre, but cluster provisions permit building houses on one-quarter-acre lots provided that the completed development shall have no more houses in it than it could contain if developed with one-half-acre lots. The space saved is to constitute an open area accessible to all residents of the clustered area, often maintained by a residents' association.

Cluster zoning is very popular with planners. It permits the preservation of open space and reduces development costs. Placing houses closer together reduces the amount of road surface and utility line required per house. Smaller lots also mean less money spent per house on grading and other site-preparation costs.

Although clusters have been built in many communities, the cluster plan is often greeted with some public suspicion. The community sees the combination of closely spaced houses and open-space blocks, and suspects that sooner or later the open blocks will fill in with housing. In point of fact, the permanency of the open blocks is easily protected with appropriate legal documents at the time the cluster development is approved by the community, but it can be difficult to convince a community that this is the case. With the passage of time and the accumulation of favorable experience, community resistance to clustering is diminishing.

Performance Zoning

Performance zoning is relatively new and not yet in widespread use, but its use is growing, and it holds much promise. Performance zoning codes stipulate what may or may not be done in terms of end results instead of giving detailed regulations on the exact form of development. It can be regarded as an attempt to achieve the same goals as conventional zoning but in a more flexible manner.

In Largo, Florida, a conventional, or Euclidean, system of 20 zoning districts has been replaced by a performance zoning system. Five residential categories differ only by the maximum density permitted. Intensity of use is controlled by limits on floor area ratio (FAR) and the percentage of the site that can be under impervious cover. There are no limitations on the type of housing, side-yard and rear-yard setback, and building height.

Four separate commercial zones have been created. The zones are distinguished by their FAR and impervious-cover requirements. For the downtown zone, a FAR of 0.90 and an impervious cover of 100 percent are permitted. On the other hand, for the flood-prone zone, the FAR is limited to 0.12 and impervious cover to 40 percent. There are no height limitations and no side- or rear-yard setback limitations. Gail Easley, the community's assistant director of planning, explained the decision to go to performance zoning in this way:

One particular problem [with conventional zoning] . . . is the proliferation of zoning districts. As the number of districts grows, it becomes harder to distinguish among them; as the distinctions become less clear, the purpose of any given district becomes blurred, and the formal distinctions become less defensible. An increase in the number of districts results in fewer uses being permitted in any single district. This decreases the likelihood that an available site will be properly zoned to meet a developer's needs. This, in turn, increases the probability that a zoning amendment will be sought.[22]

But not every municipality that has tried performance zoning has been equally pleased with it. Tallahassee, Florida, adopted performance zoning in 1992 but went back to a modified conventional system in 1997. In their view, performance zoning was too cumbersome compared with traditional zoning.[23]

Development Agreements

The state of California passed enabling legislation that permits municipal governments to enter into "development agreements." These essentially bypass the existing zoning, though they must be in conformity with the comprehensive plan. The contract between the developer and the municipality specifies what the developer may do and also what he or she is required to do within the project area. The developer benefits by being permitted to do things not permitted under the existing zoning. The developer of a multistage project also gets the security of knowing that zoning and other controls will not change during the development process or "build out" period, because the municipality is legally bound by the contract. The municipality benefits by being able to require things of the developer as a condition for signing the contract.

In the case of Colorado Place, an office development in Santa Monica, the developer benefited by being allowed to build above the 45-foot height limit specified in the zoning ordinance and also by being able to include in the project some uses not permitted under the existing zoning. The city benefited by requiring that the developer build some off-site low-income housing and provide and maintain a small on-site park and a child-care center.

Exactions

In recent years a variety of charges, often referred to as exactions, have become part of the land development scene. Numerous communities have resorted to exactions, sometimes quite substantial, before giving permission to develop. In some cases they are required only if there is to be a rezoning or zoning variance. In other cases the exactions are charged for development within the existing zoning law. In general, the exaction is charged to pay the costs that the development is presumed to impose on the community.

In some cases the exaction may be for a closely related cost, for example, nearby road construction needed to carry the additional traffic that new commercial development will generate, or school or park construction that the population of a new residential development will require. In other cases the connection may be more tenuous. For example, San Francisco decided that new office development increases the demand for housing in the city. Since 1981 builders of office structures of over 50,000 square feet of floor space must earn housing credits by either building new units themselves or contributing funds to housing rehabilitation or affordable housing projects. The number of credits is was based on estimates of how many square feet of office floor space are required per worker, what percentage of the San Francisco office workforce lives in the city, and how many workers live in the average housing unit.

FORM-BASED ZONING

The most recent major development in zoning has been the introduction of form-based zoning. The idea originated in the 1980s but has become widespread only in the last decade or so. As will be seen, form-based zoning codes are more flexible than traditional zoning in some ways but considerably less flexible in other ways.

Traditional zoning codes specify which uses are permitted and provide basic numbers for matters like floor area ratio (FAR), maximum building height, minimum parking space, and setbacks from property lines. For most places that use traditional zoning, the number of zones is quite large and there is a tendency for the number of zones to increase with the passage of time. Though traditional zoning imposes many requirements, it does not specify directly what the ensuing development will look like. Form-based zoning, by contrast, places the emphasis on the physical form of the development—on what the area in question will actually look like—and, as compared to conventional zoning, is much more flexible about permitted uses. It is consistent with neotraditional design, as discussed in Chapter 10, and, not surprisingly, many of its proponents are of the neotraditional school.[24]

One of its originators and most prominent proponents has been the neotraditional architect and urban designer Andres Duany (see Chapter 10). One way he has presented the form-based approach is through the idea of an urban *transect* (a term the dictionary defines as "to cut across" or to "dissect transversely").[25] Imagine a line drawn from the rural periphery to the center of a city or metropolitan area. The line will pass through a variety of types of development, each of which has a more or less characteristic form, as shown in the diagram on page 162. Along this transect, moving inward from the periphery, are defined six zones:

> Rural preserve
> Rural reserve

Suburban

General urban

Urban center

Urban core

The first two zones in the list make the transect complete, but it is the last four zones that are important for this discussion.

The proponents of the form-based approach take the view that for each of these zones, there is a desired form and that the goal of land-use controls is to move development toward that form. The form-based zoning code defines areas on the map and then specifies a number of design criteria that the developer must meet in each zone. It is intended to specify quite closely what the area will actually look like and be like to spend time in. So far as the aesthetics and the feel of an area, the use of a form-based zoning code shifts a considerable amount of the decision from the individual builder or developer to the planner or urban designer. To the extent that form-based codes often originate in a community "visioning" process, the public—or at least that part of the public that participates in the process—has a much greater say in the final product.

As a document, the form-based code looks very different from a traditional zoning code. The traditional code is predominantly words and numbers. It may contain an occasional diagram to help the reader understand the numbers or any calculations that must be made from them. The form-based code, on the other hand, is heavily pictorial, for its message to the developer is "this is what it should look like." Because there are only a few zones, rather than the multiplicity of zones in a traditional ordinance, it is likely to be a simpler and more readily comprehended document.

What are some of the items that are regulated? Like a traditional code a form-based code will specify maximum heights. Unlike a traditional code it will often specify minimum heights, for one of the goals of most form-based codes, in keeping with neotraditional design philosophy, is compact, walkable development. Like a traditional code, a form-based code will specify setbacks. But where the traditional code will simply specify a minimum setback, the form-based code may specify exactly what the setback must be, or in some zones it may specify that there be no setback—that the building come right up to the building line. Form-based codes will also specify items not found in traditional codes, such as placement of entrances and details about doors, windows, and courtyards. In some cases form-based codes may specify which materials are acceptable for the cladding of the walls of buildings or which materials are acceptable for roofs when roofs are visible from the street. The form-based code will include specifications about sidewalk width, radius of curbs, and the planting of trees, in some cases even down to acceptable species.

Transect Intensities: Elements that determine urbanism exist in a range that can correspond to the gradient of the Transect. Most of the elements listed here are addressed in the SmartCode prescriptions.

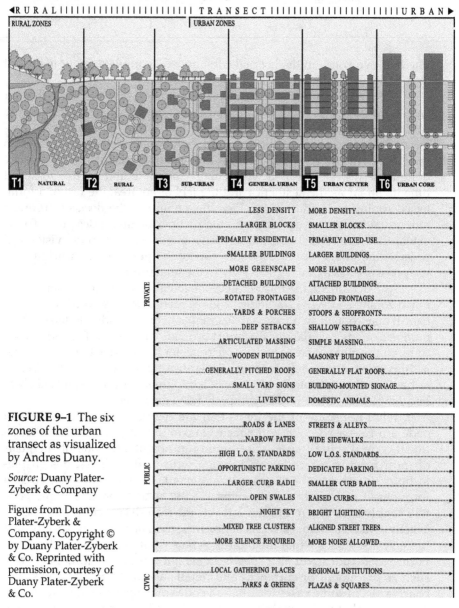

	LESS DENSITY	MORE DENSITY
	LARGER BLOCKS	SMALLER BLOCKS
	PRIMARILY RESIDENTIAL	PRIMARILY MIXED-USE
	SMALLER BUILDINGS	LARGER BUILDINGS
	MORE GREENSCAPE	MORE HARDSCAPE
PRIVATE	DETACHED BUILDINGS	ATTACHED BUILDINGS
	ROTATED FRONTAGES	ALIGNED FRONTAGES
	YARDS & PORCHES	STOOPS & SHOPFRONTS
	DEEP SETBACKS	SHALLOW SETBACKS
	ARTICULATED MASSING	SIMPLE MASSING
	WOODEN BUILDINGS	MASONRY BUILDINGS
	GENERALLY PITCHED ROOFS	GENERALLY FLAT ROOFS
	SMALL YARD SIGNS	BUILDING-MOUNTED SIGNAGE
	LIVESTOCK	DOMESTIC ANIMALS
	ROADS & LANES	STREETS & ALLEYS
	NARROW PATHS	WIDE SIDEWALKS
	HIGH L.O.S. STANDARDS	LOW L.O.S. STANDARDS
PUBLIC	OPPORTUNISTIC PARKING	DEDICATED PARKING
	LARGER CURB RADII	SMALLER CURB RADII
	OPEN SWALES	RAISED CURBS
	NIGHT SKY	BRIGHT LIGHTING
	MIXED TREE CLUSTERS	ALIGNED STREET TREES
	MORE SILENCE REQUIRED	MORE NOISE ALLOWED
CIVIC	LOCAL GATHERING PLACES	REGIONAL INSTITUTIONS
	PARKS & GREENS	PLAZAS & SQUARES

FIGURE 9–1 The six zones of the urban transect as visualized by Andres Duany.

Source: Duany Plater-Zyberk & Company

Figure from Duany Plater-Zyberk & Company. Copyright © by Duany Plater-Zyberk & Co. Reprinted with permission, courtesy of Duany Plater-Zyberk & Co.

In the ways just described, the form-based code is clearly much more restrictive and directive than the traditional code. On the other hand, it is much less restrictive with regard to permitted uses and will generally specify only very broad categories of use, such as residential. Unlike the traditional code there is not the multiplicity of zones, but just a few basic types. In that sense the form-based code is less complicated.

More often than not, form-based codes are applied to only a part or parts of the municipality. Form-based zoning is likely to work best where there is still a substantial amount of room for building. If an area is largely developed, the amount that can be achieved with a form-based zoning code will be limited. Perhaps the best environment for form-based zoning is a new community, where the planner or urban designer starts with a clean slate. Form-based zoning is relatively new, so at this point it is premature to pass judgment on it.

The writer has heard developers complain, perhaps justly at times, that if only zoning were more flexible, they could do better and more creative work. Will we someday hear them complaining in the same way about form-based zoning? Planner and land-use lawyer Donald L. Elliot suggests:

> As with most good ideas, the strengths of form-based zoning are also its weaknesses. Its advantages in communicating intended patterns of development also make form-based zoning a relatively static tool. Unlike PUDs, which can always be negotiated to reflect the latest trend in development and architecture, or performance zoning, which might be satisfied in different ways as new technologies emerge in the future, form-based zoning is more of a snapshot tied to the present. Although proponents make a fairly strong case that there is a semi-objective difference between "good" and "bad" design forms, only time will tell whether they are right. . . . If all the neighborhoods met the requirements . . . theoretically resulting in a residentially perfect city—would it become a cliché? Would we see buyers start to demand something else just to be different? . . . The jury is still out as to whether form-based zoning is more or less time bound than other forms of zoning.[26]

OTHER TYPES OF LOCAL LAND-USE CONTROLS

In addition to the subdivision and zoning regulations already described, there are a number of other controls that are not quite so widely used. Several are described here very briefly. In some cases these other types of controls are part of the zoning ordinance. In other cases they are separate.

Site-Plan Review

Typically, site-plan review applies to developments over a certain size. The community vests its planning or zoning agency with the responsibility of reviewing site plans for such considerations as internal circulation, adequacy of parking, and buffering from adjacent uses, and makes site-plan approval necessary before building permits may be granted. Site-plan review does not supersede zoning but rather is another layer of review. It is applied to commercial and multifamily development.

Architectural Review

In architectural review, building plans are reviewed for aesthetic considerations. A town with a predominantly colonial style of housing might perform a review to ensure that new development would be in keeping with
the established style. Architectural boards of review are often found in
older, upper-income residential areas where preservation of the past and
of property values weighs heavily. They are also frequently found in new
planned developments. Often they will become involved in what seem like
small issues, for example, whether or not a satellite dish antenna can be
placed in a yard or what colors are acceptable for the exterior of houses.
Feelings about review boards vary. Some applaud them for maintaining
the visual quality of the town or development. Others regard them as a
dead hand of conformity that makes the community a less interesting and
stodgier place. There is a trade-off. If you want variety and spontaneity,
you must risk some instances of bad taste.

Historic Preservation

Many communities designate historic districts and then exercise control
over development within them. Controls may dictate that new structures
be in a style and at a scale consistent with the past. They may dictate that
when repairs are done, historic appearance be maintained. For example, if
adjacent buildings have old-fashioned, leaded-glass windows with small
panes, a picture window would not be permitted. In some cases, community development funds may be used to help property owners maintain
the character of their buildings. Often, responsibility for historic preservation will be vested in the planning agency. In other cases, some responsibility will lie with a separate agency, such as New York City's Landmarks
Commission. Although there is historic preservation activity in all parts of
the United States, it is probably most prominent in New England, where a
great deal of colonial-era development remains to be preserved. Historic
preservation is unquestionably motivated by a love of the past, but where
tourism is important, there is an economic motivation too.

COMBINING CAPITAL INVESTMENT
AND LAND-USE CONTROLS

Since capital expenditures and land-use controls are the two principal
methods by which municipalities may affect land use, the enlightened community strives to coordinate them so that they reinforce each other. Capital
investment in transportation, public facilities, and infrastructure can shape
the land market. Land-use controls can permit what is desired and, within
the sorts of limitations described, can prohibit what is not desired.

For example, consider the case of Westchester County, New York's, so-called Platinum Mile. The name was chosen by local promoters with the usual lack of modesty that attends such christenings, but it is reasonably accurate. Along the border between two municipalities, the city of White Plains and the town of Harrison, is a massive collection of corporate headquarters and other office development. All told, these facilities provide many thousands of jobs and constitute hundreds of millions of dollars of tax base. It is the sort of complex that most communities would be delighted to have. How did it come into being?

First, the basic preconditions were there. One fact was a good location within the New York metropolitan area. This made it possible to capture firms that were moving out of New York City but wished to remain within the metropolitan area. It also made the area attractive to firms that were moving into the metropolitan area but did not need a Manhattan location, with its very high costs.

But given the existence of these preconditions, it was still necessary to turn them into reality. At the end of the 1950s, White Plains had been planning to build a bypass along its border with the town of Harrison. The road was to have been called the White Plains Arterial. At this time the Interstate Highway System was being laid out by the federal government in coordination with the states. City officials were quick to see the opportunity. They dropped the concept of the bypass and pushed to get the pathway of the arterial incorporated into the design for the Interstate Highway System.

The city was successful, and so interstate highway I–287 now runs between the two municipalities, increasing accessibility and greatly increasing land values and the potential for development. The crucial role of capital investment is clear. However, we note that 90 percent of the cost of building the interstate came from the federal government. Only the remaining 10 percent was paid by state and local governments. State and local funds were used to construct wide service roads on either side of the interstate and a series of overpasses across the interstate linking these roads. Thus a motorist leaving the interstate at one of several interchanges would have quick access to any point in the entire strip.

Having used capital investment—whether local funds or "foreign aid" from the federal government—to create demand on the site, it now remained to control land uses to produce a desirable result. The strategy used was to permit that which was desired and to prevent other land uses from blocking desirable development. Clearly, zoning to permit office development was one part of the strategy. Requiring large minimum sites for development prevented land from being chopped up by small, scattered development. Where there is good highway access in a relatively populous area, retailing is clearly a possibility. But strip commercial development would foreclose the possibility of office park development, both by eating up road frontage and also by creating an environment that would not be attractive to corporate headquarters and other "upscale" office development. That eventuality was blocked by simply prohibiting retail uses. Thus as a gardener favors the plants he or she wants by weeding out others, land-use controls were used to favor particular types of development by blocking other types.

FORCES BEYOND LOCAL CONTROL

The preceding parts of this chapter were written from a local perspective—what a municipality can do to shape its own pattern of development. But many land-use decisions are outside of municipal control.

For example, decisions made by state highway departments about highways are powerful shapers of the pattern of development. Not only do they involve many acres directly, but they also create powerful economic forces that, in turn, shape land uses. Municipal governments have some hand in these decisions, but they are often not the most powerful players. State highway departments, state legislators, and governors may all have more influence over decisions than do the municipality's officials and residents. In addition, major corporations and institutions may play very powerful roles in shaping state highway decisions. The major corporation that indicates that its decision whether to locate in an area or to close up its operations in an area depends on decisions made about highway construction may carry more weight with the state highway department and state government than the preferences of a town or county government. Institutions may also play a powerful role in highway decisions. In one case that the writer witnessed, a major university became a decisive force in a decision to construct a new highway. With a payroll of several thousand, a big enrollment, and tens of thousands of alumni scattered throughout the state, the university was the "five-hundred-pound gorilla" in the conflict over whether or not to build. The university's president was a much more powerful figure in the decision-making process than was any elected official in the region.

In many cases, the impetus for new road construction wells up largely from individuals and private organizations.

That was the case with the planning for Interstate 73 in Virginia, part of a larger plan for a route between Detroit and Charleston, South Carolina. Much of the impetus came from individuals, businesses, and property owners who saw the new route as an economic opportunity and beat the drum for it for many years. Of course, citizen activism cuts both ways. A citizens group, Virginians for Appropriate Roads, waged a long legal fight against the interstate until losing a final appeal in 2010.

In this age in which state and municipal governments actively pursue economic development and court firms with major financial incentives, decisions made in corporate boardrooms can have major effects on the pattern of development (see Chapter 13). Not only does the building of commercial facilities directly shape the pattern of land use, but state and municipal governments will make decisions about land use and public capital investment with an eye to their effects upon attracting industrial and commercial investment and, in many cases, in part on the basis of negotiations with those firms.

Other decisions by higher levels of government may have profound effects on the local land-use pattern. The building of state or federal facilities, an action generally not bound by local land-use controls, can have powerful effects on the municipal land-use pattern. So, too, can land acquisition by higher levels of government.

Higher Levels of Land-Use Control

In the last several decades, the state governments and the federal government have asserted some control over land-use decisions that were formerly left up to local governments. This assertion has been termed "the quiet revolution." The phrase comes from the title of a book by Bosselman and Callies. They state,

> The *ancien regime* being overthrown is the feudal system under which the entire pattern of land development has been controlled by thousands of individual local governments, each seeking to maximize its tax base and minimize its social problems, and caring less what happens to all others.
>
> The tools of the revolution are new laws taking a wide variety of forms but each sharing a common theme—the need to provide some degree of state or regional participation in the major decisions that affect the use of our increasingly limited supply of land.[27]

Much of the force for such laws comes from environmental concern, which as noted earlier increased greatly during the 1960s. In general, land-use controls emanating from higher than local levels of government do not supersede local controls. Rather, they add another layer of control. Thus the applicant must satisfy not only the local jurisdiction, but also the higher-level jurisdiction. Higher-level controls are found most often where there is a clear public interest beyond the borders of the single community. Very often, also, higher-level controls are found in environmentally fragile areas, for example, coastal zones.

Why Is Higher-Level Control Necessary?   One might ask why higher-level control of things like wetland development is necessary. After all, do not individuals as residents of a locality have the same degree of concern with environmental quality that they have as citizens of the state?

Part of the answer comes down to the issue of *externalities*.[28] If a community grants a rezoning that enables a shopping center development to obliterate a wetland, the fiscal gains of that development accrue to that community. So, too, may many of the employment gains. At least some of the increases in land values are also likely to be captured by community residents. On the other hand, the unfavorable effects may be felt outside the community. For example, increased storm-water runoff may have no significant effect on the community but may cause flooding downstream. Expanding the level of decision making to the state reduces the chance that gains for a few individuals will swing their decision and increases the chance that widespread effects will be given their due weight.

The other big reason for higher-level controls over environmental issues is technical complexity. Most local governments do not have the time and expertise to do the data gathering and analysis required for good decision making. A variety of state-level controls on development are mentioned in Chapters 14 and 15.

SUMMARY

Two major ways in which a municipality may shape its pattern of land use are through (1) public capital investment and (2) legal controls over the use of privately owned property.

Public capital investment creates specific public facilities, which make up part of the total land-use pattern. More importantly, public capital investment shapes how the development of privately owned land occurs.

Subdivision regulations essentially control the manner in which raw land is subdivided and placed on the market for development. Though subdivision regulations have been the object of less discussion than zoning, they represent a powerful means of control over the development process. The rigid "Euclidean" zoning, which came into being in the early twentieth century, has now been supplemented with a variety of techniques to make it more flexible, more subject to negotiation, and more adaptable to the planning of large developments as single entities. These devices include "bonus" or "incentive" zoning, transfer of development rights (TDR), planned unit development (PUD), cluster zoning, and a number of others. The newest major innovation is form-based zoning. This technique, very much favored by neotraditionalists, is much more flexible with regard to permitted uses, but much more prescriptive and restrictive with regard to the physical form of development.

Although the right to zone has been clearly established since the 1920s, the limits of the zoning power are still subject to some change as a result of the process of litigation and the establishment of legal precedent. In particular, since the 1960s the courts have redefined municipal obligations to nonresidents as a result of suits brought against suburban communities.

For the most effective shaping of the land-use pattern, public capital investment and land-use controls should be coordinated. Public capital investment affects the demand for land and structures, and land-use controls channel and shape the way that demand forces play themselves out.

NOTES

1. The market value of a bond moves inversely with interest rates. In general, the further away is the maturity date of the bond, the more its market price will vary with changes in interest rates.

2. Public finance texts sometimes use the term "user benefit equity," meaning that with bonds, the same population that receives the benefits from the project also pays the cost of the project through the debt service on the bonds.

3. State and local governments can borrow short term to smooth out the flow of funds and compensate for the fact that revenues tend to come in more irregularly than bills for expenses. These short-term borrowings include revenue anticipation notes (RANs), bond anticipation notes (BANs), and tax anticipation notes (TANs).

4. Charles J. Hoch, Linda C. Dalton, and Frank S. So, eds., *The Practice of Local Government Planning*, 3rd ed., International City/County Management Association, Washington, DC, 2000, p. 418.

5. Some municipal governments have gotten around debt limitations by the use of leasebacks. Here, the government wanting a facility encourages a firm to build and to own it but then signs a long-term lease on the facility. In effect, the municipality has taken on a long-term financial obligation just as if it had issued bonds, but the obligation does not count as part of its general obligation debt. Though this device seems like a transparent evasion of the debt limit, it has so far been sustained by the courts.

6. The term *district* basically refers to what we might term *quasi-governments*, that is, public bodies that have some but not all of the powers of government. For example, school districts have the ability to impose and collect property taxes, to issue tax-exempt bonds, and in some states to use the power of eminent domain. Other types of districts include water and sewer districts, transportation districts, and the like.

7. There is an extensive literature on intergovernmental grants. For an overview, see Ronald C. Fisher, *State and Local Public Finance*, Thomson South-Western, 2007.

8. For an account of the subdivision process, see Charles J. Hoch, Linda C. Dalton, and Frank S. So, eds., *The Practice of Local Government Planning*, International City/County Management Association, Washington, DC, 2000, chap. 14.

9. For a general account of the zoning process, see ibid., chap. 14.

10. Fishel, William A., *The Economics of Zoning Laws: A Property Rights Approach to American Land Use Controls*, Johns Hopkins University Press, Baltimore, 1985.

11. To pursue the matter of profit and loss from changes in zoning, see Donald G. Hagman, Den J. Misczynski, Madelyn Glickfield, et al., eds., *Windfalls for Wipeouts: Land Value Capture and Taxation*, American Society of Planning Officials, Chicago, 1978.

12. "Operation Rezone Brings Prison Terms, More Trials," *Planning*, October 1996, pp. 20–21.

13. Other criteria may sometimes be used, particularly for commercial property. For example, assessors may use estimated cost of replacement or income-generating potential.

14. When fractional assessment is used, an "equalization rate" is generally computed so that the assessed value can be converted into "full value." This is particularly important when funding such as state aid for public education is conditioned by the property tax base of the receiving community. In recent years there has been a general trend toward full value assessment to avoid such complications.

15. Typically, properties owned by nonprofit institutions, as well as properties owned by government itself, are exempt from property taxation.

16. Jane Jacobs, *The Death and Life of Great American Cities*, Vintage Books, Random House, New York, 1961. See, in particular, the section titled "The Conditions for City Diversity."

17. Kirk Johnson, "Where a Zoning Law Failed, Seeds of a New York Revival," *New York Times*, April 21, 1996, p. 1.

18. For an example of the use of transfer of development rights in regard to historic preservation, see "Large Tower Would Use Depot's Rights," *New York Times*, September 17, 1986, sec. B, p. 1. See also George M. Raymond, "Structuring the Implementation of Transferable Development Rights," *Urban Land*, July–August 1981, pp. 19–25. For recent uses in a number of jurisdictions, see Rick Pruetz, AICP, *Saved by Development: Preserving Environmental Areas, Farmland, and Historic Landmarks with Transfer of Development Rights*, Planners Press, American Planning Association, Chicago, 1997.

19. Rick Pruetz and Noah Standridge, "What Makes Transfer of Development Rights Work? Success Factors from Research and Practice," *Journal of the American Planning Association,* vol. 75, no. 1, Winter 2009, pp. 78–88.
20. Lisa Chamberlin, "Open Space Overhead," *Planning,* March 2006, pp. 10–11.
21. See Seymour I. Schwartz and Robert A. Johnston, "Inclusionary Housing Programs," *Journal of the American Planning Association,* vol. 49, no. 1, Winter 1983, pp. 3–21. See also Barbara Taylor, "Inclusionary Zoning: A Workable Option for Affordable Housing," *Urban Land,* March 1981, pp. 6–12; and Gus Bauman, Anna Reines Kahn, and Serena Williams, "Inclusionary Housing Programs in Practice," *Urban Land,* November 1983, pp. 14–19.
22. Gail Easley, "Performance Controls in an Urban Setting," *Urban Land,* October 1984, pp. 24–27. See also Tam Phalen, "How Has Performance Zoning Performed?," *Urban Land,* October 1983, pp. 16–21.
23. "Tallahassee's Performance Zoning Gives Way to Euclid," *Planning,* December 1997, p. 26.
24. For a relatively early presentation on the subject, see Peter Katz, "Form First: The New Urbanist Alternative to Conventional Zoning," *Planning,* November 2004. Current material on the subject can be found on the website of the Congress for the New Urbanism.
25. Andres Duany and Emily Talen, "Transect Planning," *Journal of the American Planning Association,* vol. 68, no. 3, Summer 2002, pp. 245–266.
26. Donald L. Elliot, *A Better Way to Zone: Ten Principles to Create More Livable Cities,* Island Press Washington, DC, 2008, p. 33.
27. Fred Bosselman and David Callies, *The Quiet Revolution in Land Use Controls,* Council for Environmental Quality, Superintendent of Documents, U.S. Government Printing Office, Washington, DC, 1973, p. 1.
28. An economist's term that refers to effects that are visited on "third parties," that is, parties who are not participants in the transactions and whose interest, therefore, may not be taken into account by the participants in the transaction.

SELECTED BIBLIOGRAPHY

CULLINGWORTH, J. BARRY, *The Political Culture of Planning,* Routledge, Inc., New York, 1993.

ELLIOT, DONALD L., *A Better Way to Zone: Ten Principles to Create More Livable Cities,* Island Press, Washington, DC; 2008.

HAAR, CHARLES, *Land Use Planning: A Casebook on the Use, Mis-Use and Re-Use of Urban Land,* 3rd ed., Little, Brown & Co., Boston, 1980.

HOCH, CHARLES J., DALTON, LINDA C., and So, FRANK S. EDS., *The Practice of Local Government Planning,* International City/County Management Association, Washington, DC, 2000.

KAISER, EDWARD J., GODSCHALK, DAVID R., and CHAPIN, F. STUART JR., *Urban Land Use Planning,* 4th ed., University of Illinois Press, Urbana, 1995.

TALIN, EMILY, *City Rules: How Codes Create Places,* Island Press, Washington, DC, 2011.

NOTE: For the reader interested in keeping up with trends in land development and land-use control techniques, the magazines *Urban Land, Planning,* and *Real Estate Review* are good and highly readable sources. For a more technical and formal current source on land-use regulation, see the journal *Zoning Digest.*

CHAPTER 10

Urban Design*

> Mind *takes form* in the city; and in turn, urban forms condition mind. For space, no less than time, is artfully reorganized in cities: in boundary lines and silhouettes, in the fixing of horizontal planes and vertical peaks, in utilizing or denying the natural site, the city records the attitude of a culture and an epoch to the fundamental facts of its existence. The dome and the spire, the open avenue and the closed court, tell the story, not merely of different physical accommodations, but of essentially different conceptions of man's destiny. . . . With language itself, it remains man's greatest work of art.[1]

The design of cities has been the conscious task of many throughout history. However, only in the 1950s, with the advent of university degree programs, did the term *urban designer* and the profession of urban design emerge with a distinct label.

Cities develop over time because of the conscious and unconscious acts of people. Urban designers assume that in spite of their vast scale and complexity, cities can be designed and their growth shaped and directed. A major example of human ability to shape the urban environment is the work of Baron Haussmann from 1855 to 1868 in Paris during the time of Napoleon III.

During this period, Haussmann was responsible for creating a new pattern of boulevards that reshaped the character of Paris. The facades of buildings along the grand boulevards were required to be uniform, giving a sense of rhythm and order to the streets. The grand tree-lined boulevards

---

*Parts of this chapter were written by Charles W. Steger. He was formerly Dean of the College of Architecture and Urban Studies at Virginia Polytechnic Institute and State University and is now president of the university.

he created became and remain some of the major public spaces of Paris. He addressed the problem of the flow of traffic and the appropriate uses of land. He shaped the skyline and the proportion of space by limits on height and rules governing the space between buildings. The vistas shaped by the boulevards focused on major public buildings and on gardens, giving new character to the nineteenth-century city. This plan for Paris, using grand boulevards as a major orienting force, was copied throughout the world.

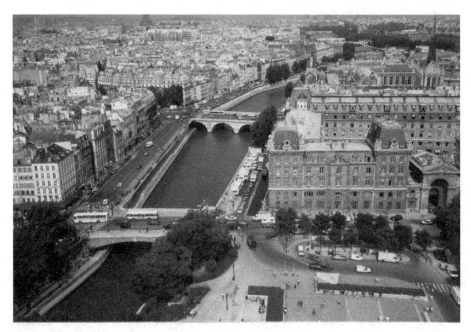

Haussman's design a century later. A view down the Seine from Notre Dame cathedral.

WHAT IS URBAN DESIGN?

Urban design falls between the professions of planning and architecture. It deals with the large-scale organization and design of the city, with the massing and organization of buildings and the space between them, but not with the design of the individual buildings.

Several factors distinguish urban design from architectural design. Urban design deals with a large scale, such as entire neighborhoods or cities, and with long time frames, frequently 15 to 20 years. For example, Haussmann's work in Paris required 17 years. This is a sharp contrast to the 1, 2, or 3 years usually required for the construction of a single building. Urban design also deals with a large number of variables, such as transportation, neighborhood identity, pedestrian orientation, and climate.

This complexity, combined with the long periods of time involved, results in an environment characterized by high uncertainty. The control over specific development is less direct than with a single building. As a result, many of the techniques employed by urban designers differ from those of the architect.

Although the urban designer and planner have complementary roles, they do have separate and distinct functions. Most commonly, the modern urban designer deals with a part of the city. Very often, the site on which the urban designer works has been allocated as part of a larger planning process. It is after that allocation is made that the urban designer examines the site in terms of massing and spatial organization. The planner, by contrast, must typically consider the entire city. In fact, very often he or she must look beyond the bounds of the city and understand how the city functions as part of a larger region, for example, how the transportation system of the city relates to surrounding suburbs and communities. Thus the planner plays a central role in allocating the uses of land among the competing functions. Planners are more likely than urban designers to be involved in the political process whereby public policy is formulated. Planners and urban designers are each involved with a spectrum of social, cultural, and physical design issues. The difference is a matter of degree.

Numerous urban designers are employed by developers on a variety of residential, commercial, and mixed-use projects. But many urban designers are also employed by public bodies. For example, during the period of Urban Renewal (see Chapter 11), sites were acquired, cleared, and planned by Urban Renewal agencies. Parcels were then sold or leased to developers, who put up buildings or groups of buildings in accordance with the agency's overall plan. In this case the urban design was done by designers on the public payroll, and the architectural design was done by individuals or firms on the developer's payroll.

The Battery Park City development illustrated in this chapter represents a large and highly successful urban design effort done under public auspices. The development organization, Battery Park City Authority (BPCA), was set up as a public benefit corporation by the New York State legislature in 1968. Its purpose was to develop 92 acres to be created by landfill on the Hudson shore of Manhattan adjacent to the World Trade Center and the city's financial district.

Streets, blocks, open spaces, utilities, a 1.2-mile-long esplanade along the Hudson River, and the allocation of land uses were all laid out by the project's designers.

The buildings, designed by independent architectural firms, conformed to height, bulk, and other guidelines provided by BPCA.

One characteristic of major urban design efforts is the long time horizon. BPCA came into being in 1968. Funds were obtained through a bond issue in 1972, and the landfill was completed in 1976. Work was suspended for several years because of New York City's financial difficulties, and BPCA

Commercial development at Battery Park City (top) and residential section and river-front promenade (bottom).

BATTERY PARK CITY

The ground plan of Battery Park City, built on 80 acres of land fill on Manhattan's west shore. The large open area to the right of the mid-section of Battery Park City is the site of the World Trade Center.

was reorganized in 1979. In 1980, construction of the first building began. By 1990, the development contained about 4,000 apartments and roughly 10 million square feet of commercial floor space. Another 8,000 apartments and several million square feet of commercial space still remained to be built. From concept to completion, the project took a quarter of a century.

In years to come, the role of the urban designer is likely to grow because of an important trend in land development in the United States: A growing percentage of all development is taking place within PUDs or other large-scale, unified developments, rather than as lot-by-lot filling-in under traditional Euclidean zoning. One reason for this shift is that better results are often obtained with a unified design approach. Another reason is the emergence of large development organizations that can put together the huge blocks of capital that such projects require.

But even more important have been changes in the market for residences and commercial space. The emergence of a large and prosperous older population created a market for retirement communities that contain not only houses and apartments but community and outdoor recreation facilities as well—all to be put together in an attractive and a unified design. Comparable comments can be made for the residential demand of affluent "yuppies," who want their squash courts and jogging paths close at hand. (See Chapter 7 for further discussion of planned communities.) Many businesses prefer a business park location because it permits the sharing of common facilities like parking and telecommunications and because a well-designed development gives an "upscale" image that impresses clients and customers. It must also be admitted that a large-scale project may sell partly because its size and physical separation provide a degree of social isolation. Personal safety, security for personal or business property, and even protection from urban unpleasantness like panhandling can be powerful selling points.

THE URBAN DESIGN PROCESS

Although each city and its problems are unique, there are some general sets of activities in most urban design studies. Following are four basic phases and some subphases.

1. Analysis
   a. Gathering of basic information
   b. Visual survey
   c. Identification of hard and soft areas
   d. Functional analysis
2. Synthesis
3. Evaluation
4. Implementation

REBUILDING THE WORLD TRADE CENTER SITE

In the diagram on page 175 the main north–south route, West Street, divides Battery Park City from the rest of Manhattan. Battery Park City is to the west of the street. Just to the east of West Street, about midlevel in the diagram, you can see the World Trade Center Site.

At this writing, 10 years after 9/11, much progress has been made on rebuilding the site. The mass transit infrastructure, including the Port Authority Trans Hudson (PATH) and the New York City subway station, has been restored and the memorial park for the 9/11 victims has been completed. The Freedom Tower, to be called 1 World Trade Center and standing a symbolic 1,776 feet tall, was topped out at the end of 2011 and is expected to be ready for occupancy in 2014. A smaller tower at the opposite end of the site, 4 World Trade Center, was partially constructed. Present plans call for two more office towers not yet begun.

The tower will be a massive structure. The thick-walled concrete, two-hundred-foot-high base will be windowless but will be sheathed with glass to give a reflective effect. The base itself has been the object of some argument, appearing sensible and prudent to some and bespeaking fear and timidity to others.[2] Above the base will rise a chamfered tower, meaning that the corners are cut at 45-degree angles producing an eight-sided shape, containing approximately 2.6 million square feet of floor space. Above the occupied floors in the chamfered section will rise an unoccupied communications tower about 400 feet in height. It will be the tallest building in North America.

From the beginning to the present, the redevelopment of the site has been bedeviled not only by disagreement about issues of architecture and symbolism, but also by serious issues of law, financial feasibility, and questions about what path the overall development of lower Manhattan should take. One major legal issue was a question of liability. About two months before 9/11, New York real estate developer Larry Silverstein had leased the site, including the World Trade Center Towers, from the Port Authority of New York and New Jersey for a period of 99 years. He insured the towers for $3.5 billion per event. The legal question after 9/11 turned on the meaning of the word *event*. Was the attack on the Towers one event or two events? Silverstein, of course, argued that it was two events. Equally predictably, the insurance companies argued that it was one event. Ultimately, the courts found for the insurance companies. That decision left Silverstein with $3.5 billion less to invest in the site than he would otherwise have had.

The decision to build so much commercial floor space in lower Manhattan has occasioned considerable argument. In the last several decades the rate of office construction in Manhattan has slowed. In the 1960s and 1970s Manhattan added roughly 60 million square feet of office space per decade. In the decade 2000 to 2010 somewhat under 20 million square feet of office space was added. In the first part of this decade office construction, with the exception of the World Trade Center site, has been slow. The apparent weakness in demand makes investors wary.

In fact, just to make the Freedom Tower commercially feasible, the Port Authority, after prolonged negotiations with Silverstein, agreed to lease 600,000 square feet in the tower at $59 per square foot per year. New York City agreed to lease another 600,000 square feet, lower down in the building, at $56.50 per square foot. Without the political decision to relocate thousands of public sector workers into the new tower, it is doubtful that the tower would have been built.

For several decades the market for commercial space in lower Manhattan has been weaker than in midtown Manhattan. It is generally believed that the major reason for this is the narrower streets, the more irregular street pattern, and the smaller blocks. It is the oldest part of the city, and some of its street pattern goes back to the time when New York was New Amsterdam. This softness in the lower-Manhattan market for commercial floor space is readily apparent on a visit to the area if you simply observe the number of older office buildings that have been converted to rental or condominium apartments. Therefore many believe that more office space is simply the wrong way to go in lower Manhattan. Rather, they argue, the main thrust of new delopment should be residential because its access to Manhattan's numerous cultural attractions, its good public transportation, and its great views of the Hudson River, the East River, and New York harbor make lower Manhattan an outstanding residential location, particularly for smaller households.

Proponents of a residential strategy might argue that building thousands of apartments, many of which will be occupied by young, well-educated people whom the urban geographer Richard Florida characterizes as members of the "creative class," in the long run would do more for the economic growth of the city than would more office space. This view may be right or wrong, but it does indicate that there is still room for basic policy choices. It is also true that there is much uncertainty about which way the market will play out. As with Battery Park City, full development of the project will be a multidecade process.

Analysis

① *Gathering of Basic Information.*   Basic information is gathered on such items as land use, population, transportation, natural systems, and topography. In addition, the designers make a careful examination of the varied character of the site and the structure of neighborhoods and business areas. Problems and design goals are identified. For a residential development the designer might consider

1. Suitability of the topography, that is, slope or flood plains
2. Land area required for the new units
3. Amount of traffic generated and necessary roadways to accommodate it
4. Adequacy of public utilities
5. Parking space requirements
6. Additional requirements for schools, parks, and playgrounds
7. Relevant zoning and subdivision ordinances

For a commercial development, the designer might also consider the buying income of surrounding residential areas, likely "absorption rates" for commercial space, and the competitive strength of nearby commercial areas.

② *Visual Survey.*   In *The Image of the City*, Kevin Lynch describes the concept and key elements of the visual survey.[3] The idea is that as each of us walks around the city, we create a mental map of it. This mental map makes us feel less anxious about finding our way about. Lynch developed a vocabulary of symbols that enables the urban designer to characterize in graphic form the key elements of the urban fabric. The visual survey is now considered a standard part of any urban design study and is used as a tool by designers to communicate their perceptions of the structure and organization of a city or neighborhood to one another. The visual survey examines and identifies components of the city such as the location and views of landmarks and activity nodes. It reveals where the boundaries between neighborhoods are and whether they are clear and distinct or amorphous. The survey also explores the sequence of spaces a pedestrian might encounter in walking from one part of the city to another.

③ *Identification of Hard and Soft Areas.*   Cities, and the neighborhoods and districts that comprise them, are in a constant state of change. Although this dynamic condition may not be seen easily from one day to the next, over the time span of 5, 10, or 15 years it becomes quite apparent.

The delineation of hard and soft areas helps the designer to know what parts of the city can accommodate growth and change and what parts are essentially fixed because they may be occupied, for example, by a historic landmark or cemetery. A good example of a hard area is a public park near the central business district of a large city. It is extremely unlikely that any development will be allowed to take place in that area. A soft area may be a neighborhood or business district with an increasing number of vacancies. Such information is of considerable value in the later stages of the urban design process when plans must be evaluated for feasibility.

Functional Analysis. The functional analysis examines the relationship of activities among the various land uses and the way that they relate to circulation systems. This study builds very heavily on the work of the land-use planners. However, the urban designer carries the study into three dimensions.

For example, in virtually every major downtown there is a problem of excessive congestion and traffic on the streets. It is therefore important to consider the real consequences of plans in three dimensions and the way that they might change over time.

Synthesis

From the synthesis phase emerge design concepts that reflect an understanding of the constraints of the problem and that propose optimum solutions, given the many trade-offs that must be made. The designer is confronted with the resolution of many conflicting demands. For housing units there is an inherent conflict between pedestrian and vehicular traffic. If traffic flow is too fast or too heavy, it will hamper pedestrian crossing unless either traffic lights or pedestrian bridges are installed. Each of these solutions takes additional resources.

It is in the synthesis phase that the data gathered and the analysis of the problem must be translated into proposals for action. Prior to the complete development of the urban design plan, there are several preceding activities. The first component of the synthesis phase is the evolution of concepts that address the problem. In the initial phases, there may be a number of concepts proposed. There is usually more than one way to solve a particular set of problems. Concepts are followed by the development of schematic design proposals. These proposals are more specific in nature. Schematics are followed by preliminary plans.

Evaluation

Evaluation occurs at many levels, ranging from meeting technical demands to the ability to gain public acceptance. It is the time at which the preliminary plans generated in the synthesis phase are compared with the original goals and problem definitions.

After the design proposals are complete, it is essential that they be evaluated in light of the original problem or issue they were intended to address. One of the more complicated tasks associated with evaluation is determining what criteria should be employed. There are two basic questions: (1) how well the solutions fit the problem and (2) how readily the proposals can be implemented.

The task is further complicated by the fact that cities are dynamic and that their problems are constantly changing. Developing solutions for problems that are in a state of flux is like shooting at a moving target.

Implementation

During implementation, the strategy for actual financing and construction is devised. Detailed phasing studies and tools such as zoning ordinances are called into play to realize the project.

Once an urban design plan is developed, the principal tools through which it is implemented are land-use controls and capital expenditures. The land-use controls available to the urban designer include not only the traditional, or Euclidean, zoning ordinance, but also a variety of modern techniques described in Chapter 9.

Capital expenditures shape the pattern of land development, as noted earlier, by altering land values through the provision of access and utilities. When there is public participation in a project, capital expenditures combined with the power of eminent domain may be used to assemble the land for the project.

WHAT IS GOOD URBAN DESIGN? _____

In its most general sense, urban designers intend to improve the quality of people's lives through design. They accomplish this through the elimination of barriers as well as the creation of opportunities for people to move about the city in a free, safe, and pleasant way. For example, one should be able to walk through a reasonable portion of an urban area in inclement weather without major difficulty.

Minneapolis, with its long, cold, snowy winters, has accomplished this goal with a system that links the second stories of downtown buildings with climate-controlled skyways. The skyways plus the connecting corridors in commercial and public buildings form a five-mile system. People may travel several blocks from parking structures or apartments to offices or stores without having to go down to street level. Some residents "skywalk" for exercise and recreation.

Clearly, the Minneapolis skyway system has helped the downtown remain competitive with outlying developments, such as the Mall of

America located to the south of the city. But skyway systems do have a downside. According to urban designer Wendy Jacobson,

> Both skyways and underground pedestrian systems can drain city streets of the activity that makes them lively, interesting, and safe. With few exceptions, North American cities lack the density of pedestrian activity to fuel both an active street frontage and a competing above- or below-grade system. Something has to suffer and in most cases it is the street.
>
> Privatization is also an important issue. Although they may appear to be public spaces, most skyways and underground walkways link privately owned development. Unlike public streets, access to these systems is normally restricted to certain times and may even be restricted to certain people—those appropriately dressed, for example.[4]

Note that the privatization issue raises questions similar to some of those raised in connection with private communities discussed in Chapter 7. When this writer raised the vitality-of-the-street question with a planner in Minneapolis, he was told that the department believed that the pros of the system substantially outweighed the cons. Thus the city continues to accept applications for new skyways.

Another cold-weather city with an extensive skyway system is Calgary in Alberta, Canada. Its system is named Plus 15 for the required clearance of the skyway over the street. Calgary officials are also aware of the problem of competition between the street and the skyway level. In fact, they note that comparable retail floor space at the skyway level rents for more than it does at the street level. But on balance they are sufficiently pleased with Plus 15 that for every square foot of skyway that a developer builds, the city allows the developer to build 20 more square feet of building floor space than the zoning would normally permit.

People like to see other people and to be seen. Many cities provide incentives for developers who will create public plazas in conjunction with new developments. Such spaces provide an opportunity for people to sit in the sun at lunch and observe the general activity of the street. William Whyte, in *The Social Life of Small Urban Spaces*, reports a systematic study of the factors contributing to successful urban spaces.[5] He concludes that some form of movable seating and the opportunity to purchase food and drink are key elements.

Another way to evaluate the success of urban space is the way in which it assists in orienting the user. For example, can users find their way from one place to the other without confusion or fear? Are the signs easily understood? Are major pedestrian areas well lighted in the evening so that users can make their way easily and safely? Jane Jacobs made this point forcefully in the early 1960s in *The Death and Life of Great American Cities*.[6]

Other functional criteria such as safety are also important. For example, separation of pedestrian and vehicular traffic reduces accidents.

Above, skyways on Minneapolis's Nicollet Mall. The narrowed street is open to buses, taxis, police, and emergency vehicles but closed to passenger cars. Below, the view from Marquette Avenue. The skyways are planned, built, and maintained privately (current cost is about $1 million each), subject to the granting of an encroachment permit. Because they are designed by different architects for different builders, there is considerable variation in their appearance.

Yet the spaces and circulation areas must be organized so that they can be readily accessible to emergency vehicles and delivery vehicles.

Good design achieves its intentions and often more. For example, the developer's intention in constructing a mixed-use project may simply be to achieve a profitable combination of commercial and residential structures. Yet if the project is well situated and aesthetically attractive, its benefits will spill over onto adjacent areas. The project might increase pedestrian traffic and hence enhance property values in adjacent retailing areas. Its presence might also enhance the value of adjacent neighborhoods by making the area more interesting and varied.

A myriad of factors can affect the success of an urban design project. A list of a number of the more important criteria for judging urban design follows:

1. Unity and coherence
2. Minimum conflict between pedestrians and vehicles
3. Protection from rain, noise, wind, and so on
4. Easy orientation for users
5. Compatibility of land uses
6. Availability of places to rest, observe, and meet
7. Creation of a sense of security and pleasantness

But it must be admitted that urban design is not an exact science, for there is always the element of personal taste. One person's peace and tranquillity will be another person's boredom and sterility. One person's excitement will be another person's soul-destroying cacophony. The area that suits a single person in his or her twenties may seem quite unsuitable 10 years later when the same person has a spouse and two children.

The Neighborhood Concept

A very central concept in urban design, and a place where one can see many of the previously noted criteria applied, is the "neighborhood." Though we now take the idea of neighborhoods and of planning for neighborhoods for granted, it is actually not an old idea. One of the first clear articulations of the neighborhood concept in the United States was that by Clarence Perry done in the 1920s for RPA (see Chapter 3).[7] A neighborhood is a unit that matches the daily scale of most people's lives. Traditionally, the neighborhood planning unit is the area that would contain a population sufficient to supply the pupils for one elementary school. Perry wrote in terms of 1,000 or 1,200 pupils, which in the 1920s implied a total neighborhood population of 5,000 or 6,000.

Typically, the neighborhood plan will provide for residences, a school, shopping facilities for goods that one buys frequently (grocery,

drug, and stationery stores but not department stores or automobile dealers), playgrounds, and perhaps small parks. The street pattern will serve
the resident population but discourage through traffic. Major thoroughfares will often serve as neighborhood boundaries. In some communities,
for example, Reston, Virginia, the residents are further isolated from traffic
by separate paths for pedestrians and cyclists. The well-designed neighborhood is likely to be laid out with common areas so that residents encounter
each other in ways that promote social relationships. The neighborhood
is thus structured to provide conveniently and safely much of what most
people need and use in their daily lives.

One complaint about the planning of many suburban areas is that the
separation of land uses and, particularly, the large expanses of tract housing eliminate much of what we associate with neighborhoods. One does
not meet one's neighbor walking to the corner store because there is no
corner store and, given the spread-out nature of many suburbs, one is not

The neighborhood concept circa the 1920s. The separate boys' and girls' playgrounds
seem archaic today, but the plan otherwise has many modern features—separation of
commercial and residential areas, a curvilinear street pattern to discourage through
traffic, the preservation of community open space, concentration of high-density
housing near public transportation. Note that the neighborhood is built around a
public school.

Right, a pedestrian bridge connecting the town center with an adjacent residential area in the planned community of Reston, Virginia. Below, a view of the town center across Lake Ann (an artificial lake). Much of the town is designed to facilitate transportation by foot and bicycle.

likely to walk to many destinations. Similarly, children do not casually encounter each other walking home from the neighborhood school because
there is no neighborhood school. Rather, they are bused to and from a con-
solidated school several miles away.

REPLANNING SUBURBIA: THE NEOTRADITIONALISTS _____

Ask a group of planners to name one urban designer, and the chances are
that a considerable number of them will name Andres Duany. The Cuban-
born Duany is the most prominent exponent of *neotraditional design,* also
sometimes referred to as the *new urbanism.*

Most of U.S. population growth is going into the suburbs, and Duany
and other neotraditionalists insist that, by and large, the suburbs have been
planned wrong.[8] They tend to lay the biggest share of the blame on the traffic engineers but still reserve a good deal of blame for the planners. Using
Duany's phrase, highway engineers "want cars to be happy," with the result that there has been an overemphasis on planning for the automobile.
Meeting traffic flow and parking goals took precedence over designing for
people and for walkable environments. New urbanists fault suburban planning for an excessive separation of land uses, particularly residential use
from other uses, and for laying out land uses at too coarse a grain. The result
is that distances between uses become too great for convenient walking and
therefore people are forced into excessive dependence on the automobile.

Neotraditionalists argue that excessive dependence on the automobile degrades the quality of life in many ways. Older people lose their independence in the suburbs, not when they are too infirm to walk but when
their eyesight no longer permits them to drive. At that point, people who
are otherwise able to live independently become dependent. At the other
end of the age spectrum, suburban children have much less autonomy
than city children have because they have to be driven everywhere.

Neotraditionalists argue that designing for the automobile produces pedestrian-unfriendly patterns that inhibit walking even when
the straight-line distances are not great. For example, even if the main
road has only two lanes, turning lanes may double the road's width near
intersections. The combination of wide streets and absence of sidewalks
makes walking unpleasant and sometimes a bit threatening. In traditional
urban areas, streets meet at right angles, thereby forcing cars to slow down
considerably to turn. By contrast, a rounded corner with a wide radius
that permits cars to negotiate the turn without much slowing can make
crossing intimidating, particularly for someone who, for reason of age or
disability, cannot move very fast. Yet highway engineers often favor this
type of intersection because it speeds the traffic flow.

Neotraditional planning is so named because much of what the
neotraditionalists advocate harks back to traditional city and town

planning practices, which were rejected in modern suburban planning. Neotraditionalists advocate the mixing of uses at a fine grain. They note that zoning originated to separate incompatible uses but that there is much less need for this technique today than at the turn of the twentieth century. For example, much manufacturing today is quiet and clean, and there is no reason why it cannot be located relatively close to housing. It is important that buildings in an area be in scale with each other, but not that they all be for the same type of use or for the same type of inhabitant. Like Jane Jacobs (see Chapter 9), they argue that excessive homogeneity of use and building type leads to sterility and inconvenience. They suggest that apartments over stores and accessory apartments on single-family lots (for example, the garage that has been converted to a one-bedroom apartment) would go a long way to solving the problem of the shortage of low and moderate-income housing. And they note that, regrettably, most suburban zoning codes prevent construction of these types of units.

Neotraditionalists place great importance on pedestrian-friendly streets. The traditional city street with, say, two lanes for traffic, one lane on each side for parked cars, and sidewalks is pedestrian friendly. Because it has only two lanes of traffic that move at a moderate speed, it is easy to cross. The lines of parked cars offer the pedestrian on the sidewalk a sense of security because there is a barrier between him or her and the moving vehicles in the street. Buildings should be brought up close to the street, and parking beyond what can be accommodated on the street should be located behind the building. Neotraditionalists see the typical shopping center or office park design in which the building is set back and isolated from the street by a large parking lot as a design disaster. Even the most unattractive building "gives more to the street," according to Duany, than does a sea of parked cars or, when the cars are not there, a sea of asphalt. Neotraditionalists like alleys, for these permit parking to be placed behind buildings. The alley avoids the need for the typical suburban residential design in which half of the frontage of a house consists of a garage door. The neotraditionalist vision of good design necessarily implies fairly small lots, for widely spaced houses discourage walking.

WHAT IS WRONG WITH THE POD AND COLLECTOR PLAN

The pod and collector system, with each pod connecting separately to the collector as in the top half of the figure, is a common suburban design approach. It looks good on paper, but, Andres Duany argues, it works badly. First, every trip from a point in one pod to a point in another pod becomes an automobile trip on the collector. This is a pre-scription for traffic congestion. The problem is not that there is a short-age of total road surface, but that this design forces a large part of the traffic onto a small fraction of the total road surface.

Walking for purposes like shopping is discouraged because there is no direct path from the houses in the pod at the upper right to the mall or the stores fronting on the collector. Walking for purposes of visiting, say, between the single-family houses and the apartments, is also dis-couraged for the same reasons. Even walking from one store to another is discouraged, for the customer at the mall cannot easily walk to the strip shopping because the only link between them is the collector. Thus in addition to concentrating automobile trips as just noted, the pod and collector system also increases the total number of automobile trips.

The half of the drawing below the collector shows the traditional pattern that Duany regards as far superior. The same elements—single-family houses, apartments, stores, and a public school—are contained in each half of the drawing. But circulation is very different. In the bottom half, most trips for shopping and social purposes can be made through secondary streets without having to go out onto the collector. In addition, many trips are easily made on foot. Residents of the single-family houses and apartments can walk to the mall by a reasonably direct path along secondary streets with sidewalks. Similarly, schoolchildren can walk to and from school on secondary streets. The student who stays after school for an activity and misses the school bus can walk home rather than have to wait to be picked up by a parent. The design promotes a greater degree of social integration because the two different types of housing, apartments and single-family houses, are not isolated from each other in separate pods.

In Virginia neotraditional thinking has made some headway with the state's legislature. Street Acceptance Requirements enacted in 2007 will not permit the state's Department of Transportation (VDOT) to accept roads for servicing and maintenance if they do not link to the roads in adjacent subdivisions or commercial development. In short, they will not accept cul de sac roads. Thus the sort of geometry in the top half of the figure on page 189 would not be permitted. The regulation also requires that roads be able to accommodate pedestrians, meaning sidewalks on one or both sides, depending upon the density of the development, and minimize environmental impact. That latter provision will mandate narrower streets than are generally found in recent subdivisions. That, in turn, should mean lower average vehicle speeds. The requirements are very much out of the neotraditionalist playbook.

Of course, as in most matters in planning there is some room for disagreement. Many people like living on cul de sacs because there is no through traffic. Many people also believe that cul de sac streets are less prone to crime because there is only one way out and strangers are more conspicuous on a street that has no through traffic. Whether research would show this supposition to be true is not known.

Another prominent neotraditionalist is California-based Peter Calthorpe. His general design philosophy is similar to Duany's, although Calthorpe places somewhat more emphasis on public transportation and the building of a sufficiently large, compact downtown to support public transportation. His name is associated with *transit-oriented development (TOD)*, meaning a high-density area laid out so that every residential unit within it is within a 10 minutes' walk of a transit stop. A series of these "pedestrian pocket" developments strung out along a transit line would give the line sufficient ridership to divert a significant number of trips from automobiles to buses or light rail. (See Chapter 12 regarding the collection and distribution problem in public transportation.) This is particularly important in many parts of California, where rapid population growth and heavy dependence upon the automobile have led to serious problems with traffic congestion and air quality. The project for which he is best known in California is Laguna West, south of Sacramento, though *Planning* magazine suggests that he may have had more of an effect on the shape of development in California and elsewhere through his work on a number of town and county transit-oriented master plans.[9]

Neotraditionalists rest much of their case on the market. They point out that people will pay very high prices for a fine-grained, pedestrian-friendly pattern. Note, for example, the high price of residential real estate in Georgetown (Washington, DC) or Marblehead, Massachusetts, or Greenwich Village and Brooklyn Heights in New York City.

This writer finds much of the neotraditional design philosophy attractive, but it must be admitted that not everyone else does. Much of the large-lot suburban zoning that the neotraditional planners decry is not so much the planners' choice as it is the will of the public.

The planners are often more open to a variety of urban design innovations than are the citizens. The fears of citizens about who their neighbors might be, whom their children might go to school with, and what might happen to their property values if less expensive structures are built nearby often make these citizens very resistive to smaller lot sizes and mixing of land uses. A substantial segment of the public prefers large-lot development, sharp separation of land uses, and the automobile-dependent way of life that goes with it—just so long as there is plenty of parking and traffic moves quickly. Frank Lloyd Wright's decentralized, automobile-based vision embodied in Broad Acre City (see the final section) spoke to the taste of a great many people. Seeing the pattern of post–World War II suburban development in the United States, it seems rather prophetic.

Neotraditionalism has received some criticism from the left on the grounds that it is elitist and does not do much for the problems of the central cities. The argument is that houses in neotraditional communities such as Kentlands (see page 192) are expensive and that relatively few neotraditional developments have occurred in central cities. In this writer's view, this criticism is not entirely fair. It is true that housing in most neotraditional communities is expensive, but the fact is that unsubsidized new housing in most of the United States is expensive. By spring 2004 several years before the bursting of the housing bubble, (see Chapter 11) the median new single-family house in the United States cost $221,000. The average figure was still higher, at $270,000.[10] New communities thus will almost inevitably have expensive housing. It is true that most neotraditional development occurs

Two scenes from Kentlands, a Duany-designed new urbanist community near Gaithersburg, Maryland. The development is characterized by closely spaced housing, sidewalks on all streets, alleys behind most housing so that garages and trash cans are out of sight, and generally meticulous attention to urban design details. The town center and adjacent areas contain multifamily rental units, a senior citizens facility, and a variety of service and retail businesses.

in suburbia or beyond, but it has to be understood that creating a neotraditional community takes a substantial number of acres and, by and large, substantial blocks of undeveloped land in central cities are rare.

As is true with planned communities in general, doing a neotraditional community requires a very large block of capital up front and generally protracted negotiations with the municipality over rezoning and other design questions.

EDGE CITY

At the very opposite end of the design spectrum from neotraditionalism is the *edge city*. Unlike neotraditionalism, which is a very clearly articulated design philosophy, the edge city embodies no single design philosophy, nor does it have a clear spokesperson such as Andres Duany. Rather, the edge city is an evolving form of development based on a variety of economic forces and on the understandings that developers and investors have of those forces.

The term *edge city* was coined by journalist Joel Garreau to describe this new form of development that has been springing up all over America in the last three decades or so. Using Garreau's somewhat arbitrary definition given below, there are more than 200 edge cities in the United States. Some of those identified by Garreau include Tyson's Corner outside Washington, DC; Buckhead in Atlanta; the Schaumburg area outside Chicago; Dearborn–Fairfield Village outside Detroit; the Galleria area outside Dallas; Irvine Spectrum outside Los Angeles; the Stamford–Greenwich area in Connecticut; Mitchell Field–Garden City in Nassau County, New York; and the King of Prussia area west of Philadelphia. He defines an edge city as meeting the following five requirements:

1. Has 5 million square feet or more of leasable office space—the workplace of the information age [to convert that figure into jobs, you could use a rule-of-thumb figure of about 250 square feet per worker].
2. Has 600,000 square feet of leasable retail space. That is the equivalent of a fair-sized mall.
3. Has more jobs than bedrooms. When the workday starts, people head toward this place, not away from it. Like all urban places, the population increases at 9 A.M.
4. Is perceived by the population as one place. It is a regional end destination for mixed use—not a starting point—that "has it all," from jobs to shopping to entertainment.
5. Was nothing like a "city" as recently as 30 years ago. Then it was just bedrooms, if not cow pastures. This incarnation is brand new.[11]

What are the market forces that favor the development of edge cities? The peripheral location means that the developer(s) can build a large, unified design at one time and do so without having to absorb the residual value of existing structures (see Chapter 11). The large size may offer substantial economies of scale in planning, construction, and marketing.

Its position on the periphery of the metropolitan area gives employers in the edge city access to a large and suitable labor force. Retailers and providers of personal services prosper in the edge city because they are easily accessible to a large, affluent suburban population. The different activities in the edge city may provide profitable synergy. For example, workers in the office buildings will also be customers for retailers and service businesses in the mall. The edge city is an understandable adaptation to a suburbanized population with a very high rate of automobile ownership and access to high-capacity, high-speed highways. The most basic requirements for the formation of an edge city are good highway access, a large and at least moderately prosperous population within easy driving distance, and a large block of available land.

Some edge cities, such as Irvine Spectrum, are planned as a single entity. Others are planned in stages. In either case, the process is very different from traditional urban development under Euclidean zoning. The developer must assemble a sizable piece of land and present the government of the municipality or municipalities with a unified plan. Development is a complex negotiated process, rather than a matter of the developer's acquiring a single parcel and then either building what is allowed by the zoning code or petitioning for a rezoning or variance for that one parcel.

Though the edge city contains many of the same commercial elements as the traditional urban downtown, it differs radically in physical form. The edge city is much more spread out than the traditional downtown. The spread-out form is an adaptation to virtually total reliance on the automobile. Garreau notes that developers regard 600 feet as about the biggest distance that people can realistically be expected to walk without complaint. Thus the typical form of the edge city is a building or perhaps two or three buildings closely grouped and surrounded by some acres of parking space. Larger groupings generally are not done because they would stretch out walking distances beyond what an automobile-owning populace would accept.

Just as the edge city is automobile friendly, it is also pedestrian unfriendly. Irvine Spectrum in southern California, shown on the map on page 195, dwarfs the traditional downtown. Its size alone renders it essentially unwalkable. So, too, does its design. There is no continuous pattern of streets with sidewalks, nor are buildings and their surroundings laid out for walking. Rather, they are laid out for driving, and the visitor is expected to make only the trip from parking space to building on foot. To the extent that there are pedestrian facilities, they are jogging trails or scenic paths intended for recreation, not transportation. Edge cities do mix a variety of commercial uses, though generally at a coarser grain than

Cincinnati, OH

Irvine Spectrum, Irvine, CA

0   4,000   8,000

FIGURE 10-1 Downtown Cincinnati and Irvine Spectrum edge city are shown at the same scale. Note that the longest dimension of Irvine Spectrum is approximately four times that of the longest dimension of the Cincinnati downtown and that the area of Irvine Spectrum is approximately nine times that of the Cincinnati downtown.

Source: Reprinted by permission of the *Journal of the American Planning Association*, 64, no. 3, Summer 1998.

the proponent of neotraditional design would prefer. But they separate work from residence very effectively and thus render virtually every trip to work an automobile trip—again, the antithesis of the neotraditional philosophy.

The edge city is only several decades old. Though numerous architects, planners, and others have speculated about the future of urban form, none really foresaw the edge city. In some ways, Frank Lloyd Wright, with his vision of Broad Acre City, anticipated the dispersed pattern of settlement and the overwhelming reliance on the automobile that characterize the larger environment in which the edge city has developed. But neither he nor any other writer anticipated the edge city itself. Joel Garreau notes that because the edge city is a new form, we cannot say what it will ultimately evolve into. Just as the nineteenth-century city that burgeoned as a result of the industrial revolution often evolved into a much cleaner and pleasanter form in the twentieth century, so too may the edge city evolve into a more gracious and subtle form in years to come. But that is only speculation.

Perhaps we will get our first view of what a transformed edge city might be like from Tyson's Corner, in Fairfax County, Virginia. Tyson's Corner is located just outside the Washington, DC, Beltway (I–495) and just to the north of its intersection with I–66. If you think of the DC Beltway as a clock face, Tyson's Corner would be at 9 o'clock. For the relationship of the city to the Beltway and I–66, see the map on page 242. Tyson's Corner is not a separate municipality, but rather a Census Designated Place (CDP) occupying 4.9 square miles and with a year 2000 resident population of 18,450. Those might sound like the statistics for any number of towns in America, but Tyson's Corner is very different from an ordinary town. On a typical weekday its daytime population is probably seven or eight times its resident population, for an estimated 117,000 people work there. Add to that numerous shoppers, and the weekday daytime population exceeds 150,000. Tyson's Corner contains an estimated 167,000 parking spaces and 46 million square feet (1.65 square miles) of commercial floor space (primarily office and retailing). It is considerably more densely developed than Irvine Spectrum, shown on page 195. Like the typical edge city, it is almost entirely designed for the automobile. There is not a continuous grid of streets and sidewalks as there is in the ordinary city or town, and wide, curved intersections designed to speed auto traffic further discourage foot travel. It is definitely not pedestrian friendly.

But plans to change Tyson's Corner into something more typically urban are underway. One central element in the plan is to connect Tyson's Corner to the Washington, DC, Metro system. An extension to the existing system will have four stops spaced about a half mile apart in Tyson's Corner

Transit-Oriented Densities

Tyson's Corner's "super-blocks" today

The figure at top shows the route of the metro line with its four stops, average spacing a little more than one-half mile, that would form the main axis of the redeveloped Tyson's Corner. Note that the intensity of development would be greatest immediately around the stops and then decline out to a distance of about one-half mile. The two figures below show the existing (top) and proposed (bottom) street patterns. The area outside the dark background shows the present street pattern, primarily suburban subdivisions, outside Tyson's corner.

Future smaller, walkable blocks

The top picture shows the entrance to the Galleria shopping center in Tyson's corner. Note the massive amount of parking space in front of it. It is clearly designed for almost exclusive automobile access. The bottom picture shows a designer's vision of what a much more urban and pedestrian friendly Tyson's corner might look like in 2050.

and will continue westward to several other municipalities and then to Dulles Airport. At this writing the rail work in Tyson's Corner is well underway and the financing for the extension out to Dulles Airport is being worked out.[12] The Metro link between Tyson's Corner and Washington, DC, with its mass of employment, will greatly increase Tyson's Corner's attractiveness as a residential location.

Additional housing will be multifamily, and a substantial share of it will have to be at least moderately high-rise, for there simply is not the space for a significant amount of single-family housing. A more fine-grained and pedestrian-friendly street pattern is a key part of the plan; so, too is a system of walkways, trails, bicycle paths, shuttles, and other nonautomobile-accessible measures designed to turn Tyson's Corner into a densely developed, pedestrian-friendly, highly accessible place. The obvious place to find the space for new streets and new housing will be in some of the areas now devoted to parking. Charging for parking will be part of the plan to shift people away from driving and onto public transportation.

VISIONS OF THE CITY OF THE FUTURE

In the twentieth century, visions included Frank Lloyd Wright's Broad Acre City, R. Buckminster Fuller's milewide geodesic dome for Manhattan, Le Corbusier's Ville Radieuse (the Radiant City), and Paolo Soleri's megastructure, among many others.[13] Behind each of these concepts was an idea about how city dwellers should respond to social and technological change.

For example, in the Ville Radieuse, Le Corbusier envisioned high-rise residential towers in a parklike setting. Major roadways would link together sectors of the city. Two of his key ideas are reflected in this urban design proposal. The first stemmed from his idea of returning the land to human use. It is for this reason that his buildings are raised off the ground on columns or pilote; in this way, buildings are not barriers to pedestrian movement along the ground. The second idea is how the organization of the city would change with widespread automobile ownership. Major roadways connect the high-rise housing with commercial and industrial sectors of the city. Le Corbusier sought to find ways for people to be in closer contact with nature and to use advances in technology to free themselves to reflect on their future and place in the world.[14]

The organization of buildings and patterns of land ownership conceived for Ville Radieuse are in sharp contrast to Frank Lloyd Wright's concepts for Broad Acre City.[15] In Ville Radieuse the land would be owned in common, whereas Wright would have each individual or family own a one-acre lot. Homes and industry would be connected by major roadways. Wright felt that individual ownership of land by broad segments of the population was important in preserving a democratic society. His political and social philosophies were translated into the design proposals contained in the plans for Broad Acre City.

Le Corbusier's "Voisin" plan for Paris 1922–1925 (top). Building very high would permit extreme population density while leaving 95 percent of the land vacant. Though never built, this plan exerted enormous influence on design, for both better and worse, in many countries. Below is the planned community of Roehampton in Great Britain. Note the Le Corbusier influence in the large amounts of interior open space and the use of columns referred to as *pilote*.

The differences in the two plans reflect the different political philosophies of the two men. Wright placed great value on the independence and autonomy of the individual, as suggested by each person owning a plot of land. In contrast, Le Corbusier saw a role for collective ownership of property, suggesting that the overall welfare of society is enhanced if individuals see themselves as part of a larger group and fit into a precise grand design.

Le Corbusier's vision seems very much at odds with Americans' major emphasis on individual choice and minimum regulation but, perhaps surpisingly, his thought was very influential in the United States. He was and is highly regarded within much of the architectural profession and he had a great deal of influence on the design of individual buildings as well as on urban design in general, notably on public housing.

Other visionaries have suggested more radical approaches to structuring the future city. Drawings and models by Paolo Soleri depict megastructures with heights as great or greater than the tallest skyscrapers and covering as much as several hundred acres of ground. The structures would contain both housing and employment for a population of 100,000 or more. Soleri has labeled this general set of studies "arcology." Analagous to ecology, which is the study of animals in their natural homes, arcology is the study of how best to build urban structures to accommodate homes, manufacturing, and public facilities in a fashion compatible with nature. In addition to suggesting new ways of organizing living space, Soleri's proposals contain predictions of completely automated manufacturing facilities that might be placed underground. Soleri constructed a small, new community called Arcosanti in the desert north of Phoenix, Arizona, to test, on a very small scale, some of the concepts embodied in his megastructure designs.

One task for the urban designer is to combine aesthetic considerations with what we have learned about the relationship between physical design and human behavior to obtain a result that actually improves the quality of people's lives. We have learned through experiences with programs such as Urban Renewal and federally assisted housing that although physical design does affect human behavior, it is far from the most powerful determinant. Rather, it is one aspect of a complex array of physical, social, economic, cultural, and psychological factors that are present in our everyday lives.

For example, public housing experience has taught us that high-rise construction does not necessarily work out well for all populations. It is hard for a mother living on the twelfth floor to keep an eye on her children as they play outdoors. The relative anonymity of a high-rise seems to make high-rise public housing prone to crime and may also make it more difficult for residents to build a feeling of community and mutual help. On the other hand, high-rise development may work very well for a young,

Paolo Soleri's "hyperstructure" in ground-level view (top), and cross section (bottom). The figure at the upper right is the Empire State Building at the same scale. The structure would be 3,444 feet (1,050 m) high, 10,367 feet (3,160 m) across the base. Population would be 520,000 or about 171,000 per square mile of ground covered, roughly seven times the population density of New York City. Soleri's work is informed by an extremely strong environmental consciousness. The hyperstructure would house and employ a large number of people but with a small "footprint" on the earth and a low per capita energy consumption. Though hyperstructures are not likely to be built in the near future, Soleri's designs have influenced a generation of planners and architects. Influences of his thought can be found in the Houston Galleria and the Atlanta Hyatt-Regency.

affluent population, as many a successful condominium developer could testify. The negative sociological effects that we now know to be associated with some high-rise, high-density housing were not anticipated by Le Corbusier. Rather than take his proposals as ideas to be applied literally to all urban areas and all urban populations, it is best to consider them as options to be explored and evaluated.

Recent Thinking About the Urban Future

Today, concern with sustainability (see Chapter 14) seems to be the most prominent single concern in thinking about possible urban futures. For example, the British firm Foster and Partners led by the architect Norman Foster has planned Masdar, a satellite city for Abu Dhabi, the capital of the United Arab Emirates (UAE).[16] The city, on which some work has been done, would occupy about 2.3 square miles located about 13 miles southeast of Abu Dhabi, would have a resident population in the range of 45,000 to 50,000, and would also have enough economic activity that a substantial number of workers would commute to it from Abu Dhabi. Perhaps the most striking feature of the city is that it would be carbon neutral; that is, all of the energy used would be generated by nonfossil fuel means. Freshwater, for example, would be provided by a solar powered desalinization plant. Energy for lighting, transportation, and the like would be solar and wind generated. Great attention has been paid to achieving as much cooling effect as possible from breezes and green spaces within the city. The streets would be narrow, which would minimize the surface that absorbs the sun's heat, and no motor vehicles would be allowed. The absence of motor vehicles and the high population density would make the city as pedestrian friendly as possible. Public transportation would be underground and provided by small, electrically powered six-passenger vehicles. The vehicles would be programmed by their riders so there would be no fixed schedule and fixed route service as in a traditional bus or metro system. Foster and Partners envision the economic base of the city as being a mix of manufacturers producing environmentally friendly products and as a center for scientific research and technological innovation. The entire city would be surrounded by a wall that separates it from the desert around it, a feature that seems unusual by Western standards but apparently is desirable to the firm's client, the government of the UAE.

Will the city happen as Foster and Partners envision it? The planning for the city began in 2007 before the financial crisis and the current recession, so economic conditions are one uncertainty—will sufficient capital be available and will the demand for business location there be as strong as the planners anticipate? A much larger uncertainty appears to be the so-called Arab Spring that began in 2011 and that may bring about huge political and social changes throughout the Arab world from which the UAE may or may not be able to insulate itself. But regardless of the fate of this particular project it illustrates some of the concerns that are paramount with those who are now thinking about the urban future.

COMING TO TERMS WITH THE AUTOMOBILE

If one wanted to pick a single theme that defined much of urban design in the twentieth century, *coming to terms with the automobile* might be the best choice. Neotraditional planning is clearly planning for an automobile-owning population. It is an attempt to incorporate the automobile into the urban fabric while not letting the automobile destroy that fabric. The edge city and Frank Lloyd Wright's Broad Acre City both represent a total accommodation to the automobile, and neither would make any sense without the automobile. One could not live in either city without an auto-mobile, and little remains of the traditional urban fabric in either one. Le Corbusier's Voisin plan, though it is radically different from Broad Acre City or the edge city, is also an accommodation to the automobile. Travel in it is by automobile. There is no continuous web of small streets and side-walks, and the distances between the huge structures would discourage walking for purposes other than recreation. Paolo Soleri's megastructure comes to terms with the automobile in a very different way: It banishes the automobile entirely. Vertical travel is by elevator, and horizontal travel is by foot. It is largely meant as an alternative to the sprawling, automobile-begotten metropolitan area of the twentieth century. Even the Foster plan for Masdar takes the autoomobile into account in the sense of banishing it and replacing with something less intrusive and more environmentally benign, but which, like the automobile, provides individual self-scheduled mobility.

If one looks back to the neighborhood drawing on page 185, one sees that it, too, makes a particular accommodation to the automobile. Curvilinear internal streets permit automobile access to all parts of the neighborhood, while the larger streets on its edges carry longer-distance traffic around it rather than through it. In fact, though it antedates the neotraditional movement by at least half a century, it has a certain amount in common with neotraditionalism. Radburn, discussed in Chapter 3, is also an accommodation to the automobile. Like the neotraditionalists, the designers of Radburn acknowledged that automobile ownership and use would be nearly universal, but they sought to keep it in its place and to protect the fabric of the community from it.

The automobile is irresistibly attractive to most people. If there were ever a product that was essentially self-advertising, it is the automobile. It works well in low-density environments but poorly in high-density environments. It is an enormous space hog, both when in motion and when at rest. The automobile takes as much square footage as a studio apartment just to park it. For all these reasons the automobile is not easily reconciled with the urban environment, and it is not surprising that accommodating urban life to it has been and remains a central issue in urban design.

SUMMARY

Urban design generally occupies a middle position between architecture and planning. Rather than focusing on the design of the individual structure, the urban designer concentrates on the massing and organization of buildings and on the spaces between them. The physical focus of the urban designer may be somewhat smaller than that of the planner, who is often concerned with the entire city or even the city as part of a larger metropolitan system.

The urban design process is broken into four main phases: (1) analysis, (2) synthesis, (3) evaluation, and (4) implementation. Judging a particular piece of urban design is always a somewhat subjective matter. However, there are some generally accepted criteria, including the following:

1. Unity and coherence
2. Minimum conflict between pedestrians and vehicles
3. Protection from rain, noise, wind, and so on
4. Easy orientation for users
5. Compatibility of land uses
6. Availability of places to rest, observe, and meet
7. Creation of a sense of security and pleasantness

The urban designer, in producing a design that not only looks good but also functions well, must consider many factors beyond the purely physical. These include financial, political, psychological, and sociological considerations.

The chapter summarizes neotraditional design (the New Urbanism) and the edge city as opposing visions of urban design. It then briefly touches on visions of the future of the city by Le Corbusier, Frank Lloyd Wright, and Paolo Soleri. It concludes with a note on the current interest in sustainable design and the observation that perhaps the greatest challenge to urban design in the twentieth and twenty-first centuries has been that of reconciling urban places to that most antiurban of technologies, the automobile.

NOTES

1. Lewis Mumford, *The Culture of Cities*, Harcourt Brace Jovanovich, New York, 1970, p. 5, originally printed in 1938.
2. Nicolai Ouroussoff, "A Tower That Sends a Message of Anxiety, Not Ambition," *New York Times*, February 19, 2007, p. B1.
3. Kevin Lynch, *The Image of the City*, MIT Press, Cambridge, MA, 1960.
4. Personal communication.
5. William H. Whyte, *The Social Life of Small Urban Spaces*, The Conservation Foundation, Washington, DC, 1980.
6. Jane Jacobs, *The Death and Life of Great American Cities*, Vintage Books, Random House, New York, 1961.
7. Clarence A. Perry, "The Neighborhood Unit Formula," reprinted in *Urban Planning Theory*, Melville C. Branch, ed., Dowden, Hutchinson & Ross, Stroudsburg, PA, 1975, pp. 44–58.
8. Andres Duany, Elizabeth Plater-Zyberk, and Jeff Speck, *Suburban Nation*, North Point Press, div. of Farrar Straus and Giroux, New York, 2000.
9. Gary Delsohn, "Peter's Pockets," *Planning*, February 1994, pp. 18–21.
10. U.S. Bureau of the Census/U.S. Department of Housing and Urban Development Press Release, May 26, 2004. Data on housing prices can be found on the Web at www. census.gov./newhomesales.
11. Joel Garreau, *Edge City: Life on the New Frontier*, New York, Doubleday, 1991, p. 6.
12. Maps and details on the Metro extension can be found at www.Dullesmetro.com. Information on planning for Tyson's Corner as it evolves can be obtained from the Fairfax County Planning Department through Fairfaxcounty.gov. Wikipedia has a good article giving background on Tyson's Corner and providing a number of useful links.
13. Le Corbusier's vision comes from the period shortly before to shortly after World War I. Frank Lloyd Wright began work on the Broad Acre City concept the 1930s. Buckminster Fuller began work on the geodesic dome as a type of structure in the 1930s. The proposal for the dome over midtown Manhattan dates from the 1960s. So, too, does Soleri's megastructure.
14. Although Le Corbusier did not build very much himself, his ideas have had a huge influence on both architecture and urban design during much of the twentieth and twenty-first centuries. Probably the best summary of those ideas is his book *Towards a New Architecture*, Dover Publications, New York, 1986 (first published in 1931).
15. Frank Lloyd Wright, *The Living City*, Horizon Press, New York, 1958.
16. Information on Masdar can be found by Googling Masdar or Foster and Partners.

SELECTED BIBLIOGRAPHY

ALEXANDER, CHRISTOPHER, *A Pattern Language*, Oxford University Press, Oxford, 1977.

BARNETT, JONATHAN, *An Introduction to Urban Design*, Harper and Row, New York, 1982.

BOHL, CHARLES C., *Place Making: Developing Town Centers, Main Streets and Urban Villages*, Urban Land Institute, Washington, DC, 2002.

BRAMBILLA, R., and LONGO, G., *For Pedestrians Only*, Whitney Library of Design, New York, 1977.

CALTHORPE, PETER, *The New American Metropolis: Ecology, Community and the American Dream*, Princeton Architectural Press, New York, 1993.

DUANY, ANDRES, and PLATER-ZYBERK, ELIZABETH, *Towns and Town-Making Principles*, Rizzoli, New York, 1991.

DUANY, ANDRES, PLATER-ZYBERK, ELIZABETH, and SPECK, JEFF, *Suburban Nation*, North Point Press, div. of Farrar, Straus and Giroux, New York, 2000.

KATZ, PETER, *The New Urbanism: Toward an Architecture of Community*, McGraw-Hill Book Co., New York, 1994.

LARICE, MICHAEL, and MACDONALD, ELIZABETH, EDS., *The Urban Design Reader*, Routledge, New York, 2006.

MORRIS, A. E. J., *History of Urban Form*, John Wiley, New York, 1972.

MOUGHTON, CLIFF, CUSETA, RAFAEL, SARRIS, CHRISTINE, and SIGNORETTA, PAOLA, *Urban Design: Method and Technique*, Architectural Press, New York, 2004.

PUSHKAREV, B., and ZUPAN, J., *Urban Space for Pedestrians*, Regional Plan Association of New York, MIT Press, Cambridge, MA, 1975.

REGIONAL PLAN ASSOCIATION, *Urban Design Manhattan*, New York Regional Plan Association, 1969.

TRANCIK, ROGER, *Finding Lost Space: Theories of Urban Design*, Van Nostrand Reinhold, New York, 1986.

URBAN DESIGN ASSOCIATES, *The Urban Design Handbook: Techniques and Working Methods*, W. W. Norton, New York, 2003.

VAN DER RYN, SIM, and CALTHORPE, PETER, *Sustainable Communities: A New Design Synthesis for Cities, Suburbs and Towns*, Sierra Publishing Co., Jackson, CA, 1991.

WALTER, DAVID, and BROWN, LINDA LOUISE, *Design First: Design Based Planning for Communities*, Architectural Press, New York, 2004.

CHAPTER 11

Urban Renewal and Community Development

For several decades, community development has been a major preoccupation of planners. It covers a wide range of goals and activities.

1. *Facilitation of economic growth or, in more desperate cases, measures to retard the loss of economic activity.*

2. *Attempts to increase the quality—and sometimes the quantity—of the municipality's housing stock.*

3. *Attempts to sustain or improve some particular commercial function of the city, most commonly retailing.* (Note the link here with item 1.)

4. *Improvement of some physical aspect of the community such as its parks, recreational facilities, parking facilities, or street pattern.*

5. *Furtherance of urban design goals.* This is often tied to some of the previously listed goals. For example, attempts to beautify—or de-uglify—a downtown street might be tied to attempts to increase downtown retailing activity, which might be part of a larger effort aimed at employment expansion.

6. *Provision of a variety of services.* Examples might be provision of social services such as day care, job training, or drug rehabilitation. Service provision is likely to be directed primarily to less affluent segments of the community's population.

Although the term *community development* is of post–World War II origin, it is not a totally new departure for planning. Planners' concerns with housing go back to the nineteenth century. Then, too, the facilitation of economic growth had been a major motivation behind city planning for decades.

This chapter begins with an account of Urban Renewal, a program that is now history. The reader may wonder why this look backward is necessary. Although the Urban Renewal program is over, many of its main elements are still central to the urban development process.

Urban Renewal is instructive in that it illustrates how hard it can be to formulate policy that is free of major side effects and actually does what it is intended to do. For its critics, who grew to be very numerous indeed, Urban Renewal was a classic illustration of the old expression "The road to hell is paved with good intentions."

URBAN RENEWAL

Urban Renewal began with the Housing Act of 1949 and was officially ended in 1973 (though some funding of projects that were started before 1973 continued far into the 1980s). The goals of the program, as expressed in legislation and congressional debate, included

1. Eliminating substandard housing
2. Revitalizing city economies
3. Constructing good housing
4. Reducing de facto segregation

The method used was clearance and rebuilding directed by local agencies and supported by large federal subsidies. It was and still stands as the largest federal urban program in U.S. history, and it reshaped parts of hundreds of communities.[1] Statistics published in 1973 when the program was terminated showed that more than 2,000 projects had been undertaken on 1,000 square miles of urban land. Some 600,000 housing units, the dwelling places of perhaps 2 million people, had been demolished and those people forced to move. Roughly 250,000 new housing units had been built on the same sites. Approximately 120 million square feet of public floor space and 224 million square feet of commercial floor space had been built on renewal land.[2] As a measure of economic impact, the floor space figures translate into workplaces for almost one-half million employees. The assessed value of land and structures in renewal areas increased by a factor of 3.6 from what it had been before the program started. Today the figures for new construction would be much larger because the 1973 figures, which actually represented the facts as of about 1971, caught many renewal areas after the demolition phase but well before the construction phase was complete.

By 1973 the Urban Renewal program had spent approximately $13 billion in federal funds, a figure that would be about seven to eight times as large if converted into current dollars.[3] To this figure should be added several billion dollars in local funds. Beyond that were the private investments on Urban Renewal sites. These far exceeded the total public investments.

The Origins of Urban Renewal

The rationale for Urban Renewal stems from two very simple economic circumstances. To build on virgin land, the builder need pay only the cost of the land plus the cost of construction. But to build on land containing structures that must be demolished, the builder must also pay the residual value of those structures. A building may be obsolete. Its owner or any objective observer might agree that under present circumstances, it would never make sense to build a building like it on the present site. Nonetheless, if the building yields some stream of income to its owner, he or she will not give up the building without compensation.

Consider the following example. Mr. X owns a 90-year-old tenement near the core of the city. The building contains 12 apartments, which rent for an average of $200 per month—a low figure, which represents the fact that these apartments are close to the bottom of the city's housing market. Mr. X is approached by a developer who is interested in the land under the building but must acquire that building to get at the land. A rule of thumb for rental properties is that buildings are valued at 100 times the monthly rent roll, so Mr. X responds with an offer to sell for $240,000 (12 × 200 × 100). If the building occupies a 50-by-100-foot lot, that works out to about $48 per square foot, or roughly $2 million per acre. Even if the developer thinks Mr. X may come down considerably, that number makes vacant land on a suburban highway at even a million dollars an acre look good.

The second factor that impedes development in built-up areas is the land assemblage problem. Typically, urban land ownership is highly fragmented. A single city block is likely to be owned by many separate individuals or business organizations. In fact, in many cities the basic unit into which land was originally subdivided is the 25-by-100-foot lot (25-foot frontage and 100-foot depth). For the developer setting up a major project, it may be necessary to deal with dozens of different owners. In some instances their titles may have legal problems that cannot be resolved without substantial delays. In other cases the owner of a small parcel may exploit his or her capacity to block a large project by holding out for a price that far exceeds the fair market value of the land. Compared with the urban fringe, where land is generally owned in much larger blocks, the situation can be very discouraging.

These impediments to urban redevelopment were recognized during the latter part of the Great Depression, and the federal government became interested in taking steps to improve the competitive position of the central cities. In December 1941, hardly good timing for proposing a new civilian program, Guy Greer and Alvin Hansen published an article suggesting the creation of City Realty Corporations.[4] These organizations would be able to use eminent domain to assemble land and would have funds from higher levels of government for the acquisition and clearance of sites. The proposed corporations would thus be able to deal effectively with both the residual value and the land assemblage problems.

The idea lay dormant through World War II but was revived shortly thereafter. The Housing Act of 1949 brought the program into being very much as Hansen and Greer had envisioned it. The act provided for the creation of Local Public Agencies (LPAs) analogous to the City Realty Corporation. The LPA would have the power of eminent domain to acquire sites. Two-thirds of the LPA's funding was to come from the federal government, and the remaining third from the municipality. However, some of the local share could be services in kind (services of city personnel, donation of city-owned land, etc.) so that in cash terms, the federal government paid more than the nominal two-thirds. The LPA would use its legal powers and financial resources to acquire, clear, and otherwise prepare sites (grading, provision of utilities, widening and straightening of streets, etc.). These sites would then be sold or leased to private developers at substantially below cost.

By absorbing the residual value as well as many other development costs, the program would greatly accelerate the redevelopment process within the designated renewal areas of cities. By using public powers to acquire and clear large sites, the program would permit far more coordinated and imaginative development than would otherwise be the case.

In order to work as described, Urban Renewal introduced a new practice into law. It previously had been understood that eminent domain could be used to take private property and convey it to a public body for public use, for example, the building of a public school. But under Urban Renewal, government took property from one private party, say, the owner of a dilapidated tenement, and ultimately conveyed it to another private party, the developer building on the Urban Renewal site. This arrangement seemed questionable on constitutional grounds, and a property owner took an Urban Renewal Agency to court. But in 1954 in *Berman v. Parker*, the Supreme Court sustained the agency. Had the case gone the other way, the Urban Renewal process as it was then structured would have come to a virtual halt, another indication of the decisive role that the courts often play in planning.

In 2005 the Supreme Court, in effect, reaffirmed *Berman v. Parker* in the *Kelo v. New London* decision. However, the political uproar that followed the *Kelo* decision caused many states to ban private-party-to-private-party transfers so that at present, the question of how many re-development projects will proceed is not clear. The *Kelo* decision and the states' responses to it are discussed in detail in Chapter 5.

Intention and Reality

Congress intended Urban Renewal as a housing program, as the goals listed earlier indicate. The initial legislation confined renewal activity to sites that either were or would be largely residential. In fact, the initial legislation stipulated that for each new unit of housing built, at least one old unit of housing must be torn down. The intent to eliminate slums by replacing bad, old housing with good, new housing was very clear.

The goals, though praiseworthy, contain some internal contradictions and some not-so-pleasant side effects, which become apparent on reflection. For instance, rebuilding the city's economy is likely to be furthered by a program that demolishes substandard housing and replaces it with a purely commercial development. But where does that leave the goal of adding good, new units to the city's housing stock? Who could be against eliminating substandard housing? Rephrase that as reducing the supply of low-cost housing, driving down vacancy rates, and thereby tightening the housing market in which the poor must find shelter, and it does not sound so good. Achieving a higher degree of racial integration is a praiseworthy goal. One way to achieve racial integration in a poor, black neighborhood is to knock down dilapidated older housing occupied by low-income blacks and replace it with high-quality—and more expensive—housing to be occupied by middle- or upper-income households, most of whom are not black. Of course, that is a rather stiff price to pay for integration. And, whether real integration will occur or whether the two populations will simply live in the same area but have little to do with each other is a question too.

Urban Renewal was major urban surgery, and as such it had many side effects, not all of which were desirable or foreseen. Doing good is not simply a matter of having good intentions.

One fact that soon became apparent as the federal funds began to flow was that local intentions and federal intentions were not always the same. With the passage of time, local desires began to change both federal law and federal practice. From the federal point of view, housing was central. But many localities did not care about housing. If rundown housing occupied by lower-income households was demolished and replaced with commercial development, the municipality solved both a housing and a tax base problem. The population that lived in the housing to be demolished would not vanish from the face of the earth. But if that population settled in adjacent communities after being dehoused by "the federal bulldozer," it became someone else's problem. From the local perspective, that solved the problem. Of course, from the federal perspective, that was no solution at all. At best, it was a "zero-sum game" played with federal funds. Clearly, what constitutes a problem and what constitutes a solution vary, depending on whom one considers to be one's constituency.

What happens when federal and local goals differ? The "locals" wanting the federal money do some compromising and accept some conditions that they do not like. On the other hand, the federal official whose job it is to spend the allocated funds wants to see agreements with LPAs signed and projects under way. So he or she does some compromising too. In time the program gets bent from its initial shape into something that both the locals and the "feds" can live with. In the case of Urban Renewal, that meant relaxing the residential requirements and permitting many projects that had a predominantly commercial emphasis.

But that was hardly the end of the story. With the passage of time, some of the program's side effects became apparent, and both those who suffered from them and their allies began to exert pressure for change.

The most easily identified and numerous victims were those people who lost their housing because of Urban Renewal. In the typical project all the land was acquired at the beginning. Before clearance could begin, all those who resided on the site had to relocate. There then followed a clearance phase during which all the demolition was accomplished. The construction phase might then spread out over a number of years. It might not even begin for several years after clearance was completed. When the construction phase was completed, the number of new units might or might not approximate the number of units demolished. In either case the new units were not likely to do the original residents much good. First, there was the question of where they were to live in the intervening years. Equally important was the cost issue. Good, new housing costs a lot more to rent than bad, old housing. Urban Renewal typically took place in the urban core, where the housing that was demolished was old, relatively inexpensive, and largely occupied by poor people. Most of them could not afford the new housing even if they could wait for it. As Martin Anderson, probably Urban Renewal's most effective critic, noted,

> The people are poor. A great many of them are Negroes and Puerto Ricans. Good quality, conveniently located housing is scarce; good quality, conveniently located housing for $50 or $60 a month is almost impossible to find. It is difficult to picture hundreds of thousands of low-income people, many of them subject to racial discrimination, moving from low quality into higher quality housing at rents they can afford. And then, one might ask, why, if all this good housing at low rents is available, didn't they move before urban renewal nudged them along.[5]

Studies of people dispossessed by Urban Renewal often found that they were worse off than before. The process of forced moving tore up individuals' connections to friends, relatives, neighborhood organizations, and the like, and generally left people less happy with their life situation than previously. The only way people seemed better off was that their standard of housing was somewhat better. That effect was almost inevitable since renewal often tore down the most deteriorated units in the municipal housing stock. Of course, with the tightening of the housing stock, they often paid more for their new housing than they had for their old housing.

The effect of Urban Renewal on the city's economy also came under some criticism. There was no question that Urban Renewal did stimulate economic development as described earlier. The question that critics raised was how much damage the process did to the existing economic structure. The first argument was that simply the announcement of impending renewal froze investment both within and nearby the designated area. Within the area no investor would commit funds, for obvious reasons. But even outside the area, investors would be inhibited because they did not know how much competition—subsidized with federal monies—would soon be coming to the renewal site. Whether it was old housing, old retailing space, or old commercial space, spending money on its renovation or modernization would be riskier if new, competing structures were soon to rise on the nearby site. Another argument was that when businesses were forced to close because their buildings were condemned, they often never reopened. The loss of customers to competitors or the expenses of reopening simply overwhelmed them. It was also said that renewal generally demolished relatively cheap commercial space. This is the space often occupied by struggling new enterprises that cannot afford newer space. Thus it attacks the "incubator" role of the city and may do long-term damage, which does not show up in short-term statistics.[6]

Ultimately, Urban Renewal accumulated so many enemies that in 1973, Congress terminated the program, although, as noted, funding pursuant to contracts signed previously continued into the 1980s.

Urban Renewal in Retrospect

On the negative side there seems little argument about the human costs of Urban Renewal. The paralyzing effect of impending renewal action seems less important in retrospect, for once the project has been completed, the effect disappears. Somehow, the argument regarding the incubator role of the city also seems less powerful in retrospect, for many cities still retained large amounts of cheap space after Urban Renewal.

On the positive side, what can be said? Probably the biggest gain has been that Urban Renewal projects gave many cities the ability to compete with their suburbs. For example, White Plains, New York (as noted in Chapter 9), has grown as a retailing center in an age when most cities have been losing retail sales and jobs to the suburbs. Clearly, it was the new and efficient street pattern and the availability of large, cleared parcels of land with marketable titles at below cost that made it possible for White Plains to swim against the tide. Without Urban Renewal most of the retailing activity now in downtown White Plains would be out on the highway.

One of Manhattan's big selling points as a commercial and residential location is its preeminence as a cultural center. A part of that preeminence resides in Lincoln Center, a cultural complex built as an Urban Renewal project on several blocks of deteriorated residential structures.

The Boston waterfront, redeveloped as part of the city's Urban Renewal program, pulls in millions of tourist dollars and also makes the city more attractive as a residence for a young and affluent population, which might otherwise settle in the suburbs. In that sense it acts as a promoter of "gentrification," a trend that most cities, rightly or wrongly, seem to welcome.[7]

Writing in the 1960s, Charles Abrams stated of Urban Renewal,

> It [Urban Renewal] allows room for more squares and parking spaces and is a useful tool for the long overdue rebuilding of cities enslaved to the 20- to 25-foot lot, and the gridiron pattern. It provides the opportunity for enlarging the street system surrounding the new projects, the closing of streets where necessary, the diversion of traffic, the addition of streets or widening of intersections. It facilitates running the new highways into the city's shopping centers and the creation of off-street parking and enclosed parking space. In short, the renewal project supplies a multipurpose opportunity in place of the piecemeal efforts to correct traffic problems, provide playgrounds and open spaces, provide neighborhood amenities, and new housing public and private.[8]

In referring to the failure of firms that were unable to compete successfully, economist Joseph Schumpeter applauded the "creative destruction" of capitalism. At its best, Urban Renewal was creative destruction. It tore away an old and obsolescent urban fabric and replaced it with something newer and brighter and, often, more economically viable. But such destruction is not without pain to individuals and enterprises. Reasonable people may differ over whether the gains justified the pain.

Although the Urban Renewal program is no more, its basic elements of the use of public funds and the power of eminent domain to solve the land assembly problem and the transfer of property so acquired to private parties who will invest in its development are still fundamental to many public redevelopment projects. The transfer of property from one private party to another has become more problematic as a result of the public and then the legislative reaction to the *Kelo* decision discussed in Chapter 5.

Baltimore's Inner Harbor redevelopment done jointly by the city and the Rouse Corporation. The development includes tourist attractions such as the restored USS *Constellation* (below), restaurants and retailing, large amounts of office space, and hundreds of hotel rooms to accommodate tourists and business travelers. The project works because the mix of uses is mutually reinforcing. Thus such redevelopment can be done only as a unified effort involving many adjacent parcels of land.

The Stamford, Connecticut, Urban Renewal area as it appeared in the 1960s before redevelopment began (top) and as it appeared two decades later at full development (bottom). Note the ready access to Interstate 95 and the revised street pattern.

COMMUNITY DEVELOPMENT _____

A year after the termination of Urban Renewal, Congress passed the Housing and Community Development Act of 1974. This omnibus act replaced Urban Renewal as well as a variety of urban "categorical" programs, that is, programs that provide funds for specific categories of activity, such as sewage treatment, recreation, or housing. The act provided Community Development Block Grants (CDBGs) to permit localities to pursue a wide range of activities including, but not limited to, activities that had been pursued under the Urban Renewal program. The intent of the block grant approach, as opposed to the categorical approach that it superseded, was to reduce the federal role in local affairs by allowing municipalities more discretion. In that sense it was in keeping with the more conservative political philosophy of the Nixon administration in contrast to preceding Democratic administrations. Community Development (CD) funds were distributed on a formula basis, which counted population, age of housing stock, and poverty. Thus virtually every municipality in the nation received some funds. Municipalities were free to expend funds on a wide range of projects, including many types of service provisions as well as capital expenditures. Among the purposes for which CDBG funds could be used were acquisition of real property, public facilities and improvements, parks and playgrounds, centers for individuals with disabilities, neighborhood facilities, solid-waste disposal facilities, parking facilities, public utilities, street improvements, water and sewer facilities, pedestrian malls and walkways, flood and drainage facilities, clearance activities, public services, rehabilitation of public residential structures, rehabilitation financing, temporary relocation assistance, and economic development.[9]

The act emphasized services for the poorer segment of the population, but in many communities there was a tendency to spend most of the funds on bricks and mortar. Bricks and mortar last longer and are more visible. Then, too, services are hard to discontinue, so if the source of funding is cut off, the municipality that spent most of its CD funds on services could find itself out on a financial limb.

According to the legislation, municipalities were not to use CD funds for expenditures they would make in the absence of such grants, nor were they simply to use CD funds for tax relief. In the terminology of public finance, CD funds were to be "stimulative," not "substitutive."[10]

The legislation also required the predominant share of CD funds to be used in a manner that primarily benefited low- and moderate-income persons. Essentially, this requirement means either spending CD funds in areas that have substantial proportions of low- and moderate-income residents or spending the funds on facilities or services that will be used by or that will benefit these persons. Presumably day care or land clearance for a factory or warehouse would so qualify; repairing the seawall at the municipal yacht basin would not.

The act required each community to include as part of its grant application a Housing Assistance Plan (HAP), which spelled out community housing needs and laid out plans for dealing with them. The act also imposed significant "citizen participation" requirements on communities. The regulations state

> There shall be involvement of low and moderate income persons, members of minority groups, residents of areas where a significant amount of activity is proposed or ongoing, the elderly, the handicapped, the business community, and civic groups. . . . The applicant shall make reasonable efforts to insure continuity of involvements. Citizens shall be provided adequate and timely information. . . . Citizens, particularly low and moderate income persons and residents of blighted neighborhoods, shall be encouraged to submit their views and proposals.[11]

Clearly, these requirements were motivated in part by criticisms of Urban Renewal, which accused these programs of riding roughshod over the residents of renewal areas. Even if the federal government were to make no effort to enforce these rules directly, they would have considerable force. Any citizen or any group that felt slighted in the community planning process could bring suit against the municipality on the grounds that it had failed to provide an adequate citizen participation process. A successful suit might well enjoin the municipality from spending further federal or perhaps even local funds until this fault was remedied.

Community Development Versus the Urban Renewal Approach

In general, Community Development has differed from Urban Renewal primarily in its gentler approach and in its emphasis on rehabilitation and preservation, as opposed to Urban Renewal's clear-and-start-from-scratch approach. For example, in the realm of housing, CD programs have expended substantial funds on grants or low-interest loans to homeowners and to the owners of rental properties for rehabilitation and modernization.

One program that has been highly successful in some cities is *urban homesteading.* In declining residential areas, cities often come into ownership of residential properties, primarily through foreclosure for unpaid property taxes. (This is not likely to happen in thriving areas since the higher market values will cause the owner who cannot pay taxes to sell out rather than simply walk away.) In the homesteading program the house is essentially given to a new owner, who promises to "bring it up to code" within a given time period. If the new owner succeeds in doing so, the title then passes to him or her without charge. In effect, the cost of acquiring the property is the expenditure required to bring the building up to the standards set forth in the municipality's building code. That expenditure may be primarily financial, that is, money spent on contractors, or it may largely be labor by the new owner, so-called sweat equity.

In the city of Baltimore, the program has worked quite successfully on old row houses. The lure of homeownership has been strong enough to attract an adequate number of urban homesteaders, but according to city officials, the potential profitability has not been so great as to bring in many speculators. Not only does the program improve housing quality, but also it fills neighborhoods with individuals and families who have a strong commitment to those neighborhoods. It thus contributes greatly to neighborhood stability, a goal that in the long run is probably more important than simply the maintenance of building quality.

In commercial areas many CD programs have taken a less radical approach than Urban Renewal. Low-interest loans have been made to local businesses, sometimes for operating purposes and sometimes for renovation and expansion. Pedestrian malls designed to attract shoppers have been constructed. Of course, some expenditures quite reminiscent of Urban Renewal have been made, for example, the construction of parking structures and street widening and realignment. But in general, the emphasis has been on preservation, rehabilitation, improvement, and gradual change. The intent has been to achieve the same goals as Urban Renewal but with less damage to the existing urban fabric.

In many cases, municipal governments have given up the idea of competing head-to-head with suburban retailers on the grounds that it is impossible to match the automobile access and parking advantages of the suburban shopping center (the case of White Plains, noted earlier, is an exception in this regard). Instead, there has been more of an emphasis on strengthening those assets of the city that are not so readily matched by suburban areas. Such assets might include cultural facilities and areas designed largely for pedestrian traffic, where the denser and more varied pattern of land uses gives the city an advantage over the suburbs. For example, the revitalized downtown in Roanoke, Virginia, includes a museum, a theater, a number of specialty shops, and a small farmers' market, all laid out for pedestrian access. There has been no serious attempt to compete with outlying shopping centers.

In a number of cities, waterfronts that have long since lost their shipping functions have been converted to areas where one strolls, has lunch or dinner, shops, or uses some cultural or entertainment facility. The Boston Waterfront, Manhattan's South Street Seaport, and Baltimore's Inner Harbor are examples. Very often there is an element of historic preservation in such efforts. For example, South Street Seaport includes a number of restored buildings as well as several old, restored sailing vessels tied up at city-owned piers. Again, one might view this as an attempt to capitalize on an asset that the city has and the suburbs generally do not have, namely, the charm of the old.

THE HOUSING QUESTION

Housing, defining the term broadly, is probably the most important issue in urban planning. Housing constitutes the biggest single land use in most cities and towns; in many places it occupies more land than all other uses combined. In many cities housing and the land under it constitute more than half of the entire real property tax base. There are few, if any, planning issues that touch most people more deeply than the condition of their immediate neighborhoods, because that is where they spend most of their time. Moreover, housing is often the single largest item in a family's budget, and a house is the most expensive possession that most people acquire. Equity in a house often constitutes the major share of the estate a person passes on to his or her descendants.

We may all agree that housing problems are important and that they need to be solved, but when asked what the housing problem is, different people will give very different answers. Though we may speak generally of the nation's housing market, it really represents the sum of thousands of separate housing markets. If you live in St. Paul, Minnesota, the state of the housing market in the San Francisco Bay area is likely to be of marginal interest to you at best.

For some, the quality, quantity, and cost of housing available to low-income Americans may be the nation's biggest housing problem, though some economists will argue that it is really not a housing problem at all, but rather a problem of income distribution. If you are renting now but want to become a homeowner, you might have concluded until recently that the nation's biggest housing problem was that in many housing markets, prices had risen more rapidly than had personal income.

If you are a middle-aged homeowner who wants to build an accessory apartment in your garage for an aging parent, your biggest housing problem may be what you see as the excessive rigidity of the zoning codes that will not let you do this.

If you are a homeowner in a bucolic exurban town that is fast turning into a suburban town, your biggest housing problem may be that too much of it is being built too near you.

If you are a homeowner in a nice suburban house that you have lived in for 25 years, you may not think that there is any housing problem at all. You are comfortably housed now, and when you retire and sell, that big capital gain will make it very easy to buy a nice condo in Florida. You won't get upset if housing prices rise because the faster they rise, the better off you are. In the writer's experience as a planner in the suburbs, it is very difficult to get homeowners concerned about housing shortages for exactly the reason just suggested.

Where is public policy in all this confusion about what our housing problems really are, you might ask. The answer is *almost everywhere.* Policies often point in different directions because different elements of public policy are responses to different constituencies.

In 2006 the federal government spent about $38 billion on subsidies for the housing of low-income people. In addition to that, it provided about $8 billion in preferential tax treatment to the builders of low-income housing. (In general, preferential tax treatments are referred to as *tax expenditures* because they achieve a somewhat similar result as do direct expenditures, but they are delivered instead through provisions in the tax code.) Certainly, on balance such expenditure and tax policies can be characterized as pro-poor. However, at the same time, federal tax expenditures in connection with property taxes, mortgage interest, and the treatment of capital gains on the sale of owner-occupied housing were worth more than three times that amount, and these sums, for reasons explained in Chapter 17, clearly favor the prosperous. The fact that these two packages of policies point in different directions is not to say that either is bad. Helping low-income people obtain better housing certainly seems praiseworthy. Then, too, many would say that encouraging homeownership is also praiseworthy. But if the federal approach had been designed by a single intelligence, say, that of a wise and benevolent despot, it probably would look rather different and would be more internally consistent. But it was not designed by a single mind. It came out of the workings of many minds—out of the democratic political process.

At the local level, policy may not be entirely consistent either. A town may limit the amount of land it zones for multifamily housing and require larger building lots for single-family housing than most planners and urban designers would consider necessary. That treatment tends to raise rents and house prices. At the same time, the town may also have inclusionary zoning requirements that compel builders to set aside a certain number of units for low- and moderate-income renters or buyers. Of course, these policies are somewhat contradictory, but they respond to different constituencies, they may have been enacted at different times, and their inherent contradictoriness may not be readily apparent to the citizen-voter who has many different things besides local housing policy on his or her mind.

Finally, as big as public direct expenditures and tax expenditures connected with housing are, they are dwarfed by private expenditures on housing. In 2006 (the last year before housing prices headed downward) the nation spent almost $2 trillion on the purchase, ownership, and operation of housing.[12] That was, very roughly, one-fourth of after-tax personal income in the United States. Inevitably, then, government's ability to influence housing is limited.

PLANNING FOR HOUSING

For housing that is to be built purely by the private market, meaning without direct subsidy of any kind, the main step a community can take is to provide the opportunity for the market to work. At the physical level this means providing infrastructure, namely, roads, public water, and sewers. Land cannot be developed for housing without road access, and it cannot be developed at more than very low density without public water and sewers. Beyond these absolutely essential items, other public investment will affect the rate of new housing construction. For example, recreational facilities or an elementary school may make a developing area more desirable.

Land-use controls will limit the quantity of the housing stock by setting an upper limit on the number of units per acre. That affects price. Controls also affect price by the types of units they permit. Garden apartments cost less per unit than do row houses. Row houses, in turn, cost less per unit than do free-standing, single-family houses on small lots. These cost less than houses on large lots. Land-use controls that require particular amenities, for example, recreational facilities, for new developments will raise prices. Subdivision requirements affect the site-preparation costs, which in turn will be reflected in the price of the finished units.

What can the community do to provide low- and moderate-income housing? As stated, it can provide the infrastructure to support and the land-use controls to permit the building of less expensive housing types. It can encourage builders to seek out and use federal and state subsidies for low- and moderate-income housing. It can make it community policy not to use its land-use control and other legal powers to obstruct the building of subsidized housing. Similarly, it can take an accommodating rather than a resisting stance toward group homes. This last item is not an idle point: In many communities, citizens' resistance to group homes can be ferocious. Also, the municipality can use CD funds, or even funds raised through its own tax efforts, to subsidize low- and moderate-income housing. For example, CD funds have been used to make low-interest rehabilitation loans to low- and moderate-income homeowners and to the owners of low-rent apartment houses. This may be done through a revolving loan fund or through the banks, with the municipality picking up a portion of the interest cost and perhaps also guaranteeing the loan. The municipality's zoning laws can provide density bonuses to developers who will include a certain number of units reserved for low- and moderate-income buyers or renters (see Chapter 9).

If particular forces threaten to reduce the supply of affordable housing, municipal governments may sometimes be able to take preventive steps. For example, one trend in many suburban areas where land prices are high and the supply of vacant building lots limited has been that of *tear downs*. Typically these occur in older neighborhoods. A would-be homeowner purchases a house that may be of good quality and in scale with other houses in the neighborhood simply to obtain the lot. That house is then torn down and replaced with a much larger house, sometimes referred to derisively as a *MacMansion* or *monster home*. Residents often object because such large homes are out of scale with the surrounding development. But another effect is to reduce the supply of so-called starter homes and thus make it more difficult for less affluent people to make the transition into homeownership. Many municipalities have resisted this process with a variety of regulatory tools. In some cases, zoning laws and building codes have been adjusted to limit height, bulk (the cubic footage of the structure), and the maximum floor area ratio, among other building characteristics.[13] Other municipalities have required design review if the new house is to be substantially larger than the one it will replace. However, like so many other matters in planning, such restrictions can be argued both ways. The goals of such restrictions seem quite reasonable, but they do constitute an infringement on the rights of the would-be buyer and may also impose a loss on the homeowner who wants to sell his or her home. The possibilities for litigation seem to be considerable.

A number of municipalities ranging from New York City to Santa Monica have attempted to render housing more affordable through rent controls. Economists, by and large, are against the practice. They argue that rent controls encourage disinvestment in those units subject to controls and that fear that controls will be extended to new units reduces the rate of new construction. Thus they conclude that controls reduce housing quality and exacerbate housing shortages. However, regardless of the wisdom of controls, no list of policies that address the question of affordability would be complete without mentioning them.

A single community generally cannot do a great deal with regard to low- and moderate-income housing. Federal monies for housing are in relatively short supply. Even if the community makes every effort to see that its land-use controls do not preclude lower-cost housing types, the fact is that any new unsubsidized housing is expensive. The ability of the community to subsidize housing through either CD funds or its own revenues is limited by other demands on the budget and the willingness of the majority of citizens to be taxed for that purpose. Still, as indicated above there is a certain amount that can be done if the community wants to do it, but as noted, not every community wants to do it.

Federal Requirements

The particular federal program that has propelled literally thousands of communities into preparing formal housing plans has been the CDBG program. One requirement for the receipt of funds, whether to be used for housing or other purposes, is the Housing Assistance Plan (HAP). At present, the rules require the community to certify in its application for CD funds that it is following a HAP approved by HUD. Briefly, HUD requires the plan to contain an inventory of the community housing stock and numerical goals for its improvement. It also requires the plan specifically to provide an analysis of the housing needs of lower-income renters. Finally, the plan must state how the goals are to be met.

Exactly what aspects of the housing stock and the housing market the study covers may vary substantially from one community to another. If the study is oriented primarily toward matters that are eligible for federal funding, it is likely to focus on the quality and cost of units available for less affluent households.

Good objective measures of housing stock quality are hard to come by. Several decades ago the U.S. Bureau of the Census had its census takers enumerate "deteriorated" and "dilapidated" units but subsequently decided that such judgments were too subjective to provide good data. However, the bureau does provide data on the number of units that do not contain complete kitchen and bathroom facilities. Imperfect as this measure is, it has been used as a "proxy" for housing quality. Another measure of housing quality, though it has nothing to do with the physical quality of the unit, is overcrowding. The U.S. Bureau of the Census defines overcrowding as a situation in which there is more than one resident per room.

Finally, much attention has been paid to the question of whether low- and moderate-income households can afford housing. For this judgment, planners tend to rely on rent–income ratios, a data item that is also supplied by the U.S. Bureau of the Census. At one time it was thought that a household should not have to spend more than 25 percent of its income on rent. Recently, housing economists have used 35 percent as a rule of thumb. Either figure is somewhat arbitrary.

Thus the community can make some estimates of the number of units that may be substandard and the number of households in need of rental assistance. Vacancy rates may also give some indication of whether the community should be seriously concerned with increasing the total number of units.

A More Comprehensive Approach to Planning for Housing

The community, in studying its housing situation, need not be bound by the necessities of federal approval and federal subsidies. One long-term issue to be considered is simply the numerical adequacy of the entire municipal housing stock. Projections of population and employment can be used to approximate future housing needs. A general understanding of market dynamics is also important. Units are added by new construction, sometimes by the subdivision of existing units and sometimes by the conversion of nonresidential to residential units. Units are lost through fire, demolition, abandonment, and the conversion of residential to nonresidential units (e.g., the conversion of a single-family house into an office). Market forces such as personal income, rents and prices in adjacent communities, land costs, the competition between residential and commercial uses for space, and so on shape the long-term change in the municipal housing stock.

For a long-term analysis, attention should be paid to supply factors, including land, utilities, street capacity, and the like. Thus a really comprehensive study would go well beyond the low- and moderate-income housing questions and attempt to understand the dynamics of the entire housing market. We might also note that housing for low- and moderate-income residents and housing for more prosperous residents are not totally separate matters. If neighborhood conditions deteriorate, we may witness a flight of the prosperous and their replacement by low- and moderate-income households. Conversely, if demand for housing is strong and the supply of housing limited, we may see prosperous households displacing poor households, the gentrification process visible in many cities.

THE HOUSING BUBBLE AND THE PROBLEM OF ABANDONMENT

At the end of the 1990s, housing prices in the United States began to rise very rapidly. The most widely quoted housing price index, the Case-Shiller index, showed that from 2000 to the second quarter of 2006, housing prices in the United States rose by 90 percent. After adjusting for inflation, that was a real increase of 61 percent over a six-year period.[14] In the second quarter of 2006, housing prices peaked and then headed downhill rapidly. What had looked to some as a trend that might continue indefinitely turned out to be a bubble, one that burst in 2006. Financial bubbles have been with the human race for many centuries. Perhaps some of the cause is inherent in the human psyche and best explained by psychologists and behavioral economists. One factor behind bubbles in housing or other assets is easy money, meaning credit that is readily available at low interest rates, for that facilitates the buying of assets to hold as a speculation for later sale. The U.S. economy at the turn of the twenty-first century was bubble-prone. There was the so-called dot.com crash of 2000, in which the NASDAQ index lost about three-fourths of its value.[15] About two years later the U.S. stock market as a whole went over the top, and the major stock indexes lost close to half their value.

The housing bubble was undoubtedly driven by many of the same psychological and monetary forces that had driven the two stock market bubbles. But it also had another driving force, which takes some explaining.

Some decades ago most mortgages were issued by banks, which then held the mortgages to maturity. The bank thus wanted to be reasonably certain that the borrower would be able to repay the mortgage. That meant requiring a substantial down payment and also taking a careful look at the borrower's income and other financial assets and obligations.

In recent years the mortgage finance picture changed radically. More and more mortgages came to be *securitized*: After the mortgage was issued, it was bundled with many other mortgages into a bond (security) that was then sold to an investor. The buyer could be anywhere, maybe in the United States or maybe in Paris or Zurich or Hong Kong. In the 1990s and into the first decade of this century, the process of securitization became more and more complex, and it turned out that there was lots of money to be made by securitizing mortgages.

A prototypical transaction might look like this: A buyer gets a mortgage from a mortgage broker. The broker makes a variety of fees for originating the mortgage and is thus highly motivated to originate as many mortgages as possible. The broker almost immediately sells the mortgage to an investment bank which combines that mortgage with other mortgages into a bond or bonds. These bonds are referred to generically as *Collateralized Debt Obligations (CDOs)*—the collateral being the houses for which the mortgages were written.[16] The investment bank then sells the CDOs to investors and makes a profit on this sale. In some cases CDOs are made up not of mortgages directly but of other CDOs, sometimes referred to in the trade as CDOs squared, and then sold to investors. Note that because they no longer hold the mortgages, neither the mortgage broker in this illustration nor the investment bank has any direct financial interest in whether the homeowners will be able to continue to make their monthly mortgage payments in the years to come. The investors, though, do have a long-term interest in whether the homeowners continue to pay on their mortgages. Investors were reassured by the good bond ratings that bond-rating agencies such as Moodys Investors Service or Standard and Poor's gave to the CDOs. Unfortunately, many CDOs were rated much higher than they should have been.[17]

With all of the money to be made in securitization, mortgage lending became looser and looser. Mortgages were made with no down payment. Some mortgages were made without the buyer having to document his or her income. These "no doc" loans were commonly referred to in the business as "liar loans" for evident reasons. Some mortgage brokers spoke of NINJA loans, NINJA being an acronym for "no income, no job or assets." Some mortgages allowed the buyer to make interest-only payments for some months. Some mortgages, called "reverse amortization" mortgages, allowed buyers for some time to make payments of less than the interest, with the difference being added to the principal. Some mortgages carried low interest rates, referred to as "teaser rates," that "reset" to a higher rate after a few years. And so on.

Thus some people who were financially naive or did not understand the contracts they were signing got sucked into purchases that they couldn't afford. Others felt that the prices of housing would keep rising and so if they couldn't make the payments, they could always sell the house, settle the mortgage, and walk away with some profit. In some cases lenders may have had the same view, which caused them to be less careful about to whom they lent. As long as housing prices kept rising, everything seemed fine. In fact, lots of people made quick money "flipping houses"—that is, buying a house, holding it for a short time, and reselling it at a higher price.

The bubble was also, to some degree, inflated by well-intentioned public policy whose downside was not anticipated. For some years it was federal policy to expand homeownership as much as possible. And, in fact, owner-occupied housing as a percentage of all housing reached its all-time peak, about 68 percent, just before the housing bubble burst. The Community Reinvestment Act (CRA), which required banks to invest a substantial part of their deposits in their own market areas, put pressure on banks to make mortgage loans that they might otherwise have hesitated to make. Then, too, Congress and the federal government put pressure on the Federal National Mortgage Association ("Fannie Mae") and the Federal Home Loan Mortgage Corporation ("Freddie Mac") to facilitate mortgage lending to homebuyers who were not qualified for conventional loans.

While Fannie and Freddie did not themselves issue any of the exotic subprime mortgages described here, they did buy billions of dollars' worth of CDOs that contained such mortgages and thus indirectly helped fuel the bubble. Part of their motivation was simply profit. They saw the high interest rates on these securities but failed to realize how risky they were. Fannie and Freddie were at the time privately held GSEs (Government Sponsored Enterprises) and until the bubble broke returned handsome profits to their investors. When the bubble burst and the value of CDOs plummeted, both organizations were saved from defaulting on their bonds only by a very large infusion of federal money. The federal government was not legally bound to save them, but not to have done so would have made the financial crisis of 2008 much worse, for a huge number of individuals and financial organizations held Fannie's and Freddie's bonds. Fannie and Freddie were both taken over by the federal government under a conservatorship and have remained so since late 2008. As of mid-2011 the federal government's losses on Fannie Mae and Freddie Mac were estimated to be in the $165 billion range. This figure might go higher if the value of many securities that the federal government purchased from Fannie and Freddie decline further.

When the bubble burst homebuyers who couldn't make their mortgage payments no longer had the option of selling and walking away undamaged. If they could sell at all in a falling real estate market, it meant taking a loss, sometimes a very big one. Many homeowners, especially recent ones, found that their houses were now worth less than what they owed on them—they were "underwater" or "upside down" in real estate jargon. Some people in this condition struggled to make their payments. Others abandoned their houses, either because they could not make their payments or because they chose not to sink more money into a losing investment and instead just "walked." One loads up the moving van and, as the last act, places the keys in an envelope and mails them to the bank—hence the expression "jingle mail."

As it became apparent that many people would default on their mortgages, it also became apparent that many billions of dollars of CDOs were worth a lot less than their face value. This spread panic throughout the U.S. financial system, caused credit markets to lock up, and helped push the United States into recession. That of course caused many people to lose their jobs and that, in turn, added to the flood of mortgage defaults. The effect on financial markets quickly spread beyond the United States in part because so many of the CDOs had been bought by investors, both individual and institutional, outside the United States.

The effects of all this "bad paper" coming from the U.S. housing market hit financial markets in indirect ways, too. For example, many buyers of CDOs insured them against default with Credit Default Swaps (CDSs). When large numbers of CDOs defaulted, many issuers of CDSs were pushed toward insolvency and they, in turn, pulled their creditors down.

The collapse of AIG, the world's largest insurance company, came about in large measure because it had sold huge numbers of CDSs on which it could not make good. The U.S. government's bailout of AIG to the extent of well over $100 billion was made not out of sympathy for AIG but because the company had so many financial commitments all over the world that its collapse would have been an international financial catastrophe. It was too big to be allowed to fail.

Why so many investors and financial institutions all over the world were willing to buy so many securities made up of such shaky material is a serious question. The complexity of the financing—that is, the lack of transparency—was one factor. Overly optimistic bond ratings were another. No doubt the matters of psychology and crowd behavior previously noted were part of the answer. In any event, a great many very smart people bought a great deal of very bad paper.

This is a very abbreviated account of the mortgage crisis. Its effects on the U.S. economy—and, given the extent of globalization, the world economy—have been huge. It should be noted that the financial meltdown that began in September of 2008, though apparently precipitated by the mortgage crisis, did have its roots in other financial excesses as well.[18]

The problems stemming from the collapse of the housing price bubble and the financial crisis proved to be very persistent. By 2011, three years after the financial crisis, new housing construction in the United States was in the range of one-half million units per year, a little less than one-third of what it averaged during the first six years of the previous decade. Housing prices in many areas were still declining, albeit at a much lower rate than before, and millions of homeowners were still underwater. Economists were concerned that as long as many homeowners were underwater they would be very cautious financially, which would reduce aggregate demand and slow the recovery from what was coming to be called "the Great Recession."

One reason that new construction was so slow was that many markets were flooded with foreclosed properties that sold at such low prices that new houses could not compete with them. The foreclosure process was also bedeviled with serious legal problems. One concerned the Mortgage Electronic Registration System (MERS). States had long required fees and the filing of papers when properties changed hands. But banks and other mortgage lenders found this expensive and cumbersome, especially as the volume of transactions increased during the housing boom of the preceding decade. So many of them took to simply registering them electronically with MERS, a relatively small company located in Reston, Virginia, and staffed primarily by computer specialists, not mortgage specialists. When foreclosure cases began piling up in the courts, people who didn't want to be pushed out of their homes resisted by claiming that their mortgage holding firm (the mortgagee) did not have a valid claim on the property because it had not registered the mortgage properly according to state law. Where mortgages had been sold a number of times they could also argue that because of the absence of a complete paper trail there was uncertainty about who had the right to foreclose.

Another source of delay in the foreclosure process was what came to be called "robosigning." When banks were overwhelmed with massive numbers of foreclosures, many turned to law firms that specialized in foreclosure work, or that came into existence to meet the demand for such work. It turned out that in many cases firms' employees signed off on foreclosure paperwork at such high rates of speed that they could not possibly have read the documents they were signing. Homeowners resisted foreclosure on these grounds, too and, understandably, many judges were sympathetic to them. A group of states' attorneys general became involved in the matter with proposals for financial penalties and proposed procedural rules.

At this writing the situation is not resolved. Mortgage lending standards have tightened and sizable down payments and proof of ability to repay are now required. The days of the no-doc and other exotic mortgages are over. It is also clear that it will be quite awhile before the huge overhang of foreclosures will be ended.

In 2011, banks and other mortgage lenders were still traumatized by the bursting of the housing bubble and unwilling to lend much without very firm guarantees. As a result, over 90 percent of all residential mortgages were guaranteed by Fannie Mae or Freddie Mac. Without those two agencies the mortgage market would have been close to dead. The federal government has attempted to reduce the number of foreclosures by means of programs that encourage banks to renegotiate the terms of mortgages by some combination of reduced interest rates, stretched-out durations, and reduced principal amounts. The largest of these is the Home Affordable Modification Program (HAMP). By 2011 the HAMP program had been involved in the renegotiation of about one-half million mortgages, which did put a little dent in the foreclosure problem, but it has not been regarded as a major success and by the end of 2011 the rate of HAMP renegotiations had slowed considerably. The amount of money that HAMP offered banks for each mortgage renegotiated was small and the paperwork was substantial. Then, too, it became apparent that many homeowners whose mortgages were renegotiated soon fell into default again, in part because of weak job markets. In many cases the mortgages that banks were asked to renegotiate were ones that the banks did not own but merely serviced. In that case the bank might need consent of the parties who had bought the CDO that contained the mortgage. That could pose problems in itself, especially if the CDO had been resold and the trail of ownership was complicated. As of mid-2011 there were in the range of 3 million houses in the United States facing the probability of foreclosure.

The Implications for Municipalities

With the previously described background, let us turn to the implications, for municipalities and their housing stock, of the decline in housing prices and the high rates of mortgage defaults. When mortgage defaults are few, banks simply foreclose (regardless of whether they hold the mortgage or merely service it for its holder), the property is resold, and the entire foreclosure event is of little or no concern to the municipality. When housing prices are falling and defaults are frequent, as became the case in so many municipalities in 2008 and 2009, the situation becomes a matter of great common concern.

Abandoned properties, especially if there are many of them, lose value very rapidly. They are often prey to vandalism. In many cases scavengers will come in and strip the property of plumbing fixtures, pipes, electrical wiring—anything that can be resold—and often do a great deal of damage in extracting what they want. There can be problems with squatters and drug users. Arson or accidental fires can also be a problem. If the original owners feel angry or victimized about having to move, they may damage the property through neglect or vandalism. Abandoned and neglected properties drag down the market value of nearby properties, which puts more property owners underwater and makes them more pessimistic that the situation will ever improve. That, of course, will push some of *them* into abandonment, and the situation feeds on itself. To say that abandoned houses can by their presence cause more abandonment is just a variation on the old real estate cliché that the three most important characteristics of a property are location, location, and location.

Not only does neighborhood quality become a problem for local governments, but defaults can be a serious financial problem for local governments and school districts, for whom property taxes are a very important revenue source. Abandoned properties don't pay property taxes.

Just how hard municipalities were hit by the recent foreclosure crisis varied greatly. In general, places that had experienced the greatest run-up in prices in the preceding years were most vulnerable. Places where a large part of the housing stock was very new also tended to be hard-hit because many homeowners and speculators had little equity and quickly found themselves underwater (negative equity) when prices slumped. California and parts of the Southeast and Southwest were especially vulnerable for these reasons. So too were places that resembled the "boomburgs" noted at the end of Chapter 2 for the same reasons. But other types of areas were also hit hard. For example, the Cleveland and Detroit areas were hit very hard in part because job losses made many people unable to make their mortgage payments.

What Can Governments Do?

Dealing with the problem is very difficult for a local government both because of the large sums of money involved and because the roots of the problem lie outside the purview of the local government. The roots are clearly in national trends—credit market conditions, housing prices, and labor market conditions. If housing prices in one municipality decline, that will exert a downward pull on housing markets in nearby communities. If unemployment is up in one municipality, that will inevitably make for weaker labor markets in nearby communities, and so on.

Municipal governments can do some things to deal with the foreclosure and abandonment problem. A municipality may focus law enforcement efforts on the area to reduce arson and vandalism. Where properties are beyond saving, it may take steps to expedite their demolition. It might use Community Development funds to strengthen adjacent areas to keep the blight from spreading. Where the municipality comes into possession of abandoned properties, it might use some variation on Baltimore's urban homesteading program to put in owners who will maintain and improve the property. To the extent that mortgages are held by local banks, a municipal government might use its influence to encourage borrowers and lenders to try to work out terms that avoid foreclosure. But, in truth, the amount that a municipality can do is limited. Few if any municipalities have the funds necessary to save large numbers of homeowners from foreclosure even if they have the political will to do so.

SUMMARY

The Urban Renewal program began with the Housing Act of 1949 and was terminated by Congress in 1973. Local public agencies used a mixture of local and federal funds plus the power of eminent domain to acquire and clear redevelopment sites. Sites or portions of sites were then made available to developers at a fraction of their cost. The combination of heavy subsidy and eminent domain was intended to solve two major obstacles to urban redevelopment: problems of residual value and site assembly.

As Urban Renewal progressed, it acquired many enemies, primarily because of its displacement effects. By the time Congress ended the program, it had demolished approximately 600,000 housing units, forcing perhaps 2 million people, most of them having low or moderate income, to relocate. It also forced the closure of thousands of small businesses, many of which never reopened. The destruction of the social and economic fabric of neighborhoods was ultimately considered to be an unacceptably high cost.

The year after Urban Renewal was ended, Congress passed the Housing and Community Development Act of 1974. In place of Urban Renewal's clear-and-rebuild approach, Community Development programs have tended to emphasize preservation and improvement. The urban homesteading program noted in connection with the city of Baltimore typifies the emphasis on preserving the existing urban fabric that characterizes many CD programs. As a reaction to what were regarded as the excesses of Urban Renewal, CD legislation contains numerous requirements for citizen participation, particularly that of low- and moderate-income citizens.

Housing plans may be narrowly keyed to federal funding programs, or they may take a broader approach. In the latter case, estimates of housing demand based on employment and demographic studies are compared with projections of future supply in order to estimate future needs. In general, housing is one of the more frustrating items with which the planner deals. The sums of money on the public side are very small compared with total expenditures. Thus the capacity of government programs to affect the basic housing picture is limited. In addition, housing issues are often major sources of social and political controversy within the community.

The chapter ends with the problem of massive foreclosures brought about by the bubble in housing prices that began to collapse in 2006 and an account of the reckless mortgage lending that was one cause of the bubble.

Widespread foreclosures and the consequent abandonment of housing pose very difficult problems for municipalities because of the threat they pose to the overall state of the municipality's housing stock and the erosion of the municipal tax base that they cause. The chapter notes some of the limited steps that municipalities can take to deal with the problem as well as a number of steps the federal government has taken to strengthen the market for housing and reduce the number of foreclosures.

NOTES

1. It can be argued that two other federal programs or policies have actually had more effect on cities than did Urban Renewal. These are (1) the construction of the Interstate Highway System and (2) the structure of the IRS code and the tax benefits it provides for homeownership. However, as powerfully as these may affect cities, they are not specifically urban programs, nor were their urban effects foremost in the minds of the legislators who enacted them. In fact, it seems likely that their urban consequences, though now well recognized, were largely unanticipated.

2. Congressional Research Service, Library of Congress, "The Central City Problem and Urban Renewal Policy," prepared for the Subcommittee on Housing and Urban Affairs, Committee Banking, Housing and Urban Affairs, United States Senate, Washington, DC, 1973. Note: Subsequent figures on Urban Renewal expenditures or any other federal housing or urban development programs can be found in the Annual Yearbook, Department of Housing and Urban Development (HUD), Washington, DC.

3. This is a very rough estimate. From 1961, the midpoint year between the start of Urban Renewal and 1973, and the termination of the program in 2011 Bureau of Labor Statistics figures show that the cost of living increased by a multiple of 7.5. That would suggest that federal expenditures on Urban Renewal would be in the $90 to $100 billion range in current dollars.

4. Guy Greer and Alvin W. Hansen, "Urban Redevelopment and Housing," National Planning Association, 1941.

5. Martin Anderson, The Federal Bulldozer, MIT Press, Cambridge, MA, 1964, p. 64.

6. The hypothesis, an old one in urban economics, is that the city incubates small,

growing industries. When they reach a certain degree of maturity, they then move out to more peripheral areas, which provide lower costs, albeit in a somewhat less rich and varied business environment. The city survives, even though it loses one mature industry after another, because it is constantly generating new industries. For an account of this idea, see Wilbur Thompson, A Preface to Urban Economics, Johns Hopkins Press, Baltimore, 1965.

7. The term gentrification comes from gentry and refers to the movement back into older neighborhoods of people of higher economic or social status than the present occupants.

8. Charles Abrams, "Some Blessings of Urban Renewal," in Urban Renewal: The Record and the Controversy, James Q. Wilson, ed., MIT Press, Cambridge, MA, 1966, p. 560.

9. This partial listing is drawn from regulations published in the Federal Register, March 1, 1978, p. 8441. The Federal Register is a daily publication of the federal government and provides detailed regulations for the implementation of legislation passed by the Congress. It runs to many thousands of pages per year.

10. Enforcing such a distinction is not always easy. If the community intended to build a playground in any case but allocates part of its CDBG to that purpose, how can we ever say with certainty how the general purpose funds thus freed have been used? Can we say with certainty that the funds freed by the CD grant have not been used for a purpose that is not an approved CD activity? In fact, can we say with certainty that the knowledge that it was to receive a CDBG did not cause a municipality to tax its property owners at a somewhat lower rate than it would otherwise have done?

11. See Federal Register, March 1, 1978, p. 8462.

12. Table 658, *Statistical Abstract of the United States*, 2006, 126th ed.

13. Terry S. Szold, "Mansionization and Its Discontents," *Journal of the American Planning Association*, vol. 71, no. 2, Spring 2005, pp. 189–200.

14. The Case-Shiller index is constructed from the prices of houses that have sold more than once during the time period for which the index is done, thus eliminating the effect of new construction and isolating, in effect, the change in market value of the existing housing stock. If the price of newly constructed housing were figured in, the rate of the price increase would be even greater.

15. The acronym is from the National Association of Securities Dealers. The index is heavily weighted to computer and other high-technology stocks.

16. The terminology can be confusing. A bond that is backed by mortgages can be referred to as a Mortgage Backed Security (MBS). But an MBS is one type of member of the larger class of Collateralized Debt Obligations (CDOs). The collateral in the case of the MBS is the mortgages. Therefore, what one person refers to as

an MBS might be refferred to by another person as a CDO.

17. It has been suggested that one reason for this was conflict of interest. Bond rating agencies made a great deal of money from rating CDOs, and the party that wanted the CDO might indicate, subtly or otherwise, that if the rating agency was overly severe in its ratings it would take its business elsewhere. It is true that for many years bond rating agencies faced this same potential conflict of interest with municipal bonds and, so far as is known, there was no problem. On the other hand, the amounts of money involved were much smaller and so the temptations were smaller.

18. For a very concise and user-friendly explanation of the causes of the crisis, see Paul Krugman, *The Return of Depression Economics and the Crisis of 2008*, W. W. Norton Co., New York, 2009. See also Nouriel Roubini and Stephen Mihm, *Crisis Economics: A Crash Course in the Future of Finance*, The Penguin Press, New York, 2010 and Andrew R. Sorkin, *Too Big to Fail: How Wall Street and Washington Fought to Save the Financial System—and Themselves*, Penguin, New York, 2010.

SELECTED BIBLIOGRAPHY

DALTON, LINDA C., HOCH, CHARLES J., AND SO, FRANK S., *The Practice of Local Government Planning*, 3rd ed., International City/County Management Association, Washington, DC, 2000, chap. 11.

FORD, LARRY R., *America's New Downtowns*, Johns Hopkins University Press, Baltimore, 2003.

PAUMIER, CY, *Creating a Vibrant City Center*, Urban Land Institute, Washington, DC, 2004.

WILSON, JAMES Q., ed., *Urban Renewal: The Record and the Controversy*, MIT Press, Cambridge, MA, 1966.

CHAPTER 12

Transportation Planning

In this chapter we consider transportation planning as practiced at the municipal and metropolitan levels. Before we begin, some background on transportation trends since World War II will be useful.

RECENT TRENDS IN URBAN TRANSPORTATION _____

In 1945 the United States had a population of 133 million people who owned 25 million automobiles. By 2008 the U.S. population had grown to 304 million, a factor of about 2.3. Automobile registrations had grown to 137 million, a factor of 5.5. But that figure greatly understates the growth of privately owned automotive transportation, for sport-utility vehicles (SUVs) and vans are classified as light trucks and counted separately. In 2008 there were approximately 101 million vehicles described as "two axle four tired trucks," which effectively means SUVs, vans, and pickups, a very large percentage of which are used for personal transportation.[1]

One powerful force behind the increase in automobile ownership was the large increase in average real personal income in the years following World War II. Not only did the general prosperity enable more people to own automobiles, but that same prosperity also facilitated a great wave of suburbanization. The postwar suburbanization and the increase in automobile ownership were complementary phenomena. Widespread automobile ownership facilitates suburbanization. On the other hand, moving from the central city to the suburbs increases one's need for an automobile.

 The public transportation situation in the postwar period was very different. As the term *public transportation or transit* is used here, it refers to buses, subways (refered to as "heavy rail" in the transportation statistics), light rail (a term for trolleylike vehicles), commuter rail, and the like. It does not include intercity rail or bus, air transportation, or taxicabs. Ridership reached an all-time high in 1945, when wartime employment peaked, gasoline was rationed, and civilian production of automobiles had been suspended for several years. From 19 billion trips by fare-paying passengers in 1945, the total declined to a postwar low of 5.6 billion in 1975. By 2009 that figure had risen to 10.4 billion, in part because of heavy federal investment in public transportation over the last three decades and partly because of increases in the price of gasoline.[2] Despite this increase, transit still constituted a smaller percentage of all trips in 2009 than it had in 1975.

Public transportation usage is distributed very unevenly in the United States. Of the 10.4 billion total annual trips 3.2 billion—almost 31 percent—are provided by a single agency, the Metropolitan Transportation Authority (MTA), which covers New York City and the New York State portion of the New York metropolitan area. Chicago is second at just over one-half billion trips a year, and Los Angeles is third at just under half a billion. For much of the nation public transportation is minimal. Subway (heavy rail) transportation is even more unevenly distributed. A single system, the New York City subways, account, for 2.4 billion trips per year, over two-thirds of the national total.[3]

The decline in public transportation is not hard to explain. Increased automobile ownership eliminated millions of potential transit customers. Suburbanization meant the movement of millions of households into areas where, because of reduced congestion, the automobile works better than in central cities. Conversely, the dispersed suburban land-use pattern makes the provision of public transportation, which depends on high volumes on fixed routes, more difficult. The spreading out of residences and workplaces with the process of suburbanization complicates both the *collection* (getting the rider to the public transit vehicle) and the *distribution* (getting the rider from the vehicle to his or her final destination) problems.

Public transportation is also bedeviled by the trade-off between the spacing of stops and average speed. The more closely spaced the stops are, the lower is the average speed. But increasing the distance between stops makes the collection and distribution problems more severe. Because of the need for frequent stops, public transportation tends to be slow. In 2009 the average speed for all public transportation vehicles in the United States was 14.9 miles per hour (mph). Buses averaged 12.5 mph and commuter rail with its less frequent stops and its own right-of-way averaged 31.2 mph.[4] These figures, which do not include waiting times, have not changed appreciably or many years, nor can they readily be changed; minimum loading times and the maximum acceleration and deceleration rates that are acceptable are not a matter of what technology is capable of, but rather what is safe and comfortable for passengers.

The ideal environment for public transportation is seen in a number of the large, older, eastern cities—with masses of jobs concentrated in the urban core and masses of apartments concentrated near transit stops. This arrangement simplifies the collection and distribution problems and provides a large enough market to sustain frequent service. The high densities also make automobile usage less attractive. But that pattern of development is very much the opposite of the dominant land-use trends since World War II. Transportation to work is emphasized here because it is the mainstay of public transportation demand. When public transportation use declines, it is generally the journey to work that holds up best. Trips for shopping, recreation, and the like fall off more rapidly.

Measured in percentage terms, the biggest growth area in transit has been in *paratransit,* also referred to as *demand response systems.* These systems, with names like Dial-a-Ride, send a vehicle in response to a call. They do not operate on fixed routes or have a fixed schedule. Such systems may serve a specialized population such as individuals who are disabled or elderly, or they may service an area in which it is not economically feasible to provide scheduled, fixed-route public transportation. In that sense, these systems are a kind of publicly supported taxi service to serve those with few other transportation choices.

As Table 12–1 makes clear, the great majority of commuters get to work by automobile, most of them driving alone. From 1990 to 2000, total commutation to work increased by 13.2 million people. Of that increase, 12.9 million was in the *drove alone category.*

TABLE 12–1 Transportation to Work in 1990 and 2000 (figures in millions)

Mode	Persons in 1990	Persons in 2000
All modes	115.1	128.3
Car, truck, or van	99.6	112.7
Drove alone	84.2	97.1
Public transportation	6.1	6.1
Bus	3.4	3.2
Subway or elevated	1.8	1.9
Railroad	0.6	0.7
Selected other		
Walk	4.8	3.8
Work at home	3.4	4.2
Ride bicycle	0.5	0.5

Note: Comparable figures from the 2010 census are not available at this writing. Given that there has not been a very large change in public transportation usage over the last decade it is unlikely that they will be very different.

Sources: *1990 Census of the Population, Social and Economic Characteristics,* Table 18; and 2000 census, Summary File 3 (SF 3), Table P30, U.S. Bureau of the Census, Department of Commerce.

The Question of Intercity Rail Transportation

In the last several years there has been an upsurge in interest in intercity rail service as well as the intracity service just discussed. Increases in motor fuel costs in 2007 and 2008 were one factor. Highway congestion, noted in connection with smart growth, and concern about global warming were others, for intercity rail has a considerably smaller carbon footprint than either automobile or air transportation. Finally, there has been a demonstration effect. The American who rides on, say, France's TGV or Spain's AVE and experiences a smooth, quiet trip that leaves and arrives on schedule and cruises at 170 mph is likely to ask the simple question "why can't we do that here?"[5]

As a result of the increased interest, the 2009 economic stimulus bill contained some funding for intercity rail service and for studies of a number of possible major routes. There have been state initiatives as well, the most ambitious of which is California's Proposition 1A, which passed in November 2008. The California High-Speed Rail Authority quotes part of the proposition as follows:

> To provide Californians a safe, convenient, affordable, and reliable alternative to driving and high gas prices; to provide good-paying jobs and improve California's economy while reducing air pollution, global warming greenhouse gases, and our dependence on foreign oil, shall $9.95 billion in bonds be issued to establish a clean, efficient high-speed train service linking Southern California, the Sacramento San Joaquin Valley, and the San Francisco Bay Area, with at least 90 percent of bond funds spent for specific projects, with federal and private matching funds required, and all bond funds subject to independent audits?[6]

A bit of history about U.S. intercity passenger service is useful here. After about 1920 U.S. intercity rail transportation began to decline, largely as a result of competition from an increasing number of privately owned automobiles operating on a newly improved road network. After World War II the situation for intercity rail became even worse as automobile ownership steadily increased, the pattern of land use became more dispersed, and competition from the airlines grew for the longer intercity routes. What happened to intercity passenger rail was similar, albeit at a larger geographic scale, to what happened to intracity public transportation. Other attractive modes became available and the land-use pattern changed in a way that made the collection and distribution problem more and more difficult.

In May 1971, responding to the continuous deterioration of intercity rail passenger service, Congress created the National Railroad Passenger Corporation to promote passenger rail service. At present almost all intercity rail service in the United States is provided by the corporation, operating under the name AmTrak. AmTrak basically pays a number of railroads to provide service. Because most of the service is over the railroads' freight lines, the kind of very high-speed service that is found in Europe is not possible here.[7] A European-level of service would require a higher-quality roadbed and also separate tracks so that passenger service would not be interrupted by the needs of the railroads' most important business, freight transport. Altogether AmTrak provides service over about 21,000 route miles. Like transit, passenger rail cannot survive without subsidy. Currently, AmTrak receives $2.6 billion a year in federal assistance.

AmTrak is generally supported by environmentalists and those in the political center and left. It is tenaciously opposed by conservatives, who see it as a poor use of public funds and an unjustified government intrusion into what should be left to the marketplace.

From a planner's perspective the key factor here is concentration. To the extent that such rail transportation can be developed, it promotes more compact development by making central locations more valuable. As was noted in connection with transit, the land-use pattern that favors intercity rail and that intercity rail will, in turn, reinforce is exactly the opposite of the direction that land-use development has taken from the 1920s to the present time.

Whether intercity rail service will make the comeback that its proponents hope for remains to be seen. This writer has his doubts. Cost is one matter. The proposed California system—which would, if built as fully envisioned, provide high-quality service all the way from Sacramento in the north to the Los Angeles area in the south—is currently estimated at a construction cost of $45 billion, and if the experience with many other projects is a guide this figure is probably low.

At present, federal and state budget deficits have largely dried up the funding for intercity rail projects, at least for the near term, a matter discussed in more detail Chapter 15. Another concern is the development of new automotive technologies, a matter on which a huge amount of money is now being spent. To a lesser degree, developments in aviation technology for shorter trips, say in the two to three hundred mile range, will also be a factor. After all, one cannot think about how well an enterprise will do without thinking about what its competition might do.

PAYING FOR TRANSPORTATION

To understand transportation policy, it is important to understand how private and public transportation are financed. In terms of direct costs, private transportation is largely self-financed. Vehicle purchase, fuel, maintenance, insurance, parking, and other costs are paid directly by vehicle owners and operators. Roads and highways are, by and large, paid for by a variety of taxes and charges levied on automobile users. Such charges include license fees, registration fees, and state and federal gasoline taxes. For example, federal contributions to road construction come from the Highway Trust Fund, which is supplied largely by federal excise taxes on the sale of motor fuel.

It has been argued, however, that the automobile exacts a variety of hidden costs that are not so covered—air pollution; death and injury from accidents; and a more scattered pattern of land use that results in increased costs of public services. If one dislikes the suburbs, one might argue that suburbanization is a cost the automobile has imposed on America. Conversely, if one prefers the suburbs to the city, as millions of Americans evidently do, one can say that suburbia is a blessing the automobile has conferred on America. But regardless of these arguable matters, the fact is that in a direct sense, automobile transportation is primarily paid for by those who use it.

The economics of public transportation are very different. In 2009 total expenditures on public transportation in the United States were $55.2 billion (about $5.30 per trip). Fares came to about $12.3 billion (about $1.18 per trip).[8] The difference, about 78 percent of the total, was paid for by nonfare revenues of transit agencies such as tolls and taxes, and by a variety of grants and subsidies from local, state, and federal governments. Without heavy subsidization, public transportation would virtually disappear in the United States.

We subsidize public transportation for several reasons. There are people who cannot use private transportation, and society must provide them with some means of personal mobility. Such people include those too young to drive, those too old to drive, those who have some disability that prevents them from driving, and those who cannot afford automobile ownership. We also subsidize public transportation because we think it improves circulation in urban areas by reducing the number of private vehicles in use. Shifting people from cars to buses or trains may also improve environmental quality by reducing the total amount of emissions. Heavier reliance on public transportation also permits a more compact urban design, which many planners favor. These last several points suggest that subsidizing public transportation confers benefits on nonusers as well as users.

Finally, some suggest that we ought to subsidize public transportation as a matter of income redistribution. The argument is that by providing at below cost a product used more heavily by low-income people, we are, in effect, transferring income to them. This is the weakest of the arguments because subsidizing transit is a very inefficient means of transferring income. Not all poor people use public transportation, nor are all users of public transportation poor. In fact, patrons of at least one type of transit, commuter rail lines, have above-average incomes.

TRANSPORTATION PLANNING AND LAND USE

Land use and transportation planning are very much a chicken and egg situation. In the short term, land use shapes the demand for transportation. Many a highway has been built because population or commercial growth produced congestion and delays that generated political pressures to deal with the situation. On the other hand, the provision of roads changes land values and thus alters the intensity with which land is used, and, with that outcome, alters the entire pattern of land use. The Interstate Highway System, to take the largest example, was designed to facilitate movement of vehicles from one existing urban center to another, something it does very successfully (see Figure 12–1). However, it has also done a great deal to reshape urban areas, an effect that was not one of the motivations behind its construction. Beyond that, it has reshaped the balance between metropolitan and nonmetropolitan areas in the United States by making formerly isolated rural areas far more accessible than they were a generation ago. In fact, it is believed that much of the movement of manufacturing activity out of metropolitan areas and into rural areas occurred for just this reason. Thus the system has had a major impact on the economies of both metropolitan and nonmetropolitan areas.

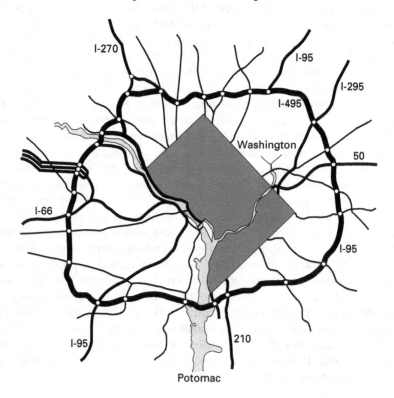

FIGURE 12–1 The Interstate Highway System with its ring road, or "beltway," design creates masses of highly accessible land outside the city, particularly where radial routes coming out of the city intersect the beltway. Though not intended in that way, this feature of the system has been a powerful force for moving people and jobs out of the central city.

In the ideal case, transportation planning and land-use planning go hand in hand. At the national level, this has clearly not been the case. At the state level, it sometimes is and sometimes is not. In the best case, state highway departments will take into account the fact that their decisions not only affect how the population now in place is served but also shape land use for decades to come. Highway planning and more general land-use planning are coordinated. In the less satisfactory case, the highway engineers tend to think in terms of meeting demand rather than a combination of meeting demand and shaping the future of land use.

It is often at the municipal level that transportation and land-use planning are most closely coordinated. The issues are simpler, and the numbers of people involved are smaller. Thus coordination is easier. The fact that both the planners and the highway department report to the same mayor and the same city council can prevent them from going off in different directions.

One current example of a close integration between transportation planning and land-use planning is the Atlanta Beltline, now in the early stages of development. If the project materializes as designed its core element will be a 22-mile light-rail loop largely on disused railroad rights-of-way around Atlanta's central business district. The loop is planned in conjunction with a series of parks and connecting multiuse trails. It will also be coordinated with affordable apartment and single-family housing developments and a number of "economic development" areas. The intention behind the plan is to take what is now a barrier and blocker of development—the disused rail lines—and turn them into an attractor of people and jobs. Numerous disused rail lines have been turned into trails and linear parks, but this is the first, or certainly one of the first, plan that would use abandoned rail rights-of-way as a major element in replanning a substantial part of a city. The Beltline is included in Mobility 2030, the Atlanta Regional Commission's overall plan for transportation in the multicounty Atlanta area (See Chapter 16 for a description of the commission). The origin of the plan is unusual. It began in 1999 with a masters thesis at Georgia Tech by Bryan Gravel. The next year he and two other students sent summaries of the thesis to a number of legislators and other prominent Atlantans. The idea proved compelling and within a few years work was underway. The first section of park was opened in 2009, and work on the parks and trails component continues.

THE TRANSPORTATION PLANNING PROCESS

Transportation planning is a basic function of many planning agencies, for adequate circulation traditionally has been a major planning goal. As practiced in the last several decades, particularly at the multijurisdictional level, it is perhaps the most elaborate and mathematically well-developed area of planning. The modern multijurisdictional transportation planning process represents a fusion of engineering, economics, and urban planning, all facilitated by modern computing equipment. The field in its present form was brought into being by a coincidence of forces shortly after the end of World War II. The rapid increase in automobile ownership and the suburban housing boom created a massive demand for increased highway capacity. The Highway Act of 1954 provided 50 percent matching subsidies for urban highways and funds for transportation planning. It also required planning as a condition of eligibility for the matching subsidies—still another example of the conditioning of the local planning scene by federal funding requirements. In 1956 Congress passed the National Defense Highway Act, which initiated the building of the Interstate Highway System. (See Chapter 17.) Federal legislation and funding thus set off a wave of highway building in the decades after the war. The digital computer, which was invented at the end of the war and became a practical planning tool a decade to a decade-and-a-half later, made it possible to "crunch" huge amounts of data and thus make feasible the modern style of highway planning.

The following pages focus on highway planning at the metropolitan level. At smaller geographic levels, the process is necessarily simpler and less mathematical. More than most other planning processes, transportation planning necessitates a multijurisdictional effort, for the flow of travelers is no respecter of municipal boundaries. Thus the same communities that may do their land-use planning in relative isolation will often be part of an area-wide metropolitan transportation planning process.

Modeling Metropolitan Area Transportation

The goal of the transportation planning process is to assist governments in providing an adequate transportation system at an acceptable cost. This involves modeling the behavior of the present system, estimating future travel demand, and estimating how changes in the system will affect travel behavior and the operation of the transportation system in the future.

The following approach described was first used in the 1950s in the Chicago Area Transportation Study (CATS).[9] Variations of it were subsequently done in many other major metropolitan areas. The general approach has also been used in many smaller area studies.[10]

Major transportation planning projects usually involve a four-step procedure for estimating travel movements. Then the merits of different possible changes in the transportation system can be evaluated.

Going through the steps requires building a geographic database. In general, the area in question, say, a metropolitan area, is divided into zones. In the Chicago study and many studies patterned after it, a rectangular grid is imposed on the region, and data are collected for each square in the grid. A typical grid might cover several thousand square miles. In other cases, particularly in smaller studies, the zones may be irregular, with shapes determined by terrain features, neighborhood boundaries, or other characteristics of the land-use pattern.

The data gathered for each zone include both population and economic information. The former includes such items as the number and type of housing units, number of residents, age structure of the population, household income, number of automobiles owned, and similar items. The economic information includes such items as the number of people employed in the area in various occupations and the number of square feet of floor space and land area devoted to retailing, wholesaling, manufacturing, office operations, and other activities. Each of these broad categories may be broken up into a number of subcategories. Sometimes, just total nonresidential floor space is used. It is often a good predictor of how many trips will be attracted to the zone, and it is much less costly to develop than the more detailed category-by-category data.

The Four-Step Process. Once the database is in place, any given transportation alternative can be evaluated. In general, a four-step process is used.

1. *Estimating trip generation.* Before deciding where people will go from a given point of origin, it is customary to estimate how many trips a given place will generate regardless of where those trips are destined. For estimating trip generation from a residential area, variables such as household income, number of persons in the household, number of vehicles owned by the household, and possibly population density might be used to estimate average trips per household per day. Usually the number of vehicular trips is positively related to the first three items and negatively related to the last. The reason for the last relationship is that trips that may be made on foot or by mass transit in a dense area are likely to be made by auto in a sparsely populated area, where trip distances are longer and parking and congestion problems are minimal.

2. *Estimating trip distribution.* After trip generation has been resolved, the next issue is to distribute the trips. Suppose a given zone in a region contains 1,000 households, whose average size, vehicle ownership, and income are known. The total number of trips that they will make can thus be estimated, but the question is how the trips will be distributed among possible destinations. A variety of estimating methods have been developed over the years. The most commonly used is the gravity model, originally developed in the 1920s to analyze shopping patterns. (The original formulation was known as Reilly's Law of Retail Gravitation, and in the past, gravity models were sometimes known as Reilly models.) The force of gravitation between two objects is proportional to the product of their masses and inversely proportional to the square of their distance. By analogy, the force of trip attraction between, say, a housing complex and an office complex would be proportional to the product of the number of households and the number of square feet of office floor space and inversely proportional to some function (perhaps the square or some value near the square) of the distance between them. In principle, then, one might estimate the relative number of trips made from origin A to destinations B and C by computing the relative force of attraction between A and B and between A and C. This process is illustrated in the box on page 247. For a region with a large number of zones, the database and the number of calculations are huge. Thus such a planning exercise was impossible before the computer.

Such an exercise could be done for an actual distribution of housing and floor space or for a hypothesized one. Distance might be taken as straight-line distance from the center of one zone to the center of another. Or it might be taken as actual road mileage, travel time, or some composite of both.

3. *Estimating modal split.*   Where there is more than one mode of transportation available, say, automobile and bus, it is important to apportion by mode the trips distributed in the previous stage. Over the years considerable experience has been accumulated, and a number of mathematical estimating techniques worked out. In general, the two main criteria that determine which mode an individual takes are quality of service and cost. Quality of service is largely a matter of travel time. Quite frequently there is a clear trade-off between speed and cost. For example, in public transportation, commuter rail service is much faster than bus transport, and also substantially more expensive. Knowing the income distribution of the population using public transportation would thus help make estimates of how that population would divide between the two modes.

4. *Predicting trip assignment.*   Once the choice of mode has been settled, the last issue is predicting how trips will be distributed between alternate routes from the same origin to the same destination. Again, the question is resolved by mathematical modeling. Consider that there are two routes, A and B, from zone X to zone Y. Imagine, also, that we begin by assuming that all traffic takes route A. As travelers shift from A to B, travel times on route A fall while those on route B lengthen. Mathematical models are used to predict when equilibrium will be reached.

A SIMPLE GRAVITY MODEL ILLUSTRATION

Assume that in the trip-generation step, we have determined that the area shown as the origin will generate 1,000 trips to work per day. This will go to the three destinations shown in the accompanying figure. The force of attraction of each destination is proportional to its square feet of floor space divided by the square of the distance. Then the trips will be distributed as shown in the calculations below the figure. If there are actual data on trips, the model can be made to approximate reality by adjusting the exponent of distance to some value other than 2.0 or by adjusting the values of distance.

$$\text{Trips to A} = 1{,}000 \quad \dfrac{\dfrac{20{,}000}{4^2}}{\dfrac{20{,}000}{4^2} + \dfrac{70{,}000}{8^2} + \dfrac{80{,}000}{10^2}} = 398$$

$$\text{Trips to B} = 1{,}000 \quad \dfrac{\dfrac{70{,}000}{8^2}}{\dfrac{20{,}000}{4^2} + \dfrac{70{,}000}{8^2} + \dfrac{80{,}000}{10^2}} = 348$$

$$\text{Trips to C} = 1{,}000 \quad \dfrac{\dfrac{80{,}000}{10^2}}{\dfrac{20{,}000}{4^2} + \dfrac{70{,}000}{8^2} + \dfrac{80{,}000}{10^2}} = 254$$

In general these four modeling steps are used in the following way. First, the existing state of the transportation system is modeled mathematically, using the steps just described. Then the model is calibrated to produce results that correspond to the actual flow of traffic. The data used for calibration will come from measurements of traffic flow, for example, those made by counters that are tripped by the weight of a vehicle passing over a rubber hose. Once the model duplicates the observed travel behavior, alternative situations can be modeled. For example, a planner might assume an increase in the number of households in a given zone.

The model can be run again, and the region will show a slightly different pattern of trips. The transportation planners might then postulate changes in the road pattern to see how these will affect the pattern of trips. Since the speed of travel on a road depends on its volume of traffic, such simulations will give planners insight into how potential changes in the road system will affect travel times. Travel in metropolitan areas has morning and evening peaks, corresponding to commuting hours. Traffic flow is very different in peak and nonpeak hours. The model can be run to simulate different times of the day.

In the past it was common to assume a single scenario for metropolitan-area growth, often an extrapolation of present trends, and use the model to explore different transportation alternatives to provide service for that pattern. More recently, it has become common to evaluate different patterns of land use in order to both think about how to service them and also to inform land-use planning for metropolitan-area development. This takes us back to the point made before, that transportation planning and land-use planning, in the ideal, should be done as part of the same process. According to Keith Bartholomew and Reid Ewing, much of this scenario exploration is done with a view toward achieving a more compact pattern of development and, as a function of that, reduced fuel use.[11]

The Policy Decision

Computer modeling can and does help examine possible improvements and additions to the transportation system but by itself cannot make any decision. How is the actual decision about policy reached?

One technical aid to decision making is benefit–cost analysis. This is a process of systematically enumerating the benefits and costs of a particular option, say, a new link in the road network or an extension of a transit line, and assigning to them monetary values. The ratio of benefits to costs can then be calculated. Where many projects are competing for limited funds, the benefit–cost ratios may be used as a means of deciding which ones to fund.

On the benefit side of a proposed improvement might be listed time saved by travelers. Doing this means that a monetary value must be assigned to time, and in fact, a large number of studies have been done by transportation analysts to find out how travelers value their time. Other benefits might include lives saved and injuries avoided if the new route is safer than the old one. Savings in vehicle-operating costs would be considered if the new route were shorter or reduced stop-and-go traffic. Costs would include land acquisition costs, construction costs, and repair costs, among others. Typically, the three biggest items in highway benefit–cost studies are construction and land costs, time savings, and vehicle-operating costs.

Benefit–cost analysis has its subjective side. For example, how does one assign precise values to human life and health? Measures such as estimated lifetime earnings and the awards of courts in negligence cases have been used. The favored technique at the present time is a statistical one that combines information on wage rates and fatality rates in different occupations to determine how much more people demand to be paid in order to accept a certain amount of risk of loss of life.[12] For example, if a person would accept a death risk of one chance in 1,000 for a wage difference of $1,000, then one might say that implicitly the person places a value of $1,000,000 on his or her own life. This method may seem to be cold-blooded or even a bit bizarre, but if we are going to make expenditures to reduce the risk of death or injury, there is no way to get around placing a monetary value on life, even though we all concede that no one really has that kind of godlike wisdom. There are also many other items that cannot readily be converted into dollar terms. For example, urban design and aesthetic issues do not lend themselves well to being "monetized." Nonetheless, benefit–cost analysis is far superior to reliance on pure intuition.

Transportation questions often generate citizen involvement and can become highly emotional and political. New construction takes people's property and can have great impact on neighborhoods. A freeway through a neighborhood can be a formidable barrier between the remaining halves, greatly raise the noise level, lower the air quality, and generally make life there a good deal less attractive. Changes in the flow of traffic may bring windfalls to some businesses and large losses to others. Citizens whose daily travel, particularly the commute to work, is slow and frustrating constitute a powerful force for public investment in new roads and, in more densely developed areas, for public transportation as well.

Some citizens' disillusionment with highway building has come from what planners and engineers refer to as "induced demand." When the capacity of the road network is increased, for example, by the opening of a new expressway, it is often observed that traffic congestion does not fall very much on the other roads and that in the peak hours, the new road may be operating at close to maximum capacity in a very short period of time. The building of new capacity has induced additional traffic; also, some people who previously traveled during off-peak hours because of congestion now travel in the peak hours. The highway planner may be satisfied with the result in that more people are now getting what they want, namely, the ability to travel where they want when they want. But to the citizen who used to drive to work in the morning rush in one hour and now drives in 59 minutes, it may appear that little has been gained.[13] The next time a highway bond issue comes up for referendum, he or she is likely to vote no.

Citizens' opposition to highway building has become formidable. In San Francisco in the early 1970s, the Embarcadero Freeway was halted in midconstruction by opposition, based largely on concerns that this elevated road would block views of San Francisco Bay. When the portion that had been built and was in use was damaged in the October 1989 earthquake, the city did not move to rebuild it. Rather, the remaining portions were torn down. Since then, the north and south portions have been replaced by an at-grade road. In the 1970s New York City planned Westway, a highway along the west side of Manhattan to divert through traffic from the city's congested street system. The project had the support of the mayor, the governor, organized labor, planners, and probably the majority of the city's population. However, it was opposed for over a decade by a determined group of citizens who simply did not want any more highways. In 1985, after $200 million had been spent on land acquisition and design costs, the city conceded defeat and filed an application with the federal Department of Transportation (DOT) to have some of the funds that would have been spent on Westway switched to mass transportation projects. The term *freeway revolt* has been used to describe rising resistance to highway building. Not only does resistance come from affected residents, businesspeople, and property owners, but some also comes from environmentalists, who in general do not favor anything that will increase automobile use.

A variety of business interests may weigh heavily in the decisions about highway construction. Firms wanting the better access that a new highway would bring may lobby for it. Major property owners who do not want their property bisected by a new highway may make every effort to oppose it. In some cases a new roadway may go through whichever neighborhood or municipality is politically weakest and therefore least able to resist it.

The details of how a new highway or highway improvement will be funded may be critical. A local government may know that on a pure calculation of benefits and costs, alternative A is distinctly superior to alternative B. But if alternative B will be paid for primarily by state and federal funds, whereas alternative A will require a substantial local contribution, the local government is likely to go for alternative B. All projects look more favorable if funded with OPM (other people's money).

Modeling, benefit–cost studies, and other types of analysis can and do help move the decision process in the direction of greater rationality. But the ultimate decision comes out of the political process.

Planning for Public Transportation

The approach to planning public transportation infrastructure is similar in principle to that of highway planning. The same sorts of computer studies done for automotive travel can be done for transit. Then, too, benefit–cost analysis is as applicable to transit as it is to highways and streets.

In recent years the public in large cities and metropolitan areas has generally been more favorably disposed to transit improvements than to the building of new highways. Improving transit tends to decongest the streets by reducing automobile travel. It appeals to environmentalists for reasons of air quality and fuel consumption. Those concerned with urban design often favor transit because it leads to a more compact land-use pattern that is much friendlier to pedestrians. Distances between destinations are shorter, and less land area is given over to streets. Taking a walk in a transit-oriented city like Chicago or Boston and then taking a walk in an automobile-oriented city like Albuquerque or Los Angeles is likely to convince one that there is some truth in this argument.

A major problem with transit, as noted before, is that financially it is far from self-sustaining. It must be heavily subsidized, and most of that subsidy must come from higher levels of government.

In the mid-1970s the long-term decline in transit ridership halted, and a ridership has slowly increased. This reversal was due in large measure to increased federal funding, beginning with the Urban Mass Transit Act of 1964.

But congressional support for public transportation has never been very strong. Behind this lack of enthusiasm is a basic geographical fact. To function adequately, transit requires population densities of at least 2,000 or so persons per square mile. Therefore, a substantial part of the U.S. population, including much of its metropolitan-area population, lives in areas that cannot adequately be served with transit at any conceivable level of public expenditure. Thus many members of Congress do not have constituencies that care much about transit.

At this writing the construction of light-rail systems proceeds at a modest pace in a limited number of U.S. cities. *Planning* magazine noted that some light-rail mileage has been constructed in eight U.S. cities since 1981 (San Diego, Buffalo, Portland, Sacramento, San Jose, Los Angeles, Baltimore, and St. Louis). In general, these routes are of modest length and operate with heavy subsidy. They are designed to take advantage of and to promote high density, corridor-type development. Construction costs for light rail are extremely high. The city of Sacramento cited a *per mile* cost of $9.6 million for its 18.3 miles of light-rail routing and claimed that this was the lowest per mile cost of any federally funded light-rail system.[14] Costs have gone up substantially since then.

In the past both light-rail and heavy-rail (commuter railroad) systems have been built on a radial plan to carry suburban workers to downtown jobs. With the increasing decentralization of employment, there has been discussion of building circumferential light rail to carry workers from suburban residences to jobs in suburban subcenters, but as yet there has been little action in this regard. The high cost of construction and the formidable collection and distribution problems noted earlier make this type of system extremely expensive.

In this writer's view, the future of public transportation probably lies much more with buses than with light rail. The capital costs are generally much lower, and routings can be changed to accommodate changes in the pattern of residential and commercial growth.

A relatively recent compromise between light rail and buses is Bus Rapid Transit (BRT).[15] The bus operates on its own right-of-way, generally with longer spacing, say, a half-mile to a mile between stops, than does an ordinary bus. The stop resembles a railroad stop more than a conventional bus stop, particularly in that it has boarding from a platform at the same level as the bus floor, rather than the usual step up from street level with an ordinary bus. This considerably shortens loading times. In some cases the system may be set up to automatically shift traffic lights to green (signal priority) as the bus approaches intersections. In some cases there is a buses-only lane. Capital costs are higher than with conventional bus systems but lower than with light rail. The system has greater flexibility in that the bus can also run on ordinary streets and those routes can readily be adjusted.

BRT systems generally provide travel speeds intermediate between traditional bus and commuter or light rail. For example, Cleveland's Health Line (so named because one end of the line is at the Cleveland Clinic medical complex) does the 9.4-mile trip in 34 minutes, or at 16.6 mph. The conventional bus line it replaced took 46 minutes at about 12.2 mph. The line, which now carries about 375,000 passengers per month, is clearly a success and shows that BRT can, with sufficient time and effort, be retrofitted into an existing urban pattern. In Everret, Washington, a BRT system averages about 22 mph over a 17-mile route. It uses a combination of transit-only and signal priority lanes.

As is the case with light rail, BRT can serve as the spine for transit-oriented development (TOD) discussed in Chapter 10. The overall design of the node places a residential population of several thousand as well as a mix of commercial uses in a pedestrian-friendly street pattern within walking distance, say one-quarter mile around the stop.

Marketing seems to be a key item in implementing a BRT system. Bus transportation, perhaps because it has generally been associated with poorer customers, has less prestige than rail. Thus BRT developers will try to make the system as distinct from traditional bus service as possible. This may be done by making their vehicles look as different as possible, by referring to them by another name, say rapid transit vehicles (RTVs) rather than as buses, by providing distinctive looking bus shelters, and even using a horn that sounds like a locomotive horn rather than a bus horn. Some of that may sound silly or trivial, but experience indicates that image has a significant effect on ridership.

CHANGES IN THE FEDERAL ROLE

For planners concerned with transportation, the most important event of recent years was the passage of the Intermodal Surface Transportation Efficiency Act (ISTEA) of 1991. Often pronounced as "ice tea," the act retains the basic structure of very substantial federal transportation aid to the states and localities financed largely by the Highway Trust Fund. But the act also contains features to integrate transportation planning with land-use and environmental planning.

For several decades it has been widely understood that the building of transportation facilities, especially highways, has had a huge effect on how and where people live. But, in too many cases, highway planning has been based almost solely on pure transportation issues with little respect for its effect on the overall pattern of settlement and on the natural environment. ISTEA requires

> states and cities to incorporate nontransportation into their transportation planning. In effect, ISTEA moves the side effects closer to the center of the planning process by forcing states and localities to look ahead and if possible, eliminate the negative consequences of road building.[16]

In areas where current air quality is not up to federal standards, so-called nonattainment areas, the metropolitan planning organization will not be able to receive federal funding unless it produces a plan that deals with automotive emissions. These plans might involve car and van pooling, increased investment in transit, elements of land-use planning designed to place jobs and housing closer to each other, and the like. Foot and bicycle paths might also be part of such a plan.

A total of $24 billion over the life of the act was earmarked for "flexible" funds that could be allocated to a wide range of transportation projects ranging from highways to bike paths. Ten percent of each grant had to be earmarked to safety and another 10 percent to "enhancement." The latter might include scenic, recreational, or other improvements along or near the transportation route in question. Funding for such enhancements was continued for another six years by the Transportation Equity Act for the Twenty-First Century (TEA-21) of 1998 and again by the ponderously named Safe, Accountable, Flexible, Efficient Transportation Equity Act: A Legacy for Users (SAFETEA-LU) passed in 2005.

SAFETEA-LU provided $244.1 billion in funding over a six-year period, of which approximately one-fifth was for transit and flexible uses.[17] Most of its funding came from the Highway Trust Fund. Since 2011 federal highway funding has continued at roughly the same levels as previously but on the basis of short-term appropriations.

FINE-TUNING THE SYSTEM

By the late 1980s the Interstate Highway System of some 40,000 miles was virtually complete. A future comparable episode of highway building in the United States does not appear to be possible. In recent years the attention of highway engineers and planners has turned to the question of extracting more performance from existing road networks. One set of techniques is referred to as transportation system management (TSM).

One TSM technique is the high-occupancy vehicle (HOV) lane to encourage carpooling. Another is the use of traffic metering techniques. With these, entry from a feeder road onto a main artery is controlled so as to maintain good traffic flow conditions on the main route and thus maximize its carrying capacity. Charging higher transit fares or vehicle tolls during peak hours is another technique. In Los Angeles all businesses with over 100 employees are required to develop a program to reduce single-occupant automobile trips to work. Promoting telecommuting, offering financial incentives to carpool, subsidizing transit fares, and the like might be elements of such a program. The common element is that programs take a managerial rather than a construction-based approach to increasing system capacity and improving the quality of travel. A number of TSM techniques are listed in Table 12–2.

Within the general category of TSM are a range of travel demand management (TDM) techniques that are intended to improve transportation system performance by reducing travel demand. For example, encouraging telecommuting reduces total travel demand. Encouraging bicycle commuting would reduce total automobile traffic, particularly during morning and evening peaks. Note that TSM and TDM are overlapping concepts. The HOV lane listed earlier as a TSM technique could also be considered a TDM technique.

TABLE 12–2 Transportation System Management (TSM) Techniques

1. Improved vehicular flow:
   Improvements in signalized intersections
   Freeway ramp metering
   One-way streets
   Removal of on-street parking
   Reversible lanes
   Traffic channelization
   Off-street loading
   Transit-stop relocation
2. Preferential treatment of high-occupancy vehicles:
   Freeway bus and carpool lanes and access ramps
   Bus and carpool lanes on city streets and urban arterials
   Bus preemption of traffic signals
   Toll policies
3. Reduced peak-period travel:
   Work rescheduling
   Congestion pricing
   Peak-period truck restrictions
4. Parking management:
   Parking regulations
   Park-and-ride facilities
5. Promotion of nonauto or high-occupancy auto use:
   Ride-sharing
   Human-powered travel modes
   Auto-restricted zones
6. Transit and paratransit service improvements:
   Transit marketing
   Security measures
   Transit shelters
   Transit terminals
   Transit-fare policies and fare-collection techniques
   Extension of transit with paratransit services
   Integration of transportation services
7. Transit management efficiency measures:
   Route evaluation
   Vehicle communication and monitoring techniques
   Maintenance policies
   Evaluation of system performance

Source: U.S. Department of Transportation, Urban Mass Transportation Administration, *Transportation System Management: State of the Art,* Washington, DC, 1977.

THE GROWING ROLE OF TOLLS AND PRIVATIZATION _____

Economists will tell you that the way to utilize resources efficiently is to get the prices right. If something is free, then it will be used down to the point where the last user gets just the most trivial amount of benefit from it, but the cost that last user imposes may be much more than trivial. If the resource is priced right, then the last user gets just as much benefit as the cost he or she imposes. In the jargon of economics, there is an efficient adjustment at the margin.

One recent trend has been a growing use of tolls. More roads are being tolled and in many cases the toll is adjusted by time of day. That makes sense in terms of efficient use of the road, for the more crowded the road is, the more an additional car slows down the other cars and thus the higher the cost that last car imposes. It also maximizes toll collections by raising the charge during the morning and evening peaks, when demand is greatest.

One new wrinkle in the matter of toll roads is that the building and operation of toll roads is attracting private capital. One notable example in the east is the Dulles Toll Road that connects the Washington, DC, Beltway (I–495) with Dulles Airport. People value their time, sometimes quite highly, and investors are realizing that there is money to be made in selling people time savings. From the municipal or state perspective, the privately built toll road achieves the public goal of improving traffic flow without the expenditure of public funds and the creation of public debt.

Private capital is being attracted not only to the construction of toll roads, but also to the operation of existing roads on a toll basis. In a case that received widespread notice, the city of Chicago sold a 99-year lease for the toll rights on the Chicago Skyway to a group of investors for $1.8 billion. The city took the position that the money would be used for investments that would have a long-term payoff for the city and that the sale was thus well advised. The skeptic could argue that politicians, who stand for election on a two- or four-year cycle, have a short time horizon and that in the long term, selling that significant revenue source will turn out to be a mistake.

The trend toward the privately built or operated toll road has been given a considerable boost by SAFETEA-LU. The law permits investors to build toll roads using tax-exempt revenue bonds. The term *revenue bond* means a bond whose interest and principal are paid out of the revenues earned by the project built with the bond. The term *tax-exempt* means that the buyers of the bonds do not have to pay income tax on the interest payments that they receive from the bonds. That, in turn, means that the bonds can be issued at lower interest rates, thus reducing the debt service costs of the investors in the toll road. That constitutes an implicit federal subsidy (a tax expenditure as discussed in Chapter 11) in the building of the road. On a billion-dollar road the cumulative interest cost savings from the tax-exemption feature might come to several hundred million dollars.

Another feature of the law expands the types of roads that states can subject to tolls. In a number of states, major roads in metropolitan areas have high-occupancy vehicle (HOV) lanes, open only to vehicles with at least two or three occupants during the morning and evening rush. SAFETEA-LU permits states to convert these HOV lanes into high-occupancy toll (HOT) lanes.[18] Vehicles with the required number of passengers will still be able to use the lane free of charge, but the lane will also be open to single-occupant vehicles if they pay a toll. The most high-tech HOT lane is one that uses *dynamic tolling*. The charge for using the lane can vary as often as every six minutes and the rate is posted on electronically operated signs along the roadway so that motorists can adjust their choice of HOT lane or untolled lanes accordingly. A transponder in the automobile is tripped electronically when the car is in the HOT lane and the motorist is billed periodically. The system brings in revenue and puts any excess capacity in the HOT lanes to use, thus reducing congestion on the remainder of the roadway. The dynamic tolling feature permits optimizing traffic flow, for as the number of vehicles in the HOT lane rises sufficiently to cause significant congestion, the fares rise to discourage use of the lane. It was feared that these so-called Lexus Lanes would be used only by upper-income drivers, but a multiyear experiment on HOT lanes on San Diego's I–15 has not shown this to be the case. HOT lanes are now in use in California, on I–10 in Houston, in Denver, and are now in the planning stage in the Washington, DC, area. In the case of the DC area, HOT lanes planners are now thinking in terms of charges that may top $1 per mile at peak times, a clear indication that they believe motorists will pay substantially to ease the pain of their daily commute.

SMART HIGHWAYS, INTELLIGENT VEHICLES, AND NEW MACHINES

Transportation system performance may also be improved in coming years by the application of electronic and other control and decision-making technologies. The *smart highway*, as the term is now used, means equipping the roadway with sensing devices and computing equipment so as to permit instantaneous decision making that optimizes traffic flow. For example, motorists can be diverted to other routes, entrances to main routes can be metered, speed limits can be adjusted, and the like.

Toll booths are notorious for slowing the flow of traffic. However, recent electronic technology permits toll collection without cars needing to slow down. A transponder in the car registers its entrance onto the toll road and debits the driver's account automatically. Such systems are now in use across the United States from parts of the New York metro politan area to Los Angeles. Some systems, such as the one in the Los Angeles area, charge higher tolls during the morning and evening peaks with a view toward diverting some traffic to nonpeak hours and also maximizing revenue.

Intelligent vehicle technology, probably combined with smart highway technology, holds much potential, both for improving safety and for increasing the capacity of a given road network. Radar or other distance-sensing devices combined with computing and control technologies would permit building vehicles whose acceleration, braking, and steering are controlled automatically. Much of the technology is here now. For example, collision-avoidance devices using either radar or infrared technologies are now showing up in higher-priced automobiles and, if they follow the pattern of other improvements, may well become standard.

A system whose reaction time is measured in microseconds and that never gets bored or sleepy could permit much safer and faster traffic flows. Drivers might guide their vehicles on local roads but once on the main route shift to automatic control and then relax and read the newspaper as the car proceeded on its way.

Just as airliners are guided by air-traffic-control decisions made on the ground and a combination of human and machine decisions made in the cockpit, we can envisage a system in which drivers, computing and control equipment in the vehicle, and the smart highway together guide vehicles on the ground. The gains in safety and faster traffic flow might be considerable.

Under the pressure of higher fuel prices and government pressure to reduce carbon dioxide emissions, the fuel economy of conventionally powered automobiles has risen substantially. Many cars run in the 30 mpg and over range compared with the 13 or 14 mpg common in the early 1970s. All-electric cars such as the Nissan LEAF and plug-in hybrids such as the Chevrolet Volt, which run on electric power much of the time, have the capacity to lower fuel costs drastically. If you owned an electrically powered car that got 2 or 3 miles per kilowatt hour (kwh), and you paid a typical residential rate of, say, 12 cents per kwh, then you would pay, in effect, 4 to 6 cents per mile for fuel.[19] That would be a big change in the economics of automotive transportation.

Another wildcard in the deck is natural gas. Motor vehicles have been run on liquefied natural gas (LNG) for decades, so at the vehicle level there are no big unresolved technical issues. LNG is held back by the lack of a national distribution system to make it as available as gasoline and by environmental problems connected with extracting natural gas, noted in Chapter 15. The United States has a large supply and at present it is much less costly than oil. Whether LNG will become a major factor in automotive transportation remains to be seen.

It is widely believed that in the longer term, the fuel cell, in which hydrogen and oxygen are combined in the presence of a catalyst, will bring about still higher mileage and lower emissions. The widespread use of the fuel cell is still many years off, for the big question to be solved is where the hydrogen to power the fuel cell will come from. Until that question is solved, mass use of the fuel cell cannot happen. The hydrogen-fuel-powered vehicle itself would emit no pollution, since all that comes out of the tailpipe is water from the oxidation of hydrogen. How much pollution the system as a whole would emit would depend on the energy source used to produce the hydrogen. The same is true for electric vehicles. Their net contribution to atmospheric pollution depends how the electricity that charges them is generated.

Although technologies that improve the speed, safety, and fuel efficiency of the automobile are obviously desirable in their own right, not everyone will be happy about their urban design implications, for whatever improves the performance of the automobile/highway system will be inherently decentralizing and will move us in the opposite direction from the compact, fine-grained pattern advocated by designers like Duany and Calthorpe (see Chapter 10). It will also, as suggested before, make the automobile a more formidable competitor for proposed intercity rail systems.

Whether there will be major changes in specifically urban vehicles remains to be seen. The European-built Smart Car, which is about as long as a full-sized car is wide, is now showing up much more often in the United States. In 2001 the Segway was introduced, accompanied by a massive publicity campaign. Stabilized and controlled by gyroscopes and position sensors backed with the computing power of several PCs, it transports a single rider at speeds up to 12 mph. Its inventor, Dean Kamen, saw it as the wave of the future and claimed that "it will be to the car as the car was to the horse and buggy." That prophecy has not come true. Perhaps the Segway did not have that clear an advantage over a variety of lower-cost and lower-tech forms like the motor scooter and the bicycle. At present Kamen and General Motors are working on a second-generation Segway tentatively named PUMA, an acronym for Personal Urban Mobility and Accessibility. This version, powered by a lithium-ion battery, would have a maximum speed of 35 mph and a range between rechargings of 35 miles. It would carry two people side by side in a seated position and provide them with some protection from the weather. It would appear to have sufficient performance for many urban commuting situations, but if it is to share the roadway with much heavier vehicles safety might be a problem.

Whether the PUMA, if it reaches the market, will be more successful than its predecessor is an open question. But just the fact that a major automobile manufacturer is looking into it suggests that substantial innovation in specifically urban individual transport may be in our future.

SUMMARY

Since World War II, per capita ownership of automobiles in the United States has more than doubled, partly because of the increase in real income. Increases in automobile ownership have gone hand in hand with the process of suburbanization, each reinforcing the other. In terms of direct costs, private transportation more or less pays for itself, whereas public transportation requires heavy subsidization. The decline in public transportation since World War II was attributed partly to increased automobile ownership and partly to a more spread-out pattern of land use.

The present pattern of land use shapes the present demand for transportation, and transportation investment decisions shape the future pattern of land use. In the best of circumstances, land-use and transportation planning proceed as coordinated rather than isolated processes.

Large-scale transportation planning is a four-step process:

1. *Estimating trip generation.* Without considering destinations, the planners, using such variables as household size, household income, and number of vehicles per household, estimate the total number of trips that will originate from each zone.

2. *Estimating trip distribution.* Using a gravity model or other mathematical model, the planners will then estimate the number of trips from each zone to each zone.

3. *Estimating modal split.* If more than one mode of transportation is available, say, automobile and bus, the planners will use mathematical models to estimate the number of travelers using each mode from each origin to each destination. The main variables in such models are cost and travel time.

4. *Predicting trip assignment.* Where there is more than one route from one zone to predicting another zone, the final item to be modeled is the number of trips that will be made via each route.

After the model is built, it is calibrated, that is, adjusted, so that its output duplicates the actual travel behavior of the region. Then the model can be used to examine different transportation alternatives. Benefit–cost analysis is frequently used to evaluate and rank different investment possibilities. Ultimately, though, deciding on major investments is a political matter because transportation system investments can have large consequences for land values, neighborhood quality, and the entire pattern of development.

For the planner, the most important recent federal initiative in transportation has been the Intermodal Surface Transportation Efficiency Act (ISTEA) of 1991 and its successors. Its intent was to bring about better coordination between transportation planning and urban and regional planning.

For reasons discussed in the chapter, another period of massive highway building comparable to that which produced the Interstate Highway System is unlikely in the foreseeable future. Much attention has thus turned to transportation system management (TSM) and travel demand management (TDM) techniques as a way of obtaining more performance from the existing road network. In the next several decades, we will probably also see substantial change in automobile transportation as a result of a combination of "intelligent vehicles" and "smart highways"—sometimes referred to more formally as the intelligent transportation system—from the increasing application of sophisticated pricing systems to roadways and from new technologies for vehicle propulsion and guidance.

NOTES

1. Federal Highway Administration, *Highway Statistics Annual*, 2008, www.FederalHigh wayAdministration.gov.
2. *Public Transportation Fact Book*, 2011, American Public Transportation Association, Table 2, www.APTA.com.
3. Ibid., Table 3.
4. Ibid., Table 8.
5. Train à ʼGrande Vitesse (train of great speed) and Alta (high) Velocidad Española.
6. Association for California High-Speed Train's website, www.highspeedtrains- forca.com.
7. AmTrak's best-known train is the Acela, which runs between Boston, New York, and Washington, DC, the so-called *Bowash* corridor, probably the largest potential passenger rail market in the United States. The 456-mile trip takes about 7 hours, for an average speed of about 68 mph. The service is popular, carrying over 2 million passengers per year. But for the two reasons noted in the text, its speed is no better than half that of comparable trips on Europe's fastest routes.
8. *Public Transportation Fact Book*, Tables 19 and 20.
9. *Chicago Area Transportation Study: Final Reports* (3 Vols.), published jointly by the State of Illinois, County of Cook, City of Chicago, and the U.S. Department of Commerce, Bureau of Public Roads, 1959–1962.
10. John W. Dickey, *Metropolitan Transportation Planning*, 2nd ed., McGraw-Hill Book Co., New York, 1983, chap. 6.
11. Keith Bartholomew and Reid Ewing, "Land Use-Transportation Scenarios and Future Vehicle Travel and Land Consumption," *Journal of the American Planning Association*, vol. 75, no. 1, Winter 2009, pp. 13–27.
12. For a discussion of this technique, see Michael J. Moore and Kip W. Viscusi, "Doubling the Estimated Value of Life: Results Using New Occupational Fatality Data," *Journal of Policy Analysis and Management*, vol. 7, no. 3, 1988, p. 476.
13. Anthony Downs, "The Law of Peak-Hour Congestion," *Urban Problems and Prospects*, Rand-McNally, Chicago, 1976.
14. Harold Henderson, "Light Rail, Heavy Costs," *Planning*, October 1994, pp. 8–13.
15. Christopher Swope, "L.A. Banks on Buses," *Planning*, May 2006, pp. 33–36.
16. F. K. Plous, Jr., "Refreshing ISTEA," *Planning*, February 1993, pp. 9–12.
17. Federal Highway Administration, Office of Legislation and Intergovernmental Affairs, Program Analysis Team, "A Summary of Highway Provisions in SAFETEA-LU," Washington, DC, 2005, www.fhwa.dot. gov/safetea-lu/summary.htm.
18. Janusz Supernak, "HOT Lanes on Interstate 15 in San Diego: Technology, Impacts and Equity Issues," San Diego State University, 2005. This article, and many others on the subject, is readily available by Googling HOT Lanes.
19. In 2011 Nissan claimed that its all-electric LEAF got 100 miles from 34 kwh.

SELECTED BIBLIOGRAPHY

DICKEY, JOHN W., *Metropolitan Transportation Planning*, 2nd ed., McGraw-Hill Book Co., New York, 1983.

MEYER, MICHAEL D., and MILLER, ERIC J., *Urban Transportation Planning*, 2nd ed., McGraw-Hill Book Co., New York, 2001.

VANDERBILTI, TOM, *Traffic: Why We Drive the Way We Do (And What It Says About Us)*. Alfred A. Knopf, New York, 2008.

CHAPTER 13

Economic
Development
Planning

Many thousands of municipalities, probably the majority of counties, and all 50 states make serious efforts to promote their own economic development. There are well over 15,000 organizations in the United States devoted to promoting local and state economic development. The exact amount of money spent on local economic development is not known. But when the operating expenses of economic development agencies, direct expenditures on economic development, and a wide variety of indirect expenditures in the form of tax abatements are added together, the figure may be as high as several tens of billions of dollars annually. The present U.S. political scene is characterized by a high level of intermunicipal and interstate economic competition.[1]

Such competition is driven partly by labor market considerations. Citizens expect local and state governments to foster job growth so as to tighten labor markets, thus pushing up wage rates and pushing down unemployment rates. Local and state governments are also driven to economic competition for tax reasons. Caught in the squeeze between the cost of providing services and citizens' resistance to being taxed, broadening the tax base by bringing in new commercial and industrial activity looks like an attractive course of action. Interplace economic competition has a certain amount of "positive feedback" built into it. If one state or municipality offers firms an attractive subsidy for locating there, or launches a massive publicity campaign to promote itself as a good location, other states and municipalities are likely to respond in kind. Thus offer begets counteroffer, and interplace economic competition becomes more intense over time. This interplace competition has promoted economic development planning as a major subspecialty of the planning profession. Planning schools offer courses in economic development planning, and the American Planning Association has for several years had an economic development planning division. Before we turn to the subject of economic development planning, some historic and national background will be useful.

HISTORIC ROOTS

Planning for economic development is an old American tradition. In many ways it antedates the sort of city planning we have discussed in this book. In the nineteenth century a great many cities took steps to strengthen their competitive position vis-à-vis competing cities. Quite naturally, much of the push came from the city's merchants, for it was they who would profit most from municipal economic success. Most often, such planning efforts were directed toward the transportation infrastructure—to increasing the accessibility of the city. In a day when overland transportation costs per ton-mile were a large multiple of what they are today, a significant reduction in those costs could give the merchants in one city or town an overwhelming advantage over competitors in other cities.[2]

Probably the best-known example in the nineteenth century was the building of the Erie Canal. In the early 1820s a group of New York City merchants perceived that obtaining good access to the Midwest would confer a tremendous economic advantage on the city. The way to do this in the prerailroad era was to build a canal connecting the Hudson River to Lake Erie. Private capital was quickly raised for the task, and within a few years the canal was completed. By the 1830s, a decade or so after its completion, the canal was carrying close to 1 million tons of freight per year, giving New York an enormous commercial advantage over its two main rivals of the time, Boston and Philadelphia. The great age of canal building in the United States, roughly 1800 to 1830, was largely a matter of municipal initiative, each city trying to steal a march on its competitors.

The age of canal building ended abruptly with the coming of railroad technology, but the same story of municipal competition was repeated. Many of the early railroads were built with municipally raised funds, and the competition between cities and towns to be on a rail line was intense. In many cases municipalities purchased railroad bonds to provide the capital to build a line that would put them on the map commercially. In other cases municipalities guaranteed bonds to make them marketable.[3]

When the U.S. rail system was fairly well developed, competition switched to other areas, particularly manufacturing. For example, the movement of textile manufacturing from New England to the southeastern United States resulted in part from recruiting efforts of local merchants and municipal governments.

PERSPECTIVES ON LOCAL ECONOMIC DEVELOPMENT _____

To understand the present situation in local economic development, it is necessary to make clear two different perspectives. For several decades, local economic development efforts were heavily shaped by federal funding and federal legislation.

Thus there is a national perspective to be considered. There are also strong local motivations, and what is good for a particular municipality or state may or may not be good for the nation as a whole.

The Federal Presence in Local Economic Development

In the years after World War II, a new term was added to the economic vocabulary of the nation: *structural unemployment.* It refers to a long-term mismatch between the supply of labor and the demand for labor. The mismatch may apply to skills. For example, in the 1960s numerous former farmers and farm workers were unemployed because the postwar mechanization of agriculture had forced them off the land, and they lacked skills for doing other kinds of work. At the same time, the burgeoning computer industry was experiencing shortages of programmers, systems analysts, and technicians. In recent years manufacturing employment in the United States has declined sharply while health care has been a major growth area, so high unemployment rates among industrial workers have at times coexisted with severe shortages of nurses. To a great extent this type of structural unemployment is the result of technological change. The faster the change occurs, the more serious the problem is likely to be.

The other aspect of structural unemployment is geographic. An area may lose jobs because firms have moved out or because changes in technology have reduced their labor needs or because they have gone out of business. If the loss of employment is not matched by corresponding out-migration of population, a sustained condition of high unemployment may result. In general, capital is more mobile than population, so that structural unemployment does in fact occur in just this way. A company's board of directors can in a single, rational, bottom line–based decision decide to close a plant here and transfer its production operations to a site elsewhere in the nation or, for that matter, elsewhere in the world. It is not so easy for a comparable part of the population to decide to pull out of a labor-surplus area and move to a labor-short area.

The structural unemployment problem did not become apparent immediately after World War II. In welcome contrast to the Great Depression, the postwar period was one of great prosperity. Thus for a time it appeared to many that the only important economic function of government was to maintain this desirable state of affairs by competent management of national (macroeconomic) economic policy.

After a few years, however, it became apparent that even though the nation was generally prosperous, not all regions or all subgroups of the population were doing well economically. The first region for which serious concern developed was Appalachia, its economy seriously weakened by declining employment in coal mining and handicapped by a rugged topography that made it difficult to develop an efficient transportation network. Lying between the prosperous Eastern Seaboard and the then thriving industrial Midwest, the Appalachian region seemed to be in a permanent depression of its own.

Beginning in 1961 Congress began to attack the problem at the national level. The basic approach was to direct federal funds to both the skills and the geographic mismatch sides of the structural unemployment problem. The skills part of the approach involved public money for what was then termed *manpower training*. Given that it does not have a spatial component, it is beyond the scope of this book. The geographic side of the problem was attacked by programs that directed federal funds to economic development in lagging areas, generally identified on the basis of federal statistics on personal income and unemployment rates. A prototypical project might have been a municipal industrial park, part of whose costs were paid by federal grants. This would permit the municipality to offer sites in the park to businesses at below market rates in order to tip the playing field toward lagging places. The first agency devoted to this purpose was the Area Redevelopment Administration (ARA), established in 1961. It was replaced in 1965 with the Economic Development Administration, which exists to the present time. The Department of Housing and Urban Development (HUD) operated the Urban Development Action Grant (UDAG) program, which funded projects in urban areas. That program no longer exists, but many downtown hotels and convention centers built with the aid of such findings are still operating.

On the tax expenditure side of the budget (see Chapter 9), the federal government has for a number of decades aided local economic development efforts through the mechanism of Industrial Revenue Bond (IRB) funding. There are no payments from the federal government. Rather, provisions in the Internal Revenue Service (IRS) code permit local governments to, in effect, make tax-exempt loans to companies, and this lowers a company's debt service burden. Unlike grant programs, these loans are not specifically targeted to poorer places. Essentially any municipality can make use of them, so just what their overall effect is on the structural unemployment question is not entirely certain.

DOES PUBLIC INTERVENTION MAKE SENSE?

Whether such federal subsidies to local development make sense from the national viewpoint has been the subject of considerable argument. From an economist's viewpoint, subsidies were being used to move economic activity into an area that was not its most efficient location in order to achieve some gains in equity. This so-called efficiency–equity trade-off deserves a short explanation, since it underlies much argument about what the proper role of government is in influencing the location of economic activity.

In brief, the argument is as follows: If the location in question were the most efficient location for the firm, ordinary market forces would cause it to locate there without any government action. If a subsidy (say, in the form of an industrial park site delivered at a fraction of actual cost) is necessary to cause the firm to locate there, by definition, the site is not the most efficient location. Thus following this logic, there is a loss of efficiency for the whole economy stemming from the use of subsidies to influence economic locations. This situation occurs simply because encouraging a firm to locate at other than its most efficient location means that the cost of producing a given bundle of goods or services will be higher. In return for this efficiency loss, there is an equity gain in the sense that economic activity is directed to areas of more than ordinary need. This, then, is the efficiency–equity trade-off. Those who support powerful public intervention in locating economic activity generally, either explicitly or implicitly, place heavy weight on equity. Those who generally oppose such public intervention are apt to place heavy weight, again, explicitly or implicitly, on efficiency.

In general, liberals have tended to favor place-related programs. Conservatives have generally opposed such programs, taking the view that it is the proper role of the national government to provide conditions under which private economic activity can flourish but that the marketplace itself should decide how and where capital is invested.

Federal activity with regard to structural unemployment peaked during the administration of Jimmy Carter (1977–1981) and declined thereafter under both Republican and Democratic presidents. Despite the slackening of federal interest in and funding for local economic development, competition between states and localities has increased in intensity. Voters in every state and most municipalities want more jobs for the local labor market and more tax revenues from industrial and commercial development. Then, too, state and municipal economic development activity seems to have the self-generating quality noted earlier. If one community offers subsidies or tax breaks for new firms, then another community may feel compelled to do the same just to not fall behind.

STATE ECONOMIC DEVELOPMENT EFFORTS _____

For many years the states have supported local economic development efforts. State departments of commerce provide information on the state and try to guide firms to municipalities within the state. States have offered a huge variety of financial incentives, such as investment tax credits, low-interest loans, infrastructure grants, labor force training grants, and the like, to encourage firms to locate or expand within the state's borders. A majority of states have overseas trade offices in Europe, the Far East, or both to help develop overseas markets for their firms and also to encourage investment in their state by overseas firms. Most important, states have become increasingly involved in major industrial and commercial relocations and expansions and are increasingly willing to spend large sums of money to attract economic activity.

For example, in the 1990s Mercedes-Benz opened an automobile assembly plant in Vance, Alabama, and BMW opened one in Spartanburg, South Carolina. The subsidy for Mercedes was estimated to be in the $250 million range, and that for BMW at about $150 million. On a per job basis, the Mercedes subsidy was about $168,000 and the BMW subsidy in the $65,000 range. The subsidies were a mixed bag of direct payments to the companies, public investment on infrastructure for the companies, and a variety of preferential tax treatments.

In some cases states have offered major packages to firms not to move in, but simply not to move out. Perhaps this trend is inevitable. Bids to move will be matched by bids to stay.

> Illinois officialdom breathed a collective sigh of relief last June [1989] when word came that Sears, Roebuck and Company had chosen the Chicago suburb of Hoffman Estates as the new location of its 6,000-worker merchandise group. Sears had announced earlier in the year that it would leave its landmark building, the Sears Tower, in downtown Chicago.
>
> Although keeping Sears cost the state some $178 million and didn't create a single new job, Gov. James R. Thompson hailed the decision as "a great victory" for his state.[4]

The state of Illinois no doubt had numerous other good uses for the $178 million (almost $30,000 per job saved) it spent on relocating Sears. But it had little choice about making the expenditure. One reason for its having little choice was that the Sears distribution center, with its 6,000 jobs, would be quite a prize for any economic development agency and had undoubtedly attracted other substantial offers. Illinois thus had no choice but to make a counteroffer. In a purely political sense, Governor Thompson had no choice either, for if Sears had moved out of the state, he would have been bludgeoned with that fact day and night in his next election campaign.

For the state or locality that provides a big subsidy package in order to attract a new industry, the net payoff may be positive or negative. On the positive side, there are incomes from new jobs and increased tax revenues from the additional economic activity and property development. On the other hand, economic growth generally promotes population growth, and so there will be additional expenses for schools, social services, handling the increased flow of traffic, and the like. Whether, after taking account of the costs of subsidization, the increased revenues will be more than or less than the additional expenses will vary from case to case. Whether or not a new firm will raise average wages in an area may also be problematic. One would expect the general tightening of labor markets caused by increased employment to raise the average wage. However, if the wage profile of the new firm is substantially below the average of employers already in place, the new firm may have the unexpected effect of lowering the average wage.

Beyond using their own funds to attract firms, states will often pursue federal investment within their boundaries. That attempt might mean using the influence and power that the state's congressional delegation has to push for having parts of a multibillion-dollar weapons system made in their state. It might mean pushing for the opening of a new federal facility built in their state rather than somewhere else. Or it might mean having the state's congressional delegation do everything it can to resist a decision to close a military base in the state. Pursuit of federal funds for highway construction is another example, for accessibility is an important consideration when firms make location decisions.

In the present climate of high unemployment and very big state government deficits the necessity to compete with other states by holding down tax rates becomes an argument for cutting services, laying off state employees, and weakening the power of public sector unions. It has also become an argument for adopting "right-to-work" laws in states that do not have them.[5] Viewed at a national level, cutting back on state expenditures to lower state taxes my be a zero-sum game; however, viewed from the perspective of a single state it makes some sense. Tax rates are far from the biggest consideration when firms decide to relocate or expand, but they are of some importance. The same can be said for right-to-work laws. If all states had them the net effect might not be much different than if no states had them. But if one state has a right-to-work law it will give it an advantage over a state that does not have one, for, all other things being equal, most firms prefer locations where labor unions are weak.

LOCAL ECONOMIC DEVELOPMENT PROGRAMS _____

At the local level there is intense interest in economic development. Of the more than 15,000 organizations in the United States devoted to economic development, the vast majority operate at the local level—city, county, town, or neighborhood.

Communities have several motives for pursuing economic development. One is employment. Increasing the size of the local economy seems like an obvious way to reduce unemployment. In fact, economic development often decreases local unemployment by considerably less than one might expect. One big reason is that new jobs encourage in-migration and so many of the jobs are taken by new residents. This has been well known among regional economists for perhaps half a century but often is lost sight of in the political process.[6]

Another major motivation at the local level is property tax relief. The property tax is by far the largest source of locally raised revenue for substate levels of government. It is also by far the largest locally raised source of revenues for school districts. Most local governments and school districts find themselves under pressure on the subject of property taxes because they are caught between citizens' resistance to tax increases and demands for services. One obvious way out of the dilemma is to expand the tax base so that a given tax rate produces more revenue. In many localities the property tax motivation is actually more important than the employment motivation. For one thing, essentially all citizens pay property taxes, whereas at any given time only a minority of citizens are unemployed.[7] Then, too, there is no ambiguity about who captures the tax benefits. If a facility is built within the city or county or town or school district lines, that body receives the tax payments. On the other hand, the labor market and business stimulation effects are likely to spread far beyond the municipal boundaries. Small communities within metropolitan areas often sense that they are part of the metropolitan labor market and are too small to affect it very much. However, it is possible for them to calculate quite clearly how much a new project will add to their tax rolls.

There are other motivations as well. Economic growth is likely to be good for various sectors of the business community. Real estate brokers will benefit from an increased number of transactions. Property owners will benefit from increased demand for land and structures. Retailers will benefit from increased sales resulting from increased personal income. Construction firms—and their workers—will benefit from increased construction activity. In short, there is a good deal of general support from business and labor for local economic development efforts.

Several decades ago the prime focus of many, if not most, economic development agencies was manufacturing, and in fact the field of economic development was sometimes casually referred to as "smokestack chasing."

In the early post–world War II period manufacturing accounted for close to one-third of total U.S. enployment, and it was believed that much of it was relatively "footloose" in the sense that a manufacturer selling to a regional or national market had a potentially large choice of locations. Therefore it seemed logical for it to be the first target for many economic development agencies. But manufacturing's predominance did not last.

For several decades manufacturing employment in the United States held more or less steady in absolute numbers but declined as a percentage of total employment as the U.S. economy grew. Since about the year 2000, manufacturing employment in the United States began to decline in absolute numbers as well. It currently accounts for somewhat less than 10 percent of total U.S. employment. Thus today one is more likely to find municipalities and their economic development agencies pursuing retailing, business and personal services, office, recreation, and other categories where there is significant employment growth.

A number of municipalities, states, and regional agencies have developed research parks to attract high-tech firms. These firms may do high-tech work like software development or scientific research and some may do, on a small scale, cutting-edge manufacturing, where technical prowess and the ability to attract small numbers of very highly trained and qualified personnel is more important than low labor costs. For most such parks the core resource is the presence of a major university with strength in science and engineering. For example, Virginia Tech in Blacksburg, Virginia, is associated with a very successful facility called the Corporate Research Center. The center is located about a mile from the center of the campus. Its employees can pursue degrees at the university (a powerful recruiting tool) and have access to the university's library and computer facilities. The location facilitates consulting arrangements with the school's faculty and provides a convenient venue for faculty members who may work for or be principals in firms at the park. Finally, putting a large number of high-tech firms together where they use a variety of common facilities provides a venue for the casual exchange of useful ideas and information.

A Crucial Difference

Most of the planning discussed in this book does not involve intermunicipal competition. If town A improves its park system, that effort will not make the park system in town B worse. In fact, it may stimulate town B to improve its park system. But if town A through infrastructure improvements, tax abatements, or other inducements causes Universal Valve and Faucet to locate there instead of in town B, its gain is town B's loss. In that sense of intense head-to-head competition and sometimes zero-sum outcomes, local economic development efforts represent a unique area of public policy and planning.[8]

The Relationship Between Planners and Economic Developers

Planners and economic developers necessarily have considerable interaction, for both are concerned with public investment in infrastructure, land-use controls, environmental regulations, and anything else that affects the what and where of industrial and commercial development. Sometimes the relationship between the community's planners and its economic developers will be a happy one, but sometimes it will not. To the planner, bringing in new firms and encouraging the expansion of firms already in the community will be one of a number of goals. To the economic developer, these may be, in practice, the only goals. Thus the planners' *we want development but it has to fit into the master plan* perspective can conflict with the developers' *do whatever it takes to bring them in* position. When a potential investor wants to do what the economic developers think is the right thing but in what the planners think is the wrong place, the scene is set for disagreement. The issue can go either way, depending on the priorities of the municipality's political establishment.

That planners and economic developers have many professional links is hard to deny. At one time the author and a colleague surveyed a large number of directors of economic development agencies. One question was, "If economic development was not your first profession, what was your previous profession?" The most common single answer was *urban planner.*

What a Community Can Do to Promote Its Economic Growth

In a very general way, there are four major things a community can do to facilitate its own economic growth. As will become apparent, there is a certain amount of overlap among them.

Sales and Promotion.   The community can engage in a variety of public relations, advertising, selling, and marketing efforts. In effect, it can view itself as a product and then make a concerted effort to sell that "product." For a firm seeking a location, there is no feasible way to gather objective information about all the possibilities. The community that makes itself highly visible thus gives itself an advantage.

Subsidization.   The community can subsidize development in a variety of ways. One form is tax abatement. Since the main tax used by local government is the property tax, abatement most commonly takes the form of reduced property taxes for new commercial or industrial development. Some communities will set up revolving loan funds or other credit-granting arrangements to facilitate business growth. If the municipality levies sales, inventory, commercial occupancy, or business taxes, it may offer reductions in these.

The enterprise zone is a variation on this theme. The city, town, county, or state designates an area as an enterprise zone. Within this zone a variety of tax breaks are offered for new investment. These may include property tax reductions, sales tax reductions, reduced corporate income tax, and so on. In addition, direct grants may be offered. Another inducement may be the waiving of some land-use regulations to permit higher densities. The technique has most commonly been used in the attempt to restore deteriorated central-city areas.

The use of municipal funds for subsidies, whether through direct expenditure or through the tax expenditure route such as a property tax abatement, has some inherent problems. If the municipality gives assistance to one firm, it has to find the money to do so. If that pushes up its tax rate, it has simultaneously made itself more attractive to one firm but less attractive to every other firm. The question is which effect predominates? That is not always easy to decide.

Subsidizing is bedeviled with the matter of information asymmetry. In the ideal case a subsidy would be given only if it were decisive. If the firm were going to invest in the community in any case, then the subsidy is just a windfall to the firm and serves no community purpose. Assuming that the subsidy is decisive, the subsidy should be exactly the minimum size to get the firm to do what the municipality wants it to do. Any money beyond that minimum amount is also a windfall. Determining whether the subsidy is decisive and whether, if so, it is the minimum amount necessary is no easy matter. It is in the interest of the firm to get as big a subsidy as possible, and so the firm will take the position that of course it is necessary and it has to be very large. The firm knows its own motivations and, if it has been shopping for a new location, what offers are available from other places. But this information is generally not available to the municipality or its economic development agency. The firm reveals what it chooses to reveal. On the other hand, the municipality and its development agency as public bodies have to operate in a relatively open manner. In effect, it is a poker game in which one player is allowed to hold his cards close to his chest and the other has to play with his cards face up on the table. The chance that the municipality will get the offer just right is small.

Special Small Area Finance Arrangements.   There are a variety of arrangements a municipality may use to direct funding to the economic development of selected areas when that suits its larger economic development strategy. One is tax increment financing (TIF). Here the increase in property tax revenues resulting from new development in the area is reserved for reinvestment in that area. A related device is the business investment district (BID). Here, property owners within the district are charged a surtax above the prevailing property tax rate, with that surcharge dedicated to investment within the district. The BID surcharge may be politically acceptable even in a generally antitax environment because the link between who pays and who benefits is so clear.

Making Sites and Buildings Available.   Availability of sites or buildings is a key factor in determining whether a community can attract new commercial activity and retain existing activity. What constitutes a usable site? Consider a planning agency in a suburban or metropolitan fringe area setting up preliminary criteria for identifying potential industrial or commercial land. A first cut might be to rule out any land with a slope of more than 5 percent, for steep slopes push up site-preparation and construction costs. Subsoil conditions such as drainage problems or rock outcroppings that add to construction costs might be a second cut. If the municipality is traversed by a river or stream, land in the flood plain might also be eliminated from consideration. Availability of utilities such as water, sewers, and electric power is also a criterion. For light manufacturing, retailing, wholesaling, and office activities, adequate road access would also be a requirement. For heavy manufacturing, rail access as well is likely to be needed. In addition to having an adequate number of acres available, there is also the matter of site geometry. For heavy industry, a minimum site depth of 800 feet might be a good rule of thumb. For light manufacturing, minimum depths of 400 to 600 feet are desirable.

To ensure that adequate sites will be available in the foreseeable future, there are various steps a municipality can take. The most direct step is the public provision of sites. Numerous cities, towns, and counties have municipal industrial parks. The community uses public funds (and sometimes the power of eminent domain as well) to acquire and develop sites. The prepared sites are then sold or leased long term to firms, which erect and operate manufacturing or other commercial buildings on them. Very often, there is a significant public subsidy in such operations in that the rent or sales price covers only a fraction of the costs incurred in site acquisition, grading, drainage, building of access roads, running water and sewer lines, and so on.

Some communities will go even further by erecting a building and then seeking a firm or firms to occupy it. Very often the structure put up is a "shell building." The community puts up the outer shell of the building and then waits until it has found a firm to use the building before it completes the interior. Again, there may or may not be an element of subsidy in the process. In either case, the community bears the risk, namely, that the building will not sell or rent.

Another community might take a somewhat more tentative approach and engage in land banking, that is, acquiring land or perhaps options on land with a view simply to hold it as a potential commercial site. Of course, such a method is expensive. The financial cost to the community is the loss of interest on whatever funds are tied up in the land. If the community sinks $1 million into land banking and the current rate at which the community borrows is 5 percent, the carrying cost is $50,000 for this year, a burden that must be borne by the municipality's taxpayers.

حاشية

Incubator Buildings.   Many economic development programs try to foster small-business development through the use of incubator buildings. This is a building that provides space for business start-ups. The idea is to reduce costs by use of shared facilities and in some cases also by some degree of subsidy if that space is rented to firms at below cost. The economic development agency may also provide technical assistance for beginning entrepreneurs, perhaps by arranging mentoring relationships with other businesspeople in the community.

تمرين اكثر

Revolving Loan Funds.   The revolving loan fund starts with a block of capital either from public or local business sources and uses it to make small loans to small local businesses. As those loans are repaid, funds become available for additional loans: There may or may not be some subsidy in the form of reduced interest rate. Such funds, because their goal is community development rather than profit, are generally willing to make some loans that a commercial lender would not. A revolving loan fund might also help firms by offering loan guarantees so that they can obtain commercial credit. At this time when many banks are feeling especially cautious and many small businesses find it hard to borrow money, such founds might have an expanded role—provided, of course, that they are able to raise sufficient capital.

Use of Land-Use Controls and Provision of Infrastructure.   Beyond the direct provision of land, the community can use its land-use control powers to ensure that adequate privately owned land will be available for commercial development. One obvious step is simply zoning an adequate amount of land in the appropriate categories. The zoning should be applied to land that actually has real development potential, land that meets the sorts of topographic and geometric standards previously described. It also means land that either already has been or has the potential for being provided with adequate access and utilities. As noted in Chapter 8, the zoning should be coordinated with the land uses shown on the comprehensive plan.

The infrastructure question is addressed through the community's capital budget. For sites with near-term development potential, capital funds can be spent to provide utilities and access. For sites with longer-term potential, it is hard to justify immediate expenditure. However, providing infrastructure to these sites can be an item on the community's capital improvements program scheduled for some years hence.

None of these measures will guarantee that a given parcel of land will be used for commercial or industrial use or that it will not be put to some other use. However, by declaring its intent through master planning, zoning, and capital budgeting, the community decreases the odds that lands with economic potential will be preempted by other uses. Assume that a block of 100 acres has good potential for economic development in the long term but that its chances for such development in the next few years are small. The owner has the chance to sell 5 acres out of its center for residential use now. However, dividing the site in that manner will greatly reduce its ultimate commercial or industrial potential. By telegraphing its long-term intentions as described, the community encourages the property owner to take a long-term rather than a short-term view of the situation.

Cooperation and Competition

At one time local economic development was an almost entirely competitive activity, a sort of intermunicipality "war of all against all," to use a phrase Thomas Hobbes originally said in a very different context. But in recent years that has changed. For many municipalities, especially as regards manufacturing, the most serious competitor is not the next town or the next county, but a producer 10,000 miles away. As a result there are now a very large number of multijurisdictional agencies that seek to promote an area, rather than a single jurisdiction. These agencies may share advertising and public relations expenses and have a policy of seeking to guide prospective investors to whichever jurisdiction in the area best meets the needs of that investor. For such agencies the old habit of trying to seduce firms away from neighboring jurisdictions is no longer acceptable.

Pursuit of Investment by Higher Levels of Government

As do state governments, local governments also pursue investment by higher levels of government. Occasionally the higher level of government is the federal government. More often, it is the state government.

For example, many counties, particularly in rural or semirural areas, have decided that prisons make a good source of jobs. They are labor-intensive activities, and employment in them is not subject to the vagaries of the business cycle. If there is a site that is suitable for a prison and not too close to a center of population, the municipality may well exert itself to get the next state prison built there. Other state facilities, too, may be the subject of considerable competition by local governments. Local governments frequently seek to influence federal and state investment in highways, for good highway access is often a necessary though not sufficient condition for attracting private capital investment.

Larger Considerations

How much can a municipality do to promote its own growth? As stated, a municipality can do a considerable amount to make itself known to potential investors, it can (with the caveats noted) use subsidies, and it can do a certain amount in terms of sites and infrastructure. But there are also larger matters that are not within municipal control or are only partly within municipal control. When firms are questioned about how they make location decisions, two items that come up very frequently are market access and the local labor market. Market access is primarily a matter of location, and that is beyond municipal control. Labor market considerations are a mixed bag. The size of the labor market, prevailing wages, and labor force quality all weigh heavily with potential employers. The last item is a mix of skills, education, and some intangibles like "work ethic." For many firms, quality of life questions weigh heavily in the location choice. This is partly because the executives and owners making the location decision care about where they will live and also partly because of recruitment considerations. If the recruitment of highly skilled personnel who are in high demand is critical to the success of the firm, then being located in an area that will be attractive to these potential employees is very important. What constitutes a good quality of life is a subjective matter, but items like climate, an attractive natural environment, recreational opportunities, cultural opportunities, the quality of public education, and personal safety are likely to be important to a very large number of people.

Some of the items listed in this section are entirely beyond the ability of a municipality to affect and some can be affected to some degree. To a large extent, the municipality and its economic development agency have to play the hand that they are dealt.

The importance of these larger questions also suggests that sometimes investments that are not directly aimed at economic development may have a bigger development payoff than investments that are directly targeted to economic development. For example, investment in a museum or concert hall, or in public parks, or in a system of bicycle paths by their contribution to the quality of life as perceived by potential employers might have a bigger payoff than, say, direct subsidies for investment in the municipality. Similarly, investment in public education might pay off in terms of both the perception of and the actuality of labor force quality. Two researchers studying employment in U.S. central cities concluded that the "only consistent correlate with long term economic success is the level of educational achievement of the workforce."[9] This finding is broadly consistent with the view of the urban geographer Richard Florida that the most important determinant of a city's economic success in the long term is its ability to attract and retain members of what he refers to as the "creative class."

Of course, investing in education will not always have a guaranteed economic development payoff. For one thing, people do migrate. Many a small town has the unhappy experience of seeing some of its graduating high school seniors take their diplomas and head for more promising labor markets very shortly thereafter. Formulating an economic development strategy that makes the most efficient use of limited municipal funds is no easy task.

A Systematic Approach to Economic Development Planning

The following is a brief account of how a municipality might approach economic development planning.[10]

    1. *Needs assessment.*   In this phase the municipality decides the purpose of the program. The two most common goals are providing additional employment opportunities and strengthening the municipal tax base. If the main goal is jobs, the municipality should consider whether the goal is simply to increase the total number of jobs or whether it is seeking particular types of jobs, perhaps to address high rates of unemployment or underemployment among particular sectors of its labor force. Being clear about the goals of the program is particularly useful if choices have to be made about the expenditure of public funds on competing projects.

    2. *Market evaluation.*   In order to develop an effective marketing program, the municipality's economic development agency tries to make an objective assessment of the municipality's competitive strengths and weaknesses. This means examining wages and the availability of labor, taxes, land and construction costs, utility rates, the composition of its existing commercial and industrial establishment, strengths and weaknesses in its transportation infrastructure, its educational and cultural establishment, and a variety of quality-of-life items. Such an assessment will help the municipality target its sales and marketing efforts toward those types of firms that are most likely to be interested in relocating to or expanding in that municipality.

    3. *Assessment of the consequences of an economic development program.* Economic development will involve fiscal effects, both new revenues and also new expenditures. It may also affect traffic flow, environmental quality, housing markets, and many other aspects of community life. Anticipating and planning for those effects is part of a systematic approach to economic development.

    4. *Plan formulation.*   The plan might include some or all of the following elements:

        a. An advertising and marketing program.
        b. A plan for the use of subsidies such as property and other tax abatements, low-interest loans or loan guarantees, or public absorption of some of the costs of site acquisition and development.

    c. A program of capital investments in water, sewer, road, and other facilities necessary to support industrial and commercial development. If the municipality decides to take an entrepreneurial role, it might include planning for the development of a municipal industrial or commercial park or the construction of a shell building.

    d. A land-use element. This might involve adjusting the municipality's land-use controls to provide adequate industrial and commercial sites and possibly also the purchase or optioning of land for future economic development.

SUMMARY

Planning for economic development dates back many decades. Early efforts tended to focus on transportation and generally were initiated by the commercial elite of the city.

Beginning in the 1960s the federal government began to subsidize local economic planning and development efforts with a view to combating structural unemployment. This policy continues to the present time, though it peaked in the Carter presidency and has become progressively less significant under both Republican and Democratic presidents.

Virtually all states strive to foster their own economic growth through a variety of programs involving marketing, subsidization, and the use of capital expenditures. Many thousands of municipalities also promote their own economic development using marketing and subsidization. Very often, the community will use its capital budget and its land-use policies to ensure the availability of an adequate number of suitable sites.

Steps in a simple systematic approach to planning for economic development include the following:

1. Needs assessment
2. Market evaluation
3. Assessment of the consequences of development policy
4. Plan formulation
5. Plan review and updating

NOTES

1. For an overall description of interplace economic competition and the general workings of local economic development agencies, see the first several chapters of John M. Levy, *Economic Development Programs for Cities, Counties and Towns*, 2nd ed., Praeger, New York, 1990. For a current picture of the field, see *Economic Development Quarterly*.

2. For a picture of the economics of transportation in the United States at the beginning of the nineteenth century, see Alan Pred, *City Systems in Advanced Economies*, John Wiley, New York, 1977.

3. Alfred Eichner, *State Development Agencies and Employment Expansion*, University of Michigan Press, Ann Arbor, 1970.
4. Robert Guskind, "The Giveaway Game Continues," *Planning*, February 1990, pp. 4–8.
5. Right-to-work laws permit workers who do not wish to belong to unions to not join even though the plant or company is unionized. They are generally found in politically conservative states, especially in the South. This is in contrast to the union shop in which all employees in unionized categories are required to be members.

   Right-to-work laws weaken unions both by reducing the number of unionized workers and also by limiting the amount of dues the union can collect, for large dues will cause more workers to choose not to be members.
6. The measured unemployment rate may be very little changed for two reasons: There is the migration effect noted in the text. Also, new jobs may draw in residents who had dropped out of the labor force and thus were no longer counted as unemployed. For a summary of experience on this point, see Gene Summers, *The Invasion of Nonmetropolitan America by Industry: A Quarter Century of Experience*. Praeger, New York, 1976. See also Wilbur Thompson, "Economic Processes and Employment Problems in Declining Metropolitan Areas," in *Post Industrial America: Metropolitan Decline and Job Shifts*, George Sternlieb and James W. Hughes, eds., Center for Urban Policy Research, Rutgers University, New Brunswick, NJ, 1976.
7. Homeowners pay property taxes directly. Renters pay them indirectly since they are a cost that the landlord must cover and thus are passed on to the renter. As a rule of thumb, property taxes account for about a fourth of the total rent. All people also pay property taxes indirectly whenever they make a purchase, since property taxes are a cost that retailers, wholesalers, service businesses, manufacturers, etc., must cover. As a political matter, homeowners tend to be acutely aware of property taxes while renters generally are not.
8. The term comes from game theory and refers to a game in which the total sum of winnings necessarily must equal the total sum of losings, say several people playing poker together.
9. Edward W. Hill and John Brennan, "American Central Cities and the Location of Work," *Journal of the American Planning Association*, vol. 71, no. 2, Autumn 2005, pp. 411–432.
10. Not all communities approach economic development in this systematic manner. In many cases, for a variety of political reasons, communities jump into economic development programs without much planning, and the program largely amounts to a matter of shooting at targets of opportunity. See H. J. Rubin, "Shoot Anything That Flies; Claim Anything That Falls," *Journal of the American Planning Association*, vol. 56, Spring 1988, pp. 153–160; and John M. Levy, "What Local Economic Developers Actually Do: Location Quotients Versus Press Releases," *Journal of the American Planning Association*, Spring 1990, pp. 153–161.

SELECTED BIBLIOGRAPHY

BLAKELY, EDWARD J., *Planning Local Economic Development: Theory and Practice*, Sage, Newbury Park, CA, 1989.

FITZGERALD, JOAN, and LEIGH, NANCY GREEN, *Economic Revitalization: Cases and Strategies for City and Suburb*, Sage, Thousand Oaks, CA, 2002.

GLASMEIER, AMY K., *The High Tech Potential: Economic Development in Rural America*, Center for Urban Policy Research, Rutgers University, New Brunswick, NJ, 1991.

MALIZIA, EMIL, *Local Economic Development: A Guide to Practice*, Praeger, New York, 1985.

MITCHELL, JERRY, *Business Improvement Districts and the Shape of American Cities*, State University of New York Press, Albany, 2008.

VAL, AVRAM BEN-David, *Regional Economic Analysis for Practitioners: An Introduction*, 4th ed., Praeger, New York, 1991.

WATSON, DOUGLAS J., and MORRIS, JOHN C., eds., *Building the Local Economy: Cases in Economic Development*, Carl Vinson Institute of Government, University of Georgia, Athens, 2008.

WHITE, SAMMIS B., BINGHAM, RICHARD D., and HILL, EDWARD, *Financing Economic Development in the 21st Century*, M. E. Sharpe, Inc., Armonk, NY, 2003.

CHAPTER 14

Growth Management, Smart Growth, and Sustainable Development

Growth management is generally defined as the regulation of the *amount*, *timing*, *location*, and *character* of development. Since the late 1960s hundreds of cities, counties, and towns in the United States have instituted growth management programs. Many state plans, too, have large elements of growth management.

The goals of these programs vary. Growth management programs are often heavily motivated by environmental considerations. A related consideration may be ensuring a desirable pattern of land development in future years. Preserving an existing lifestyle and community ambiance are common motivations, as is ensuring that community facilities such as schools, roads, utilities, and recreation will be adequate for future needs. In some cases a major goal of growth management will be fiscal, ensuring that the community will not be swamped by development-imposed costs. Finally, like the exclusionary zoning discussed earlier, growth management may have an exclusionary, or "keeping the good things to ourselves," motivation. Rarely will a program be instituted for a single reason. Untangling the various motivations and saying exactly why a community has entered into growth management may be extremely difficult.

In general, growth management plans or systems are made up of elements that have been well known to planners for years. Growth management systems differ from traditional comprehensive planning not in the elements that compose them but in the synthesis of those elements. Specifically, growth management systems are generally characterized by very close and long-term coordination between land-use controls on the one hand and capital investment on the other. They are often also characterized by the use of more modern approaches to land-use control and often by a great sensitivity to environmental issues. In that all of these points are to be found in planning efforts that are not specifically labeled as growth management, it must be admitted that no absolutely hard line separates growth management from more traditional planning.

When growth management appeared in the late 1960s and early 1970s, several different terms with overlapping meanings came into being. A multivolume anthology of articles on the field, published in 1975, carried the title *Management and Control of Growth*.[1] In addition to the terms *growth management* and *growth control*, the term *no growth* also came into use.

Growth management might be taken to mean management without any implication of limiting growth. *Growth control* carries the implication that growth is not only to be managed or guided but also to be limited. The term *no growth* carries the obvious implication of an intent to stop growth entirely. With time, *growth management* became the standard term covering programs that fit all three senses of the term just noted. Growth management has its staunch defenders, who see it as a sensible and principled way to preserve both community and natural values. It also has its detractors, who see it as serving much more selfish purposes, as will be explained subsequently.[2]

Growth management policies are not common in older central cities, for there the problem is more likely to be shrinkage or stagnation rather than rampant growth. Growth *management* policies are common in suburban areas and in those cities where there is still substantial growth potential. They are also common in counties and towns outside metropolitan areas. The potential for rapid growth and a high degree of environmental consciousness predisposes communities toward the establishment of growth management policies. So, too, does a high degree of general prosperity. If people or communities are poor, they are likely to focus first on growth because growth implies jobs and revenues. In that case, environmental and quality-of-life issues seem less important. Interest in growth management was stronger a few years ago than today, for the slowdown in both residential and commercial development that followed the 2008 financial crisis drained immediacy away from it and shifted attention to economic development and fiscal questions.

THE ORIGINS OF GROWTH MANAGEMENT _____

Several strands came together to bring about the growth management movement. First was the rush to suburbanize after World War II. People moved outward in metropolitan areas partly to obtain relief from central-city conditions: to breathe cleaner air, to be less crowded, to be safer, and to be closer to nature. The person who has made such a move would in many cases want to be the last person who does so—thus the "I'm on board, now pull up the ladder" syndrome. No one who is active in suburban planning is unaware of such motivations.

These motivations were joined by the growing environmental consciousness that began, roughly, in the early 1960s. Growth-control proponents could gather strength and respectability from a general climate of environmental concern. Proposals to limit growth could now be supported on environmental grounds. At a local level it is hard to refute such arguments, for it is undeniable that any development, whether residential or commercial, will have some adverse environmental impact.

Whether environmentally based opposition to growth can be justified when the physical scale of analysis is expanded is another matter. If a town takes some action that keeps a particular area in, say, low-density residential use when it might otherwise have gone into high-density residential use, it has unquestionably reduced the environmental impact on that area. Fewer trees will be cut down, less ground will be covered with impervious cover, fewer sources of air and water pollution will be present in the area, and so on.[3] However, it is obvious that much of the growth that was prevented will be displaced elsewhere. In that case one cannot say, a priori, whether the total effect of the growth limitation has been to decrease or increase environmental impact. The environmental impact argument is commonly used by proponents of growth limitations, but the issue of displacement effects is less often discussed.

Regardless of the displacement effects issue, there is no doubt that the growing environmental consciousness of the 1960s and 1970s lent much strength to the growth management movement. Even global concern with overpopulation lent strength to the growth-control movement because of the superficial resemblance between planetary population control and local population control.

> Undoubtedly this [local effort to stop population growth] has much to do with the new Malthusian concern with the consequences of unlimited population growth at national and world levels. Some seem to think that the place to start controlling the nation's population growth is at the level of their city, metropolis or state. Others hope that, as the nation moves to zero population growth (ZPG), so will their communities. Both these views are misleading half-truths.[4]

Ernest F. Schumacher's book *Small Is Beautiful* and similar works that railed against the increasing scale and complexity of modern life also lent strength to growth-control movements.[5]

One of the first and best-known growth management programs in the United States was that enacted by Ramapo, New York, in 1969. The town, located about 28 miles northwest of midtown Manhattan, felt itself on the verge of being overwhelmed by new development. The town was at the very fringe of what was then commuting distance from Manhattan but was in easy reach of masses of new commercial development in the outer portions of the New York metropolitan region located in southern New York State and in adjacent parts of New Jersey. Ramapo was already zoned so that only single-family development was permitted, but it then added rules that made it possible to turn down development proposals that met the zoning requirements if the development did not have enough points for such infrastructure as sewers, nearby recreational facilities, public roads, and proximity to a firehouse, all items keyed to the town's 18-year capital improvements program. Opponents of the plan saw it simply as exclusionary zoning carried to a new level and took the town to court. On a split decision by the state's appellate (appeals) court, the town was sustained. The ordinance, which seems very primitive by today's standards, and which probably would not be sustained today, has since been rescinded. But it did mark judicial approval of growth management.[6]

WINNERS AND LOSERS IN GROWTH MANAGEMENT _____

In principle, many municipalities could slow growth with equal effectiveness by limiting either residential or commercial development. Slowing residential growth would slow commercial growth by limiting the size of the labor force and the number of customers. Similarly, limiting commercial growth would slow the growth of the housing stock because the presence of jobs is a major factor in the demand for housing.

In fact, most growth management systems emphasize limiting residential growth because such a policy tends to produce tight labor markets and high housing prices. That result is much more attractive to the population already in place than a commercial limitation policy, which would produce higher unemployment and lower housing prices. And, of course, it is the population resident at the time who establishes the growth management policy.

Assume that a growth management program has the effect of slowing residential growth relative to employment growth. Who wins, and who loses? The homeowner wins simply through the workings of the law of supply and demand. Restrict the supply of any item, and, all other things being equal, its price rises. The owner of rental property benefits in the same manner. A lesser supply of rental units in the long run means higher rents, which is capitalized as a higher value for the building in question. Of course, by the same token, the renter loses. The nonresident of the municipality, if he or she has the desire to become a resident, is also a loser, for it is now more difficult to find housing in the community. In a general sense, those who own developed property in the community benefit, and those who would like to own property lose. Those who would profit from community growth—for example, builders, construction workers, and real estate brokers—also lose. Owners of undeveloped land within the community are losers in the process, for there is a general relationship between the value of land and the intensity with which it can be developed. Restrict that intensity, and the value of land is diminished.[7]

Financial effects will be felt outside the municipality as well. If town X and town Y are in the same metropolitan area, they are to some extent part of the same housing market. If town X reduces its rate of housing construction, it deflects some housing demand to town Y. Thus housing prices in town Y (as well as in X) will rise, benefiting those who already own housing there and penalizing those who seek to buy there. Comparable effects may be seen for rental property.

Fiscal effects can also be demonstrated. If town X restricts residential development but accepts a new corporate headquarters, its tax rate may go down because the tax revenues from the headquarters exceed the new expenses that the headquarters will impose on the town. Town X is capturing the tax surplus from the headquarters while shifting the population-related costs to other towns. Town Y now has to pay the cost of educating the children of people who work in town X and whose place of work contributes handsomely to town X's tax base.

The "Defense of Privilege" Issue

Beyond the purely financial issue of winners and losers is a larger but less demonstrable issue. Much argument over environmental and planning issues is bedeviled with the question of "defense of privilege," with charges of hypocrisy by opponents of growth management and protestations of virtue by its proponents. Without trying to pass a blanket judgment over a complex situation, let us simply present an argument.

There are some goods whose enjoyment by one party does not diminish the enjoyment of comparable goods by another party. If I enjoy a fine steak, that enjoyment does not diminish your enjoyment of another steak. On the other hand, my enjoyment of a day on the ski slope may well diminish your enjoyment of your day on the slope because my presence makes the trails and the lift lines just a bit more crowded for you.

As the U.S. population becomes more prosperous, the possession of goods of the first type becomes less significant as a way of distinguishing between the affluent and the nonaffluent. Instead, the distinction increasingly becomes a matter of being able to enjoy goods and services of the second type—those whose value is lessened the more that others have access to the same or similar items. Increasingly, wealth becomes important not because it buys consumer goods but because it buys quiet, solitude, clean air, or access to relatively unspoiled nature. We can always produce more stereos, but the supply of mountain streams is fixed.

If one accepts this argument, it is only a short step to seeing some environmental and planning conflict in terms of the defense of privilege. The population of a prosperous, attractive community that seeks to limit growth is simply defending its privileges. It is seeking, by means of political action, to protect or enhance the value of those goods of the second type that it now enjoys. One might say that it is using the political process to impose losses on outsiders, that is, denying them temporary or permanent access to the community.

An interesting aspect of this argument is the lineup of combatants in fights over environmental issues. Very often business and labor will be allied in favor of development, and the opposition will be largely upper-middle class, perhaps as represented by a coalition of environmental groups like the Sierra Club. The lineup of players is not hard to understand. The same project that means profit to the developer means jobs to the construction worker, and so they make common cause. The upper-middle-class opposition earns its living neither by investing capital nor by doing construction or industrial labor. If one accepts the defense of privilege argument, this class opposes the project for the reasons presented earlier.[8]

A SAMPLING OF LOCAL GROWTH MANAGEMENT PROGRAMS

The city of Boulder, Colorado, which is located in a beautiful physical environment and offers what seems to many to be a superior quality of life, limits growth in a number of ways. Within the city, building permits for residential units are limited to 400 units a year, about 1 percent of the city's total housing stock. If there are applications for more than 400 units, each applicant gets a proportional share of what he or she has requested. Given the long-term decrease in the average number of persons per unit, the 400-unit cap means an end to population growth in Boulder.[9] This limit is becoming moot in that vacant land in the city suitable for residential development is in short supply. In fact, the city planning department estimates that at recent rates of growth, the city will reach "buildout" in another decade or so. As of the end of the first decade of this century, building permits were in the 250–300 per year range.

Ordinarily, growth pressure that cannot be accommodated in the city would be accommodated in peripheral development. But that possibility has been blocked in Boulder's case because the city, along with some other jurisdictions, has bought up land outside the city line for permanent open space, in effect, a greenbelt. The squeeze on Boulder housing prices is further intensified, since Boulder, like many other municipalities, restricts housing development more than it restricts commercial development. Thus the workforce grows faster than the housing stock. The Boulder planning department estimates that about 54 percent of all jobs in Boulder are held by workers who commute from municipalities located in the area but beyond the greenbelt.

Boulder, recognizing that its tight housing market produces very high housing prices, tries to eliminate this side effect of growth management with an affordable housing program. If a new development has five or more units, then 20 percent of those units must be "affordable." That means, for example, that a free-standing unit must be within reach of a couple earning about $86,000 per year. There are adjustments for household size and whether the unit is new or a resale and whether it is free standing or detached. The seller of the units may meet up to half of his or her affordable-housing obligation by making a payment in cash in lieu of actually providing the unit. The size of the *in lieu* payment is substantial, amounting to an average of about $120,000 for each detached unit that the seller would otherwise have to provide. Since one unit out of every five must be affordable, this means that the $120,000 is, in effect, carried by four ordinary units, which is a burden of about $30,000 per unit.

For the limited number of low- and moderate-income people lucky enough to get an affordable unit, the system works. For the lower-income or moderate-income person who is not lucky in this way or the person who falls above the income limits for an affordable unit but does not have a big income, the Boulder housing market is a tough nut to crack. In 2009 the average selling price of a single-family house in Boulder was in the $530,000 range.

Bucks County, Pennsylvania, in the Philadelphia metropolitan area, reacted to growth pressures in a somewhat different manner. Here the county has no direct control over local land use since, under Pennsylvania state law, zoning powers reside at the municipal level. The county planning department designates development districts largely on the basis of projected population change. Within those districts it recommends infrastructure (such as sewer lines, water mains, and roads) to facilitate development consistent with the natural environment and expected or planned population change. It suggests that the county outside those districts be considered a "holding zone," with land-use controls that hold population to very low density levels. This purpose is achieved by large-lot zoning requirements and tax policies that encourage farmers to keep their lands in agricultural use.[10]

In the areas designated for development, Bucks County suggests a performance zoning approach with some Euclidean elements (see Chapter 9). Rather than specifying the nature of residential development in great detail, as does the conventional or Euclidean ordinance, the county will simply suggest zoning districts that specify the amount of permissable impervious cover and the number of units per acre. Whether, for example, the units in question are to be single family or multifamily is a matter for community determination. The impervious cover requirements are cast in terms of percentage of the site covered. The intention is to control land use in terms of what is really important (in this case, population housed in an area and volume of storm-water runoff) rather than to specify a large number of details of secondary importance. From a design point of view, performance zoning achieves the overall goals of zoning but gives the designer far more freedom and should encourage much more interesting and varied designs. It relies on the marketplace rather than the zoning ordinance to achieve functional, aesthetically sound development.

As in the Boulder case, one side effect of the growth management program is higher house prices. The holding-zone approach prevents some peripheral growth that would relieve pressure on the housing stock. Because residential development is limited more strictly than commercial growth, there is also the labor market pressure noted in the Boulder case.

Although the county's role with regard to zoning is only advisory, the county is not entirely toothless. Under state legislation passed in 2001, if a municipality's land-use plans are not in conformity with the county's recommendations, the chance that the municipality will receive state aid for infrastructure development is reduced. Thus there is a substantial financial motivation for local governments to go along with county plans.

Many jurisdictions have seen the growth management problem as a largely financial issue—how to provide the infrastructure for growth before growth occurs and how to pay the infrastructure costs that growth imposes. As noted in Chapter 9, an exaction is a payment that a jurisdiction demands in return for permitting development to take place. Fairfax County, Virginia, uses a system of "proffers," a variation on the exaction theme, which requires developers to offer to pay the infrastructure costs of major projects. The county is immediately west of Washington, DC, and has experienced extremely rapid growth, particularly in office activity. It is very concerned with providing the infrastructure to keep up with this development. Because demand for commercial space is strong, the county has considerable leverage in its dealings with developers.

The county uses the ability to grant or deny rezonings as a means of obtaining proffers. For example, in the Fairfax Center area, which, roughly speaking, is a 3,000-acre development node in the county, the master plan recognizes three levels of development. There is a base level, which is essentially single-family large-lot development; an intermediate level; and an overlay level, which permits intensive commercial and multifamily residential development. Under Virginia state law, government cannot literally demand a contribution from a private party. Thus if the developer builds "by right"—that is, under the existing zoning—he or she cannot be compelled to contribute to infrastructure or other costs that the development may impose upon the county. However, if the developer wants a rezoning, the county can choose not to grant the request unless a proffer is made. The making of the proffer is thus, in a sense, voluntary. The developer makes it in the hopes of receiving something of value in return, namely, the higher profit obtainable from developing at a greater density. The proffer may take the form of actually doing off-site physical work such as improving an intersection or widening a roadway. In other cases it may take the form of a cash contribution to a housing, parks, road, or recreation fund. In order to provide affordable housing, the county requires that developers of large residential projects either include a certain number of low- and moderate-income units within the project or make a contribution to the housing trust fund to help build such units elsewhere.

Fort Collins, Colorado, uses a technique designed to direct growth into specified areas and also to require new development to pay its own infrastructure costs first. The city is located within a county, and over the years it has grown by annexation. Under the terms of a joint city–county agreement, a 65-square-mile "urban growth area" has been defined. The understanding is that all land within the growth area is ultimately subject to annexation. Within this area, urban services are provided, and urban development standards—paved roads, public water, public sewer facilities, and the like—apply. As urban development takes place, the city annexes the area. In addition to providing necessary infrastructure on-site, developers are required to provide off-site infrastructure such as roads and sewer and water lines. How much they are required to provide is based on traffic and other studies, for which they themselves are required to pay.

In the Fort Collins case, rather than contribute to a development fund, the developer is literally required to provide the specified infrastructure. A subsequent developer may be required to make payments to a prior developer if he or she makes use of the infrastructure the former has provided. For example, if developer A builds a mile of road to serve his or her project and developer B subsequently builds in such a manner as to make direct use of that road, a compensating payment from B to A may be required.

The Fort Collins approach, as seen by the city's planning agency, is "growth management" as opposed to "growth control" in the sense that the effort is to shape growth rather than limit it. In fact, in the late 1970s a growth limitation initiative analogous to Boulder's was soundly defeated by Fort Collins's voters.

STATE-LEVEL GROWTH MANAGEMENT

Many states exercise considerable control over the process of growth, particularly in environmentally sensitive areas. These controls constitute much of Bosselman's "quiet revolution," noted in Chapter 9.

Hawaii

The first statewide land-use controls were instituted in Hawaii in the early 1960s. The motivation behind them was that the land area of the islands is small, growth pressures were strong, and agriculture was important to the state economy. According to Bosselman, the goal was to keep Honolulu, the main center of population in the state, from sprawling out, Los Angeles–like, into the adjacent Central Valley of Oahu. Under legislation passed in 1961, all land in the state falls into one of four major categories: urban, rural, agricultural, and conservation. Within the urban areas, county zoning regulations prevail. In effect, counties may (but do not have to) permit urban-type development in any area that the state designates as urban. In rural and agricultural areas, land uses are controlled by the State Land Use Commission, a board set up when the system was created. In the conservation district, land use is controlled by the state's Board of Land and Natural Resources.

Perhaps it is no surprise that the first statewide system developed in Hawaii. A small, scenically beautiful state, subject to major growth pressures and having a limited supply of highly productive agricultural land, would appear to be an ideal candidate for such a system. The fact that much of the growth pressure came from outsiders, people from the U.S. mainland, may also have contributed to the passage of the act.

Partly as a result of the limitation on urban growth, Hawaii is characterized by very high housing prices. But is that bad? The person who already owns property in the state is likely to take a very different view than the person who lives on the mainland but thinks it would be nice to buy a condominium in Honolulu for retirement. Again, we see that planning decisions, no matter how well intended, create winners and losers.

Florida

The state of Florida faces serious environmental problems in several regards. Its population growth has been extremely rapid in the last several decades and is likely to continue at a brisk pace when the present foreclosure crisis is resolved and the economy returns to a normal level of activity. Its swampy areas are environmentally fragile, as is often the case with tropical soils. Its groundwater supplies are readily threatened by saltwater intrusion because much of the state lies very close to sea level.[11]

In 1972, after considerable lobbying by environmental groups, the state legislature passed the Environmental Land and Water Management Act, as well as several ancillary pieces of legislation. In "areas of critical state concern" and on "developments of regional impact," the state can overrule local land-use decisions if they fail to take into account effects that extend beyond the locality's boundaries.[12] John M. DeGrove quotes the key language of the legislation defining areas of critical state concern as

1. An area containing, or having significant impact upon, environmental, historical, natural, or archeological resources of statewide importance
2. An area significantly affected by, or having significant effect upon, an existing or proposed major public facility or other area of major public investment
3. A proposed area of major development potential, which may include a proposed site of a new community, designated in a state land development plan

The "new community" provision is particularly germane to Florida because much of its population has been accommodated in major new developments, frequently carved out of environmentally sensitive former wilderness. Developments of regional impact are defined as projects that "because of [their] character, magnitude or location, would have a substantial effect on the health, safety or welfare of the citizens of more than one county." Thus, for example, a regional shopping center that would affect the pattern of vehicular traffic in adjacent counties could be classified as being of regional impact. So, too, could a power plant or an industrial facility whose emissions could have measurable effects on the air quality in adjacent counties.

In 1985 the state enacted the Growth Management Act, which added another level of control through "concurrency requirements."[13] These requirements stipulate that before new development can occur, local governments must demonstrate to the state Department of Community Affairs (DCA) that the infrastructure required to support the development is in place. For example, before new housing is built, it must be shown that the water and sewer capacity necessary to support it exists. Similarly, it must be shown that the road capacity exists to handle the additional traffic at an acceptable level of service. If the capacity cannot be shown to exist, then DCA can prevent the project from going forward. Concurrency requirements thus constitute a powerful tool both for imposing some higher-level control and also for avoiding environmental degradation and congestion. But the actual workings of the concurrency requirements are another demonstration that in planning all things are more complex than they first appear. One goal of state planning is to avoid excessive sprawl. Suppose a developer would like to develop on skipped-over parcels in an already developed area (sometimes referred to as "infill"). Traffic congestion in that area, however, is already such that without new road construction, the area cannot meet concurrency requirements. The developer may then choose to invest in a less developed area where traffic flow is not congested and there is no concurrency problem. In that case, the concurrency requirements promote sprawl. To deal with this problem, the Environmental Lands and Management Act (1993) contains provisions for the creation of Transportation Concurrency Exemption Areas (TCEAs). These can be created if the local government will commit itself to improving public transportation or engaging in various transportation demand management initiatives. (See Chapter 12.) The 1993 act also permits local governments to average traffic conditions over an entire "district" rather than have a project blocked because of conditions on one segment or link.

Florida's growth management program has always faced substantial opposition. When a program in effect says to a landowner or a developer, "You can't do that here" or "Maybe you can do that here someday, but not now," it is imposing a financial loss, and sometimes a very substantial one. In 2009 the Florida legislature passed a bill, SB 360, that appeared to significantly weaken the state's growth management abilities. A majority of Republican legislators voted for it and a majority of Democrats voted against it. Virtually every environmental group in the state, as well as the American Planning Association, opposed it and there was hope that the state's Republican governor, Charlie Crist, who looked to many as having a good environmental record, might be persuaded to veto it. But, in the end, he went with his party.

It is said that "the devil is in the details," and in this case one big detail is that the new law defines as "a dense urban land area" any area with a population of more than 1,000 persons per square mile. Thus an area that was developed with, say, single-family houses on acre lots would easily qualify as urban, and hence could be exempted from concurrency requirements. The act also defines a number of cities and parts of eight counties as urban. The net result appears to be to weaken the overall effect of concurrency requirements and thus permit a more scattered and sprawling pattern of development.

Oregon

Oregon has had a state growth management plan since 1973. At this time Oregon was growing at about twice the rate of the United States as a whole, with much concern about the consequences of such rapid growth. The state, considered as a whole, was not and is not densely populated, but growth was highly visible because most of it was occurring in one area, the Willamette Valley south of Portland. The phrase "Don't Californicate Oregon" appeared on bumper stickers at about this time. The state's then governor, Thomas McCall, was a strong environmentalist and a proponent of limiting population growth. Under the plan, all cities and counties are required to make their own land-use plans conform to the goals of the state plan. Though the state plan has 19 separate goals, the core elements in the plan are closely related ones of preservation of natural resources and containment of urban growth. The state Department of Land Conservation and Development is required to certify that local plans are in conformity. An important feature of the plan is the use of Urban Growth Boundaries (UGBs). Land-use controls and public capital investment are designed to encourage growth within the UGBs and to discourage it outside. Local governments are encouraged to promote fairly dense development within the UGBs to minimize sprawl. By increasing the amount of development proximate to central areas, growth boundaries contribute to revitalization of central-city areas.[14]

The effects on housing prices may be a problem. Ordinary economic theory would suggest that increasing the demand for land inside of the UGB (by making development outside of the UGB more difficult) should push up housing costs. At the same time, reducing the amount of development outside the UGB might push up land and housing prices there too.

The 19 goals include, in addition to the items mentioned earlier, a variety of provisions connected with shoreline preservation, estuary preservation, economic development, air quality, energy conservation, and citizen participation, among others. The goals themselves were evolved in a public process involving many thousands of citizens, thus gaining some support for the inevitable political and legal battles over limiting growth. The plan also receives considerable political support from a nonprofit organization, the 1000 Friends of Oregon, an organization that came into being in 1975, partly founded by Governor McCall. More generally, the plan gains support from the strong pro-environmental ethos that characterizes the Pacific Northwest in general.

New Jersey

The state of New Jersey has good reason to pursue a state growth management program. With approximately 8 million people living on little more than 8,000 square miles, it is the most densely populated state in the nation.

Although the state does not have any very large cities within its borders, it is subject to development pressures from the New York metropolitan area on its northeast and the Philadelphia metropolitan area to the southwest. The resulting suburban sprawl is readily visible, particularly in the parts of the state that fall within the New York City commutershed. The state uses a variety of approaches to pursue the goals of channeling growth into designated development areas. The goals are to help protect the natural environment and also to minimize the cost of servicing population growth. Meeting those goals will also give New Jersey residents convenient access to the natural world.

The state plan is only advisory to municipal governments, but it does provide a financial carrot for local governments in that state agencies must use the state plan in making decisions about capital investments. Thus the state's power of the purse with regard to roads, water and sewer mains, the location of public facilities, and the like reinforces the plan.

Coastal areas of the state fall under the authority of the Coastal Area Facility Review Act (CAFRA), passed in 1973. Under this act, development along the state's Atlantic and Delaware Bay shores and along some of their tributaries requires both local government and state approval. Thus the state has a say over development on much of the most ecologically fragile and desirable land in the state.

Beyond that, there are two areas of the state subject to regional authorities. The 30.4-square-mile Hackensack Meadowlands area, best known to sports fans as the home of Giants Stadium, falls under the authority of the Hackensack Meadowlands Development Commission, established in 1969 and now renamed the New Jersey Meadowlands Commission. The area contains parts of two counties, Bergen and Hudson, and 14 municipalites. The area, which is across the Hudson River from Manhattan, is traversed by two rivers, the Hackensack and the Passaic. For years much of it was basically a swampy wasteland and dumping ground for the region. Yet given its position in the New York metropolitan area it was obviously a very valuable location. Clearly it needed a coordinated planning system, and that was provided by the Meadowlands commission.

The legislature that established the commission gave it the key power to override local zoning. It also let it establish a system of property tax sharing. That was important because it meant that development could be channeled to the places where it made most sense without other areas fighting it because they didn't want to lose the tax revenues (a somewhat similar system has been used in St Paul–Minneapolis; see Chapter 16). To deal with the inevitable problems of intermunicipal rivalry a Meadowlands Municipal Commission composed of the mayor of each of the 14 towns was set up, and its concerns are taken very seriously by the Meadowlands Commission.

Forty years later the results are impressive. The area is home to much commercial development as well as considerable residential development, though not quite as much as the commission would like. Highway development and traffic management have been coordinated in the area, which experiences a huge amount of commuting, both internal to New Jersey and between New Jersey and Manhattan. Much of the wetland area has been restored. Brownfields (see Chapter 15) have been redeveloped, green building standards have been promoted and widely applied, and economies of scale in the provision of various public services have been achieved through intermunicipal cooperation.

Farther south, about 1 million acres (roughly 1,600 square miles and one-fifth of the state's total land area) fall under the jurisdiction of the Pinelands Commission. The area contains 52 municipalities and parts of seven counties. Throughout the area, local plans must conform to the commission's plan. Thus the commission has control over the density of development and types of land uses permitted in this large and environmentally fragile area.

All of the preceding program does not guarantee that New Jersey will be able to control the process of sprawl, for there are very powerful forces behind sprawl—in particular, the economic dynamism of those parts of the state near New York and Philadelphia, and the public demand for housing and for what H. G. Wells a century ago (see page 14) called that "private imperium." However, this program does give the state a fighting chance to contain sprawl and to achieve an orderly pattern of development in those parts of the state where there are still substantial blocks of land that remain to be developed.

Numerous other states have growth management plans at the state level. Most plans have some of the elements noted before. Many designate development areas and seek to divert growth into those areas. Many use the state's ability to make capital investments as a carrot to induce municipal governments to make their plans conform to the state's overall plan. State plans generally place emphasis on protecting environmentally fragile areas, whether they be shorelines, wetlands, estuaries, or, in the case of Vermont and other mountainous states, land at high elevations. A number of states also seek to protect areas of particular scenic or historic value from excessive development, and they use a mix of regulation and financial incentives for this purpose.

GROWTH MANAGEMENT—PRO OR CON?

Growth management, like any other planning technique, is subject to use and misuse. At best, it can be used to step into the future in a planned manner and emerge with good results—with a sensible and an attractive pattern of development, with the public treasury in good shape, with community services adequate to the tasks demanded of them, and with the natural environment disrupted to a minimal degree. At worst, growth management techniques can be used to block legitimate growth, to defend the privileges of those already privileged, and to displace the inevitable costs of development to other jurisdictions.

Quite probably, the best results will be obtained when the government doing the managing corresponds in size to a natural labor market or housing market. If the primary purpose of the growth management system is environmental, it seems likely that all other things being equal, the best results will be obtained if there is a correspondence between the physical jurisdiction of the managing unit and the realities of the environmental processes. In this case the displacement effects of growth management decisions will be taken account of to a substantial degree. On the other hand, if the jurisdiction is small with regard to the economic, social, or physical effects resulting from its actions, the temptation to consider only parochial interests and to ignore the numerous effects of local decisions on outsiders may be hard to resist.

THE CHALLENGE OF SMART GROWTH

In the mid-1990s the term *smart growth* appeared on the planning scene and rapidly became the buzzword of the day. The term was first used in connection with the Maryland state plan under then governor Parris Glendenning. Whether smart growth is inherently different from growth management as just described or whether it is basically growth management under a more attractive name—who could be in favor of "stupid growth"?—is arguable. In either case, smart growth refers to a set of issues that will be with us for years to come.

From 1990 to 2000, U.S. population grew by about 32 million people. That rate of growth, about 3 million per year, continued well into the first decade of this century. (It may have slowed somewhat at the end of the decade as a weakening U.S. labor market reduced immigration, but that is probably only temporary.) Most of that growth has occurred in those parts of metropolitan areas outside the central city, what we refer to as the suburbs even though not all of these areas are suburban in character.

Much of the concern with smart growth has been driven by a concern with suburban sprawl, a condition that derives directly from that population growth. There is no standard, unambiguous definition of sprawl, but many of us may take an I-can't-define-it-but-I-know-it-when-I-see-it position. Reid Ewing suggests that indicators of sprawl are the following:

1. Leapfrog or scattered development
2. Commercial strip development
3. Large expanses of low-density or single-use development (as in sprawling bedroom communities)[15]

He then goes on to argue that these readily observable signs do not tell the entire story and that there are some functional indicators as well. The most important of these is "poor accessibility." In an area of sprawl, getting around is inconvenient. One must drive past undeveloped areas to get to one's destination. On roads characterized by strip development, one must pass many commercial uses before getting to one's destination. Because potential destinations are scattered about, it is difficult to combine errands or trips—each destination may be in a different direction.

Ewing also suggests that lack of "functional open space" is also an indicator of sprawl. Though the area will have large amounts of undeveloped land, most of it is in private hands, perhaps with access blocked by other development, and thus unavailable for recreational or other public use.

If we use a definition like Ewing's, then sprawl is not a matter of low density alone, though there may be a correlation between sprawl and low density of development. A 10-square-mile area with a population of, say, 10,000 might be an example of sprawl if it met some or all of the preceding criteria. On the other hand, if the same number of people were grouped in several centers with jobs, shopping, and other destinations generally within short distances of residences and if there were substantial blocks of undeveloped land accessible to and open to the public, then by a definition like Ewing's, we would not call it sprawl. We might, in fact, consider it to be an exemplar of desirable low-density development.

The biggest force behind smart growth has been citizen concern over one aspect of sprawl, namely, traffic congestion. The suburban resident who finds that his or her commuting time is increasing because of growing congestion on major roadways and who finds that trips to shopping, to visit friends, and to entertainment and recreation are making him or her feel as if the car is becoming a second home is likely to feel that something needs to be done. Often that something is planning for smart growth. Other forces behind the push for smart growth have been concern over preservation of the natural environment and concern with what some suburban residents may regard as excessive urbanization of their environs. Because smart growth does not have a precise definition, the term means different things to different people, and it is thus a large political tent that can contain many people with different tastes and agendas.

One element in a smart growth agenda might be using land-use controls, tax policy, and perhaps some public subsidies to encourage compact development. In the same vein, the smart growth program might place an emphasis on infill development and reuse, whether of old buildings or of previously used industrial and commercial sites. A smart growth program might also involve buying up or acquiring development rights for some undeveloped land to ensure a supply of future open space and to channel development into selected areas. Urban growth boundaries, such as those used around Portland, Oregon, might be part of a smart growth agenda.

Those who favor smart growth are likely to be fans of the New Urbanism (see Chapter 10). New Urbanist design emphasizes relatively close spacing between structures and a fine-grained mixture of land uses. Both of these should facilitate trips by foot or bicycle and also reduce the average length of automobile trips.

Because smart growth is an attractive but not a precisely defined term, there will inevitably be disagreement about just which policies really are smart. For example, a county in the fast-growing fringe of a metropolitan area decides to buy up big blocks of farmland (or the development rights for that farmland) in order to channel growth and preserve open space. Proponents of the move argue that the move is good for the county's present and future residents and also good environmentally because it preserves the habitats of many species. But opponents argue that it simply diverts growth to further out-locations—in effect, it simply promotes leapfrog development at a larger scale. It is not always easy to say who is right. Smart growth, because it is such a nice term, may sometimes be used as a flag of convenience by those whose real game is simply NIMBY (Not in My Back Yard).

Smart growth policies may be pursued at many geographic scales—municipal, county, or state. Because the term originated in Maryland, we take a quick look at Maryland's Smart Growth Program begun in 1997. The background conditions that propelled the state into the program were two-fold. First, Maryland is a small state with a higher than average population density—over 500 people per square mile compared with somewhat under 100 people per square mile for the average of the coterminous ("lower") 48 states. In fact, only 4 states—Massachusetts, Rhode Island, Connecticut, and New Jersey—have higher densities. Second, a large percentage of the state's population lives within the greater Washington–Baltimore area and thus is sensitive to all of the sprawl-related considerations previously mentioned. Maryland defines the goals of smart growth as

1. Save our most valuable remaining natural resources.
2. Support existing communities and neighborhoods.
3. Save taxpayers millions of dollars in the unnecessary building of the infrastructure required to support sprawl.[16]

The core of the state's effort is the creation of Priority Funding Areas. The state directs its expenditures on physical infrastructure and also on some other categories such as subsidies for industrial development into priority areas in order to channel growth there. Priority areas are defined by the state as

1. Every municipality in the state.
2. All the area of Maryland that lies inside either the Washington, DC, or the Baltimore beltway. Baltimore is entirely within the state of Maryland; and

the District of Columbia, not legally a part of any state, is bordered by both Maryland and Virginia.

3. Enterprise zones, neighborhood revitalization areas, "heritage" areas (see later) and industrial areas.

Though the preceding sounds like a lot, it is only a small share of the state's total land area.

The use of the state's capital budget to concentrate development in these areas is backstopped by a number of other programs. The Rural Heritage program uses state funds to buy conservation easements on rural properties with an emphasis on preserving large contiguous blocks. A brownfields program (see Chapter 15) seeks to reduce the investment risks on disused urban industrial properties and thus to promote infill development. A "Live Near Your Work" program assists workers in buying homes near their jobs. Its goals are neighborhood stabilization and infill development.

Looking back over a decade, the program has produced modest results. The program works primarily through a variety of tax and other incentives, and working against that are very powerful economic and political forces predisposing toward sprawl. Then, too, not all local governments synchronize their planning and land-use control decisions with the smart growth program. According to Freece and Knapp, it has had more success in preserving open space than in encouraging further development within existing communities.[17] But beyond limited accomplishments in Maryland, the program has served as a model for work in other states and helped place the concept of smart growth on the nation's planning agenda.

PLANNING FOR SUSTAINABILITY

In recent years there has been much interest among planners in the matter of planning for *sustainable development*. In the United States part of the interest is homegrown, and part comes from Great Britain, the Netherlands, and other nations in western Europe where much higher population densities give many planning questions a sense of greater urgency. Most discussions of planning for sustainable development hark back to a 1987 report of the World Commission on Environment and Development—also known as the Brundtland Commission, for the name of its chair, Gro Harlem Brundtland, who was then prime minister of Norway. In its report the commission defines sustainable growth as follows:

> Sustainable development is development that meets the needs of the present without compromising the ability of future generations to meet their own needs.

That is a very general statement, and much thought and argument have been devoted since then to defining exactly what it means. On the surface it might be taken to have a simple environmental meaning. For example, in regard to forestry, it might mean not cutting more board feet of timber in one year than the forest can grow in one year. However, with the passage of time, sustainability has come to be defined more broadly. Although there is no single, unambiguous definition for sustainable development, a very rough, general agreement appears to have emerged in the last decade or so. Most writers define sustainable development planning as planning that addresses three overall goals in a coordinated manner. These goals are *environmental* quality, social *equity*, and *economic* development, easily remembered as the three "Es."[18]

The environmental requirement is readily understood as meaning planning for development that does not degrade the quality of the environment from one time period to the next. However, it should be understood that determining exactly what constitutes degradation is not always so easy. For example, suppose years of farming have thinned the topsoil somewhat in a particular area, but, at the same time, years of fertilizer use have increased the nitrate and phosphate content of the soil. Experts might disagree about whether, on balance, the soil is now better or worse than it was.

Social equity is more ambiguous. Most proponents of sustainable development take it to mean greater equality of wealth and more opportunity for poorer and less advantaged people. To defend the idea that social equity ought to be included in the concept of sustainable development, one might argue that over the long term, any social or economic system must achieve a satisfactory degree of equity or the internal stresses generated by inequity will render it unstable. Whether that is really true can be argued. There is no question that inequity and the perception of inequity have been at the root of many social and political upheavals such as the French or the Russian Revolutions. On the other hand, there have been inequitable systems that have shown remarkable stability. The caste system of India strikes most Westerners and many Indians as grossly inequitable. But the social and economic order that the system rests on has shown great stability over many centuries and is only now changing at a moderate pace under many pressures of modernity. One might even argue that some social and economic systems may become unstable as they become more equitable, because that change expands people's perspectives and whets their appetite for more change ("the revolution of rising expectations"). The point that equity is a prerequisite for long-term stability can be argued either way. The skeptic might contend that equity has been added as a criterion, not because it is intrinsically necessary for sustainability, but because those who argue for planning for sustainability also, as a group, favor more egalitarian systems—that equity has been tacked on much as a rider is tacked on to a bill in Congress.

It can be argued that at times, sustainability goals and equity goals may be in conflict, just as environmental and equity goals may be in conflict (see Chapter 15). Therefore, planning for sustainable development should address such conflicts. But that is a separate argument from the question of whether equity issues are inherently part of the question of sustainability. However, regardless of argument and counterargument, equity is now firmly ensconced as one of the three main elements of the term *sustainability* as commonly used in the planning profession.

If one accepts equity as a key element in planning for sustainability, then the requirement for economic development makes considerable sense. If equity concerns make it desirable to redistribute a certain amount of wealth, that goal will be easier to achieve if average wealth is growing than if it is stable. In a steady-state situation, any redistribution of wealth would necessarily be a zero-sum game and would meet powerful resistance.[19] This observation is no more profound than saying that it is easier to be generous if you are wealthy than if you are poor.

In principle the idea of planning for sustainable development can be applied at any scale ranging from the municipality, or perhaps even a part of a municipality, up to the planet itself. Actions to promote sustainable development at one geographic scale will inevitably have effects on the environment at other geographic scales. Then, too, what looks sustainable or not sustainable at one scale may look different at another scale. For example, the development of Manhattan (the most densely populated urban place in the United States) might look very bad from a sustainable development perspective, if viewed solely at a municipal scale. Most of the natural environment has been paved or built over; the original land form has been substantially changed; creeks, streams, and marshy areas have been filled in; and biodiversity has been vastly reduced.

On the other hand, when viewed from a larger geographic perspective, Manhattan looks environmentally virtuous. The 1.54 million people living on Manhattan's 22.7 square miles have much less environmental impact than the same number of people would if spread out over, say, 750 square miles (at a typical suburban density of 2,000 people per square mile). Transporting one person to work by subway consumes considerably less energy than transporting one person to work by car. It takes less energy to heat one apartment than it does to heat one single-family house. Fewer trees must be cut down to build one high-rise apartment than would have to be cut down to build single-family houses for an equivalent number of residents.

The amount of impervious cover is one aspect of environmental impact. Manhattan has 508 miles of streets. Multiply that by 5,280 (the number of feet in a mile). Then divide that figure by the population of Manhattan, roughly 1,540,000. The result is that there is approximately 1.7 feet of street length per Manhattan resident. Contrast that with how many feet of street there would be per resident on a suburban street of single-family houses built on 100-foot-wide lots. Thus in considering sustainable development, one may come to very different conclusions depending on whether one thinks in terms of what happens at a particular location on the map or whether one thinks in terms of accommodating a specific number of people or specific amount of economic activity.

With all of the preceding caveats, we turn now to planning for sustainable development in a single municipality.

Implementing a Local Sustainable Development Program

Advocates of sustainability are fond of the motto "think globally, act locally" with the implication that a multitude of local actions can have global effects. If the three Es of sustainability are *environmental quality, social equity*, and *economic development*, as noted before, what can a locality do to promote them?

The municipality can use its land-use controls to protect environmentally fragile areas and, more generally, to provide for its total of residential and commercial activity with a minimal footprint. Implementing green building standards (see Chapter 15) can reduce the amount of power used for heating and cooling. Solar access zoning and an accommodative rather than a resistive stance toward wind-generated power if it is technically feasible in that area can contribute to slowing down the progress of the greenhouse effect. Urban design that minimizes vehicular mileage can also help, as can land-use policy that favors housing types that consume less energy. The potential for a district energy system (see Chapter 15) could be considered. Brownfield redevelopment can be favored over green field development.

In this writer's opinion there is not a great deal that can be done with regard to equity at the local level; the really big questions like the distribution of income and access to medical care are clearly national issues, but a certain amount might be achieved in connection with housing, as discussed in Chapter 11. As noted there, how much a single municipality can achieve in this area is limited by tax rate considerations and the fact of intermunicipal ecnomic competition. If the municipality has an economic development program it might try to tune the program to meet the labor market needs of some of its least privileged residents rather than just focusing on total jobs or total additions to the tax base.

So far as economic growth, the municipality can pursue an economic development program as discussed in Chapter 13. But, as implied in that chapter, there is a question as to whether local economic development efforts contribute very much to aggregate economic growth or whether they largely redistribute a total that is more or less determined by other factors at the national and international levels (monetary policy, fiscal policy, tax policy, trade policy, and the like).

The box lists a wide range of categories of local sustainability practices in current use.

A LIST OF SUSTAINABLE PLANNING TECHNIQUES

In 2001 Edward J. Jepson, Jr., surveyed some hundreds of municipal governments to see what steps they were taking to pursue sustainable development.[20] He asked them about 39 categories of actions. These categories are shown in the list that follows to provide a sense of the range of sustainable development. Those whose meaning is not self-evident or explained elsewhere in this book are explained in the notes that follow. The measures listed here address the three Es as well as local self-sufficiency and include both direct actions and steps to gather information to support subsequent actions.[21]

1. Agricultural district provisions
2. Agricultural protection zoning
3. Bicycle-access plan
4. Brownfield reclamation
5. Community indicators program
6. Community gardening
7. Cooperative housing
8. Eco-industrial park
9. Ecological footprint analysis
10. Environmental-site-design regulations
11. Green-building requirements
12. Green procurement
13. Green maps
14. Green-print plans
15. Greenways development
16. Heat-island analysis
17. Import substitution
18. Incentive/inclusionary zoning
19. Infill development
20. Life-cycle public construction
21. Living-wage ordinance
22. Low-emission vehicles
23. Neotraditional (New Urbanist) development
24. Open-space zoning
25. Pedestrian-access plan
26. Purchase of development rights
27. Rehabilitation of building codes
28. Right-to-farm legislation
29. Solar-access protection regulations

30. Solid-waste life-cycle management
31. Tax base/revenue sharing
32. Transfer of development rights
33. Transit-oriented development
34. Transportation-demand management
35. Urban-growth boundary
36. Urban forestry program
37. Urban-system analysis
38. Wildlife habitat/green corridor planning
39. Wind-energy development

Notes: Explanations are for items not mentioned elsewhere in this text and whose meanings are not readily apparent. 5. Use of community social, economic, or environmental indicators in making plans. 7. Closely spaced housing with many shared facilities. 8. Industrial parks designed to incorporate good ecological practices. 11. Requiring new buildings to use practices that minimize energy use and other environmental impacts. 12. Taking environmental considerations into municipal purchasing decisions. 14. Municipal planning and mapping that show natural areas slated for acquisition and preservation. 20. Costing public construction to include all phases of the project from inception through demolition and disposal. 22. Favoring low-emission types when purchasing municipal vehicles. 27. Writing building codes to favor rehabilitation and reuse. 36. Tree planting to reduce CO_2 in the atmosphere and to facilitate heating and cooling of buildings. (The term has also been used in connection with maintaining small amounts of seminatural habitat within a municipality.)

Note that items 7, 18, and 21 specifically address equity concerns. Item 17 addresses local self-sufficiency.

Earlier in the chapter we noted that *growth management* relies in large measure for its implementation on planning tools that were in existence for many years before the term came into being. Similarly, many of the techniques that are used in planning for sustainable development have also been around for some time. For example, many localities have been planning and appropriating monies for open-space acquisition for decades. Another example is that many municipalities have had a long-standing commitment to making provisions for affordable housing. To the extent that planning for sustainable development is a new idea, it is the overall concept and the long time horizon, not the individual techniques, that distinguish it from previous planning efforts.

SUMMARY

Growth management is often defined as the regulation of the amount, timing, location, and character of development. Growth management programs generally use techniques that are common to much of planning. Thus such plans are distinguished from more traditional plans by their intent and scope rather than by their implementing techniques.

Growth management programs became widespread in the 1960s as a reaction to the rapid suburbanization of the postwar period and the growth of environmental consciousness and concern. Growth management also gained strength from concern with national and global population growth even though the logical link with these concerns and local population growth is weak. Such programs raise a variety of equity issues, for controlling the rate and character of growth inevitably produces a variety of winners and losers, a point discussed in some detail in this chapter.

A number of subsequent growth management plans have been instituted in various parts of the country. Some, such as Boulder's, attempt to place a cap on growth, or to hold growth to some predetermined annual percentage rate. Others, such as Fort Collins's, seek to shape the pattern of growth without attempting to limit the rate.

Many states have instituted growth management programs, beginning with Hawaii in the early 1960s. In general, state growth management programs cover only parts of the state, frequently for environmental reasons. State controls on development usually do not supersede local controls. Rather, they constitute an additional level of control intended to see that larger-than-local issues are given adequate weight in the making of development decisions.

The term *smart growth* came into use in the 1990s, first in connection with Maryland's state planning efforts. Interest in smart growth has largely been generated by the perception of growing suburban sprawl and, in particular, by traffic problems associated with sprawl. Whether smart growth is a new idea or merely growth management under a more attractive name is a matter of some dispute among planners.

The concept of *sustainable development* harks back to the work of the Brundtland Commission in 1987. At the local level it shares many techniques with growth management and smart growth. One way it differs is in the very long time horizon, and perhaps another way is that its proponents are concerned with all scales of development from local to global. Still another difference is the very prominent position that it gives to equity issues, though as noted, whether the link between sustainability and equity is entirely logical can be argued either way.

NOTES

1. Randall W. Scott et al., eds., *Management and Control of Growth*, Urban Land Institute, Washington, DC, 1975. Three volumes appeared in 1975; two more have since appeared.

2. For some early recognition of the dark side of growth management, see articles by Wilbur Thompson and Willard R. Johnson in vol. 1, ibid.

3. One might ask what sources of air pollution purely residential development involves. According to EPA estimates, about one-half of U.S. air pollution comes from motor vehicle exhausts. Thus the vehicular traffic associated with residential development is a major source of air pollution. Smaller amounts of air pollution may come from home heating systems. In some areas of the country, for example, Denver, Colorado, emissions from wood-burning stoves have been a major source of air pollution.

4. William Alonso, "Urban Zero Population Growth," *Daedalus*, vol. 102, no. 4, Fall 1973, pp. 191–206. The article is reprinted in Scott, *Management and Control*, vol. 1, chap. 5.

5. Ernest F. Schumacher, *Small Is Beautiful: A Study of Economics as If People Mattered*, Harper & Row, New York, 1975. Previously published in Great Britain.

6. A more detailed description of the Ramapo ordinance and litigation, as well as references to the large planning literature that developed around Ramapo, can be found in any of the first six editions of this book.

7. William Fischel, "The Property Rights Approach to Zoning," *Land Economics*, vol. 54, no. 1, February 1978, pp. 64–81, and subsequent books and articles by Fischel.

8. For a presentation of the view that environmental controls have been used to defend privilege, see Bernard J. Frieden, *The Environmental Protection Hustle*, MIT Press, Cambridge, MA, 1979.

9. The average number of persons per housing unit has been declining ever since the end of World War II. One factor has been the increase in real per capita income in the United States. In the last several decades, a second factor has been the increasing percentage of older adults in the population, a group that typically lives in one- or two-person households. That trend may have been temporarily reversed by the recession, the slowdown in new construction, and the increased number of young adults living with parents.

10. Many counties in or near metropolitan areas use preferential tax treatment to keep land in agricultural use. In general, this means taxing it at a rate appropriate to its value in agricultural use rather than its market value as sold for nonagricultural use, say, residential or commercial development.

11. In low-lying areas near the sea, a drop in the water table, caused by excessive use of groundwater or a reduction in surface water available for aquifer recharge, will cause saltwater from the ocean to move in. This can cause changes in vegetation and wildlife and also render groundwater unfit for drinking.

12. For details see John M. DeGrove, *Land, Growth and Politics*, Planners Press, American Planning Association, Chicago, 1984, chap. 4.

13. Teresa Austin, "Pay as You Grow," *Civil Engineering*, February 1992, pp. 64–65.

14. Arthur C. Nelson, Raymond J. Burby, Edward Feser, Casey J. Dawkins, Emil E. Malizia, and Robert Quercio, "Urban Containment and Central City Revitalization," *Journal of the American Planning Association*, vol. 70, no. 4, Autumn 2004, pp. 411–425.

15. Reid Ewing, "Is Los Angeles-Style Sprawl Desirable?" *Journal of the American Planning Association*, vol. 67, no. 1, Winter 1997, pp. 107–119.

16. Details on the Maryland plan can be obtained from the state's department of planning website, www.mdp.state.md.us/smartgrowth/smartwhat.htm.

17. John W. Freece and Gerrit-Jan Knapp, "Smart Growth in Maryland: Looking Forward and Looking Back," *Idaho Law Review*, vol. 43, 2007, p. 446. This article can also be found on the website of 1000 Friends of Maryland. See also the National Center for Smart Growth Education and Research (www.smarthgrowth.umd.edu) and the State of Maryland Planning Department (www.State.md.us).

18. For a discussion of the meaning of *sustainable development* and some of its history, see Virginia W. MacLaren, "Urban Sustainability Reporting," *Journal of the American Planning Association*, Spring 1996, vol. 62, no. 2, pp. 184–202; and Scott Campbell, "Green Cities, Growing Cities, Just Cities," *Journal of the American Planning Association*, Summer 1996, vol. 62, no. 3, pp. 296–311.

19. The idea that no-growth conditions would tend to lock the poor in their place indefinitely has been present in the planning literature for many years. See, for example, Willard R. Johnson, "Should the Poor Buy No-Growth?" *Management and Control of Growth*, Urban Land Institute, Washington, DC, 1975, Vol. I, pp. 415–425.

   Some writers argue that the terms *economic development* and *economic growth* do not mean exactly the same thing. Economic growth clearly means an increase in total or per capita output. Economic development is taken by some to mean some movement toward a better economic situation without necessarily implying an increase in total output. For example, if the same output were achieved with less environmental impact or with better working conditions, some might argue that economic development had occurred even if there were no increase in total output. However, for purposes of this argument, the terms *economic*

development and *economic growth* can be used synonymously.

20. "Edward J. Jepson, Jr., "The Adoption of Sustainable Development Policies and Techniques in US Cities," *The Journal of Planning Education and Research*, no. 23, Winter 2004, pp. 229–241.

21. Some writers on sustainable development have included a degree of local self-sufficiency in addition to the three Es as a goal.

SELECTED BIBLIOGRAPHY

ABBOT, CARL, HOWE, DEBORAH, and ADLER, SY, EDS., *Planning the Oregon Way*, Oregon State University Press, Corvallis, OR, 1994.

BROWER, DAVID J., GODSCHALK, DAVID R., and PORTER, DOUGLAS R., *Understanding Growth Management*, Urban Land Institute, Washington, DC, 1989.

BURROWS, LAWRENCE B., *Growth Management: Issues, Techniques and Policy Implications*, Center for Urban Policy Research, Rutgers University, New Brunswick, NJ, 1978.

DEGROVE, JOHN M., *The New Frontier for Land Policy: Planning and Growth Management in the States*, Lincoln Land Institute, Lincoln, NE, 1992.

DEGROVE, JOHN M., *Planning, Policy and Politics*, The Lincoln Institute of Land Policy, Cambridge, MA, 2005.

DOWNS, ANTHONY, ED., *Growth Management and Affordable Housing*, The Brookings Institution, Washington, DC, 2004.

HOLCOMBE, RANDALL, and STALEY, SAMUEL, EDS., *Smarter Growth: Market-Based Strategies for Land Use Planning*, Greenwood Press, Westport, CT, 2001.

LAYARD, ANTONIO, DAVOUDI, SIMIN, and BATTY, SUSAN, EDS., *Planning for a Sustainable Future*, Spon Press, London, 2001.

CHAPTER 15

Environmental and Energy Planning

Environmental planning covers a wide range of concerns having to do, generally, with minimizing the damage that human activity does to the natural environment. The goals may pertain to any of the following:

Minimizing threats to human health and life, for example, by reducing the concentration of dangerous pollutants in the air or the water supply or by limiting development in hazardous areas like flood plains

Preserving resources for future use, for example, minimizing soil erosion or minimizing the emission of greenhouse gases

Achieving aesthetic and recreational goals such as preserving some areas in a pristine condition

Minimizing damage to the environment for its own sake rather than humanity's sake, for example, by preserving the habitat of a rare species that has no known or readily foreseeable use to us

Energy planning has a much simpler goal: the saving of nonrenewable energy resources. An example would be designing a subdivision so that all the houses have unobstructed southern exposures to facilitate solar heating. Often, energy conservation will help achieve other environmental goals. For example, solar heating will conserve energy, but it may also reduce the degradation of air quality by reducing the amount of fuel burned for home heating.

THE ENVIRONMENTAL PLANNING PROBLEM _____

Environmental problems can be difficult to deal with for several reasons:

1. Environmental processes may be complex and not fully understood. For example, both the physical and chemical pathways a pollutant takes through the environment may not be fully understood, nor may be its exact effects as it is dispersed and transformed.

2. Environmental problems are not respecters of political boundaries. Agricultural chemicals sprayed on fields in Kansas may find their way into tributaries of the Mississippi River and end up in the drinking water of a Louisiana community a few months later. Sulphur dioxide from smokestacks in Ohio may come down as acid rain in Vermont. In 1985 the United States and Canada held talks on acid rain because acid rains in eastern Canada result in part from oxides of sulphur and nitrogen released in the American Midwest. The ultimate environmental problem is probably the greenhouse effect largely resulting from increased levels of carbon dioxide in the atmosphere. Fossil fuel burned anywhere on the planet contributes to the problem, so that it can be fully addressed only at an international level.

3. The solution of one environmental problem may become the cause of another. For example, air quality regulations require "scrubbers," which remove a certain percentage of sulphur from the smokestacks of coal-fired electric generating facilities. However, the resulting accumulation of sulphur-containing sludge can prove to be a source of groundwater pollution.

4. Environmental issues can arouse strong emotions and produce formidable political conflict because environmental decisions may deliver both large gains and large losses to particular individuals and groups.

In general the approach to environmental problems has been piecemeal, one pollutant or one source of emissions or one land-use question at a time. This approach is not because of shortsightedness or lack of vision. The problem of achieving higher levels of environmental quality is simply so complicated that a unified approach in which all side effects are considered has yet to be devised.

THE QUESTION OF GLOBAL CLIMATE CHANGE _____

Including a section on climate change in a book on urban planning may seem like a bit of a stretch, but both changes in climate and how we respond to them will have many effects on what we do and what happens at the local level. Climate change is likely to be the overarching environmental problem, and the great majority if not virtually all other environmental problems will have to be addressed within its framework.

At the global level changes in climate, particularly changes in rainfall, are likely to have big effects on world agriculture, with major consequences for war and peace, political stability, and mass migration. Within the United States, climate change may prove negative for some parts of the nation and positive for others. For example, warming and possibly drying may be a net negative for the Southwest. At the same time, it may produce what some regard as climate improvement for, say, Minnesota and other parts of the north-central region. If, as some climatologists expect, global warming increases the intensity of tropical storms, it will likely prove negative for the Gulf Coast region. Changing patterns of rainfall affect the spatial pattern of agriculture. In all of these ways global warming may affect the distribution of population in the United States and perhaps change the patterns of regional growth shown in Table 2–1.

What we choose to do to address the problem of climate change will affect the work of the planner in many ways. Transportation uses more than a quarter of U.S. energy. Thus energy planning and transportation policy are inextricably linked and, as discussed in Chapter 13 transportation technology and the pattern of land use are closely tied. Housing is a major consumer of energy, and so choices about energy and about housing development are also closely tied. Choices about environmental policy will have to be considered both in terms of purely local issues as well as the larger issue of global warming. For example, some dams have been torn down and some additional ones are slated to go because of local ecosystem considerations such as the survival of particular species of fish. But producing electricity by hydropower is very benign in greenhouse terms compared to producing by the burning of fossil fuel. There is clearly a trade-off between two desirable but contradictory goals.

The biggest force behind global warming is the increasing level of carbon dioxide in the earth's atmosphere. As Figure 15–1 shows there is no sign that the rate of increase is slowing. While there is near-universal agreement among climate scientists about the fact of warming, there is considerable uncertainty about just how fast it is likely to proceed. There is also much uncertainty about what should be and what will be done. One overarching question on which there is no general agreement is how much to spend on reducing greenhouse gas emissions versus how much to spend on mitigating the effects of increasing temperatures and shifting weather patterns.[1] Within the context of reducing the rate of warming there is disagreement over how much to focus on the largest single cause, carbon dioxide emissions, versus how much to focus on smaller causes such as methane or fine carbon particles ("black carbon"). Within the context of carbon dioxide there are a large number of energy choices including sequestration of carbon dioxide from coal burning, direct removal of carbon

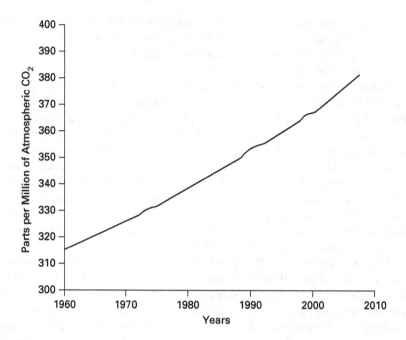

FIGURE 15–1 Atmospheric Carbon Dioxide in Parts per Million, 1960 to 2007.

Note: Preindustrial revolution CO_2 levels are estimated from ice core samples to be in the 260–280 per million (ppm) range.

Source: Measured at Mauna Loa Observatory, Hawaii.

dioxide from the atmosphere, solar and wind technologies, and expanded use of nuclear energy. One now hears a small but increasing number of voices suggesting that beyond emission reductions we should consider positive steps to increase the earth's albedo (the percentage of incoming solar energy that the planet reflects back into space), a subject that is beyond the scope of this book but that the interested reader can easily look up by Googling the word *geoengineering.*

Although there is a great deal that the United States can do about global warming, much of the problem is out of U.S. hands. At present the United States produces roughly one-fourth of the world's total carbon dioxide emissions and that share is shrinking. About 2006 or 2007 China passed the United States as the world's largest carbon dioxide emitter and the gap is growing rapidly. This country has very little leverage over China in this matter. Over 1.3 billion Chinese want their automobiles (China is now the world's largest automobile market with almost 14 million passenger cars and slightly over 20 million total vehicles sold in 2010), central heating, and electric appliances just as Americans do. And to American pleas for China to cut back, the Chinese are likely to reply, in effect, "you had your party and now we are having ours." What was just said about China may, a decade from now, apply to India. It has a population of 1.2 billion, it's birthrate, though lower than it once was, is still considerably higher than either ours or China's, and it is experiencing very rapid economic growth.

When a nation cuts back on its emissions of greenhouse gases it benefits the entire world, but the country itself captures only part of the total benefit. Thus simple economic theory would suggest that the nations of the world are, in total, likely to underinvest in greenhouse gas reduction.

The 2010 United Nations Climate Change Conference held in Cancun, Mexico, reached some agreements on a Green Climate Fund and a Climate Technology Center as well as some agreements on goals. However, there was no binding agreement on hard numbers for greenhouse gas emission nor does such an agreement appear likely, at least in the near future.

In the United States the question of reducing greenhouse gas emissions is tangled up with the question of political ideology. When Americans are questioned on the subject of global warming a majority of them say that they believe it is happening, but in some surveys at least half of those who do believe that it is happening attribute it to causes other than human activity.[2] Belief in the reality of global warming shows little if any correlation with educational level, but it is very strongly correlated with political position. Democrats, as a group, are much more likely to believe it is happening and that human activity is behind it than are Republicans. Perhaps the difference is explained by the implications of believing that the problem is serious, for if it is, that implies the need for considerable amounts of regulation and for major public expenditures.

Reductions in greenhouse gas emissions are expensive, whether it is an expense laid on firms by regulation or an expense laid on government through subsidy programs and direct expenditures. Either way, at this writing it runs afoul of powerful concerns over tax cuts, budget deficits, and our ability to compete economically in world markets.

ENVIRONMENTAL PROGRESS AT THE NATIONAL LEVEL

Much of the attack on environmental problems must be made at the federal level, and indeed, the federal government has been very active in this area.

The U.S. commitment to environmental quality, as indicated by pollution-control expenditures, has grown substantially since the passage of the National Environmental Policy Act (NEPA). For 1972, pollution-control expenditures were estimated at about $44 billion in 2004 dollars.[3] Pollution-control expenditures by 2004 were estimated at $200 to $250 billion, roughly 2 percent of the gross domestic product.

The figures include both direct public expenditures and expenditures by firms to comply with environmental regulations. The costs appear in the form of higher taxes and higher prices and, in that sense, represent a reduction in living standards. However, and more important, they also represent a contribution to our living standards by improving the air we breathe, the water we drink, and the environment in which we live. In a populous, industrialized society, environmental quality does not come cheap.

Despite the complexities noted before, considerable environmental progress has been achieved in many areas. Figure 15–2 shows trends in the emissions of six major air pollutants from 1960 to 2000 (the data series from which the chart comes were discontinued shortly after 2000). The figures should be viewed in the light of changes in the United States since 1960. Specifically, from 1960 to 2000 the U.S. population grew by 57 percent, U.S. gross domestic product (GDP) by 288 percent, and motor vehicle registrations by 200 percent. Had we made no effort at environmental regulation, we would see a picture of sharply increased pollution rather than the picture of stabilization and decline shown in Figure 15–2.

In many cases, the imposition of uniform national standards is absolutely necessary. If different standards prevailed, polluting activities would simply be shifted from places with tight standards to places with loose standards.

Progress is often most rapid when there are a few sources that can be clearly identified and a substitute product or technology can be introduced. Note that the most striking reduction shown in Figure 15–2 is that for airborne lead, a pollutant that can contribute to, among other maladies, mental retardation and developmental problems in young children. The primary source was leaded gasoline. When Congress required automobile manufacturers to market only cars that ran on unleaded gasoline, the problem was on the way to an almost total solution.

When the pollutant has multiple sources, when substitute technology is not available, or when the problem is global rather than local, solutions are much more difficult.

Much pollution is, one way or another, a result of the production and use of energy—for example, toxic runoff from mining or the release of sulphur dioxide from coal burned to produce electricity. Between 1980 and 2010 the amount of energy used to produce a given amount of real GDP (Gross Domestic Product) declined by about 55 percent.[4] That drop represents a major environmental improvement. Much of it represents the effects of technological improvement motivated by increases in energy costs, and some was the direct result of regulation.

Sulfur Dioxide Emissions

Particulate Matter Less Than 10 Microns

Nitrogen Oxide Emissions

Volatile Organic Compound

Carbon Monoxide Emissions

Lead Emissions

FIGURE 15–2 U.S. Air Pollution Trends.

Sources: Data through 1990 are from Environmental Quality; 22nd Annual Report of the Council on Environmental Quality, U.S. Government Printing Office, Washington, DC, 1992, p. 11. Subsequent data are from the *Statistical Abstract of the United States,* 122nd edition, 2002, Table 348.

A BRIEF HISTORY OF NATIONAL ENVIRONMENTAL POLICY ___

For reasons noted at the beginning of this chapter, much of the impetus for environmental improvement and planning must necessarily come from the federal government. Since 1970, federal legislation has been the major shaper of environmental planning and the nation's efforts to deal with environmental problems. In fact, to a large extent the environmental planning professions have been brought into being by legislation passed by Congress.

As discussed in Chapter 4, environmental consciousness in the United States grew substantially during the 1960s. At the end of 1969, Congress passed the National Environmental Policy Act (NEPA).

> The Congress, recognizing the profound impact of man's activity on the interrelations of all components of the natural environment . . . declares that it is the continuing policy of the federal government, in cooperation with State and Local governments, and other concerned public and private organizations, to use all practicable means and measures, including financial and technical assistance, in a manner calculated to foster and promote the general welfare, to create and maintain conditions under which man and nature can exist in productive harmony.[5]

NEPA was signed in 1970 as President Nixon's first official act that year. Subsequently, the Environmental Protection Agency (EPA) was created by executive action. During the 1970s many states enacted their own versions of NEPA, generally known as "little NEPA" acts. Within the next few years, a variety of other major environmental acts became law. These included the Clean Air Act of 1970; the Clean Water Act of 1972; the Marine Protection, Control, and Sanctuaries Act of 1972; the Coastal Zone Management Act of 1972; the Safe Drinking Water Act of 1974; the Resource Conservation and Recovery Act of 1976; the Toxic Substances Control Act of 1976; and the Comprehensive Environmental Response, Compensation, and Liability Act (CERCLA) of 1980, more commonly known as "Superfund."

In 1990, amendments to the Clean Air Act placed stricter limits on emissions of sulphur dioxide, a primary component of acid rain. Most of the sulphur dioxide discharged in the United States in 1990 came from the burning of coal in electric generating plants. The act permitted an innovation that most economists see as a more efficient way of reducing pollution than the usual flat regulatory standards. It permitted the creation of a market in pollution rights to be run by the Chicago Board of Trade.[6] So far, the program appears to have been an outstanding success, with goals reached well ahead of schedule and at much less than estimated costs.

From 1990 to 2000, the ambient level of sulfur dioxide in the air in the United States dropped by 39 percent. From 2000 to 2008 there was a 41 percent decline. The act also required the phasing out of chlorofluorocarbons (CFCs), widely used as a refrigerant, and carbon tetrachloride and methyl chloride, believed to be the main causes of ozone depletion. The deadline was originally set for the year 2000, but the first Bush administration subsequently moved the deadline up to 1995. As of the end of 1995, the United States was on the verge of a complete phaseout of CFCs, far sooner than had been anticipated only a few years earlier.

Under the Clean Air Act and its amendments, states are required to create State Implementation Plans (SIPs) for metropolitan areas not meeting federal National Ambient Air Quality Standards (NAAQS) and to implement programs to reach the NAAQS. This requirement includes measures to reduce both point source (a nonmoving source such as an industrial operation) and mobile (automotive) sources. The EPA identified 84 areas not meeting the standards.

Considerable progress has been made in many areas such as Los Angeles. The South Coast Air Quality Management District (AQMD) includes Los Angeles and Orange County, as well as parts of San Bernadino and Riverside counties. It contains about 14 million people and over 9 million motor vehicles in a 12,000-square-mile area. The area's air pollution problem, considered the worst in the nation, is compounded by its topography, for mountains ringing the area create a bowl that restricts air circulation. Although the area's air quality problem is still far from solved, officials of the agency note that ozone levels are half what they were in 1950 despite a tripling of the area's human population and a quadrupling of its automobile population. They also note the following:

> In the past decade, we have reduced by half the number of Stage 1 Smog Alerts, the level at which schools are advised to keep children from playing outside. And, we almost never reach Stage II levels, which used to occur 15 times a year a decade ago.[7]

Among the measures taken have been regulation of many types of industrial and commercial processes, as well as some personal activities such as barbecuing, and stringent emissions standards for automobiles. The AQMD is responsible for point source pollution, and other California agencies for mobile sources. The regulations are backed by fines and, in the extreme, criminal prosecution.

In October 1992, Congress passed a wide-ranging energy bill. The legislation contains provisions to reduce both the use of nonrenewable energy sources (fossil fuels) and pollution from energy use. The bill requires that small energy producers be allowed to make use of the transmission lines of electric utility companies. In effect, this use permits the small producer to sell power to the utility company, which helps create a market for small-scale wind, solar, and hydroelectric power. Few wind generators would be in existence if their builders were not able to make use of the existing electric grid. In the 2004 election, voters in Colorado passed Amendment 37, which stipulates that by 2015 at least 10 percent of the electricity used in the state must be generated by renewable means, of which the majority share is expected to be from wind-driven generators. This was the first such requirement adopted by a direct vote, but other states have adopted such requirements by legislative act.

The energy bill mandated efficiency standards for lightbulbs and home heating systems. The latter is not a trivial item. About one-third of all U.S. energy use is for space heating, and a large part of that is residential.

The bill authorized the Department of Energy (DOE) to enter into agreements with companies to develop electric vehicles. For a while very little came of this. In fact, many environmentalists viewed it as a dodge that made it possible for the federal government and the automobile industry to avoid the obviously doable step of simply raising Corporate Average Fuel Economy (CAFE) standards. At present there is a rush to develop electric vehicles, both by U.S. and overseas auto manufacturers, that is driven by both fuel costs and changed environmental consciousness quite independent of the 1992 legislation.

The bill provided for the "environmentally sound use of our nation's abundant coal resources through research and development of advanced coal technologies." The situation with regard to "advanced coal technologies" is not entirely clear at this time. A clean coal technology might simply mean burning coal in such a way that the production of pollutants like sulfur dioxide is minimized. But from a greenhouse gas perspective, the main villain is carbon dioxide, which is not reduced by scrubbers and other conventional pollution-control technologies.

During the Clinton administration (January 1993 to January 2001) there was no one overarching environmental bill passed, though there were a number of minor bills pertaining to specific items such as acquisition of land for conservation purposes. There was, however a steady stream of regulations, presidential directives, and small steps of a pro-environmental nature, many connected with issues such as endangered species, logging, mining, and road building on public lands. One program initiated under President Clinton that is familiar to millions of Americans is the Energy Star program, which promotes energy efficiency in refrigerators and other electric appliances. In general, President Clinton got good marks from environmentalists.

George W. Bush, who succeeded Bill Clinton in January 2001, was generally not beloved by environmentalists, some of whom took to referring to him as the "toxic Texan". Environmentalists were unhappy with Bush administration policy on endangered species, logging on public-owned lands, and a host of other matters. They saw him as a man who would appoint as heads of regulatory agencies people hostile to regulation, and who saw their roles as limiting regulatory action. Environmentalists were very critical about the Bush administration's position on New Source Review (NSR) for electric power plants. The administration permitted firms that made new investments equal to less than 20 percent of the value of the facility to be exempt from NSR provisions of the Clean Air Act. Thus several less-than-20-percent investments would, in effect, enable building a new plant outside the rules. Many environmentalists thought Bush energy policy placed far too much emphasis on production and far too little on conservation. To many, the Bush energy policy seemed epitomized by the chant "drill baby, drill" at the Republican's 2008 presidential nominating convention.

The big piece of legislation with major environmental consequences that passed during the Bush administration was the Energy Policy Act of 2005. This was a massive bill oriented toward increasing domestic production of energy. It included subsidies, friendly regulatory treatment, and preferential tax treatment for almost every sort of energy including oil, coal, nuclear, wind, solar and geothermal, with an emphasis on the first three. It included funds for research on a wide range of energy technologies, including both fossil fuels and renewables. The bill also established a variety of subsidies for green buildings and for the retrofitting of older structures to reduce energy consumption. Though the major weight of the bill was on the production side, it did have a significant conservation element too.

The fruits of the bill with which you may be most familiar were the "this fuel may contain up to 10 percent ethanol" signs at gas pumps. The bill mandated the addition of renewable fuels to gasoline and also provided a 45-cent-per-gallon subsidy for ethanol used as a gasoline additive. The move to ethanol seemed like a good idea at the time, both to reduce U.S. dependence on imported oil and also to reduce greenhouse gas emissions by getting some energy from a renewable source. But it has since come in for considerable criticism. Some studies have concluded that when one considers all of the petroleum used in the cultivation, fertilization, and transportation of corn and all of the electricity used in the plants that convert corn to ethanol, the net reduction in atmospheric carbon dioxide is negligible. The ethanol program has also been criticized from an entirely different perspective. As of 2011 about 40 percent of U.S. corn production (about 36 million out of a total of 91 million acres planted in corn) went for ethanol to be mixed with gasoline. That, it is argued, drives up food prices all over the world, which raises the question of whether in a world where not everyone has enough to eat we should be putting that much corn in our gas tanks.

The Obama administration, which took office in January 2009, marked a sharp change in the national administration's stance toward the environment. President Obama's choices for top federal posts signaled a much more pro-environmental stance. Most notable was his pick for head of the Department of Energy, Steven Chu, a winner of the 1997 Nobel Prize in physics. Not only were Chu's scientific credentials outstanding, but his environmental predisposition was very clear. As director of the Lawrence Berkeley National Laboratories in California, he had made the organization one of the major players in research on biofuels and solar energy and was clearly on record about the necessity of shifting away from reliance on fossil fuels.

Both in his campaign and after his inauguration, President Obama indicated a serious concern with global warming and hence a big commitment to the development of alternatives to fossil fuels and an interest in energy conservation. Because of the financial crisis of fall 2008, the new administration's first domestic priority was the passage of an economic stimulus package, the American Recovery and Reinvestment Act of 2009, a $787 billion appropriation that became law in March of that year. The bill contained substantial sums for scientific research related to environmental and energy issues, green buildings, subsidies for alternative energy development, and modernization and expansion of the U.S. electric grid. The last item was part of a move toward the replacement of fossil fuels by electricity to be generated by alternative methods including nuclear, solar, and wind. The argument was that such a goal could not be realized without the capacity to move larger amounts of power than is now possible from generating sources to distant users.

On the regulatory side, the Obama administration took a different tack from the Bush administration by showing more willingness to regulate, to go to court to enforce environmental regulations, and to reconsider some Bush-era environmental policy decisions that most environmentalists thought were overly favorable to industry at the expense of environmental quality. For example, in 2007 California had requested a waiver from the EPA that would have permitted California to demand stricter fuel-economy standards for motor vehicles than those passed by Congress. Since a number of other states follow California's lead in this regard, this would have become the nation's de facto standard. At the behest of the Bush administration, the EPA turned down the request and then for the next two years, in the face of considerable political pressure, refused to budge on the issue. Within a week of his inauguration, President Obama instructed the EPA to hold hearings to reconsider its 2007 decision. In May 2009 the Obama administration announced new, substantially higher CAFE (Corporate Average Fuel Economy) standards, which essentially reconciled national standards with the higher California standards that the Bush administration had resisted for two years.

Almost from the start of his administration, President Obama pushed hard for a "cap and trade" system to limit total carbon emissions. This would be a system somewhat analogous to the system that has been used in connection with control of sulfur dioxide (see page 314) but on an economy-wide scale. Formally the American Clean Energy and Security Act, the bill was also referred to as the Waxman Markey bill after its sponsors, Representatives Henry Waxman (Democrat from California) and Edward Markey (Democrat from Massachusetts). The basic idea of the bill was to limit the permitted carbon emissions of major industrial and commercial emitters (the *cap*) and then to allow those emitters who were under their limits to sell (*trade*) their unused emissions rights to firms that wanted to emit more than their permitted amount. That would encourage greater efficiency by motivating firms to either accumulate salable rights or reduce the number of rights that they would have to purchase.

The bill was long and complex and had numerous caveats and exceptions, many of them accommodations to the realities of legislative politics. It was easily attacked on these grounds. Many economists had favored a so-called carbon tax (so many dollars per ton of carbon emitted) on the grounds of administrative simplicity and greater efficiency, but that was a political nonstarter in the prevailing antitax political climate. Opponents of cap and trade argued that although the cap and trade was not literally a tax, it was one in all but name. They argued that, like a tax, it would push up firms' costs. That would show up in higher prices, which would lead to reduced sales, which would, in turn, cause job losses, a powerful point in a time of high unemployment. Opponents also claimed that it would cause further outsourcing of jobs to nations that did not impose comparable restrictions and therefore, in addition to costing jobs, would increase our trade deficit.

The bill passed the then strongly democratic House of Representatives in June 2009 and was then referred to the Senate, but never came up for a vote there. In November 2010 the Republican Party took control of the House with a large majority and the bill was effectively dead.

Environmentalists had been pleased with the environmental emphasis in the 2009 stimulus bill discussed previously and looked forward to continued funding from subsequent stimulus bills. But that, like the cap and trade bill, was not to be. In 2010 the federal budget deficit rose steeply and the Republican Party, and some Democrats as well, took the position that the nation's number one economic problem was the deficit. When the new Congress convened in January 2011 the Republicans in Congress, strengthened by their victory in the 2010 congressional elections and pulled rightward by a large number of new members elected with Tea Party support, moved forcefully to make major cuts in the discretionary portion of the budget.[8] In percentage terms, the Republicans proposed the largest budget cut for the EPA. The Democrats argued for smaller cuts in the discretionary budget but did not resist the basic position that it should be cut. No new stimulus program was even proposed.

In the realm of transportation, as noted in Chapter 12, environmentalists were disappointed too. At the request of the Obama administration Congress had approved a number of grants for intercity high-speed rail routes. But several governors turned down these grants claiming that they feared cost overruns and thought that they could not afford their own shares of the cost because of large, recession-caused state budget deficits. In 2010 New Jersey's Governor Chris Christie rejected federal funds for a tunnel under the Hudson River that would have doubled the number of daily commuter train trips between New Jersey and Manhattan. In February 2011 Governor Rick Scott of Florida turned away $2.4 billion in federal funding for a high-speed rail link between Tampa on Florida's Gulf Coast and Orlando in central Florida. Then the 2011 budget compromise removed all subsequent rail subsidy funding from the federal budget.

Even geology seemed to conspire against the Obama environmental agenda. The Obama administration had taken a pro-nuclear position, arguing that nuclear energy for electric power generation (nuclear provided about 20 percent of U.S. electricity at the time) would be an important step in reducing U.S. carbon dioxide emissions. But the construction of nuclear power plants in the United States posed such financial risks to investors that little or no new nuclear construction would occur without some federal government subsidization and loan guarantees. With that in mind, in February 2011 the administration had proposed that Congress appropriated $32 billion in subsidies and loan guarantees for new plant construction. In the following month, the combination of earthquake and tsunami disabled the Fukushima Daiichi nuclear plant in Japan, damaging or destroying four of its six reactors, causing significant release of radioactivity and, for a time, causing fears of catastrophic meltdown. At this writing it is too early to say with certainty how negative the effect will be on the future of nuclear energy in the United States. The fact that Germany under Chancellor Angela Merkel, herself a physicist by training, has planned to decommission all of its nuclear power plants by 2022 is suggestive.

Studies have shown that, even including Chernobyl and the 2011 disaster in Japan, nuclear power imposes smaller costs in death and illness than any fossil fuel technology (coal has the highest cost) per unit of energy produced.[9] However, perceptions are important, and when nuclear power does impose such costs it does so in spectacular way.

In 2011 Solyndra, a maker of solar panels that had taken more than one half billion dollars in federal subsidy money as part of the Obama administration's program to promote alternative energy sources, went bankrupt. That provided a field day for congressional critics of federal energy policy. In November 2011 Energy Secretary Chu appeared before a

Congressional committee and was subjected to a fairly harsh interrogation—not the usual experience for a Nobel laureate in physics.

All in all, the beginning of the second decade of this century was not a good time for administration environmental policy.

THE LINK BETWEEN NATIONAL AND LOCAL ENVIRONMENTAL PLANNING

If any one act can be said to be the founding event in the evolution of modern environmental planning in the United States it was the passage of NEPA discussed in the previous section. The act required environmental impact statements (EISs) as a precondition for large projects making use of federal funds. In brief, the NEPA process works like this:[10] The agency considering an action that might have significant environmental effects must prepare an environmental assessment (EA). This is a relatively brief document that describes the project in general and includes a "discussion of the need for proposed action, the environmental impacts of the proposed action, and alternative actions, and a listing of the persons and agencies consulted." The EA either concludes that an environmental impact statement is necessary or that there is "no significant impact," in which case an EIS is not required. The EA is a public document, and it can be expected that if there is serious public concern with the issue, it will be subject to considerable scrutiny. The process is designed for visibility and accountability. Thus an agency could not readily rule that an EIS was not necessary if, in fact, serious environmental effects could be demonstrated.

If an EIS is called for, a complex process begins. Notice of the agency's intent to prepare an EIS must be published in the *Federal Register*. This is a daily newsletter published by the federal government detailing regulations and a variety of other federal actions. The first step is a "scoping" process involving other federal agencies, lower levels of government, and the public. At this time, too, a lead agency, or agency having overall responsibility, is designated. Once the scope (hence the term *scoping*) of the work to be done has been determined, a draft EIS is prepared, either by the federal agency or by an agency of a lower level of government or a party under contract to a body of government. The latter might be a consultant. The draft EIS includes

a discussion of the purpose of and need for the proposed action, alternatives to the proposed action (for example, a highway EIS might include discussion of the merits of expanding mass transit instead), including a no action alternative, analysis of the affected environment and of the environmental consequences of the proposed action and alternatives, a list of persons who prepared the document, a list of agencies, organizations and persons to whom the document is being mailed.[11]

At this point the draft document is circulated for both official and public comment. The lead agency, after considering the comments, then produces the final EIS. There again ensues a comment period, and following this, the lead agency prepares a "record of decision." This is a summary of the agency's decision and indicates the basis for the decision, alternatives that were considered, and so on.

The process is an open one. The turn-of-the-century "muckrakers," who were fond of the expression "sunlight is the best disinfectant," would be quite pleased with the process. It prevents government from acting in secrecy, makes the process open to any concerned citizen, and makes it as practical as possible for interested parties to comment.

The EIS may be a long document, or in the case of a large project, a shelf of documents, often supported by large amounts of data. EIS requirements have brought a fair-sized consulting industry into being. EIS requirements have also provided an enormous amount of employment for attorneys. For the individual or group opposed to a particular project, the most effective action often is to sue. A common basis for suing is to claim a procedural flaw in the environmental review process. The litigant does not necessarily have to show that the project is a bad plan. If it can be shown that there has been some fault in the process itself, that is, a violation of a law or regulation, the project can be stopped until that flaw has been remedied.

To take a well-known example, New York City's Westway project, noted in Chapter 13, was killed by such litigation. In the last chapter of a decade-long saga, a federal judge found that state and federal officials had "colluded" in concealing information about the effect of the project on the Hudson River and, particularly, on striped bass in the river.

Whether the litigants actually cared about the striped bass is a moot point. The complexity of the review process presents numerous opportunities for delaying actions, in this case sufficient delays to kill the project. Critics of the environmental review process have complained that it provides too many legal weapons for naysayers and that it permits small, determined groups to thwart the will of the majority. Defenders of the process argue that the law is meant to be obeyed and that if it has not been, the project should be delayed until it is.

The field of air quality planning was essentially brought into being by the Clean Air Act of 1970 and its subsequent amendments. The preparation of SIPs and the evaluation of proposed projects for their effects on NAAQS (see page 315) created the demand for air quality planners. For the biggest moving source, the automobile, Congress itself set the emissions standards rather than delegating that task to the EPA. The emission control equipment on all new cars sold in the United States is there because of requirements that, although periodically modified, date from this time.

The 1972 Federal Water Pollution Control Act (FWPCA) brought into being state and local water quality planning efforts on a massive scale. Specifically, section 208 of the act requires states to produce water-quality plans, either directly or by delegating responsibility to substate governments. Accompanying the planning requirements were substantial sums of grant money to fund the work. The 1972 Coastal Zone Management Act imposes coastal zone planning requirements on the states. We note that about half of the U.S. population lives in counties that border on a coast, that coastal areas are often ecologically fragile, and that for many reasons, coastal areas can be extremely attractive for commercial and residential development.

ECONOMIC AND POLITICAL ISSUES IN ENVIRONMENTAL PLANNING

Environmental protection and environmental planning are inevitably contentious for a number of reasons. Environmental legislation and regulation often impose large losses on some parties and deliver large gains to others. Consider shoreline protection. Suppose that protecting a certain stretch of beachfront requires that further residential development be stopped or sharply curtailed. People who already have beachfront properties are winners. Their privacy will be protected and the market value of their houses will rise because no more can be built. Conversely, people who own beachfront property that they can no longer develop are losers (see the case of *Lucas v. South Carolina Coastal Council* in Chapter 5). People who would like to buy beachfront houses but cannot do so because no more can be built are also losers.

In many places it is difficult to get a permit to open a marina. This difficulty is understandable because the dredging necessary to keep channels open, spilled fuel, and boat exhausts all damage the marine environment. This situation makes winners out of those who already own a marina because it protects them from the emergence of new competition. People who might like to open marinas are losers. So, too, are boat owners because with less competition, prices for space at marinas will be higher.

Environmental regulations that mandate additional pollution-control expenditures for a firm will increase that firm's costs and thus decrease its profitability, clearly a loss to its stockholders. In the extreme, the costs of complying with environmental regulations may put the firm out of business, a loss to the stockholders and an even larger loss to the employees.

But those same regulations will deliver benefits to firms in the business of making pollution-control equipment. Perhaps production of the product in question will go overseas to a country where environmental protections are weaker, the so-called export of pollution. Any pattern of laws and regulations that delivers gains and losses on a large scale will inevitably produce controversy and provide much employment for attorneys.

The Special Case of "Superfund"

Environmental regulation can produce unpredicted side effects. Superfund (more formally, CERCLA, the Comprehensive Environmental Response, Compensation, and Liability Act of 1980) is a case in point. The act provided authority to the Environmental Protection Agency to designate contaminated sites. Owners of these sites are required to bring them up to EPA standards. The law requires this "remediation" even if the actions that polluted the site were legal at the time they were taken. For example, a site might have been contaminated by dumping of paint solvents when such dumping was not prohibited. Beyond that, present owners of the site may be held responsible for contamination caused by previous owners of the site. Thus by buying a site that subsequently turns out to have been contaminated by a previous owner, a firm or individual may be inadvertently "buying" a liability that is much greater than the value of the site. That possibility will make potential buyers of used industrial or commercial sites very hesitant. But it goes still further than that. Suppose XYZ Corp. goes bankrupt while still owing $1 million to the bank that holds its mortgage. Normally, the bank would foreclose the property, sell it, and thus recover some of its loss. But if the site has been in industrial use for, say, the last century, Superfund's liability provisions will make the bank hesitate. If the site subsequently turns out to be contaminated, the bank may now become the unhappy owner of a site that costs $10 million to bring up to standards. Maybe it would be wiser just to accept the loss and not foreclose. But the next time the bank is asked to make a loan to a firm on an old, possibly contaminated site, it will remember what happened when the XYZ Corp. went under and say no.

The liability provisions of Superfund have brought into being the terms *greenfields* and *brownfields*. A greenfield is a site, usually suburban or rural, that has never been used for industrial or commercial purposes. A brownfield is a site, usually urban, that has been or is in commercial or industrial use. Greenfields pose no threat of unforeseen liability under Superfund, but brownfields do. This will bias the market for industrial and commercial sites against urban areas in favor of suburban and rural sites.[12] For cities struggling with problems of structural unemployment (see Chapter 12) and inadequate tax bases, that bias is very unfortunate. It was also completely unintended.

After perhaps a decade, these antiurban side effects became widely recognized, and some steps were taken to nullify them. For example, some state environmental agencies devised arrangements that, in effect, immunize firms against Superfund liability for contamination that comes to light in the future, if firms will agree to appropriate remediation of presently known contamination. Banks sometimes can protect themselves against the sort of risk described earlier by making mortgage arrangements such that in the event of default, they can foreclose on property other than the potentially risky brownfield property. In the previous example, that would mean that the bank could foreclose on some nonbrownfield property owned by the XYZ Corp. Of course, doing that presumes that XYZ Corp. has such a property and that said property is not encumbered by other liens. Insurance arrangements against Superfund liability risk have also emerged. Thus the side effects of the law have been dealt with, at least to some extent. The point of the digression, though, is that environmental legislation and regulation can create powerful and unintended side effects.

Friendly Criticism

Current environmental policy has been subject to what we might term *friendly criticism* from economists, policy analysts, risk analysts, and others who take a rationalistic, quantitative approach to environmental issues. The economist, the benefit–cost analyst, and the policy analyst would, if they could, have us balance the costs and the benefits of environmental regulation at the margin—the last dollar spent on conforming to environmental regulations would yield exactly one dollar of benefit. In a rational system, they would argue, proposed environmental regulations (or at least major ones) would be subject to benefit–cost analysis. Unless it could be shown that the proposed regulation would yield benefits at least equal to the costs that it imposed, it would not be accepted.

However, environmental policy is not always made that way. Benefit–cost studies are required for some projects, and are sometimes required of new regulations before they can go on the books. But it is also the case that laws are often written with fuzzy terminology such as "best available technology" or "adequate margin of safety." In some cases, laws and regulations may direct that the regulated industry strive for a zero-risk standard without any adjustment for the relationship between costs and benefits. Nor, generally speaking, is there any balancing between the benefit that could be obtained by expenditures on one environmental problem or hazard as against another problem or hazard. William Reilly, a former head of the EPA, noted:

No law has ever directed that [the EPA] seek out the best opportunities to reduce environmental risks in toto; nor that we employ the most efficient, cost effective means of addressing them.

But, of course, that global, rationalistic approach is exactly what the academic critic of present policy would favor. Present environmetal policy offers the critic some fine targets.

Although relatively low in total costs, EPA's rule regulating wood preservatives costs at least $5 trillion [not a misprint] per life saved and is estimated to avert only one case of cancer every 2.9 million years.[13]

If one thinks about environmental quality purely from the perspective of human health and well-being, it turns out that environmental expenditures that have a very high ratio of costs to benefits can actually increase human mortality and morbidity (illness). Statistically, more prosperous people live longer and are healthier than poor people. This is true if we compare the populations of rich and poor countries and also if we compare rich and poor people within the same country. Suppose that we require more effective but also more expensive emission controls on automobiles. We will then breathe cleaner air, which will contribute to our health. But the increased price of automobiles will leave us less to spend on medical care, more healthful food, bicycle helmets, and other things that contribute to health and safety. Which effect will predominate? One cannot answer that question a priori. Answering it takes careful study as well as the economist's balancing of benefits and costs at the margin. From the economist's perspective, then, one can both favor substantial or even increased environmental regulation and expenditures, and also be critical of some aspects of current environmental policy.

Unfriendly Criticism

After the 1994 congressional elections that gave the Republicans control of both houses of Congress for the first time since 1948, national environmental policy came under sharp attack. Based largely in the House of Representatives and presaged in the "Contract with America," the attack came from a general animus to regulation, a feeling that the federal government was simply too large and powerful, and a strong preference for the rights of private property. Much of the force behind the attack came from congresspersons from western states. They were often influenced by, and spokespersons for, a loose coalition of antiregulatory forces referred to as the "Sagebrush Rebellion." As discussed in Chapter 17, a large part of all land west of the Mississippi is owned by the federal government and managed by federal agencies such as the Bureau of Land Management. As a result, logging interests, grazing interests, mining interests, and others whose incomes derive from the use of public lands constitute a powerful antiregulatory force. This force gains support from a general ethos of "rugged individualism" that figures heavily in the political culture of many western states.

Many groups and individuals interested in scaling back federal environmental regulation in the west organized as the "Wise Use" movement. The movement, well named from a public relations standpoint, took positions on a variety of regulatory and control issues, claiming "wise use" to be a combination of commercial use and environmental conservation. Clearly the movement was not beloved by environmentalists. In controversies such as the one in the northwest over the needs of the timber industry versus the preservation of the habitat of the spotted owl, the movement could be counted on to take a relatively pro-industry position. The Wise Use movement was another weight on the antiregulatory side of the balance.

The wave of referenda and legislation on takings (see Chapter 5) that came in the wake of the *Kelo* decision is part of the same antiregulatory mindset.

LOCAL ENVIRONMENTAL PLANNING

Planning at the local level can make a contribution to the quest for environmental quality in several ways, including the following. (They are discussed in detail in subsequent sections of this chapter.)

1. Control of the intensity of development
2. Control of the type of development
3. Control of the location of development
4. Public capital investment
5. Control of the operation once development is complete

An Example of Local Environmental Planning

The issue of what to do about solid waste has bedeviled many communities. Typically, solid waste just from households averages several pounds per person per day. To this is added solid waste from manufacturing, commerce, and the like. Basically, it can be disposed of in landfills, burned, or dumped (though ocean dumping is being phased out under pressure of federal legislation). In general, landfills are not popular with people who have to live near them. Such sites involve truck traffic and may be unsightly or odiferous. Beyond these essentially aesthetic issues, they can often engender real fear in nearby populations.

If solid waste is buried in landfills, there is fear of groundwater contamination because acids in surface water or rainwater dissolve pollutants in the waste and carry them into the groundwater. Fears, quite obviously, are even greater if the landfill is to contain toxic wastes. Siting landfills is often more difficult as a political problem than as a technical problem. (This kind of controversy can also occur at the national level; witness the more than decade-long controversy over nuclear waste storage at Yucca Mountain, Nevada.)

Incineration causes fears regarding air quality. Reassurances from experts often do not carry much weight with nearby residents. For one thing, it takes a certain amount of technical background to interpret figures cast in terms like "parts per million" or "micrograms per liter." Then, too, there is often some fundamental distrust of the expert. If the town government hires a consultant who tells the citizenry that the planned incinerator poses no threat to their health, there is always the suspicion that he or she is singing the song of those who pay the consulting fee.

Having admitted that the decision on how to dispose of solid waste is politically sensitive, let us look at how the more technical side of the process might be carried out. Very often, a community is propelled into solid waste planning when the present system begins to look as though its days are numbered. If the community is now using landfill disposal, it may be that the landfill area is now nearly filled to capacity. It may be that the community is shipping its solid waste to a landfill in another municipality, which has indicated that when this waste disposal contract expires, it will not be renewed. Or, perhaps, the cost of upgrading the municipal incinerator to meet air quality standards appears to be more than the community can manage.

A planning approach might be as follows:

1. *The dimensions of the problem are established.*   Population and employment projections are used to estimate the probable load of solid waste that must be handled. The present disposal system is examined to see how long it can be expected to function adequately. For example, pounds of solid waste would be converted into cubic yards, and that figure laid off against the remaining capacity of the community's landfill.

ا بعض / بعض ٱخـتـلـف ف

2. *A preliminary reconnaissance of alternative disposal methods might be undertaken.*   These are likely to include landfill, incineration, and rail haul. The latter essentially means shipment out of the area to someone else's landfill or incinerator. This alternative is becoming less available as the cry of NIMBY, an acronym for Not in My Back Yard, becomes more common. Within the incineration alternative there are several possibilities.

ا ر / ضار / فرق

Incineration may be combined with power generation. The heat might be used for generation of electric power or simply to produce steam for heating. In both cases a big question is whether there is a good market for the energy. In the case of steam, the market has to be close by because generally it is not practical to pipe steam for more than 1,000 yards or so. After incineration, various material recovery schemes might be considered. For example, magnetic separation might be used to extract ferrous residues. Other systems might be used for glass and nonferrous metals. Some schemes for disposal of the residue after separation need to be considered. The residue might be buried in landfills. It may be possible to process the unburned residue into a useful product such as construction aggregate if a user who will enter into a long-term contract can be found.

At this stage a final selection cannot usually be made because the costs and risks of each alternative may not be fully known. However, it may be possible to eliminate some possibilities and find some other possibilities that look promising. Consider, for example, the landfill alternative. A common way to approach it would be to make a list of criteria and then find all the sites in the jurisdiction that qualify. Such a list might include minimum site size; minimum distance from residential population; minimum distance from schools, hospitals, or other institutions; minimum distance from streams and aquifer recharge areas; minimum distance from wetlands; area outside of 100-year flood plain; maximum distance from main road; acceptable site geology; and soil characteristics.

3. *Cost estimates are developed.* For example, site-acquisition costs might be estimated by examination of assessed values of land and consultations with assessors, appraisers, or real estate brokers. Operating costs on the site itself might be estimated by obtaining figures from presently operating sites. Transportation of solid waste to landfills can be a major cost, so this too might be estimated. Recent experience from the municipality itself or nearby communities could be used to obtain an average ton-mile figure. The community can be divided into a number of "wastesheds," and the distance from the center of each wasteshed to a given site measured. The population and commercial activity are then estimated and hence the ton-miles estimated.

4. *Site selection is made.* A common way to approach this final step is with some sort of scoring system. A system might assign so many points for cost, so many points for environmental impact, so many points for traffic impact, and so on. Thus potential sites identified in step 3 could be ranked from most to least acceptable. Such scoring systems are not entirely objective, for the matter of what weight one assigns to each consideration is necessarily judgmental. Nonetheless, a point system is a step in the direction of rationality. Then, too, the person who chooses to call its results into question has to state what attributes he or she thinks have been weighted incorrectly. That act in itself forces the participants in the process to be explicit and thus helps clarify discussion of the issue.

These steps are a fairly straightforward technical process. The next step—actually designating a site—is often the most difficult. Even if one site is clearly superior, the process of site selection is far from over, and the choice of site not necessarily determined. In general, opposition from nearby residents can be expected. The opposition may take the form of political and public relations activity—neighborhood organization, protest meetings, letters to newspapers and legislators, and the like. It may also take the form of litigation. The state has an environmental permit system, and groups opposed to the plan may mount legal challenges either on procedural or substantive grounds.

In practice, the location of such sites is often determined by a political process that bears some resemblance to a game of hot potato. In a multijurisdictional body—for example, a county made up of a number of municipalities—such a site may end up in that municipality that is least able to resist it.

Public participation in such a decision is likely to be substantial. State legislation pertaining to the granting of permits for such facilities is likely to require that plans be made public, that hearings or public meetings be held, and that the public be given an opportunity to comment. But even in the absence of any such legal requirements, public participation is likely to be high simply because of a high degree of interest and concern. In recent years many states have passed so-called sunshine laws, which make many government meetings and internal documents open to the public. Thus as a practical matter, most local governments could not get very far in siting such a facility without the process becoming public knowledge. In many cases, the best policy for a local government seeking to choose a site may be to conduct the entire procedure in a very open way. Doing that will not prevent conflict or even feelings of victimization on the part of the "losers," but it will at least protect the government against charges of secrecy and impropriety. A basic rule of politics is that no one likes surprises.

The reader might well ask, "Why go through the procedure outlined if politics is likely to figure so heavily in the outcome?" One answer is that the process, though not entirely rational, is not totally irrational either. One role for the planner—and not just in this situation—is to lay out options clearly and accurately in order to move the decision-making process in the direction of rationality as much as possible. In a democratic society, the planner is only advisory to the elected political body, and it is unrealistic for the planner to expect that his or her advice will necessarily be followed as given. At a practical level, if the actions of local government are challenged in court, there is no better defense than a well-documented, well-researched, systematically arrived at position.

ENERGY PLANNING

The field of energy planning emerged quite abruptly at the end of 1973. It resulted from the energy price increases and shortages that followed the Arab oil embargo at the time of the Arab–Israeli War in October of that year. For about three decades after that, interest in the field bobbed up and down, largely with the price of oil. At the present writing, interest in energy conservation is very strong not only because the price of oil is high but also because it appears that major changes in the nation's pattern of energy use and energy production are very likely and that there will be ramifications through many areas of American life. We first take a brief look at the overall picture.

Table 15–1 shows the big picture of U.S. energy consumption and production. The gap between total U.S. consumption and total U.S. production is accounted for primarily by the gap between U.S. petroleum consumption and U.S. crude oil production. About three-fourths of petroleum consumption is for transportation. Natural gas is used primarily for heating, industrial purposes and electricity generation. Consumption and production are roughly in balance.

The United States produces sufficient coal for domestic use plus a small surplus for export. Over nine-tenths of U.S. coal consumption is for generating electricity, and it accounts for about half of all U.S. electricity

TABLE 15–1 U.S. Energy Consumption and Production in Quads, 2009

	Total Consumption	Total Production
Petroleum	35	11 (crude oil)
Natural gas	23	22
Coal	20	22
Nuclear	8	8
Hydroelectric	3	3
Renewables	5	5
Total	**95**	**73**

Notes: Figures may not add up to totals due to rounding, minor adjustments, and omissions of small amounts. Renewables include geothermal, solar, wind, and biomass. Of these, biomass is the largest item. A quad is 10 to the 15th power (1,000,000,000,000,000) BTU. A BTU (British Thermal Unit) is the energy needed to raise the temperature of a pound of water 1 degree Fahrenheit.

Source: U.S. Energy Information Agency, Annual Energy Report.

generation. Table 15–1 shows five quads produced by renewables. That figure includes hydroelectric power as well as the burning of wood and waste. Wind, solar, and geothermal account for somewhat less than one quad, though that figure is growing rapidly in percentage terms. Nuclear power is used entirely for electricity generation and at this time accounts for about one-fifth of U.S. electricity generation.

There are numerous reasons for thinking that major changes in the U.S. energy picture will have to occur. But, as we will see, there are many different ways in which the ball may bounce. With oil, there are several big problems. First, more and more geologists as well as others are accepting the concept of peak oil, sometimes also referred to as Hubbert's peak, after geologist M. King Hubbert, who in the 1950s developed a model for predicting the time path of fossil fuel production. Very briefly, if no new oil sources are found, world oil production, currently in the range of 80 million barrels per day, would fall by several million barrels per day each year as the production from existing wells declined. Maintaining current production, much less increasing production, then becomes a race between the exhaustion of existing sources and the discovery and development of new sources. Judging from the rate of new-source discovery, among other factors, an increasing number of geologists are coming to believe that the world is near peak production. Some see the peak as a few years in the future. A smaller number believe that we are currently passing or have just passed the peak. People have coupled the peak oil concept with expectations of increasing world petroleum demand and come to the obvious conclusion about future prices.

But quite apart from the Hubbert's peak issue, oil imports represent a large part of the U.S. chronic trade deficit. In spring 2011 the United States was importing about 10 million barrels of oil a day at a price of roughly $100 per barrel. That's $1 billion of deficit per day. At the same time the U.S. trade deficit was in the range of $50 billion per month. Thus oil imports amounted to more than half of the total deficit. Beyond the deficit issue, our need for oil ties us into Middle East geopolitics. There has been much discussion of increasing U.S. oil production. Shale oil in some of the western states is a possibility, but extracting oil from shale is inherently dirtier and less efficient than bringing up oil from wells. The other big prospect is for expanded offshore drilling. That prospect was considerably diminished by the 2010 BP (British Petroleum) oil spill off the Louisiana coast.

Natural gas has huge potential. The United States has a large supply, and natural gas, at this writing, costs no more than one-third as much per BTU as does oil. But it has its problems, too. Building the infrastructure to distribute natural gas as widely as gasoline and diesel oil are now distributed and retrofitting tens of millions of vehicles to run on liquefied natural gas (LNG) would reqire huge expenditures and take many years. In addition there is concern that the process of hydraulic fracturing, often referred to as *fracking*, necessary to bring the gas up can cause serious groundwater pollution. In March 2011 the state of Maryland's legislature moved to ban all natural gas production pending a two-year study of the problem. New York State at that time was permitting production from existing wells but banned all new drilling. Until the fracking issue is resolved the future of natural gas is uncertain.

The story with coal, too, is mixed. On the positive side the United States has huge reserves and, compared to oil, coal is inexpensive. On the other hand, coal produces considerably more carbon dioxide per BTU than does oil and almost twice as much as does natural gas, so in terms of global warming it is a big villain. Underground mining poses hazards to life and health, and strip mining and mountaintop removal have serious environmental costs. Burning coal also releases particulates and traces of various metals contained within the coal and thus affects air quality. There has been much discussion of sequestering carbon dioxide from the burning of coal by pumping it under high pressure into permanent underground storage. Sequestration has been done on a small scale, but whether it is feasible on a major scale remains to be seen. Where the power plant was not located over a suitable geologic formation, carbon dioxide would have to be transported under high pressure by pipeline to the site from which it would be pumped underground. The scale of the undertaking would be enormous. At present, the United States burns about 1 billion tons of coal per year. Burning a ton of coal produces a little more than three and one-half tons of carbon dioxide. Thus sequestering all of the carbon dioxide now produced by burning coal in the United States would mean putting about three and one-half billion tons of carbon dioxide underground each year.

The crystal ball with nuclear power is also clouded. Nuclear power generates no carbon dioxide so in that one way it is totally benign. But there are the big problems noted earlier in this chapter, most importantly those of financing and the public perception of risk.

Renewables, particularly wind and solar, look promising—no carbon dioxide emissions and no catastrophic risks. But there are problems with these, too. Cost is one. Without subsidy neither wind nor solar is cost competitive with coal at present. And, of course, subsidy money is a very contentious matter politically. Beyond that, there is simply the question of magnitude. For an economy that currently uses close to 100 quads a year, how long and how much investment would it take to expand two sources that together now produce less than 1 quad to the point that they become a major factor in the total energy picture?

At the national level, major change seems inevitable, but that change could take many different forms. At the municipal level much of the effort will probably go into conservation and to adapting to changes in the cost and technology of transportation and residential and commercial heating.

Energy Planning at the Local Level

In the United States, about 21 percent of all energy is used in the residential sector.[14] That is primarily energy for heating, cooling, lighting, and utilities. The commercial sector uses another 19 percent, of which at least half is for the same items just listed. Thus, in total, at least a third of all U.S. energy consumption can be directly affected by the actions of local government. Of course, in many cases local action will be affected by federal grants, tax credits, regulations, and the like.

Steps that a municipality can take to conserve energy can be divided into four general categories.

1. Land-use planning
2. Changes in building characteristics
3. Changes in transportation
4. Community energy sources

Land-use planning can be used to reduce energy consumption in a variety of ways; the most obvious is by minimizing transportation requirements. One way to do this is by favoring development that reduces the average distance between the origin of a trip and the destination. However, the long-term trend in the United States, as noted in Chapter 2, has been to lower urban densities. An alternate, and probably more feasible, approach is to encourage mixed-use development. For example, mixing commercial and retailing uses with residential uses may permit shorter average commuting and shopping trips than would be the case if the three uses were strictly separated. (See neotraditional planning in Chapter 10.)

Another way that land-use planning can encourage energy efficiency is by making nonautomotive modes convenient. This might mean providing separate bus lanes along major thoroughfares. In a major metropolitan area, it might mean designing major highways with a median that would be suitable for future installation of rail lines. For example, Route I–66, which extends westward from Washington, DC, was laid out in this way. In the mid-1980s the Washington Metro was extended into adjacent parts of northern Virginia along that routing. In a smaller community, planning for energy efficiency might mean providing bikeways to separate bicycle from automotive traffic, thus eliminating a major discouragement to bicycle use. The community in the United States best known for this plan is Davis, California. There, approximately 25 percent of all passenger miles, as opposed to about 2 percent statewide, are made by bicycle. In general, land-use planning can facilitate the development of public transportation by arranging residential and nonresidential uses to reduce the "collection" and "distribution" problems noted in Chapter 12. A community might also decrease the use of private automobiles by greater expenditures for public transportation, setting up new initiatives in public transportation such as van pooling and dial-a-ride systems, and encouraging carpooling.

Building characteristics can be altered to produce very sizable reductions in energy expenditures. In some cases these changes are closely linked to land-use planning decisions; in other cases they can be effectuated independently. A land-use plan might encourage row housing as opposed to free-standing single-family units. This choice need not mean higher density in the development but might, for example, mean clustering, with the provision of common open space. Row or attached housing, in general, reduces energy used in heating because it reduces the amount of building surface exposed to the elements. To see this, just imagine two free-standing units moved into a side-by-side position. The two side walls that have been brought together become interior walls and can no longer conduct heat to the outside.

Siting buildings with regard to the sun will affect the ease with which sunlight can be used to supply part of the energy used for heating. Streets that run east–west facilitate placing houses so that they face south for maximum solar exposure. A number of communities have adopted solar access zoning, which prevents structures or trees from being placed in such a position that they block the direct access of other buildings to the sun.

There are also building-related steps that are unrelated to overall land-use planning. A number of communities impose minimum insulation requirements on new houses. Some municipalities have implemented programs designed to encourage property owners to retrofit old buildings. These may be limited to giving technical advice or may also include low-interest loans and other financial incentives. A few communities require that before a house can be resold, it must be brought up to some minimum standard of insulation, a technique that gradually forces a retrofitting of the existing housing stock.

The number of municipalities that have "green building codes"— codes that mandate a variety of energy saving and other environmentally friendly features in new buildings—is increasing rapidly. Many municipalities now build or retrofit their own structures with energy conserving features such as solar heating or photovoltaic panels.

The LEED Program

Much of the effort toward more environmentally superior buildings is structured around the Leadership in Energy and Environmental Design (LEED) program now run by a nonprofit organization, the United States Green Building Council (USGBC), headquartered in Washington, DC.

The USGBC has established a set of LEED standards for green building under which points are awarded for various green features in six major categories: sustainable sites, water efficiency, energy and atmosphere, materials and resources, indoor environmental quality, and innovation and design process. For example, in the sustainable sites category, points are given for density of development and what the USGBC terms "community connectivity," meaning ease of access to other parts of the community. Points are also given for redevelopment in a brownfield, for access to public transportation, provision for use by bicyclists, open-space restoration, storm-water management, and a variety of other items. The water efficiency category essentially pertains to water quality and water conservation issues. The energy category pertains to energy-efficient construction and renewable energy systems, and so on.

The USGBC certifies buildings in three categories, platinum, gold, and silver, depending on how many points they achieve under the LEED rating system. Building to LEED standards is more expensive than ordinary construction, but there are paybacks. For one thing, certification is appealing to the organization or individual who is environmentally conscious and wants to achieve a minimal environmental footprint.

A LEED platinum rating is something that a residential developer can use as a selling point to environmentally conscious buyers and that a corporate advertising department might relish for corporate image purposes. Then, too, there is a long-run cost issue, for a LEED-certified building will be less expensive to operate over the years and thus recover some, all, or more than all of the initial cost difference.

LEED certification can be required by a municipality for tax breaks, density bonuses, or other financial incentives. Where a municipality is purchasing a building, it could make LEED certification a contractual requirement.

The USGBC runs training programs to certify a variety of professionals in LEED standards and technology and, as of 2007, had certified about 54,000 people in this way. There are now LEED standards for a variety of building types, and the standards evolve as building and energy conservation technology evolves. The USGBC has links to numerous organizations outside the United States, including the World Green Building Council, Canada Green Building Council, and a number of others.

At the national level, the move to green buildings has been assisted by a variety of tax incentives. These include tax credits for home insulation and for renewable energy generating devices.

The green building movement in the United States received a powerful push from the Obama administration and the passage of the economic stimulus package, noted earlier in this chapter. The bill includes funding for green building construction and retrofitting for public schools, public and publicly assisted housing, and a variety of other building types. It also provides substantial funds for training to prepare workers for green building jobs.

Local Energy Production

A number of communities have begun community energy production systems. These do not literally represent energy conservation, but by their nature they tend to, and are intended to, conserve traditional energy sources. Many communities have developed or are developing so-called low head hydroelectric systems, for example, using a source that was used for power but subsequently abandoned when relatively low-cost power from central sources became available. One factor that makes such development practical is state laws that require utilities to buy power from small-scale generators and thus create a market for the output of such facilities. New England, with a large number of dams dating from the period when many mills and factories ran on waterpower, is the national center for such activity.

In many communities, solid waste, which was once disposed of in landfills or burned in incinerators, is now used as the fuel for power generation. The power is either used locally or sold back to the area utility and distributed through the utility's transmission grid. A number of municipalities have looked at the possibility of *cogeneration*, a system in which waste heat from one process is put to a second use rather than simply discharged into the atmosphere. For example, waste heat from a municipal power generating facility might be converted to steam and used to supply heat for municipal or other buildings.

There is now considerable interest in recovering heat from wastewater. How does it work? Assume water in the municipal sewer system is at 60 degrees Fahrenheit (16 degrees Celsius), a typical temperature. It is 30 degrees outside and we want to maintain the air temperature in buildings at 70 degrees. A heat exchange system captures the heat of the sewer water and brings water for building heating systems up to 60 degrees. The amount of heat required to go from water at 60 degrees to a building air temperature of 70 degrees is much less than would be required in the absence of this boost from the sewer water. The sewer water thus carries most of the base load. The remainder of the load can be carried in various ways. For example, there might be roof-mounted solar heaters for daytime supplementation and natural gas heat (the most efficient fossil fuel from a greenhouse perspective) for peak loads. Viewed as a whole, the system is basically a means of capturing the waste heat from showers, dishwashers, washing machines, and all of the other household or commercial devices that use hot water.

It is not practical to pump heating water over distances greater than a few hundred yards. Therefore an energy district based on recovered heat from sewer water fits in well with some design concepts discussed earlier such as transit-oriented development that provides a large amount of residential or commercial floor space in a small area. The energy district offers advantages of cost, reduced greenhouse gas (GHG) emissions, and space savings in buildings because the building does not need to have its own heating plant. Like other systems, it is more practical to design the energy system in from the beginning rather than to retrofit it later.

On-site solar electric generation has the potential to bring about substantial reductions in the net amount of electric power a household has to buy from its electric utility. During the day, the solar array simply feeds back into the electric power grid and runs the house's electric meter backward, reducing both the owner's bill and also the amount of power that the utility has to generate. A very big problem, however, is the high front-end cost of installing the solar array. In Palm Desert, California, the municipality used $7.5 million of its own funds to make loans to homeowners to install arrays. The loan is paid back, with interest, over a period of years by an add-on to the house's property tax bill. The commitment runs with the property so that when the house is sold, the new owner has to accept the obligation as a condition of purchase. In several other municipalities in California, there are similar programs except that the funding comes from a third party such as a bank, rather than the municipality. In either case, what would have been a major financial obstacle is converted into a manageable stream of long-term payments.[15]

SUMMARY

Much environmental planning and regulation must be done at the national level because of the scale of the problems and the great distances pollutants can travel through the environment. Local environmental planning often takes place within a framework of federal grants and regulations. Concern with environmental problems grew rapidly in the United States during the 1960s, culminating in the passage of the National Environmental Policy Act (NEPA) in 1969, the creation of the Environmental Protection Agency (EPA) in 1970, and the passage of a number of other major pieces of national environmental legislation in the 1970s. The passage of NEPA produced a massive increase in the number of planners and firms specializing in environmental planning because of NEPA's requirements for environmental impact statements (EIS) as a prerequisite for the federal funding of large projects.

At the national level, environmental planning involves the establishment of standards and the funding of such activities as the construction of wastewater treatment facilities. At the local level, much activity is related to federal legislation and funding, for example, EISs, or to planning for projects that involve joint local and federal funding, such as wastewater treatment. However, much to enhance environmental quality can also be done at the purely local level, including controls on the intensity of development, the type of development, the matching of development to the physiographic character of the area, the pattern of public capital investment, and regulation of the character of development and operation.

Energy planning arose with the oil price increases that followed the 1973 Arab–Israeli War. The original concern of the energy planner was the conservation of nonrenewable energy sources, that is, fossil fuels such as petroleum. At the local level, reductions in consumption of nonrenewable energy may be achieved by urban design that reduces trip lengths and facilitates public transportation or the use of nonautomotive modes (foot or bicycle). Energy savings can be achieved by site design, doing new construction to high standards of energy efficiency, and retrofitting older structures. The green building movement has gained strength as concern with climate change has increased and was given a substantial push by federal funding provided in the 2009 economic stimulus legislation.

NOTES

1. Bjorn Lomborg, *The Skeptical Environmentalist*, Cambridge University Press, 2001, and *Cool It*, Vintage Press, New York, 2007.
2. Numerous polls on the subject of attitudes have been done by Gallup, Pew Charitable Trust and other organizations. To see an assortment of them Google a phrase like "global warming and polls."
3. D. Morgenstern, R. A. Pizer, and J. S. Shih, "The Cost of Environmental Protection," *Review of Economics and Statistics*, vol. 83, no. 4, November 1, 2001, pp. 732–737.
4. U.S. Energy Administration, *Annual Energy Review*, 2010, available at the Energy Administration's website, TK
5. From Title I of the National Environmental Protection Act (NEPA) of 1969, PL 90–190.
6. For a detailed discussion of this process and an explanation of the economic rationale for pollution rights, see John M. Levy, *Essential Microeconomics for Public Policy Analysis*, Praeger, New York, 1995, chap. Chap. 12.
7. See the Air Quality Management District's website, www.AQMD.gov.
8. The discretionary part of the budget is what is left after payments have been made for entitlements such as Social Security and Medicare as well as payments on the national debt. The first two items are well

over half of the total federal budget. The Republican position also treated defense as if it were not part of the discretionary portion of the budget, even though in literal terms it is. Therefore, the part of the budget that they in practical terms regarded as discretionary amounted to between one-fourth and one-fifth of the total federal budget.
9. Amil Markandya et al., "Electric Generation and Health," *The Lancet* vol. 370, no. 959, September 13, 2007, pp. 979–990; and Paul R. Epstein et al., "Full Cost Accounting for the Life Cycle of Coal, *Annals of the New York Academy of Sciences*, vol 1219, February 2011, pp. 73–98.
10. For an account of this process, see *Environmental Quality*, 1983, p. 253.
11. Ibid.
12. A large literature has developed on the greenfields–brownfields issue, with a heavy emphasis on the how-to-do-it aspects of brownfields redevelopment. See, for example, David Yaussy, "Brownfields Initiatives Sweep Across the Country," *Environmental Compliance and Litigation Strategy*, vol. 10, no. 11, April 1995, p. 1; "Redeveloping Contaminated Sites: Economic Realities," *Urban Land*, June 1995; and James A. Chalmers and Scott A. Roehr, "Issue in

the Valuation of Contaminated Property," *Appraisal Journal,* vol. 61, no. 1, January 1993, pp. 28–41.
13. Bradley K. Townsend, "The Economics of Health Risk Analysis," in Levy, *Essential Microeconomics,* p. 217.
14. Energy Information Administration, *Annual Energy Review,* 2007, p. 36. The administration

divides all U.S. energy consumption into four broad categories: transportation, 29%; residential, 21%; commercial, 18%; and industrial, 32%.
15. Leslie Kaufman, "Harnessing the Sun, with Help from Cities," *New York Times,* March 15, 2009, p. B5.

SELECTED BIBLIOGRAPHY

COUNCIL ON ENVIRONMENTAL QUALITY, *Annual Report,* Washington, DC. (This series begins in 1970.)

DANIELS, TOM, and DANIELS, KAMERINE, *The Environmental Planning Handbook,* APA Press, Chicago, 2003.

MABEY, NICK, HALL, STEPHEN, SMITH, CLARE, and GUPTA, SUJATA, *Argument in the Greenhouse,* Routledge, New York and London, 1997.

MANGUN, WILLIAM R., and HENNING, DANIEL H., *Managing the Environmental Crisis,* 2nd ed., Duke University Press, Durham, NC, 1999.

MASER, CHRIS, *Sustainable Community Development: Principles and Concepts,* St. Lucie Press, Delray Beach, FL, 1997.

MCHARG, IAN, *Design with Nature,* Natural History Press, Doubleday & Co., Inc., New York, 1969. Second edition, 1992.

MOFFAT, IAN, HANLEY, NICK, and WILSON, MIKE D., *Measuring and Modeling Sustainable Development,* The Parthenon Publishing Group, New York and London, 2001.

NATIONAL RESEARCH COUNCIL, *Our Common Journey: A Transition Toward Sustainability,* National Academy Press, Washington, DC, 1999.

RANDOLPH, JOHN, *Environmental Land Use Planning and Management,* Island Press, Washington, DC, 2004.

VERCHICK, ROBERT R. M., *Facing Catastrophe: Environmental Action for a Post-Katrina World,* Harvard University Press, Cambridge, MA, 2010.

CHAPTER 16

Planning for Metropolitan Regions*

Most of the planning discussed in this book is that done by the individual municipality. But there are many planning issues that transcend municipal boundaries and are much better addressed at a larger-than-municipal scale. In this chapter we discuss planning at the metropolitan-area level.

THE POLITICAL PROBLEM

The key problem in planning for a metropolitan area is the political one. By themselves, city governments are generally too small to address adequately metropolitan-area problems. Yet it is at the municipal level that much of the power and responsibility lie. The problem, then, is to set up a metropolitan area–wide mechanism that has the capacity to do effective planning. That means an organization that can obtain sufficient support and cooperation from the established institutions of government, municipal and state. This is not an easy task. Politicians, like most other people, do not readily cede power and authority to others. They need to be convinced that they and their constituents have a community of interest with

*Portions of this chapter pertaining to Minneapolis–St. Paul were written by the late C. David Loeks, who was Professor Emeritus in Urban Affairs and Planning at Virginia Polytechnic Institute and State University, and a former Planning Director of the city of St. Paul.

the regional organization. Metropolitan planning organizations succeed only to the extent that the local and state political establishments—elected officials and their constituents—see the regional organization as useful in meeting their needs. This is necessarily so, for metropolitan-area planning takes place within the U.S. federal system, in which large amounts of authority and responsibility, such as the power to control land use, reside with local governments.

What, specifically, are the planning issues that demand a regional rather than a local approach? The listing that follows is not complete, but it includes the main items that would make most lists.

1. Transportation. Because large numbers of people cross municipal lines to work, shop, or take part in social and recreational events, a regional approach to transportation is necessary. Then, too, many transportation facilities, such as airports, by their very scale must be regional facilities.

2. Water supply, sewers, and sewage treatment and solid-waste disposal. Water-supply systems must be designed with regard to topography and hydrology, not to political boundaries. Where municipal populations are small, economies of scale in water and sewer treatment facilities may make multijurisdictional plants more efficient. Locating a solid-waste disposal facility means taking account of soil characteristics, groundwater flows, road access, and population distribution. In most cases these design requirements will not correspond to municipal boundaries. The same is true for flood control.

3. Air quality. A single municipality within a large metropolitan area cannot by itself solve its own air quality problems. There must be cooperative action within the metropolitan area or within the "airshed." (See the discussion of the Los Angeles Air Quality Management District in Chapter 15.)

4. Parks, outdoor recreation, and open space. Because population densities and land values in the core of a region are vastly greater than on the periphery, it makes sense for outlying areas to provide more of their share of open space and parkland, creating a need for multijurisdictional planning.

5. Economic development. If the region unites for this purpose, it can sell itself as a single entity to the rest of the world rather than expend funds on competition between municipalities that are all part of the same regional labor market. Thus some zero-sum game activity can be avoided. A regional approach may also achieve marketing economies of scale, for example, in having a single development office represent the entire region of London or Frankfurt or Tokyo.

6. *Housing*. Housing and land-use policies in one municipality affect housing prices, rents, and vacancy rates in the entire metropolitan area. Employment growth in one municipality affects housing demand in many other municipalities. Thus housing is a regional as well as a local issue. It must be admitted, however, for a variety of reasons noted in the last section of Chapter 11, that regional housing planning is still more of a gleam in the planner's eye than a major force in urban and metropolitan housing markets. Although there good arguments for it, the political force behind a regional approach is often weak.

Beyond these planning issues there are many services for which a regional approach makes sense, often because the former permits greater economies of scale. Thus we also see regionwide efforts in workforce training and the provision of various social services. But these services take us beyond the realm of planning as the term is used in this book.

A BRIEF HISTORY OF METROPOLITAN-AREA PLANNING

In this section we discuss three institutional approaches to planning at the metropolitan level: the regional planning agency, the authority, and the council of governments. Though they are separate approaches, they have many points in common.

The need for metropolitan-area planning was recognized at least as far back as the turn of the twentieth century. Recall that the 1909 Plan for the City of Chicago contained regional elements for both transportation and open space. However, the first big surge of interest in regional planning came in the 1920s. The primary cause was the great increase in automobile ownership that occurred during the 1920s and the related growth of the suburbs. As the compact city of the nineteenth century gave way to the metropolitan area of the twentieth century, the need for metropolitan-area planning became evident, particularly in regard to transportation and utilities.

One response to this need was the regional planning agency. One of the first, and probably the best known, of these organizations was the Regional Plan Association in New York. The plan, described in Chapter 3, covered more than 5,000 square miles in three states: New York, New Jersey, and Connecticut. By the end of the 1920s, there were about 15 regional plans in the United States. Many of them, like the plan for the New York region, were done entirely under private auspices. Such plans had absolutely no official sanction or any force of law. They affected the region only to the extent that they influenced the opinions of public officials and their constituents. Other regional plans of the period were governmentally chartered and funded so they had a certain statutory relationship to the political establishment. But even then, the power of such a group was essentially only the power of persuasion, for it is only the legislative and executive branches of states and municipalities that can make laws and appropriate monies.

The Public Authority

Another path to regional planning, also of 1920s origin, was the creation of authorities. An authority is an organization that is generally created by state government or in some cases by the joint action of two or more state governments. Rather than being a general-purpose government like that of a town or city, it is a quasi-governmental organization with some of the usual powers of government. For example, an authority often has the power to raise money through the issuance of tax-exempt bonds. It may also have the power to take property through condemnation or to override local land-use controls. In general, it has a single task or set of tasks assigned to it. In modern administrative jargon, it is set up to be very "task oriented." Authorities were not and are not created to do general-purpose planning in the sense that a regional planning agency is. However, the decisions of an authority may well shape a region and constitute planning decisions under another name.

The authority exists "at the pleasure" of the state legislature(s) that created it, and it can always, at least in principle, be abolished by the same legislative body or bodies. Its board of directors is appointed by the same legislature(s). That feature, too, constitutes a powerful element of legislative control. Yet authorities do sometimes become a force of their own and achieve a substantial degree of autonomy. Though ultimately under legislative control, authorities are much further from political control than, say, a city agency such as a public works department. They operate separately from municipal and state governments, and they are further from the reach of the voter because he or she does not vote for the board members directly. Rather, the voter votes for the legislators, who then choose the authority's board.

The first authority in the United States was the Port of New York Authority, subsequently renamed the Port Authority of New York and New Jersey. It was created jointly by the legislatures of New York and New Jersey in 1921. As discussed in the next section of this chapter, it has been a powerful force in shaping the New York region.

The fact that both regional organizations mentioned so far, the Regional Plan Association and then Port Authority of New York, were created in the New York region is not entirely coincidental. Regional planning and development efforts come into being where the disproportion between the size of the real city—the economic and social city—and the political city is great. The New York region was by far the nation's largest metropolitan area in the 1920s, and the problems of achieving coordinated action were compounded further by its being a multistate region. It is not surprising that much of the apparatus of regional cooperation should have evolved where the need for it was greatest.

Regional Planning After World War II

Regional planning in the United States after its promising start in the 1920s developed only slowly over the next several decades. But the pace of development accelerated sharply in the 1960s. One reason for the acceleration was the long period of rapid suburban growth that began after the end of World War II and continues to the present time (or, at least, until very recently). This was a resumption of the same force that had started the trend toward regional planning in the 1920s. A second factor was that we began to give environmental issues more weight, and environmental problems by their very nature tend to be multijurisdictional. But perhaps most important was that the federal government began to offer state and local governments irresistible inducements to regional planning.[1] In the 1960s the flow of federal money for highways, urban redevelopment, and environmental projects increased greatly. But to get federal grants, local governments had to meet federal requirements for regional planning. For example, the 1962 Federal Highway Act provided matching funds for highway construction, but to get those funds, the applicants had to show that their application was consistent with a regional plan. The Urban Mass Transit Act of 1964 authorized billions of dollars for mass transit systems, but again, the applicant had to show that the funds being applied for would be used consistently with a regional plan. Not only did these and other acts make regional planning a requirement for funding, but many of them also provided funds for the making of regional plans. The carrot of federal funding was a major factor in bringing into being the Councils of Governments (COGs), which today are the main instrument for intermunicipal cooperation in the United States, and which often incorporate regional planning and former regional planning agencies within themselves.

Councils of Governments. The term *Councils of Governments* is used generically in this section, but numerous other names for the same type of organization are in use, such as regional councils, associations of governments, planning districts, and area development district associations.

According to the National Association of Regional Councils, there are about 450 COGs, by one name or another, in the United States today. They range in size from three employees to over 3,000 employees. In the South and the Southwest, virtually all local governments are members of COGs, and in the rest of the nation, the great majority of local governments are members. Some municipal and county governments may belong to more than one COG. For example, every county in the state of Virginia belongs to one of Virginia's 17 Planning District Commissions. But Virginia counties in the northeast portion of the state are also physically part of the Washington, DC, metropolitan area. Those Virginia counties such as Fairfax and Prince William, which are part of the metropolitan area, also belong to the Metropolitan Washington Council of Governments (MWCOG).

To meet the National Association of Regional Council's definition of a COG, at least 51 percent of the organization's board of directors must be elected officials of its constituent municipalities. In practice, local elected officials usually make up much more than 51 percent of board membership. Those members of boards who are not elected officials are often persons who have some appointed relationship to one of the constituent municipalities, such as being a member of a planning board. The board of the COG sets policy and hires the full-time director, much as a city council hires a city manager. The director is the day-to-day director of the COG, but he or she serves under the direction of the board. Thus the COG is very much the creature of its constituent municipalities. What responsibilities it has and how far it can go in any direction are thus determined by the municipalities that it represents. For a COG to do effective work, it must have the support of its member municipalities, that is, that they perceive it as serving their purposes—as being a help and not as being a rival.

The COG serves as a venue for communication and negotiation between municipal governments. For example, imagine that the COG in its role as Metropolitan Planning Organization is putting together a grant application for highway funds. The approximate total that the region will receive is known, but the cost of every project that each municipality would do if it could is vastly greater. The collective "wish list" must thus be pared down to approximate the total of funds available. Thus there must be bargaining and compromise among the municipalities making up the COG. The COG serves as a venue for such activity and in that way helps bring about some meeting of minds among the governments of the metropolitan area or region.

COGs are not always well understood by the citizens of their member municipalities. The city or town or country government is much more visible to the citizen. Its actions tend to be much better reported in the local press or covered on the 6 o'clock news. Then, too, the citizen votes for municipal officials. The COG, as a creation of the various municipal governments, is much less visible. Politicians want visibility because they have to stand for election, and to do that successfully, they must be known. The director of a COG may take a different view. He or she may prefer to simply get on with the work of the COG outside the light of publicity. Thus many COGs function in relative obscurity.

In the following sections we present three case histories to illustrate the previous general discussion: the case of Minneapolis–St. Paul, for regional planning agencies; the case of the Port Authority of New York and New Jersey, for authorities; and the Atlanta Regional Commission, for Councils of Governments.

MINNEAPOLIS–ST. PAUL: A TALE OF TWO CITIES _____

At the turn of the twentieth century, Minneapolis and St. Paul were two separate cities with a combined population of about 460,000. But by the 1950s their combined population had risen to about 1.2 million, and the two once-separate cities had coalesced into a single urban area bisected by the Mississippi River. Both cities, like many others of the period, were rapidly suburbanizing.

The problems of suburban expansion as well as those of rebuilding the two cities' downtowns focused the attention of civic and government leadership on the question of how to guide the continuing growth of the Minneapolis–St. Paul region. The issue was brought to a head by problems connected with the expansion of the metropolitan sewer system and by the advent of the Interstate Highway System (see Chapter 17). The sewer problem required a regional approach if duplication of facilities was to be avoided and if the efforts of one municipality were not to complicate the efforts of other municipalities. Since in that region all sewer systems ultimately empty into the Mississippi River, it would not be helpful to have one municipality's discharge pipes located immediately upstream of another municipality's intake pipes. Similarly, it was understood that the highway system, which would serve the entire region, would be best designed if the region were viewed as a whole.

In 1957, after two tries and much bargaining and compromise, the Minnesota legislature passed a bill creating the Metropolitan Planning Commission (MPC). The law that created the MPC provided for a 28-member governing board, of which 21 members represented local governments. The other 7 members were appointed by the governor to represent civic, business, and community interests. The law also specified that the commission's authority was limited to planning and recommending. It had no powers to implement. The MPC had been structured to be as nonthreatening as possible to the existing political establishment.

For the next decade the MPC worked on developing a regional plan. A good part of the time was spent on developing information and promoting public consciousness of the issues and of the need for planning. The plan that emerged was a development policy designed to minimize sprawl and to concentrate urban development in the two central cities and in a number of large-scale, self-contained satellite communities. These would be separated by open space and farmland but would be linked by the metropolitan transportation system.

One obstacle to achieving intermunicipal cooperation about land-use planning is the matter of property taxes (see Chapter 9). All municipalities want land uses that return more in property taxes than they cost the municipality to service. Thus there will be intermunicipal competition over attractive commercial development. Therefore, the plan called for a tax-sharing arrangement. A portion of the property tax revenues from new nonresidential development would go into a common pool to be shared by all the municipalities in the region. This arrangement meant that there would be less motivation for municipalities to compete for fiscally desirable developments and more chance of achieving a land-use pattern that made sense in regional terms.[2] By 1966 the planning phase was just about complete, and it was time to begin implementation.

In 1967 the Minnesota state legislature created the Metropolitan Council to move from plan to reality. Within several years the Metropolitan Council was responsible for policy in a number of areas including sewers and sewage treatment, solid-waste disposal, open space, sports facilities, public transportation, and highways. The tax-sharing arrangement was set up in 1971. In 1975 a "Metropolitan Framework" law was passed, stipulating that the Metropolitan Commission would establish the following:

1. Urban service areas in which housing subdivisions would be concentrated
2. Commercial/agriculture areas in which free-standing subdivisions would not be allowed
3. Rural development zones that would not provide urban services (such as public water and sewers) except around preexisting development

Note that this approach is similar to that of many growth management systems, some of which are described in Chapter 14.

In addition to this planning work, the Metropolitan Commission also functioned as a management and service-delivery agency for various federally mandated programs in criminal justice, health care, the arts, and services for the aging. In this regard it functioned in the same way as many other Councils of Government.

In recent years much of the council's work has been on transportation. The Hiawatha line, a light-rail link connecting the Minneapolis downtown with the Minneapolis–St. Paul International Airport and the Mall of America, opened in 2004 and, unlike a number of other rail projects, its ridership, now over 30,000 per weekday, is well ahead of initial projections. Work is currently under way on the Central Corridor Light Rail route, which will run 11 miles to link downtown Minneapolis with downtown St. Paul. In addition, the council has done work on bicycle trails and bus–bike linkages, to facilitate both bicycle commuting and recreation. The council has also worked on parkland acquisition and park development, among other projects.

What Has Been Accomplished?

The council by itself does not literally put bricks on mortar, but it has created the framework in which regional planning takes place. The region benefits from a better transportation system and better public utilities, a well-planned system of open space, and higher environmental quality.

There are also economic benefits. The region has benefited greatly from investment by such organizations as the 3M (Minnesota Mining and Manufacturing) Corp. The corporation's willingness to commit itself to the region stemmed in part from its recognition that problems that affected it and its employees would be effectively addressed. The revitalization of the downtowns of Minneapolis and St. Paul has been facilitated because investors have had confidence that transportation and other problems of the downtowns would be addressed.

More generally, the Twin Cities area is widely regarded as having a high quality of life as measured by things like public services, employment, education, and recreational and cultural amenities. There is a widespread "pride of place." Some of that emanates from a raised regional consciousness and a sense of national leadership in urban planning, development, and governance.

THE PORT AUTHORITY OF NEW YORK AND NEW JERSEY _____

The first authority formed in the United States was the Port of New York Authority, which was created in 1921 by the legislatures of New York and New Jersey and was subsequently renamed the Port Authority of New York and New Jersey. In the following discussion it is simply referred to as the Port Authority.

The authority's original mission was to improve the transportation of rail freight in the region. The port area is divided by the New York–New Jersey boundary, which lies in the middle of the Hudson River. The interstate problem was compounded by commercial rivalry between the business establishments on the New Jersey and the New York sides of the port. On the New Jersey side, the problem of political coordination was further complicated because the area is divided into a large number of municipalities. An authority looked like a way to cut through the problems of multiple competing political jurisdictions. The authority also offered a way to get the public's work done without tax increases. In the words of Al (Alfred E.) Smith, then governor of New York, such an authority would be

> the one method we have discovered of getting work done expeditiously and without overtaxing our people to get it done.[3]

At first the Port of New York Authority concentrated on rail freight improvements, but it quickly became apparent that the future belonged much more to the automobile and the truck than it did to the train. The authority's basic mission soon expanded to that of building in a coordinated way the river crossings that would meld the New York and New Jersey sides of the New York region into a single metropolitan area.

The decisions about what to build and where emerged from a mix of engineering, planning, and political considerations. The decision to let the entire problem of river crossings be handled by a single public agency was a political one, driven in part by the conviction of Governor Smith that such an important public task should not be left to separate groups of investors formed for each project but should be handled publicly as a single undertaking.

The first major project was the George Washington Bridge, which spans the Hudson River from the Palisades in New Jersey to 179th Street in northern Manhattan. The decision to build there rather than to build either a bridge or a tunnel to midtown Manhattan was made for a variety of reasons. The governor of New Jersey and a variety of interests in northern New Jersey wanted the crossing in that location to open up the northeastern part of the state. Part of the decision-making process turned on a particular personality. One of the great civil engineers of the twentieth century, Othmar H. Ammann, a Swiss immigrant to the United States, was taken with the idea of such a crossing to northern Manhattan. The bridge that he conceived would be the longest single span in the world. In the late 1920s a suspended center span of over 3,000 feet was an engineering challenge that would push the bridge-builder's art to the limit. Ammann was convinced that it could be done, and he wanted to be the one to do it. A persuasive and energetic man, he was a major force behind the scenes in bringing about a consensus that the bridge could be built within a reasonable budget, that it would quickly pay for itself, and that it could be completed in a relatively short period of time. He proved right on all counts, and the bridge was finished in 1931, in less than two years and under budget.[4] Ammann, who had some of the artist in his makeup, as well as being a talented engineer, was very concerned with bridges as works of art. Commenting on the bridge in 1936, Le Corbusier said,

> The George Washington Bridge over the Hudson is the most beautiful bridge in the world. Made of cables and steel, it gleams in the sky like an arch upturned, blest. It is the only seat of grace in a disheveled city.[5]

The bridge was a major planning decision for the region. The direct, continuous, high-capacity link for motor vehicles provided by the George Washington Bridge gave a tremendous impetus to the growth of northern New Jersey. The effect might not be so great today, for suburbs are much more economically self-sufficient than they once were. But in the 1930s the economic role of the metropolitan core, Manhattan in the case of the New York region, was proportionally much greater than it is today. If one says that regional planning to a large extent consists of intervening at a few strategic points, the building of the bridge was clearly one such decision. In subsequent years the Port Authority of New York and New Jersey continued to build, producing many of the links that bind the New York area, cut up as it is by bodies of water, into a unified region.

In addition to building bridges and the Lincon Tunnel connecting New Jersey with midtown Manhattan, the Port Authority has also played a role in mass transit. It operates bus lines, and much of the bus traffic between New York City and the New Jersey part of the region uses the Port Authority's bus terminals. It also operates commuter rail service from New Jersey to lower Manhattan. Though it did not build them, the Port Authority operates the region's three major airports, La Guardia, Kennedy, and Newark.

The Port Authority also has played a major part in shaping the role of New York City as a port. In the period after World War II, the Manhattan docks lost their ocean freight business. The city's congested streets drove up the cost of moving freight, and lack of available land made it impossible to expand docking facilities to handle containerized freight, which made its appearance during that period. The Port Authority responded by developing the Port Newark–Elizabeth Marine Terminal (Port Newark) on the New Jersey side of the region. Covering over three square miles, the terminal is set up to handle containerized freight and provides very quick access to the Interstate Highway System as well as to railroads and Newark Airport. Though its construction did nothing to keep freight handling at its traditional Manhattan location, it does enable the region to retain considerable ocean freight business that would otherwise have gone out of the region entirely.

The Port Authority was not the only authority that shaped the New York region. On the New York side of the Hudson River, a number of bridges and tunnels have been built by the Triborough Bridge and Tunnel Authority (TBTA), under the direction of Robert Moses.[6] For example, in the 1960s the TBTA built the Verrazano Bridge between Brooklyn and Staten Island. Previously the only links between Staten Island (the borough of Richmond) and the rest of New York City were either a ferry trip to Brooklyn or Manhattan or a very circuitous drive to make use of the Holland or the Lincoln Tunnel. Staten Island in, say, 1960 was a rather quiet place, semirural in many parts, because of its relative isolation. The building of the bridge produced much suburbanization, a major increase in population, and much more commuting between Staten Island and the rest of the city. The Verrazano Bridge is without doubt the most important planning decision ever made in connection with Staten Island.

Above, the George Washington Bridge, shown looking west from the New York side of the Hudson River, which was the first major project built by the Port Authority. To accommodate rising traffic volumes, a lower deck was added to the bridge after World War II. Below, Port Newark, built by the Port Authority on the New Jersey side of New York Harbor near the confluence of the Hackensack and Passaic Rivers. Note the strategic location. Immediately to the west of the port is the New Jersey Turnpike, a part of the Interstate Highway System, and beyond that is Newark Airport, visible at the very top of the photo.

Up to now we have said nothing about the financing of authorities. In the case of an authority such as the Port Authority, the main instrument is the tax-exempt bond (see Chapter 9). The monies received from the sales of bonds are used to build facilities, and charges like tolls are used to pay off the bonds. For the government, whether city or state, that created the authority, this is an attractive arrangement. The bonds are not an obligation of the government, nor do they count in determining whether that government has reached its debt limit. The agency can accomplish the purposes of the government that created it without obligating or burdening that government. If the agency has sufficient revenue-generating assets within the total mix of services that it provides, it can be entirely self-financing, as is the Port Authority. Not every activity must be self-supporting, since the more profitable ones can "cross-subsidize" the money-losing ones. For example, surpluses on bridge tolls might subsidize losses on bus operations.

Is There a Downside?

The picture presented so far is that of the authority cutting the Gordian knot of multiple jurisdictions and doing its work in a condition of relative isolation from the city or state finances. Is there a downside to this otherwise attractive picture?

Although authorities are created with a specific mission, they tend to survive for very long periods of time, and over time their missions may change and grow considerably— "mission creep" in Pentagon jargon. The first goal of most organizations, whether they be governments, foundations, businesses, academic departments, or authorities, is to survive and to grow. The Port Authority, born in 1921, has outlived all of its creators. It plays many roles that its founders never imagined.

Because the authority is isolated from direct involvement in electoral politics, it may be able to operate with a somewhat longer time frame than the two- or four-year cycle that necessarily looms so large in the minds of those who have to stand for reelection. Thus its relative political isolation may enable it to accomplish some tasks expeditiously. But because it is somewhat outside the political process it may make decisions that the body politic as a whole would not choose to make. In the case of the Port Authority its transportation decisions were, in effect, huge planning decisions, but they were made at least partly outside the usual planning process. That is not a statement about whether, in retrospect, they were good or bad decisions, but simply that they were very big decisions made by a relatively small number of people who stood outside the usual political process. It has been claimed that if a large share of public spending is in the hands of authorities, they may tend to push the mix of spending toward infrastructure rather than services both because most authorities are originally created to address infrastructure issues[7] and because infrastructure like bridges and tunnels generates revenues.

Though the authority can, in principle, always be abolished by the legislature that created it, that is easier said than done. A large authority can be a considerable political force in its own right. The Port Authority, for example, has close to 8,000 employees. Its operating revenues in 2008 were over $3.5 billion, and its outstanding bonds totaled approximately $11 billion. Its capital expenditures in that year were $2.4 billion.[8] Those are the statistics of a large city government.

THE ATLANTA REGIONAL COMMISSION

Councils of Government are now the predominant mechanism for metropolitan-area planning, as well as for multi-county and other multi-jurisdiction efforts outside metropolitan areas. The Atlanta Regional Commission, which bills itself as the "oldest and largest publicly supported, multi-county planning agency in the United States," is also one of the most respected.

The history of metropolitan-area planning in the Atlanta region began in 1938. Recognizing that growth beyond municipal borders was producing problems, the City of Atlanta; Fulton County, which contains most of the city; and the city's Chamber of Commerce commissioned a consultant to study and make recommendations regarding intermunicipal cooperation in the Atlanta region. The consultant, Dr. Thomas Reed of the National Municipal League, came out strongly in favor of a regional planning agency:

> We feel that the institution of a metropolitan planning commission would be the beginning of a new day in the growth of the Atlanta region. Planned development is the only sure development. No man today trusts himself to build a structure much bigger than a chicken coop without a set of blueprints. How can such a vast and complicated affair as a great metropolitan community have orderly growth without a plan?[9]

This quote from Thomas Reed perhaps shows a bit more faith in our ability to shape the future through planning than the modern planner, with the benefit of hindsight into the unplanned effects of major programs like Urban Renewal and the Interstate Highway System, might have. In that sense it is very representative of the 1930s outlook (see Chapter 3).

The region's move toward regional planning was delayed by World War II. However, in 1947 a Metropolitan Planning Commission (MPC) was created by act of the Georgia state legislature. The membership of the commission was small, only the city of Atlanta and two counties, Fulton and DeKalb. The commission focused primarily on transportation and open space, which appeared to be the critical issues in a growing region. As the region gained population, the initial organization grew. In 1960, Clayton, Cobb, and Gwinnett Counties joined, roughly doubling the land area in the planning region, and a new organization was formed, the Atlanta Region Metropolitan Planning Commission (ARMPC). During the 1960s, regional planning for a variety of purposes grew, largely as a result of the flow of federal funding noted earlier. The result was that there were several regional planning agencies operating within the Atlanta region. Beyond the ARMPC were separate regional agencies for health, crime, and highways. To bring order out of the situation, the Georgia legislature in a bill titled Act 5 combined these various agencies into a unified agency, the Atlanta Regional Commission, which began operations in 1971. At this point, these separate regional efforts had been transformed into a full-blown Council of Governments.[10]

At present the Atlanta Regional Commission represents 10 counties and a population of over 3 million. The City of Atlanta, with a population estimated at 426,000, represents only about 14 percent of the metropolitan population and, of course, a much smaller percentage of the land area under the purview of the Atlanta Regional Commission. As is true of all other COGs, control of the board of directors is firmly vested in the municipalities that constitute the COG. Twenty-three members of the board of directors are elected officials, mayors, and county commissioners. In addition, there are 15 members at large who cannot be elected or appointed officials nor employees of the political subdivisions of the COG. However, they are not elected by the public but chosen by the 23 elected officials on the board.[11]

What does the Atlanta Regional Commission do? Its organization chart shows its staff divided among five main areas: Communications, Community Services, Comprehensive Planning, Development Services, and Support Services. From the perspective of this book, the two of major interest are Comprehensive Planning and Development Services.

As is the case with many other COGs, the Atlanta Regional Commission provides a database for the region's planning efforts. Thus population, water use, traffic, and other projections made by the council provide a common denominator for planning throughout the region. Having such a shared picture of the future is fundamental to being able to cooperate. Many of the council's planning efforts over the years have been devoted to transportation issues. The City of Atlanta was founded as a rail terminal in the 1830s, and its function as a transportation hub has been a key element in its economy ever since. Over the years its efforts in transportation have included planning for the I-285 beltway around Atlanta; Hartsfield Atlanta International Airport; and the region's commuter rail system, the Metropolitan Atlanta Rail Transit Authority (MARTA). After Congress passed the Intermodal Surface Transportation Efficiency Act (ISTEA) in 1991, which included money for so-called enhancements, the council participated in planning for bicycle and pedestrian pathways as well.

The council has also been active in water planning. This has included planning for reservoir development and for the protection of watersheds in the Atlanta region. A 1972 study by the council of the Chattahooche River corridor formed the basis for intermunicipal efforts to protect the river and for the designation of river and environs as a National Recreation Area by the Carter administration in 1978. The council has also engaged in collaborative efforts with the states of Alabama and Florida, which share watersheds with Georgia.

The Development Services section of the Atlanta Regional Commission has taken a modest role in economic development. The agency produces and supplies data and, most recently, a Geographic Information System (GIS) for firms interested in an Atlanta region location. It also seeks to assist the efforts of municipal economic development agencies and chambers of commerce. It does not, by itself, spend monies on economic development projects such as industrial parks.

As is the case in Minneapolis–St. Paul and other metropolitan areas, the chief contribution of a regional planning agency is to be found in a spirit and process of intermunicipal cooperation. In the case of the Atlanta region, the Atlanta Regional Commission has played a significant role in a variety of regional initiatives, particularly in transportation, open space and environmental quality, and water supply.

SUMMARY

The first major wave of planning for metropolitan areas occurred in the 1920s. The primary force behind it was the great increase in automobile ownership and the related increase in suburbanization. As the area of urbanization spilled out of municipal boundaries, the need for planning at an intermunicipal level became apparent.

In the 1920s two types of organizations appeared in response to this need. One was the regional planning agency, of which the best known was the Regional Plan Association (RPA) in the New York metropolitan area. Some agencies, like RPA, were entirely private organizations with no official aegis at all. Others were created by legislative act. But in either case, regional planning agencies had no power to implement. Instead, they existed purely to advise, with implementation left entirely to the governments of the region. The second type of organization that appeared in the 1920s was the authority. These were organizations created by state legislatures with a definite mission (in transportation, utilities, and the like), and with some, but not all, of the powers of government. Though authorities were not specifically "tasked" with overall metropolitan-area planning, decisions that they made about public infrastructure often turned out to be major planning decisions. In the post–World War II period, a third instrument for cooperation at the intermuncipal level appeared. This was the Council of

Governments (COG). Today there are about 450 COGs in the United States, and most municipalities in the United States belong to one. Some belong to more than one. The growth of COGs was promoted in large measure by the federal government's regional planning requirements for funding bills in transportation, urban redevelopment, environmental improvement, and social services.

The chapter concludes with three case studies: the evolution of regional planning in the Minneapolis–St. Paul region, the origins and growth of the Port Authority of New York and New Jersey, and the history of the Atlanta Regional Commission.

NOTES

1. Frank S. So, Irving Hand, and Bruce D. McDowell, eds., *The Practice of State and Regional Planning*, American Planning Association, Chicago, 1986, pp. 144–147.
2. This arrangement is widely admired by planners and experts in public finance, the former for its land-use effects and the latter on the ground that it will help equalize the per capita fiscal capacity of different municipalities in the same region. Unfortunately, such systems are rare for a very simple reason. Most municipalites are able to predict whether they will be net gainers or net losers under such a system. There is no way to compel the potential net losers to agree to join the system.
3. David C. Perry, ed., *Building the Public City*, Urban Affairs Annual Review 43, Sage Publications, Thousand Oaks, CA, 1995, p. 221.
4. For a detailed account of the politics of the bridge and Ammann's role, see Jameson W. Doig, "Politics and the Engineering Mind: O. H. Ammann and the Hidden Story of the George Washington Bridge" in *Building the Public City*, op. cit.
5. Ibid., p. 22.

6. For an account of Robert Moses's career and effects upon the city and the New York region, see Robert Caro, *The Power Broker*, Alfred A. Knopf, New York, 1974. The TBTA was merged with the Metropolitan Transit Authority (MTA) in 1965 and essentially survives as that part of the Authority with responsibility for bridges and tunnels. The other part of the Authority is responsible for the New York City subway system, city buses, and the metropolitan area's commuter rail service.
7. Katherine Foster, *The Political Economy of Special Purpose Government*, Georgetown University Press, Washington, DC, 1997.
8. Statistics from the *Annual Report of the Port Authority of New York and New Jersey*, 2008, available on the Port Authority's website.
9. From the 1938 Reed Report as quoted in *Atlanta Regional Commission: 50 Year Commemorative Report*, Atlanta Regional Commission, Atlanta, GA, 1997.
10. This chronology is adapted from *Atlanta Regional Commission: 50 Year Commemorative Report*, Atlanta, GA, 1997.
11. *Bylaws of the Atlanta Regional Commission*, adopted September 10, 1971, amended through August 28, 1996.

SELECTED BIBLIOGRAPHY

PERRY, DAVID C., ED., *Building the Public City: The Politics, Governance and Finance of Public Infrastructure*, Urban Affairs Annual Review, no. 43, Sage Publications, Thousand Oaks, CA, 1995.

CHAPTER 17

National Planning in the United States

IS THERE NATIONAL PLANNING IN THE UNITED STATES? ___

Does national planning exist in the United States? In one sense the answer is no, for there is no person or organization charged with drawing up a physical plan for the nation. There is no national master plan corresponding to the master plan that a city or town or county might have. In fact, when Congress terminated the National Resources Planning Board (NRPB) in 1943, it expressly prohibited any other agency in the federal government from assuming the board's national planning functions (see Chapter 4). No national planning agency comparable to NRPB has been set up since then.

One reason that we do not have a national plan is simply ideological. A national master plan sounds like socialism, and for most of our history, that has not been a welcome sound. Another reason may be the formidableness of the task. A national land-use plan for a small country is feasible. The Dutch do national land-use planning very well. But the Netherlands has a land area of a little more than 13,000 square miles, not much bigger than the state of Maryland. That is quite different from the 3 million square miles of the "lower 48."

Finally, and perhaps most important, we have a federal system of government in which a great deal of power resides with the states' congressional delegations. That dispersion of power makes the formation of a unified national plan extremely difficult. Dutch style top-down planning is simply not possible in the U.S. political environment. This is not a matter of democracy versus autocracy, for the Netherlands is just as much a democracy as is the United States. Rather, it is a matter of the degree of centralization of political power.

Although there is not now nor has there ever been a master plan for the settlement pattern of the United States, there is no question that the federal government has engaged in a number of acts that have had a major effect upon the pattern of development in the United States. This chapter briefly describes some of the acts that, to an extent, constitute de facto national planning.

All these acts do not fit together neatly as parts of a single grand design, but there are some commonalities. The federal style, in most cases, has not been to command but to permit and to encourage. In most cases there has been more carrot than stick, the carrot being federal money or federal land. The general direction is set by a system of federal guidelines and incentives, but the details are decided at the state or substate level. Where the federal government actually does the work, as in an Army Corps of Engineers' project, much of the initiative is local.

In general, the federal hand in shaping the pattern of development looms larger as one moves west. Federal ownership of land necessarily made the federal government a major player in determining the pattern of land development. In the immediate postrevolutionary period, most of the land east of the Mississippi was claimed by the 13 colonies, though much of that land came into the union as other states. However, west of the Mississippi, the Louisiana Purchase, lands obtained from Mexico as a result of the Mexican War, lands ceded by Great Britain in the Oregon Compromise, the Gadsden Purchase from Mexico, and the Alaska Purchase from Russia made the federal government a landowner on a huge scale. Climate has also favored a larger federal role in the west. In most of the United States west of the 100th meridian (a line that runs roughly from North Dakota southward through the Texas Panhandle), rainfall is generally under 20 inches a year and is not sufficiently reliable to support agriculture other than grazing.[1] Thus agriculture in most of the western half of the country is dependent on irrigation. That dependency makes federal water policy a key shaper of the development of the region.

THE PATTERN OF LAND SETTLEMENT

The Ordinance of 1785, passed by the Continental Congress under the Articles of Confederation, laid out the basic pattern of landownership in what was then the Northwest Territory, a tract extending from the western border of Pennsylvania westward to the Mississippi, bounded on the south by the Ohio River and on the north by the Great Lakes. The act established the six-mile-by-six-mile-square township and the one-square-mile section as the basic units for land division. In the original plan, land was to be auctioned off in blocks of one square mile (640 acres) at a minimum price of $1 per acre. The money was to provide the Congress with revenue, and the process of auctioning land in relatively small pieces would people this vast area with small, independent farmers. When the $1-per-acre price proved to be too high, Congress backed away from the plan to some extent by selling off large blocks of land to investors and speculators at a much lower price. The area then developed in a manner largely determined by the rate at which these buyers could create new settlements and resell land to individual holders. The effect of the act was to permit the rapid peopling of the area and to lay down a basic grid pattern that is still readily seen on a map of Ohio, Indiana, and other parts of the upper Midwest. The decision to sell farm-sized plots of land to individuals reinforced the rural American pattern of scattered farmsteads as opposed to a pattern commonly seen in Europe in which a rural population lives in hamlets or villages surrounded by the fields farmed by its residents.

In the latter half of the nineteenth century, the settlement of the west was very much influenced by a few other decisions of the federal government. The Homestead Act of 1862 permitted settlers to claim 160-acre blocks of public land at essentially no cost if they would reside on the land for five continuous years.[2] Ultimately, about 80 million acres, roughly 125,000 square miles, were homesteaded. Most homesteading occurred west of the Mississippi and much of it in areas that did not have adequate and predictable rainfall to support agriculture. This situation, some decades later, helped propel the federal government into taking a major role in water development throughout the west.

In the same year Congress passed the Morrill Land Grant Act, which granted each state 30,000 acres of federally owned land for each member of the state's congressional delegation. The states were to use the monies from the sale of these lands to establish at least one college that would have as its primary role the teaching of "agriculture and the mechanic arts." A great many of the state universities in the United States today are land-grant colleges. The suffix A&M in a university's name dates from the act. In the case of many other schools, the "A&M" has subsequently been lost. Again, the federal government's actions were all carrot and no stick. No state was required to create an A&M college nor told where such a college should be located. The states were simply offered an attractive option, and most of them made use of it. The scattering of major state universities in small towns across the United States is, in part, a legacy of the Morrill Act.

ESTABLISHING THE RAIL NETWORK

The railroad network that facilitated and shaped the rapid development of the United States during the nineteenth century was, itself, shaped, and its construction greatly accelerated, by the actions of Congress. In 1850 there was no national network of railroads. There were under 10,000 miles of track in the eastern United States, mostly connected to large cities but not forming a unified system. For example, the farthest west one could continuously travel by train from New York City was Buffalo. Other than along the East Coast, there were no major north-south links. Yet by 1860, national rail mileage had tripled, and most of the major cities east of the Mississippi were tied together in a network so that people or goods could travel between any two major cities entirely by rail.

A major factor in this expansion was federal land grants to railroad companies. The grants provided the right-of-way plus large amounts of land adjoining the right-of-way that the company could sell or use as collateral against which to issue bonds to pay for construction. The first such grant, totaling 3,736,000 acres (5,837 square miles), was to build a continuous link from Chicago to Mobile, Alabama. By 1860 Congress had granted a total of 18 million acres for railroad construction.[3] That area, about 28,000 square miles, is roughly the area of Vermont, New Hampshire, and Massachusetts combined.

With the rail system of the east relatively complete, the next obvious task was to span the continent with railroads. The First Pacific Railway Act of 1862 provided both the authorization and the financial incentives for a transcontinental railway.[4] The act authorized the Union Pacific Railroad to build westward from St. Joseph, Missouri, and the Central Pacific Railroad to build eastward from Sacramento, California. The act granted the railroads a 400-foot right-of-way and five square miles of land for each mile of track built (a figure that was doubled by Congress two years later). In addition, the federal government issued bonds to provide construction funds. Thus investors in the project bore relatively little of the total risk. The building of the lines was accompanied by considerable corruption and malfeasance.

> Their bookkeeping was, to say the least, primitive, and such records as existed, were destroyed, possibly by design, in a fire in 1873. But there can be little doubt that the profits were enormous.[5]

Construction proceeded rapidly over formidable obstacles, and the two lines met at Promontory Point near Ogden, Utah, in 1869, making coast-to-coast rail travel possible.

Within a decade or so, other lines crossed the continent, both north and south of the Union Pacific route. Here, too, congressional aid played a major role. In 1863 Congress granted the Atchison, Topeka, and Santa Fe 10 square miles of land for every mile of route constructed, and in 1864 the Northern Pacific railroad was given lands that totaled more than the entire area of New England.[6]

Grants of public lands to railroads continued until 1873, by which time approximately 160 million acres (250,000 square miles) of land had been given to railroads either directly by the federal government or indirectly by the federal government through the states.[7] It is hard to imagine a more powerful stimulus to railroad building. The grants provided a clear and an uncontested title to the route, and the potential sale of land to settlers and speculators made the financial prospects very attractive. U.S. rail mileage grew from about 30,000 miles in 1860 to about 200,000 in 1900, by which time the rail network as we now know it was essentially complete.[8]

WATER AND THE WEST

The combination of the Homestead Act and the spanning of the continent by railroads greatly accelerated the peopling of the western states, and this brings us to the question of water. In the eastern United States, where rainfall is generally adequate to support farming, water policy is rarely the most important public issue. In much of the west, water policy is an absolutely vital issue. In the years immediately after the Civil War, the populations of the Plains states grew very rapidly for reasons noted. These years were wetter than usual, and if many western farmers did not thrive, they at least survived. The favorable weather, in fact, caused some to believe that the very act of cultivating large areas of land would cause rainfall, a notion then expressed in the phrase "rain follows the plow."

In the 1880s the weather turned drier, and it became apparent that rain does not follow the plow. In a number of Plains states, both the farm population and the total population fell sharply as farmers abandoned their barren lands. By the end of the nineteenth century, of somewhat over 1 million families that had tried homesteading, only about 400,000 had made a successful go of it.[9]

The failure of rain-fed agriculture in the western half of the nation promoted a great interest in irrigation to "reclaim" the desert lands for agriculture. But private irrigation efforts, by and large, were not very successful. Inadequate technical knowledge, undercapitalization, and, in many cases, fraud and chicanery doomed a majority of private irrigation projects. Pressure mounted for federal action.

The Reclamation Act of 1902 established the Reclamation Service (which became the Bureau of Reclamation in 1923). Under the act, funds from the sale of public lands were to be used to pay for irrigation projects and the investment repaid (without interest) by the parties using the water.

At first the repayment period was to be 10 years, then 20 years with a 5-year grace period, and subsequently was extended even further.[10] The principle of federal subsidization of water development thus became firmly established. From the act's passage to well into the 1920s, the federal role in providing water in the west was modest. But in the late 1920s, a combination of events propelled the nation into almost a half-century of dam building and water projects that shaped much of the modern west.

In the period around World War I, people in the rapidly growing Los Angeles region recognized that growth would be brought to a halt by water shortages if a new source were not found. The nearest major source was the Colorado River, which begins in central Colorado more than two miles above sea level and follows a tumultuous southwesterly course, ending in the Gulf of California between Baja California and the main land mass of Mexico. But the river does not flow through California itself, and thus California could not make a direct claim on it. Californians took the initiative, and after much negotiation the Colorado River Compact to divide the waters of the Colorado was signed by the seven states of California, Arizona, New Mexico, Colorado, Nevada, Utah, and Wyoming. In 1928 Congress authorized the construction of Boulder Dam (subsequently renamed Hoover Dam), smaller dams downstream, and the All-American Canal. The latter was to run westward from a lower point on the river, Lake Havasu, to be formed by Parker Dam, to Los Angeles. The centerpiece of the project was Boulder Dam, on which construction began in 1931 under the auspices of the Bureau of Reclamation. Completed in 1936, the dam was a massive testimony to the civil engineer's art. It was 726 feet high, almost a quarter of a mile across the crest, and contained 66 million tons of concrete. A system of canals and aqueducts was then constructed to carry the waters of the Colorado across the width of California to serve the city of Los Angeles. Further south, the All-American Canal carried the Colorado's waters westward just north of the California–Mexico border and turned the desert of California's Imperial Valley into one of the nation's most productive agricultural areas.

The dam was a spectacular demonstration of what could be done both to supply huge quantities of water and to produce enormous amounts of cheap, hydroelectric power. At the same time, the Great Depression had left a quarter of the nation's labor force unemployed, and federal job creation looked like the best way to deal with the problem. Dam building and reclamation projects were a way to soak up unemployed labor and produce a useful product. The dust bowl of the early 1930s (a result of dry weather and overcultivation) drove hundreds of thousands of farmers off their land in states like Oklahoma (hence the term *Okies*) and sent them westward toward California. Another use, then, for funding reclamation work was to open lands for farmers displaced by the dust bowl. A great era of dam building was soon under way. The prime agency for this work was the Bureau of Reclamation, though some dams were also built by the Army Corps of Engineers.

In connection with the dam building and associated construction done on the Colorado, one writer states,

> If the Colorado River suddenly stopped flowing, you would have two years of carry-over capacity in the reservoirs before you had to evacuate most of Southern California and Arizona and a good portion of Colorado, New Mexico, Utah and Wyoming. The river system provides over half the water of greater Los Angeles, San Diego and Phoenix; it grows much of America's domestic production of fresh winter vegetables; it illumines the neon city of Las Vegas . . . whose annual income is one-fourth the gross national product of Egypt—the only other place on earth where so many people are so helplessly dependent on one river's flow.[11]

What was done on the Colorado was not unique but only a harbinger of what was soon to be done elsewhere. By the start of World War II, Grand Coulee and Bonneville Dams (built by the Army Corps of Engineers) on the Columbia River and Shasta Dam on the Sacramento River in northern California had been completed. The process of damming and controlling the rivers of the west continued with great speed after World War II. By 1971, Hoover Dam ranked only forty-seventh in size among dams built or under construction by the bureau.[12] The largest of these, the earth-filled San Luis Dam in California, had an interior volume of over 77 million cubic yards, more than 30 times that of Hoover Dam.

Construction of water projects peaked in the 1960s with the addition of about 29 million acre-feet of storage per year and then slowed in the 1970s. It has since come to an almost complete stop. What happened? First, most of the best dam sites had been developed:

> In the 1920s, a cubic yard of dam produced 10.4 acre feet in reservoir capacity. The average declined in each decade, and by the 1960s only .29 acre feet of storage was produced per cubic yard of dam.[13]

Thus newer projects showed lower benefit–cost ratios than older ones, and it became increasingly difficult to justify large federal expenditures for them.

Then, too, our notions of conservation have changed. To Theodore Roosevelt, the greatest turn-of-the-century conservationist, the idea of reclaiming the desert and making it bloom made perfect sense. The conservationist of today might ask just what prior claim we were "reclaiming." We have come to question how much sense it makes to deliver water to the farmer at 10 cents on the dollar in a nation that uses billions of federal dollars to pay farmers elsewhere to take land out of cultivation. Does it really make sense to grow rice, as is actually done, in the California desert? Then, too, it has become apparent that the great Bureau of Reclamation and Corps of Engineers' projects of the past make both friends and enemies. Farmers and the industrial users of hydropower love them. But environmentalists become concerned about converting wetlands into reservoirs, for wetlands serve as breeding areas, as sources of biodiversity, and as stopping areas for migrating birds. They are concerned that changing the flow of a river by damming it may drive some species to extinction. Fishermen and others want rivers left in their natural state. Archaeologists do not want to see historic sites submerged forever. In short, the growing strength of the environmental movement helped bring the era of great water projects to an end.

In 1986 Congress passed the Water Resources Development Act (WRDA). The law mandated much higher local contributions to federal water projects and higher user fees for federal water projects. By shifting a substantial part of the cost downward, it ended the era when state and local governments would lobby for inefficient projects simply because the project would bring them some benefits while imposing almost no costs on them.[14] The law applied to the Corps of Engineers and not the Bureau of Reclamation, but it affected the bureau nonetheless. At present both the bureau and the corps are much more attuned to issues of conservation and efficient use of resources rather than massive new projects. In the west the key issues in regard to water conflicts are likely to involve water rights and water pricing and balancing the needs of growing urban and suburban populations with the prior claims of agriculture.

In the west, water rights have generally been determined on the basis of "prior appropriation," meaning on the basis of who first claimed the right and used the source.[15] Agriculture, which employs a very small part of the total population of the region, uses a very large share of the region's total water supply. It has a grip on this supply because of the doctrine of prior appropriation. If water is to be allocated on a more economic basis, whether it be competitive bidding or simply pricing water at its true cost of delivery, that change will favor urban and industrial users over agricultural users.[16] Decisions on this apparently technical issue of how to price water will have a major effect on the future development of the west.

Western Water Policy in Retrospect

Looking back on the era of reclamation, what is one to make of it? Some, like Marc Reisner, the author of *Cadillac Desert* cited earlier, regard much of the damming and reclamation work in the west as a giant combination of hubris, delusion, and scandal. But millions of westerners who like their region and the life they lead in it take a very different view. They will tell you that even if mistakes were made along the way, they are, by and large, pleased with what was done and what it has made possible. Some of them might also tell you that it is not right to judge actions in the past by the sensibilities of today. One should not condemn those who dammed the Colorado and the Columbia in the 1930s because they lacked the particular sensibilities of the Sierra Club members of today.

Projects, some by the Bureau of Reclamation, some by the Army Corps of Engineers, and some by state or municipal public authorities, made the modern U.S. west vastly different than it otherwise would have been. Dams, aqueducts, and canals provided the water for vast metropolitan areas like Los Angeles. Hydroelectric power at a fraction of the cost of fossil fuel-generated power in the east provided a basis for western industry. Western agriculture is largely a product of public water policy. California is first among the 50 states in value of farm output.[17] In California's Imperial Valley rainfall averages two to three inches a year. Without the waters of the Colorado, it would be as dry as the Sahara.

Were it not for the great water projects, the population of the American West would be much smaller than it is, and it would be strung out along the region's rivers. Los Angeles could not exist at anything close to its present scale. Reno and Las Vegas would, at best, be small towns depending on whatever water could be brought up from the wells. The west would be a food-importing rather than a food-exporting region and its industrial base far smaller than it currently is. People would not be able to water-ski on artificial lakes in the desert.

The rest of the nation would be different too. The population of the eastern United States would be substantially larger than it is today, and the centroid of U.S. population would be farther east than it now is, for there would have been much less east-to-west migration.[18] The eastern United States would have considerably less forest than it now has, for without so much food production in the west, there would have to be much more land cultivated in the east.

SYSTEMATIC REGIONAL PLANNING

The sort of systematic planning for an entire region that one might call national planning has been done only once. That project was the work of the Tennessee Valley Authority (TVA). The Tennessee River originates in the Cumberland Mountains of the eastern part of Tennessee, flows westward, turns southward into northern Alabama, and then swings north, emptying into the Ohio at Paducah, Kentucky, a few miles upstream from the confluence of the Ohio and the Mississippi. Over half of its drainage basin is in Tennessee, but the basin also includes parts of Virginia, North Carolina, Georgia, Alabama, Mississippi, and Kentucky.

The natural regime TVA of the Tennessee River is characterized by large spring flows that produce destructive floods and low summer flows that inhibit navigation. The intensity and frequency of these events discouraged development and contributed to persistent poverty in the valley.[19]

The idea for integrated development of the valley originated shortly after World War I and was persistently and skillfully backed by Sen. George Norris of Nebraska. One selling point for a project on the Tennessee, aside from the poverty of the region, was that there already was some federal investment in the valley. Toward the end of World War I, the federal government had started to build a dam at Mussel Shoals on the Tennessee River to generate hydroelectric power and an industrial facility to use that power to make nitrates for explosives. The nitrate plant was tested and then "mothballed" in 1919. The dam was completed in 1925. The presence of that wartime investment provided a rationale for more development to properly utilize the original public investment. The nitrates that would have been used for explosives in war would be used for fertilizer in peacetime. In 1928 Congress passed legislation that would have created an organization similar to TVA, but it was vetoed by President Calvin Coolidge.

The Great Depression changed the political equation. In April 1933 President Franklin D. Roosevelt requested passage of legislation creating an authority, and Congress quickly complied.[20] Both job creation and alleviating the persistent poverty in the region were motivations. The act created a single authority to deal with all aspects of the project.

The river was dammed at a number of points to control flooding, and the same dams were used to produce hydroelectric power. The hydropower made possible electrification and furnished power for industry. In time the economic growth of the region raised the demand for electricity beyond what could be produced from the river, and in the years after World War II, TVA branched out into fossil fuel and nuclear-generated power as well. The building of locks rendered the river navigable from Knoxville, Tennessee, to the Missouri and thence to the Mississippi, thus contributing to the commercial growth of the region. Lakes created by the water projects provided recreation for the residents and brought in income from tourism.

As a project and as an experiment, TVA has both its critics and its admirers. From the political right it has been criticized as socialistic and as permitting government to compete unfairly with private power companies. In fact, early in its history, electric power companies brought suit to enjoin it from selling electric power. The appeal went to the Supreme Court, which upheld the right of the governmental body to produce and sell electric power. TVA has been criticized from the left for being too cautious and sticking to an excessively narrow agenda. The agency has concentrated on a few areas—flood control, navigation, and power—and has eschewed a more comprehensive planning and social engineering role. Its admirers will argue that the agency performed yeoman service for the region by ending flooding, rendering the Tennessee River navigable (over a 652-mile stretch from Paducah to Knoxville), and providing the region with low-cost power. It let the region compete rather than languish in a state of underdevelopment.

Congress has never duplicated the TVA, though many "little TVAs" have been proposed. One reason clearly is ideological. A writer who worked for TVA for some years suggests that another reason is bureaucratic rivalry.[21] In the TVA, various functions are all the responsibility of a single commission. Thus, she asserts, little TVA proposals have been opposed by the Corps of Engineers, the Bureau of Reclamation, and other agencies because the proposals would take functions out of the hands of those agencies. Although the TVA experiment has never been duplicated in the United States, the project has been the object of study for planners, economists, and administrators from developing nations all over the world as an example of how to do regional development.

Although the TVA has never been duplicated there have been less comprehensive efforts made at multistate planning. Of these, the biggest and best-known effort is that of the Appalachian Region Commission (ARC). Set up in 1965, the commission was designed to combat the problem of lagging development in Appalachia noted in Chapter 13. The region, defined by statistics on poverty and unemployment, extends from the southwest corner of New York State to the northeast corner of Mississippi and includes parts of 13 states. It is run by a director appointed by the president of the United States and the governors of the 13 states. The basic function of the commission is to channel federal funding to projects in the region to make it more competitive with other regions and also to ameliorate some of the social effects of underdevelopment.

After the commission was set up it was concluded that the biggest single factor holding back ecomomic development in the region was inadequate transportation, a result of the region's mountainous topography. The largest expenditure of federal funds coming through the commission has been for highway construction, and accessibility in the region has been very much improved. Funds have also been spent directly on economic development—for example, the community-owned industrial park that offers firms sites at below cost. Funds have also been spent on workforce training to improve the quality of the labor force and on medical care as well as a variety of social services. Good work has been done by ARC, but in terms of comprehensiveness and the remaking of a region, it is not comparable to what was accomplished by TVA. There was no single project comparable to the controlling of the Tennessee River that could serve as the defining element in a plan, nor was there a comparable level of funding and political commitment.

As suggested earlier in this book, the effects of Hurricane Katrina on New Orleans and some tens of thousands of square miles of the Gulf Coast suggest that a major regional planning effort for that region might make some sense, for wind and high water are no respectors of municipal or state lines. Certainly, the planning technology today is vastly more advanced than what was available when TVA was created. Back then, high technology for data crunching was the hand-cranked calculator and the slide rule. GIS systems were unheard of and our knowledge of the underlying sciences like hydrology was only a fraction of what it is today. The question is not one of technical capacity but of the alignment of political forces.

THE INTERSTATE HIGHWAY SYSTEM

The design and construction of the Interstate Highway System represent a major act of national planning. In cubic yards of earth moved or cubic yards of concrete poured, the system, taken as a whole, may well be the largest construction project in human history. The construction of a coordinated system of highways all built to the same standards and linking every major city and more than 90 percent of all cities down to a population of 50,000 or more residents, across a land of about 3 million square miles, was a major act of planning. It was done as a cooperative venture between the federal government and 49 states.[22]

The federal presence in highway construction began with the Federal Aid Road Act of 1916. This act provided federal funds to assist states in the construction of intercity highways. It established a basic pattern of shared funding responsibility and local consent to and participation in highway planning that persists to the present time.

In the 1920s and 1930s, the increase in the number of automobiles and the dispersal of population, largely because of widespread automobile ownership, outpaced the rate at which the states and municipalities could build roads. In 1934 federal legislation authorized funds for state highway planning in addition to supplementing the states' construction expenditures. This set in motion a variety of traffic studies and placed the idea of a national highway grid on the national political agenda.

In 1938 Congress requested the Bureau of Public Roads (BPR, a federal agency that subsequently became the Federal Highway Administration) to study a proposal for a system of six superhighway toll roads, three to cross the country from east to west and three from north to south. Toll roads were suggested because the federal government and the states were starved for revenues during the Great Depression, and tolls appeared to be a way to make the highways self-financing. BPR studied the matter and decided that this proposed 14,000-mile system would not be able to generate enough toll revenues to be self-financing. Instead, in 1939 BPR came back with a proposal that recommended a national highway system of 26,700 miles. A succession of planning studies over the next decade and a half produced a vision of a national highway system of roughly 40,000 miles.[23] The system would be jointly planned by the federal government and the states, would be built to the same design standards across the nation, and would be a system of limited-access roadways. Limited access was necessary to maintain a smooth, high-speed flow. The concept had been proved on a very small number of parkways beginning with the Bronx River Parkway in the late 1920s (see Chapter 3).

Although the vision of a single, integrated, limited-access system was compelling, the passage of legislation that would bring it into being was stalled by the problem of how to finance it. Studies indicated that tolls, despite their financial success on a few roads such as the Pennsylvania Turnpike, could not generate the revenue required to build and maintain a national system. It took a decade after the end of World War II before that problem could be resolved.

In 1956, at the urging of the Eisenhower administration, Congress passed the Federal Aid Highway Act of 1956. Title I of the act called for uniform design standards across the nation, established methods for apportioning highway funding among the states, and dealt with questions of procedure and administration. But the crucial part of the act was title II, which provided for a mechanism that would deliver massive funding for highway construction. The act set up the Highway Trust Fund, which would receive money from excise taxes on new vehicles and sales taxes on motor fuel. These funds would be dedicated, meaning that they could be used only for highway construction. Since the passage of the act, motor vehicle ownership, miles driven, and fuel consumed have risen rapidly, providing a growing tax base to sustain highway construction.

The design of the system was a joint effort between the Federal Highway Administration and state officials. The overall plan of the system was worked out by the federal people, but the exact routing within the states was largely determined by state officials. Design standards were uniform. There were four 12-foot lanes to be separated by a median and provided with shoulders at least 10 feet wide. The highways were designed for maximum speeds of 50, 60, or 70 miles per hour depending upon topography. Early on, it was decided not to permit any services on the highways themselves, in contrast to the practice on toll roads. The argument given for this was to preserve competition and avoid the granting of "monopoly positions." But one might speculate that this decision had the fortuitous effect of increasing support from local businesspeople, who would see the highway as a source of additional customers, rather than as a source of additional competition.[24]

The system, at this writing, covers about 42,500 miles and is virtually complete. The total cost of the system is estimated at about $129 billion. In that the entire system is a single entity built to a single set of standards providing high-quality connections between virtually all of the major urban centers in the United States, it is a huge act of planning. It has shaped the development of the nation to an enormous degree. But it must be said that there were unanticipated effects.

From the beginning it was recognized that there would be a choice between whether the interstates would go through cities or would bypass them with a circumferential road. It was understood that this choice would have important urban design consequences, and the 1956 legislation provided that where such a decision was to be made, a public hearing would be required. Within a few years enormous public opposition to cutting interstates through cities developed, and the decision was almost always to bypass.

The decision to bypass brought into being the familiar beltway pattern that we see around most major cities. And that is a profoundly deurbanizing design. The beltway creates a major locus for economic activity around the city. People who work for businesses on the beltway no longer need to live within commuting range of downtown. The beltway, in effect, becomes the new downtown. The "edge city" of which Joel Garreau writes (see Chapter 10) is made possible by the beltway design.

Proponents of the Interstate Highway System believed that it would strengthen the economy of the city by providing better access to the city's central business district both from other cities and from the city's hinterland. But it was not foreseen that this effect would be overshadowed by the larger effect of creating huge masses of highly accessible commercial space outside the central business district and outside the city itself.

In the cases of the largest metropolitan areas, congestion on the beltway and the areas around it, in time, creates demand for a second beltway. The New York metropolitan area has, in effect, a double beltway system though it has breaks in it because of topographic considerations and bodies of water (Long Island Sound and the lower reaches of New York Harbor). In the Washington, DC, metropolitan area there has been much discussion of a second beltway 10 or 15 miles farther out. This would bring many hundreds of square miles of exurbia into the metropolitan area.

The building of the Interstate Highway System accelerated the shift of U.S. manufacturing from rail-borne to truck-borne freight by providing a road network that greatly increased the efficiency of trucking. That, of course, was also a decentralizing force. It probably also accelerated the growth of the sunbelt relative to the rest of the country by tying formerly remote rural southern areas into a single, highly efficient national highway system.

One might wonder how different America would look if instead of taking the path we did, we had attempted to keep cities compact and spent much of the money devoted to interstates on a high-quality, heavily subsidized rail system. But although one may wonder about this, there was no real possibility for such a choice. The American love affair with the automobile and the process of suburbanization were well under way by the time the interstate system was begun. The rail-served, compact city configuration has its appeal, and it certainly can make a claim for environmental virtue. But it never had the mass support that might have made it a real possibility.

The system accomplishes what it was intended to do. It provides rapid, safe, high-quality automotive transportation between cities, and between cities and their hinterlands. It has also accomplished much that was not intended.

FINANCING THE SUBURBS

Few acts of the federal government have had more effect upon the physical form of metropolitan areas than legislation concerning the financing and taxation of housing. Prior to 1935, mortgage lending was very different from what it is today. To protect themselves from losses when the borrower defaulted on a mortgage loan, banks required very large down payments. That, by itself, prevented many people from becoming homeowners. There were other barriers as well.

> Lenders considered a ten year mortgage to be long term. Many mortgages ran only one, two or three years, with most of the loan amount due in one large payment at the end of the short term. At the end of this short period, the home purchaser faced great uncertainties. Could he persuade the lender to renew his mortgage? At what interest rate? If he failed to get a renewal, he often lost his home. The standard plots in melodramas of the time [the villain about to foreclose on the hapless widow] were not entirely fiction.[25]

This situation was radically changed by a single act of the federal government. In 1935 the Federal Housing Administration (FHA), which had been created the previous year, began to offer mortgage insurance. The insurance fund consisted of a small fee paid by each borrower (the buyer of the house). The fund reimbursed banks should the borrower default on the mortgage. Federal mortgage insurance effectively eliminated the risk of default and thus made banks willing to lend for 25 or 30 years and with little down payment. Shortly thereafter the federal government created the Federal National Mortgage Association (FNMA, often referred to as Fannie Mae) to buy mortgages from banks. The bank could sell the mortgage to

FNMA, thus converting the mortgage into cash. The home buyer would continue to make mortgage payments, but they would go to FNMA, with the bank acting as intermediary. By creating a secondary market for mortgages, the federal government further increased the willingness of banks to issue mortgages because the bank could now get out of the commitment if and when it saw a more profitable use for its funds. In other words, the operations of FNMA removed much of the "opportunity cost" risks of mortgage lending.[26] After World War II the Veterans Administration further encouraged home buying by insuring veterans' mortgages that carried little or no down payment.

Congressional intent in passing the required legislation was primarily to increase homeownership, something that is generally considered to be a central element of "the American dream." Another goal during the Great Depression was to reduce unemployment by stimulating residential construction. The stimulating effect during the Great Depression was not very large, but the effect on both construction and homeownership in the prosperous years that followed World War II was enormous. So far as is known, there was no spatial intent behind Congress's actions. In fact, there is no evidence that members of Congress were aware early on that these actions would have any spatial effect. But the effect of making homeownership more accessible was to promote rapid and extensive suburbanization, for the suburbs rather than the cities were where the mass of land available for building single-family houses was located.

Suburbanization and Tax Policy

The federal government has also contributed to suburbanization through tax policy. If you own a house, you can deduct from your taxable income both interest on the mortgage and property taxes on the house and the lot. If you rent a house or an apartment, you implicitly pay mortgage interest and property taxes because the landlord must cover these taxes through the rent. However, you cannot deduct these expenses from your taxable income. This favorable treatment of the owner vis-à-vis the renter creates a powerful push toward homeownership.

There was no spatial intent to this favorable tax treatment. One can take advantage of it just as well by buying an apartment in a high-rise condominium or cooperative in the city as one can in the suburbs. But because most of the land available for new construction is in the suburbs and exurbs, the net effect is deurbanization.

One should not underestimate the force of this favorable tax treatment acting year after year. For fiscal year 2008, the last full year before the financial crisis and ensuing recession, the Office of Management and the Budget (OMB) estimated the federal revenue loss (tax expenditure) for the deductibility of interest paid on home mortgages at $89 billion. It estimated the deduction for the deductibility of property taxes on owner-occupied housing as being worth an additional $13 billion. Even that is not the end of the story. Since the Taxpayer Relief Act of 1997, a couple selling their house can exempt up to $500,000 of capital gain (basically, what they sell the house for minus what they paid for it) from federal taxation. For 2006 that tax expenditure was estimated at $39 billion.[27] The three tax expenditures, adding to a total of $141 billion, have a huge effect on people's decisions about whether to buy or rent and how much housing to buy. To the extent that the tax deductions increase the demand for owner-occupied housing, they also have a substantial effect on the price of housing.

The homeowner tax deduction has enormous political support and is likely to be part of the tax code for the foreseeable future. It has been suggested periodically for at least the last four decades that the playing field could be leveled simply by extending the same deduction to renters. Essentially, each renter would be able to take as a tax deduction a prorated share of his or her landlord's property tax and mortgage interest payments. But so far the idea has not gathered much political support. Perhaps one reason is that we have long seen expanding homeownership as a national goal and thus have looked with favor upon tax provisions that pull us in that direction. Extending the benefit to renters would lessen that pull. Recently the writer heard a few planners suggest that if one favors more concentrated forms of development, leveling the playing field by giving renters the same tax treatment as owners might be a good idea. Then, too, the bursting of the housing bubble may suggest to some that perhaps we have pushed the idea of expanding homeownership a bit harder than was necessary and that a balancing of the scales would be in order.

But Is It Planning?   The question is whether one should refer to the federal government's actions just described as "planning." In the matter of restructuring mortgage lending there was, in a loose sense, a plan. The goal of the plan was to promote homeownership. In this regard the federal government was highly successful.

The issue is less clear with regard to tax treatment. Provisions exempting interest and local taxes have been part of the IRS code since its inception. The Tax Reform Act of 1986 took away the exemption on most other local taxes and most other types of interest payments (for example, interest on credit card debt or on a car loan is not tax exempt). But Congress left the homeowner treatment untouched. One reason was that trying to eliminate it or scale it back would have provoked a political firestorm, for about two-thirds of all occupied housing units in the United States are owner occupied. Some feeling in Congress that homeownership was an important national goal to be pursued through continued favorable tax treatment was probably also a factor.

The idea that the widest possible homeownership is necessarily a good thing has changed in the last several years. The most obvious reason in that homeownership has proven to be a financial disaster for many millions of people. A more subtle insight is that widespread homeownership makes labor markets less flexible because someone who cannot sell or rent out his or her home is often locked in place and cannot move to take a job somewhere else. In that way, widespread homeownership may at times contribute to higher unemployment rates. Thus it will not be surprising if Congress someday decides to take a serious look at the tax treatment of owner-occupied housing.

LAND MANAGEMENT

The federal government is involved in land management on a grand scale. As of 1989 the federal government owned 662,158,000 acres, about 1.035 million square miles of the United States, most of it west of the Mississippi.[28] The Bureau of Land Management (BLM) manages hundreds of millions of acres. Much of that land is low-value land for reasons of low rainfall, poor access, or the like. Its role is, therefore, more one of steward-ship than of planning for development.

In the United States, 231 million acres (about 361,000 square miles) are designated as National Forest, of which almost 83 percent is actually owned by the federal government. Again, the role of the federal government is largely one of stewardship. Shaping the pattern of settlement in the nation is not a primary intent. Nonetheless, decisions about how much development to permit in national forests and where to permit the cutting of timber have economic consequences that exert some influence on the pattern of settlement. And, of course, in the long term, decisions by BLM and the Forest Service about how hundreds of millions of acres are to be used cannot help but have an effect on the environmental quality of vast areas. The National Park system, often considered to have begun with the setting aside of Yellowstone National Park in 1872, now covers an area of about 119,000 square miles.

For many years this system of land management has seemed a fixed feature of the American scene. In recent years, however, particularly since the Republican Party took control of both houses of Congress in the 1994 elections, there has been pressure on the federal government to divest itself of some of its landholdings and turn these back to the states. This can be regarded as another part of the "sagebrush rebellion" noted in Chapter 15. So far the pressure has been greatest to change the ownership of lands managed by BLM. There has been somewhat less pressure regarding lands managed by the National Forest Service and much less regarding lands managed by the National Park Service. The pressure comes largely from grazing, mining, and lumber interests.

The federal position is that the legality of federal ownership has been upheld before by the courts and is beyond doubt. Federal land management agencies and many environmentalists argue that land is being held in stewardship for future generations and it is important that this stewardship continue. Many environmentalists fear that if land is turned over to the states, transfers from state hands to private hands will follow, partly as a result of local political pressures and partly because sales of land will ease pressures on state budgets. Commercial considerations will then, they fear, take precedence over the interests of future generations. But arguments can be made on both sides of the issue. Against the federal stewardship position, it can be argued that the states, being closer to the situation, may do a better job of land management. It can also be argued that if some land, for example grazing or timberland, comes into private ownership, the owners will have a powerful financial interest in its long-term management and thus will do a better job than, say, BLM. On purely legal grounds the consensus is that the federal government's position is not likely to be shaken. If change occurs, it will happen because sufficient political force has developed to cause the Congress to change the laws. That looks even less likely in the Obama era than it did in the Bush era.

WHAT'S NEXT?

If there is to be another great act of national planning comparable to those previously discussed, what might it be? One widely discussed possibility is a major remaking of the national electric grid. Concerns about climate change and about a range of issues loosely grouped under the term *energy security* have led many to visualize a clean electric energy economy much less dependent on overseas energy sources and less dependent on fossil fuels in general. Major sources of energy for this new regime would be non-fossil fuel modes such as nuclear, solar, wind, geothermal, and biomass. If the technology for carbon sequestration proves out (an unknown at this time), "clean coal" might also be part of the solution.

Conversion of major segments of the economy, like transportation, to electric power would require much more grid capacity than we now have and might also require new pathways from places of production to places of use. Other goals that have been mentioned include greater system reliability and reduced energy losses from long-distance transmission of power. If the past is any guide, the federal role would involve a general setting of directions and a combination of sticks and carrots, probably more of the latter, with detailed planning and implementation done primarily by state or local governments and the private sector. One very loose parallel might be the massive and very successful rural electrification program begun by the Rural Electrification Administration during the Great Depression.

A noted in Chapter 15, the United States has large supplies of natural gas, and the present cost is a fraction of that of petroleum. If the environmental problems connected with extraction (the pollution of groundwater by fracking, referred to earlier) can be resolved, liquefied natural gas (LNG) might replace a large part of the petroleum now used for transportation. The reduction in the U.S. balance of trade deficit and the increase in employment could be very large. For that replacement to occur, a nationwide system for making LNG as available as gasoline is now would be required. Developing such a system might well be a major act of national planning analogous to that discussed earlier for electric power.

SUMMARY

The United States has never had a national plan nor, since the termination of the National Resources Planning Board in 1943, a national planning agency. However, the federal government has, through a variety of programs and policies over the last two centuries, played a major role in shaping the pattern of settlement in the United States. In general, the federal style has been to provide guidelines and funding and to let the states, localities, and private parties fill in the details. The federal actions and legislation discussed in this chapter include the Northwest Ordinance of 1785, the Homestead Act, the Morrill Land Grant Act, land grants to railroads, the work of the Bureau of Reclamation, the Tennessee Valley Authority, the building of the Interstate Highway System, and federal mortgage insurance and the tax treatment of owner-occupied housing. It is also noted briefly that today the federal government owns and manages somewhat over 1 million square miles of the United States, primarily west of the Mississippi River.

NOTES

1. The 100th meridian passes through North Dakota about one-third of the way west from the eastern border of the state, passes through South Dakota, Nebraska, Kansas, Oklahoma, and then forms the eastern edge of the Texas Panhandle. The exceptions to this generalization about rainfall are the northwest coastal region about as far south as San Francisco and a few scattered areas in the northwest quarter of the region.

2. In some western states where the dry climate made it impossible for 160 acres to support a farm family, larger homesteads were permitted.

3. Richard Hofstadter, William Miller, and Daniel Aaron, *The American Republic*, 2nd ed., vol. 1, Prentice Hall, Inc., Upper Saddle River, NJ, 1970, p. 545.

4. The fact that several of the pieces of legislation mentioned in the chapter were passed in 1862 is not a coincidence. Both the opening up of western lands for settlement and the choice of transcontinental rail routes had important implications for the balance of power between free and slave states. Thus prior to the Civil War, congressional agreement had not been possible. But with southern representatives out of the Congress in 1862, agreement was easily reached.

5. Dexter Perkins and Glyndon G. Van Deusen, *The United States of America: A History*, 2nd ed., The Macmillan Co., New York, 1968, p. 73. The interested reader can look up further details under the heading "Credit Mobilier" in numerous U.S. history texts.

6. Ibid., p. 73.

7. Hofstadter, Miller, and Aaron, *American Republic*, p. 683.

8. Perkins and Van Deusen, *History*, p. 69.

9. Marc Reisner, *Cadillac Desert: The American West and Its Disappearing Water*, Viking, New York, 1986, p. 111.

10. On a long-term loan the sum of the interest payments can be significantly greater than the principal. Thus interest forgiveness of these loans represented a very substantial subsidy. In point of fact the actual subsidy was even greater than that would suggest because the bureau would not (or politically could not) force the farmer who became delinquent off his or her land. For a brief account of the early years of the Bureau of Reclamation, see Kenneth D. Frederick, "Water Resources: Increasing Demand and Scarce Supply," in Kenneth D. Frederick and Roger A. Sedjo, eds., *America's Renewable Resources: Historical Trends and Current Challenges*, Resources for the Future, Washington, DC, 1991. For a more detailed presentation, see Richard W. Wahi, *Markets for Federal Water*, Resources for the Future, Washington, DC, 1989.

11. Reisner, *Cadillac Desert*, p. 127.

12. *Major Dams, Reservoirs, and Hydroelectric Plants, Worldwide and Bureau of Reclamation*, released by U.S. Department of the Interior, Bureau of Reclamation, Denver, CO, undated.

13. Frederick, "Water Resources," p. 49.

14. For a detailed account of the events leading to the passage of the act, see Martin Reuss, *Reshaping National Water Politics: The Emergence of the Water Resources Development Act*, IWR Policy Study 91-PS-1, U.S. Army Corps of Engineers, 1991.

15. In the east the law has generally relied on riparian rights, a concept derived from English common law, that assigns right on the basis of immediate proximity to the water source. This worked reasonably well in the east but was not practical in the water-short west.

16. Robert Reinhold, "New Age for Western Water Policy: Less for the Farm, More for the City," *New York Times*, October 11, 1992, sect. 1, p. 18.

17. *Statistical Abstract of the United States*, 112th edition, U.S. Department of Commerce, Economics and Statistics Administration, Bureau of the Census, Washington, DC, 1992, Table 1096. Texas ranked second, also largely on the strength of irrigated land. In the case of Texas, however, irrigation waters largely come from wells in the great Ogallala aquifer. Unlike surface waters that are renewable, "mining" the Ogallala is a one-time event, for the aquifer's recharge rate is only a minuscule fraction of the rate of current withdrawals.

18. The centroid is a calculated point "at which an imaginary flat, weightless and rigid map of the United States would balance if weights of identical value were placed on it so that each weight represented the location of one person on the date of the census." In 1990 the centroid was located a few miles southwest of St. Louis. See Ibid., Table 3.

19. Frederick, "Water Resources," p. 37.

20. For an account of the legislative history, see Marguerite Owen, *The Tennessee Valley Authority*, Praeger, New York, 1973.

21. Ibid., p. 235.

22. There is no interstate mileage in Alaska.

23. This account is drawn from *America's Highways 1776/1976: A History of the Federal Aid Program*, U.S. Department of Transportation, Federal Highway Administration, Washington, DC, undated.

24. For a detailed account of the politics of the Interstate Highway System, see Mark H. Rose, *Interstate Express Highway Politics*, revised edition, University of Tennessee Press, Knoxville, 1990.

25. Carter M. McFarland, *The Federal Government and Urban Problems*, Westview Press, Boulder, CO, 1978, p. 117.

26. For further details see an urban economics text such as James Heilbrun, *Urban Economics and Public Policy*, 3rd ed., St. Martin's Press, New York, 1987; McFarland, *Federal Government*; Henry Aaron, *Shelter and Subsidies*, The Brookings Institution, Washington, DC, 1972; or a text on real estate finance such as William Brueggeman and Leo D. Stone, *Real Estate Investment*, 8th ed., Richard D. Irwin, Homewood, IL, 1989.

27. *Statistical Abstract of the United States*, 2008 Table 463.

28. *Statistical Abstract of the United States*, 1996, Table 343.

SELECTED BIBLIOGRAPHY

FREDERICK, KENNETH D., and SEDJO, ROGER A., EDS., *America's Renewable Resources*, Resources for the Future, Washington, DC, 1991.

OWEN, MARGUERITE, *The Tennessee Valley Authority*, Praeger, New York, 1973.

ROSE, MARK H., *Interstate Express Highway Politics*, revised edition, University of Tennessee Press, Knoxville, 1990.

WAHL, RICHARD W., *Markets for Federal Water: Subsidies, Property Rights, and the Bureau of Reclamation*, Resources for the Future, Washington, DC, 1989.

Note: Detailed information about the work of federal agencies such as the Bureau of Reclamation, the Department of Transportation, or the Army Corps of Engineers can be obtained by writing or calling them directly. A number of federal agencies employ a department historian, an especially good source for the student or scholar.

CHAPTER 18

Planning in
Other Nations

With co-authors Sonia Hirt
and Johann Jessen*

In this chapter we look briefly at planning in other nations. Much of the chapter focuses on Europe, not out of "eurocentricity" but because planning practices in the United States and Europe have many common elements and have exerted considerable influence on each other. Thus European experience can be an enlightening reflection on planning in the United States. We look first at several Western European cases and then briefly at the present situation in eastern Europe. The chapter concludes with a brief note on planning in Asia. It is clearly not possible to present a systematic review of planning practice around the world in a single chapter. This chapter is just a sampling.

PLANNING IN WESTERN EUROPE

Before we look at particulars, let us note a few background differences between the United States and the Western European planning scenes. These differences are generalizations, and not all apply to every country.

1. To understand the history of European planning in the second half of the twentieth century, one must take into account the effects of World War II. In many nations there was enormous destruction of urban areas. Thus in the early postwar period, there was a big emphasis on reconstruction and on rebuilding the housing stock destroyed in the war, particularly in inner-city areas.

---

*The section on Eastern Europe was written by Professor Sonia Hirt of Virginia Polytechnic Institute and State University, and the section on Germany by Professor Johann Jessen of the University of Stuttgart.

2. In the last two decades or so of the twentieth century, the planning scene in Europe was affected by another continent-wide force, this time a peaceful one. This was the coming of European unification. The European Community (EC) is increasingly becoming a single nation economically, at least until the European debt crisis of 2011. (Items 1 and 2 are related, for it was the experience of two world wars beginning only a quarter-century apart that provided much of the push for European union.)

3. Socialism was a major political force in many European nations at various times in the second half of the twentieth century, whereas the United States has never had a powerful socialist movement. That ideological difference carries with it a different set of ideas about what are the proper prerogatives and obligations of government. Another way to make this point is to note differences in the share of gross national product (GNP) spent by the public sector.[1] In the United States that percentage is in the low- to mid-30s. For most of the states of Western Europe, it is up in the 40s or 50s, and for at least one country, Sweden, has at times been in the low-60s. That larger role for the government in the general life of the nation usually also includes a larger role for planning in particular.

4. Most European nations have higher population densities than has the United States. The "lower 48" states have an average population density of about 100 persons per square mile. Great Britain and Germany have over 600 people per square mile, the Netherlands almost 1,200, France about 280, and Switzerland about 470. Thus in many European nations, there is more of an emphasis on concentrating development and on using land more efficiently simply because there is less land per capita.

5. Most, if not all, European nations take a less expansive view of the rights of property owners than do we in America. Thus a degree of control over the use of private property that would not be tolerated politically or legally in the United States is tolerated in Europe. Recall the safeguards for property rights embedded in the U.S. Constitution (see Chapter 5). The greater degree of control that government can exercise over the use of private property in Europe clearly strengthens the hand of the planner.

6. In the United States only a very small part of the housing stock is publicly built and owned (see Chapter 3). By contrast, in many of the nations of Western Europe, a very substantial share of all housing is publicly built and owned. (Generally it is referred to as "social housing.") This ownership gives government a powerful role in shaping the human-made environment.

7. In a number of Western European nations, particularly in Scandinavia, large amounts of urban land are publicly owned, thereby giving the municipality absolute control over when and how that land is developed.

8. In many Western European nations large numbers of middle- and upper-class individuals seem content to live in apartments rather than experiencing the American dream of the single-family house on a large lot. In general, the middle and upper classes also seem to show a much stronger preference for urban and central-city residence than do people in the United States. Then, too, European tax systems are not structured to favor homeownership as is the case in the United States (see Chapter 17).

9. In Europe there is generally more reliance on administrative decision and less reliance on the courts to adjudicate planning disputes than is the case in the United States. Thus municipal governments in Europe are less inhibited by fears that their actions in regard to regulating the use of privately owned land will be reversed by the courts.

10. In most European nations, with the exception of Germany, Austria, and Switzerland, political power is much more centralized than in the U.S. federal system. Recall that the U.S. Constitution reserves a great deal of power to the states (some of which the states delegate to substate units of government). Then, too, the U.S. Constitution establishes the system of checks and balances so that one of the three branches of government can block the actions of another branch (see Chapter 5). The higher degree of political centralization in Europe allows national governments to require that local plans be in conformance with the national plan.

11. Finally, there is the matter of physical size. The greater land area of the United States makes the development of a national plan more difficult than would be the case in a smaller country.

Planning in Great Britain

One might think that given many similarities in culture and in law (much of American law is derived from English common law), planning in the United States and Great Britain might be done in a similar manner. But this is not the case. In Britain the national government is much more powerful relative to subnational governments than is the case in the United States. For one point, Britain does not have a written constitution. Parliament thus can act with much more freedom than can the U.S. Congress. During the prime ministership of Margaret Thatcher,

Parliament simply abolished a number of municipal governments, including that of Greater London, and placed oversight of the affairs of these municipalities directly in its own hands.

Two other features of the British system should also be noted. In general, citizen participation and media coverage of the actions of local government are much more limited than in the United States.

> The British elect their politicians and then expect them to get on with the job: that is what they have been elected to do.[2]

That is a very different approach from the American tendency to elect the politicians, suspect that they are rascals, and watch them like a hawk.

Another feature of the British system is that questions that in the United States would be settled in court are settled administratively. A property owner who is displeased with a decision of a council (a unit of local government) may appeal it to the national level, but he or she does not take it to court. Since the passage of the Town and Country Planning Act in 1947, there has been no zoning in Great Britain. Even a project that conforms in every detail to the land-use plan of the council must have specific council approval before construction can begin. A builder cannot "build by right" as in the United States (see Chapter 9).

Planning in Great Britain Since World War II.   In the 1930s, Great Britain, like much of the Western world, suffered from the high unemployment rates of the Great Depression. The problem had a strong geographic dimension. The London metropolitan area suffered moderately, but many of the more peripheral parts of the nation experienced real economic disaster. This was particularly so where the economic base was heavily dependent on manufacturing, ship building, or mining. Thus British officials and planners in the late 1930s saw much of the national planning problem as limiting the growth of the London metropolitan area and diverting economic growth to other parts of the nation.

Little could be done to effectuate this vision during World War II (1939–1945), but even in the early stages of the war, when it was far from certain who would win, planning continued. The strategy that emerged was embodied in a series of laws passed by Parliament in the decade after the end of the war. The main thrust of the plan that emerged in the early postwar period was to

1. Limit the growth of London and a few other major cities.
2. Preserve as much as possible of Britain's remaining farmland and countryside from development.
3. Strengthen the economy and prevent population decline in lagging outlying areas.

To effectuate these goals, the national plan had three main elements:

1. A system of greenbelts surrounding London and other major cities.[3]
2. The creation of new towns
3. The use of subsidies and regulations to divert economic growth from London to lagging areas of the nation[4]

The last element, the use of subsidies and regulations to divert growth, was never very successful. For many years the policy was applied just to manufacturing, but in the postwar period, manufacturing was shrinking as a share of total employment. Even when the policy was extended beyond manufacturing, many businesses that wished to locate or expand in the London area found ways around the regulations. But elements 1 and 2 were carried out vigorously and have changed the face of Britain.

The concept of the greenbelt was enunciated in the Town and Country Planning Act of 1947 and remains policy up to this time. The greenbelts are the most striking manifestation of British planning. The American planner making an automobile trip from, say, the City of Oxford to the City of London, located about 40 miles to the east, encounters a very "un-American" sort of landscape. Oxford (population about 100,000) is densely developed by American standards, yet the instant a traveler leaves the city, he or she is in the countryside. There is no transitional suburban or exurban zone. The motorway into London passes through countryside. There are fields, woods, and an occasional house or hamlet in the distance. At the London end of the trip, the transition back from countryside to city is equally abrupt. One moment the traveler is passing through fields and pastures, and the next moment the traveler is in a dense urban environment.

Clearly, the spreading and scattered development that would have been produced by the natural working of market forces was blocked. How was this done? The Town and Country Planning Act simply froze development in the greenbelt areas. The development that already existed was permitted to remain, but new development was simply forbidden. A limited amount of compensation was paid to some landowners for losing the development potential of their land. Basically, though, the government had "nationalized development rights." Parliament had, in effect, ruled that the property owner does not have the automatic right to profit from increases in land value nor the right to be compensated should the government prevent him or her from developing the land in the most profitable use. Though the political pendulum has swung back and forth from left to right in the intervening six decades, the basic greenbelt plan has held.

One might ask what happened to all the population and housing growth that would otherwise have gone into the areas designated as greenbelts. Part was absorbed in existing urban centers. In fact, in recent years British planners have spoken of "town cramming." As demand for housing and business locations in already urbanized places increases and property values rise, there is an understandable tendency for denser development to occur in town and for every available parcel of land to be used. The trade-off is inevitable. The more congested town and the unspoiled expanse of the greenbelt are the flip sides of the same coin.

Another portion of the population growth deflected by the greenbelts was housed in new towns. Between the end of the war and 1980, over 30 new towns were begun in Great Britain. The first wave, started in the 1946 to 1951 period, included both towns located around London and towns located in lagging areas of the nation. In the period after 1960, additional towns were begun in order to relieve population pressures around other urban areas. By 1990, according to Peter Hall, new towns that were begun since the end of World War II contained about 700,000 housing units and a population of about 2 million.[5] Though new towns absorbed some of the population growth that might have gone into the greenbelt, the part that they did not absorb led to an increase in long-distance commuting, a result that was not part of the plan.

The British system of strong central government and relatively weak local governments facilitated the building of new towns. The process was set in motion by Parliament in 1946 by the passage of the New Towns Act. The building of a new town was the responsibility of a group of directors appointed by a national official, the Minister of Town and Country Planning. The committee, in turn, hired staff to do the planning and administrative work. The commission had broad powers to acquire land either by purchase or by condemnation, and to construct housing, commercial and public buildings, and the infrastructure such as roads and sanitary facilities necessary to support the town.[6] The law called for consultation with local councils (governments), but the real power was in the hands of the directors appointed by the national government, and the wishes of local governments could be overruled. The money to support these expenditures came from long-term bonds issued by the national government, subsidized in part by some deferred payment arrangements. The reader might compare this process with the building of planned communities in the United States as described in Chapter 7. In the United States, the planned community, whether it is small or covers thousands of acres as in the cases of Reston, Virginia (see Chapter 10), and Columbia, Maryland, occurs on land owned by the developer and is done as a profit-making venture. The capital involved is entirely or almost entirely private. The community is built pursuant to the permission of local government. If the necessary rezonings and other adjustments in land controls are not granted, then the project cannot be done. The land involved is acquired through voluntary sale by private landowners. In some cases, like that of Columbia, Maryland, built by the Rouse Corporation, land was purchased very discreetly through a variety of dummy organizations, for if Rouse's intentions had been known, land prices would have risen sharply, making the project impossible.

The building of the new towns was influenced in many ways by the ideas of the turn-of-the-century planner Ebenezer Howard (see Chapter 3). Howard argued that land values were created by public investment and should be captured by the public, not by individual property owners.[7] In the new towns much of the land and many of the structures were owned by the commission that built the town, and so as land and property values increased, the commission could capture that increase either as rents or, from time to time, sales of property. The monies realized from increases in property value were, in turn, used to pay off the bonds that underwrote the development of the new town.

The physical planning of the town also reflected Howard's thinking. The original town plans generally aimed for populations in the 30,000 to 60,000 range, which was similar in size to what Howard had suggested. (Some new towns, like Milton Keynes, which is about an hour's train ride north of London, have been much larger.) He favored a population size large enough to sustain a significant amount of economic activity so that the town would be more than just a bedroom community. On the other hand, he favored a small enough size so that places of business could be reasonably close to people's homes and so that an ample amount of the natural world would survive within the town. He also favored a ring road (a rail line in the original conception) that took traffic out of the town and also connected the town to the central city and the rest of the metropolitan region. Finally, the original Howard vision called for the location of some industrial activity outside the ring road to keep it from impinging on residential areas. All these design elements showed up in many new town plans.

Though greenbelts and new towns are the most distinctive features of post–World War II British planning, there were other important elements as well. Like all other nations with advanced economies, the British had to confront the postwar explosion in automobile ownership. Thus an important part of British planning in the last several decades has been a system of high-speed limited-access motorways similar in overall design to the U.S. interstate system. One of the persistent British planning problems is traffic congestion. The high rate of automobile ownership coupled with high population density make that problem inevitable.

In the years immediately following the end of World War II, much subsidized housing was built in central areas, and as part of that process, there was also a great deal of slum clearance. New housing was needed both to replace housing destroyed by bombing during the war and to make up for the slow rate of construction during the Great Depression and war years. Clearance was needed to replace much very-low-quality housing that had survived the war. Urban housing conditions in Britain had been worse than those on much of the continent for a simple historic reason. The industrial revolution began in Great Britain, and so the process of rapid urban growth got started there much sooner than in other nations.

Milton Keynes, located about 60 miles north of London, is one of the new towns built in Great Britain after World War II. The commercial center is located proximate to the train station. Most housing is in small hamlets separated by open space. The town has a dual circulation system with roads for automobiles and an extensive parallel system of bicycle and footpaths. Above, a view of the commercial area seen from across a roundabout (rotary) at the intersection of two bicycle paths. Note the underpass for these paths under the automobile road at upper left. Below, a view of one of the hamlets from the path. Automobile access is from the other side of the hamlet.

For example, the coming of rapid industrialization in Germany trailed that of Great Britain by more than half a century, and in Scandinavia the process lagged by approximately a century.[8] Thus Great Britain had masses of densely developed, low-standard urban housing dating from early in the nineteenth century. As measured by physical indexes like overcrowding and poor plumbing facilities, considerable improvement in housing quality was achieved by this combination of building and clearance.

British Planning Since the 1970s.   A great deal had been accomplished by the 1970s. But new needs were becoming apparent, and some dissatisfactions with the results of the early post–World War II planning were being voiced. Then, too, Great Britain was changing politically. There was considerable dissatisfaction with the British welfare state, what some have termed the "nanny state," and there was also a feeling that the British economy would perform better if more were left to the market and less to the state. In short, Britain was moving to the right politically. And, as noted previously, planning and political ideology can never be entirely separated. In 1979 the Conservatives, led by Margaret Thatcher, assumed power. Thatcher herself enjoyed the longest period in office of any British prime minister in a century and was then succeeded by the less colorful but quite conservative John Major. The Conservatives did not relinquish power until 1997, with the election of a Labour prime minister, Tony Blair, 1997–2007. By that time the British political center of gravity had moved far enough to the right that on most domestic policy issues, the Blair government looked remarkably like the Conservative government of a few years earlier.

But even before Thatcher took office, the planning agenda had begun to shift. It had become apparent that none of the accomplishments previously noted did much for the problems of depressed inner-city areas. In fact, it could easily be argued that the building of new towns and new housing developments (called "housing estates" in Great Britain) in peripheral areas actually increased blight in inner cities. This situation is analogous to that in the United States, in which post–World War II suburbanization sucked income and jobs out of the inner cities, leaving behind a stranded underclass that was not capable of participating in the general prosperity of the nation. Then, too, there was the issue of national economic competitiveness. Britain was growing economically at a slower rate than a number of nations on the continent and elsewhere, a fact that many attributed to the effects of regulation and heavy taxation.[9]

The Thatcher government essentially stopped making grand national plans. To use the terminology that will be introduced in Chapter 19, there was a shift from a *comprehensive* to an *incremental* planning philosophy. The British government began to focus on deteriorated urban areas and to try to involve private capital as much as possible. One Thatcher initiative was the Enterprise Zone, a concept developed by British planner Peter Hall, cited earlier in this chapter. A depressed part of a city would be designated as an Enterprise Zone, and within that part, builders and firms would be eligible for a variety of tax breaks and would be free from many ordinary planning restrictions. Note that this idea then crossed the Atlantic and appeared in the United States in the form of Enterprise Zones in a number of states and then later at the federal level in the Clinton administration's Empowerment Zones.

Another closely related Thatcher administration initiative was the Urban Development Corporation (UDC). These organizations were designated and funded by the national government. In their designated areas they had the power to take property and to override the plans of local government. Their boards of directors were heavily weighted toward businesspeople to give them a pro-business focus. The goal of the UDC was to make the area attractive to private investment by establishing the preconditions for development, such as providing cleared sites and infrastructure improvements. The parallel with U.S. urban policy, and particularly with Urban Renewal, is very strong.

The most visible single result of the Enterprise Zone and UDC approach is the Canary Wharf development on the Isle of Dogs, a part of the London Docklands area. Within the Isle of Dogs Enterprise Zone, an enormous amount of capital, most of it private, has been invested to produce a massive office and retail development. The path was not a smooth one. In fact, the Canadian development firm Olympia and York, which did a great deal of the actual construction, went bankrupt during the building.[10] Nonetheless, Canary Wharf is a very impressive development. At least for a time, it was the largest office development in Europe, with work spaces for about 45,000 people.[11]

In brief, planning in Great Britain moved in the direction of what is often termed "property led" development, meaning that the pattern of development was largely shaped by the competition for private capital investment in property. When government seeks private capital investment and a development depends on private investment, compromise becomes necessary, and some of the decision-making power necessarily shifts from public to private hands. As discussed subsequently, the trend toward "property led" development made itself felt at about the same time in a number of nations on the continent. The cause was basically the same—strain on the public purse and the desire to be economically competitive. In its emphasis on private investment and in the competition between places for private investment, the British planning scene became more similar to the American scene.

The Thatcher government also introduced a variety of American-style programs designed to foster competition and to integrate construction programs with programs designed to attack underlying social and economic problems. Among these were some grants for which cities had to compete and some investment in manpower training programs to increase the employability of the residents of poorer areas. Again, the parallel with U.S. policy is very strong.[12]

Planning policy in Great Britain did not change substantially under the subsequent Labour governments of Tony Blair and Gordon Brown.

Under the present Conservative prime minister, David Cameron, there has been a devolution of planning authority downward and a further emphasis on growth. Some of this may be ideological, but some also stems from Great Britain's current economic situation in the wake of the 2008 financial crisis. At this writing the British government faces large budget deficits and has responded by laying off many public sector employees, raising tuition at public universities, and cutting back on the "social safety net" in general. All of this is driven by a desire to reduce government deficits and defend the British pound. It is clearly not a situation that favors major planning initiatives. Within the three tiers of the British planning system, responsibility has been pushed down from the national level to the regional level and from the regional level to the local level.

At the local level there has also been some devolution downward. New rules permit a group as small as three—what one British planner characterized as "mom, dad and the dog"— to set up a neighborhood forum that can bring planning proposals forward at the local level. But, in keeping with the big priority of the Cameron government, such proposals must promote growth. Yet despite the conservative trend under Cameron the most distinctive element of British planning, the greenbelt policy, has remained intact.

Planning in France

A number of European nations have seen planning as a way to address regional imbalances. One such nation is France. Since the nineteenth century, the Paris region has grown more vigorously than the rest of the nation, and it contains disproportionate amounts of the nation's higher educational establishments, cultural resources, and administrative activities. It even contained a disproportionate share of the nation's total manufacturing employment. In many periods the Paris region accounted for a large share of the nation's total population growth. Shortly after World War II, a French geographer, Jean Français Gravier, wrote the very influential *Paris et le désert Français* (Paris and the French Desert). His main point was that the disproportionate growth of the Paris region left the rest of the nation impoverished and that something ought to be done about it.[13]

In response to this problem of Parisian dominance, the French government identified eight growth poles.[14] The actual term is *métropole d'équilibre*, denoting the idea that these regions will balance the economic and demographic mass of the Paris region, the *Ile de France*. Each of these poles consists of a city or of two or three closely located cities.

These cities form a ring several hundreds of miles in diameter. The eastern part of the ring lies close to the French–German border, and the western part extends to France's Atlantic coast. The northern part extends to the English Channel, and the southern part to the Mediterranean, France's *Côte d'Azur*. For the last five decades it has been national policy to strengthen these poles relative to the Paris region.

> Since the late 1960s, successive French governments have systematically sought to divert public investment into these poles, thus strengthening their economic potential and acting in turn as a device to attract private capital.[15]

Specifically, Peter Hall notes that investment in higher education facilities, in the nation's limited-access highway system, and in its high-speed passenger rail system has all been used to favor the growth of these regional centers.[16]

In addition to strengthening other regions relative to the Paris region, French planners also sought to divert growth from the city itself into other parts of the Paris region. Thus public funds were invested in building satellite towns and peripheral development areas. The plan was supported by the building of a regional rail system, the RER, and a circumferential highway.

The sort of national approach to planning just described, in which the planning authorities consciously make national economic and demographic (in the sense of where people will live) policy, is feasible only in a very centralized state. Historically the French central government was very strong, and local governments, though very numerous, were very weak. In fact, many local administrators, called *préfets*, were appointed by the central government. Planning was a top-down process, with the national government laying out the big picture and the local governments filling in the details, pursuant to approval by the national government. In the early 1980s there was major political reorganization in France, and some political power was decentralized.[17] For example, appointed *préfets* were replaced by elected officials. But compared with that of the United States, the French system is still highly centralized. The United States has had no national planning body since the abolition of the NRPB in 1943 (see Chapter 4).

Not only is planning much more centralized and the power of government to control land use much greater than in the United States, but

The new town of Créteil. Built at the end of one line of the Paris Métro, it is within easy commuting range of the center of the city. Above, the town center. Below, mixed residential and commercial development along the shore of an artificial lake.

the government also exercises power over development in another way. A great deal of urban development is done by development organizations of mixed private and public ownership, the *Société d'Économie Mixte* (SEM). Thus there is not the separation between development interests on the one hand and government on the other hand.

> Normally the public partner has a majority shareholding in the company. Thus political control is retained [by government] while the company structure allows for greater operational flexibility, free from the bureaucratic rules of town hall. The SEM may be set up by the commune [local government] or by a private party.[18]

The arrangement is consistent with the French vision of the proper relationship between state and private sector—a mixed system in which the relationship between government and capital is a cooperative one. In the decades after World War II, the French national planning style was termed "indicative planning," in which government and industry jointly set goals and policies.

At the local level, urban planning in France, as in many other nations of Western Europe, often has a somewhat different emphasis than in the United States. There is often more emphasis on the fine texture of the urban fabric—on historic preservation, on the details of urban design, and on pedestrian-friendly environments. There is often more emphasis on spaces that promote interaction between people. Where the design choice must favor either the pedestrian or the automobile, there is more of a tendency to favor the former than is usually the case in the United States.

In recent years observers of the French, like those of the British, have seen an increase in "property-led development." In France several factors have contributed to this increase. The decentralization of political power in the early 1980s made local governments more important decision makers in the development game. At the same time, there were cutbacks in the flow of revenues from the national to the local governments. The response of local governments was to begin competing for commercial investment. The analogy with the American situation (see Chapter 13 on economic development planning) is quite strong.

Two views of La Defense, a major public–private office development about four kilometers from the center of Paris. La Grande Arche (top), built to commemorate the 200th anniversary of the French Revolution (1789), is intended to be a twentieth-century version of the Arc de Triomphe. It is a cube 106 meters (347 feet) on edge. The sides contain offices whose windows face the interior of the cube.

The historic district of Annecy, France. Above, the canal, once used for transportation of freight, is preserved as a scenic attraction. Below, preservation of old buildings and protection from vehicular traffic help keep street life lively in this commercial area.

Planning in the Netherlands

Another European nation with a strongly centralized planning system and a commitment to national-level planning is the Netherlands. The Netherlands' population density is about 13 times that of the "lower 48." The nation's land form has been substantially changed by a long-time policy of reclaiming land from the North Sea. Thus some of the nation's population lives on land that lies a few feet below sea level and is protected from the sea by dikes. It is no surprise that the Dutch take a different attitude toward planning than do Americans. When it comes to the use of land, the Dutch have learned to cooperate with each other. They have no alternative. Then, too, with a land area only a little larger than that of Connecticut and no major physical barrier that divides the nation, planning the entire nation on the basis of a unified vision is much easier. Peter Newman and Andy Thornley note that the Netherlands has been called the "most planned" nation in Europe. The American planner traveling in the Netherlands is very likely to feel that this description is true.

As in many other parts of Europe, there is a very sharp separation between town and country. Urban development and farmers' fields meet abruptly with no intervening suburban development. The first impression one gets of the Dutch landscape is of great order, of a landscape in which very little space has been wasted, and in which every acre is earmarked for some purpose. The nation's largest city, Amsterdam, is densely developed but also orderly and charming. It is very modern and functional, yet a great deal of the old survives. The core of the city is not big; there is essentially no vacant land left, and the city is a major magnet for businesses and for tourism, as well as for permanent residential use. It is clear that if the land and property market were allowed to work without interference, the effects of extremely high land values would quickly transform the core of the city. Buildings of five or six stories, the typical height, would quickly be torn down and replaced with much taller structures. The street system would soon be overwhelmed, for it has an essentially preautomobile-era layout. In very little time the charm and the delightful pedestrian character of the city would be gone. Part of the city's charm comes from a well-preserved system of concentric canals that once performed a central transportation function but are now primarily scenic and recreational. The canals, too, would not survive if land uses were determined purely by the market. Planning controls are obviously very strict and effective.

The Dutch planning system is a top-down one. The national government produces both the laws that govern planning and, periodically, a national plan. Provincial governments, the middle layer in a three-tier system, interpret the national plan and prepare directives and the like for local governments. Local government plans must be in conformity with the national plan. At the local level there is a *struktuurplan* that lays out the overall

A section of a canal about a mile from downtown Amsterdam.

picture. The U.S. counterpart would be the master plan. To implement that, there is a detailed plan *(bestentminsplan)* that specifies the expected and acceptable use of every parcel. The U.S. counterpart would be the zoning ordinance and map.[19] The system as described here may sound a bit more rigid and autocratic than it is. In actuality there is a great deal of communication up and down, and there is opportunity for the public to comment on plans. But when the period for comments and adjustments is over, the plans are binding. Some years ago the writer attended a presentation by a Dutch planner to a group of American planning professors. When the planner had finished explaining the system described here, one of the Americans asked, in effect, "But does it really happen that way?" The Dutch planner answered that indeed it does, and he seemed puzzled by the question. The Americans understood the question perfectly, for they all knew about the role of politics, the process of litigation and appeal, and our love affair with private property. But they had difficulty believing the answer.

The most conspicuous example of Dutch planning at the national level is the Randstad Holland, the urban heart of Holland. As shown in Figure 18–1, this urbanized area consists of a grouping of six cities around an open core. This arrangement will not happen naturally, for if events are left purely to

FIGURE 18–1 The cities in the ring form the Randstad Holland described in the text. The diameter of the Randstad, about 50 miles, is similar to that of the London or New York metropolitan area. About 70 miles north of the Randstad is a huge dike behind which are polders (shaded areas), flat low lying agricultural lands reclaimed from the North sea.

the market, the central core will fill in because locations inside the core will offer good access to all the cities and thus become very valuable. Rather, the arrangement is made to happen by large-scale planning and strict controls on land use. The arrangement has several advantages. First, it gives the residents of the Randstad much better access to the natural world than they would have if the same 4.5 or so million people were all contained in a single city. The arrangement also reduces commuting times, for the average trip in a small city will be shorter than the average trip in a large city.[20] There are environmental advantages as well; for example, the ring of cities will, all other things being equal, have better air quality than would a single city containing the equivalent number of people and economic activity. Peter Hall notes that there is a considerable degree of specialization among the three larger cities of the Randstad. Rotterdam, at the mouth of the Rhine, is a port city, in fact, the largest port in Europe. The Hague is the seat of the Dutch government and also contains some international organizations including the World Court. Amsterdam is a commercial, financial, and cultural center. Much of that specialization is historical accident or is decreed by geography. But some is planned and makes the cities more efficient economically than they would otherwise be. In an economic sense, the group of cities, because they are physically close and linked by a very effective transportation system, constitutes a single economic entity and achieves some of the advantages of large scale that a single metropolis would have.[21] But the group also achieves some environmental and quality-of-life advantages that we normally associate with smaller places.

Planning in Scandinavia

Unlike the case of the Netherlands, planning in Scandinavia has been less a national matter and more a matter for the municipality and the region. One reason for this tendency is that local governments have been stronger relative to the national government than is the case in many other European nations.

In Sweden a very high level of municipal and regional control over the pattern of development has been achieved in two ways that render Swedish planning practice very different from American practice. First, municipal governments often own a sizable percentage of the land within their own borders. In fact, the central government encouraged municipal governments to own (land-bank) a 10 year-reserve of developable land. Legislation permitted municipal governments to take privately owned land for purposes of land-banking.[22] Doing this would be the equivalent of a U.S. municipal government condemning private property not for a specific public use but simply to hold it for unspecified purposes at an unspecified time. It is doubtful that any U.S. court would sustain this action or that many municipal legislatures would appropriate funds for it.

Public ownership of land gives government a very strong grip on the process of development. It controls the timing of development through the release of land for sale or lease. It also provides total control over the way that the land is developed because the developer of the land is bound by whatever contracts are part of the sale or lease agreement.

Vallingsby, a new town located in the Stockholm metropolitan area. The town is laid out around a stop on the city's metro, providing its residents easy access to employment in the city's central business district. Above is a pedestrian-oriented shopping area proximate to the metro station. Below, a short walk from the station, is a residential area fronting on a combined pedestrian and bicycle path. Automobile access is on the other side of the buildings.

Skarpnack, another new town in the Stockholm metropolitan area, located about 20 minutes from downtown Stockholm via the metro. Essentially an in-town bedroom community, it is oriented to families with children. A system of interior paths connects groups of apartments located around courtyards. Parking is located in a multilevel structure several blocks away from where the pictures were taken. Most housing is low-rise multifamily. As in Vallingsby, there are no single-family houses.

The second way in which Swedish municipal governments achieved tight control over the pattern of development was through a very extensive role in the production of housing. For many years of the post–World War II period, housing was essentially a nationalized industry in Sweden. The national government provided the financing, and local governments directed the what and the where of residential construction. Though most construction was done by private firms, the firms were, in effect, acting as contractors to local governments.

> The government adopted a strong social housing policy for the whole population and believed that people had the right to a good home regardless of income. In contrast to most other developed countries the Swedish government sought to control the whole housing stock and not just that for low income earners. A massive programme of suburban high rise took place called the Million Homes Programme and large numbers of existing town centers were also redeveloped. An organisational structure was set up to deal with the huge programme. This resulted in wide-ranging controls on residential development which extended far beyond the traditional planning system. The production of housing was steered by the public sector with the aim of removing speculation from land and housing. Central government was responsible for regulation and the supply of resources while municipalities ensured that the building took place.[23]

This approach was very much in accordance with Swedish political ideology in the postwar period. Sometimes this has been referred to as the "social democratic" model and sometimes as a "third way," one that is more socialistic than the capitalist model and more capitalistic than the socialist model.

As noted elsewhere in this book, housing is the largest single land use in most cities. In some cities it is a larger use than all other uses combined. Thus government's tight control over almost the entire housing market easily translates into great influence on the entire pattern of development.

In and around the capital city of Stockholm, the basic plan, which has been carried through and is widely admired, was to deal with growth pressures and the spreading of the city by concentrating further growth in planned communities centered around stops on an underground railroad system. Development was to be concentrated and new towns separated by green areas to be used for recreation and summer housing. In recent years the scheme has been extended somewhat with smaller developments linked by road rather than by rail. But the basic scheme of tight development surrounded by greenbelt has held. The resemblance to Ebenezer Howard's vision is strong. Since the 1980s the Swedish planning system has become a little more free-form for many of the same reasons noted in connection with Great Britain and France. Dissatisfaction with some aspects of the welfare state has caused some rightward movement along the political spectrum. Slowing economic growth has caused fiscal pressures. In short, there has been some turn toward property-led development. As noted before, where government courts private investment, there must necessarily be negotiation and compromise.

Many elements of the approach just described can be found elsewhere in Scandinavia. For example, in Helsinki, the capital city of and by far the largest city in Finland, planners have exercised a fairly tight control over the pattern of development through the mechanism of public land ownership. As of the mid-1990s, about half the land in the city was owned by the city.[24]

Perhaps the best-known Finnish planning accomplishment is the new satellite town of Tapiola, located a few miles outside Helsinki and linked to the city by frequent, high-speed bus service. The town has a linear commercial core with housing and open space on each side. There is some single-family housing but a predominance of multifamily housing. This arrangement permits a moderately high population density to coexist with a considerable amount of open space within the town. The entire town is automobile accessible, but it is also very pedestrian and bicycle friendly. Distances from residences to the commercial core are short, and there are numerous pedestrian and bicycle paths. The resident of Tapiola can reach downtown Helsinki in half an hour or so by bus, and then at the end of the business day, can return to an environment that offers real closeness to the natural world.

Planning in Germany

Modern urban planning in Germany dates back to the last decades of the nineteenth century, when the first planning laws were enacted and planning agencies were established. The first planning textbook was published in 1879. Regional planning emerged during the early 1920s when the Ruhr Coalfield Settlement Association (*Siedlungsverband Ruhrkohlenbezirk*, or *SVR*) was formed to protect the landscape in the Ruhr area, which was almost completely devastated by the rapidly expanding mining and steel industry. The SVR is said to be the world's first regional planning agency, predating the Tennessee Valley Authority (TVA) in the United States by about a decade.

General Features.   Germany is a federal state with three levels of government: the federal government (*Bund*), the states (*Länder*), and the municipalities (*Gemeinden*). The constitution, written after World War II, clearly defines the division of power among the three levels. The planning system in Germany is characterized by a strong legal framework and a decentralized decision-making structure. On the national level, there are only general legal guidelines. The legal framework consists of the Federal Spatial Planning Act (*Raumordnungsgesetz*) and the Federal Building Code (*Baugesetzbuch*), which provide the legal instruments for spatial planning on the state level and for urban planning on the local level. This framework ensures a degree of consistency of planning on the lower levels (*Länder* and *Gemeinden*). However, each *Länd* has its own regional planning system. Municipal governments enjoy a high degree of autonomy in planning and have fervently defended this against all demands for centralization of power.

The overall objective of planning and spatial policy in Germany is *sustainable development*—as it is in many other countries since this concept became popular worldwide after the UN Conference in Rio in 1992. Since 1997, it has been fixed in the Federal Building Code. The code includes

- *Improving the economic competitiveness of city regions*—efficient transport systems, modern infrastructure, dynamic and vibrant metropolitan regions, excellent universities and research facilities, etc.
- *Protecting the natural resources*—saving energy; reducing land consumption; reducing pollution of air, water, and soil, and so on; adapting to climate change: "brownfield development before greenfield development"
- *Supporting social and cultural cohesion*—affordable housing and an adequate supply of education and health care for all social groups
- *Obtaining living conditions of "equal value"*—reducing the gap between, or disparities in, both urban and rural areas and between declining and prospering regions

These objectives contain many contradictions. Therefore, urban and regional policies are mostly compromises by nature, as they are in every other country. Although the objectives are the same, the strategies selected and pursued may be completely different depending on whether you find yourself in a prospering region or in a declining region—whether you are in a small town in a rural environment or in a vibrant metropolitan region. Munich and the Stuttgart Region in the south, with their modern industries such as automobiles and electronics, are very prosperous. By contrast, the Ruhr area in the west and Oberlausitz in the east, with their declining mining and steel industry, suffer from high unemployment and little, if any, economic growth. There are also very large differences between non-metropolitan areas. Some are prosperous and booming, attracting modern industries—like Oberbayern (Upper Bavaria) and Oberschwaben (Upper Swabia) near Lake Constance—and some are remote and rural areas, with poor agriculture and no prospects for new industries and/or tourism—like parts of Lower Saxony in the west or Vorpommern in the far northeast of the country. Since the reunification of Germany, differences among regions in former West Germany have been overshadowed by the much greater differences between the poorer former East Germany and the rest of the nation.

Planning in Germany After the Reunification in 1989. When World War II ended in 1945, Germany was divided into two states, the Federal Republic of Germany (West Germany) and the German Democratic Republic (East Germany), the former becoming part of the Western Alliance and a member of NATO and the latter becoming part of the Soviet Bloc and the Warsaw Pact. These two countries were separated not only by the iron curtain, but also by antagonistic political systems. Thus, the context, the objectives, and the instruments of planning widely differed. In the decades after World War II, planning in West Germany followed very much the same lines as in other Western European countries, whereas in East Germany, collective planning on all levels was a central feature of the communist regime, as it was in all other countries of Central and Eastern Europe.

The breakdown of communism and the fall of the iron curtain in the year 1989 led to the reunification of West and East Germany. This completely changed the political geography of Europe and the regional context of almost every city in Central Europe. The reunification was a unique historical experience. It called for policies to solve problems for which there was little precedent: how to bring together two countries that, although having a common language, had very different political, economic, and social structures; different cultures; and different social attitudes. These questions were addressed at the political level by fully applying the legal, organizational, administrative, and political structures of West Germany to East Germany. There has also been a tremendous investment in the former East Germany by the German government. Much of it has been in the cities: urban renewal of the inner-city areas, maintenance and modernization of the public housing areas from the socialistic period (*Plattensiedlungen*), extension and modernization of the road network and railway system, and the like. But despite the huge efforts, the task of reunification is far from completed. The former East Germany remains much poorer than the rest of the nation, and unemployment rates there are much higher than elsewhere.

In the first years after reunification, many East Germans moved to West Germany because of the better job opportunities. The urban regions in West Germany thus faced a new boom. Urban growth and the elimination of housing subsidies at the end of the 1980s were responsible for a dramatic housing shortage. At the beginning of the 1990s, the municipalities were again confronted with the necessity of planning and building extended urban areas in the peripheries, even though for environmental reasons, there is consensus that untouched green areas should be preserved.

One feature of the German planning scene that appeared in the 1990s that has no parallel in the United States or much of Western Europe was the opportunity to redevelop a vast amount of land once in military use. The end of the Cold War and the subsequent withdrawal of the Soviet and American and Allied Forces bestowed on many German municipalities and states a substantial planning opportunity: the conversion of former military areas to urban development. Some of the garrison towns in former East Germany even now have an abundance of abandoned military land at their disposition. Extended areas, once shut off from the public for decades, are now ready to be integrated into the existing urban structure.

Strengthening the ability of metropolitan areas to accommodate growth by continuously improving the infrastructure through extending and renewing airports, extending the high-speed train net (ICE) while integrating it more closely with the transeuropean net, modernizing the motorway system, and the like are important and costly parts of the German planning system.

For about the last 20 years we have seen contradictory trends in the organization of planning in Germany: On one hand, there is a growing concern for the natural environment, which is reflected in laws for the protection of ground, water, and air; for energy saving; and for reducing CO_2 emissions. This concern introduces more and more regulatory elements into the planning process. On the other hand, there is the general trend toward a more property led development, as noted earlier in this chapter in connection with Great Britain, France, and Sweden. As the financial situation of the municipalities (*Gemeinden*) became more and more difficult, big urban projects had to be carried out largely with private capital. In order to attract private investment, deregulation necessarily became a major issue in German planning policy.

Since the turn of the century several major social and political trends have had substantial impact on urban development in Germany: First, the economic, social, cultural, and political ties among the different European countries have become closer and closer in the last decade. As a result of this European integration process, a significant part of the agenda of urban, infrastructural, and environmental policy is no longer determined on the national level, but on the European level.

Second, the population of Germany is beginning to decline and will decline more steeply in the future. Germany now has a population of 82 million people. The 2050 population is projected at 67 to 73 million people. This demographic change goes back to a consistently low birthrate (fertility is about 1.4, compared with a replacement level of 2.1). This means that not only will there be fewer people, but there will also be a significantly higher number of elderly people. That is why constantly high immigration of qualified workers from other countries is considered a crucial precondition for the economic future of Germany. Today, more than 5 million people from other countries live in Germany. In the city of Frankfurt, every third inhabitant carries a foreign passport.

Third, there is an ongoing process of deindustrialization in the German economy that started in the late 1960s. Although Germany is the world's second largest exporter of merchandise and a major producer of automobiles, machine tools, and industrial chemicals, among other items, manufacturing employment in the nation has been declining for some time, resulting in persistent high levels of unemployment, particularly among unskilled workers. Today, Germany is largely a service economy, with more than 70 percent of the employees working in the service sector.

Fourth, despite the tremendous political efforts and financial support for East Germany, there is still a big social, economic, and spatial divide between Eastern and Western Germany. Whereas most of the West German cities are still growing and prospering, a vast majority of the cities in Eastern Germany are continuously shrinking. The permanent loss of population and jobs has had dramatic impacts: an unemployment rate in the 17 to 20 percent range, a very large number of people depending on social welfare, a rapidly aging population, impaired housing markets, decreasing land prices, reduced purchasing power, and reduced local tax revenues. The effects become more and more visible. The cities are marked by extensive wasteland and derelict commercial sites, streets with many vacant shops and offices, dilapidated factory and residential buildings, underutilized or abandoned social and technical infrastructure, and neglected parks and squares.

In the prospering cities such as Munich, Hamburg, or Stuttgart, planning efforts still concentrate on managing urban growth without compromising environmental goals. Complex projects of urban restructuring are considered crucial elements that contribute to the cities' economic and cultural competitiveness in a globalized world. At present, the HafenCity project in Hamburg is one of the most outstanding examples. It is the largest waterfront project under way in Europe right now.

The shrinking cities in the East face completely different planning problems: How to create a new local economic base? What to do with an abundance of housing and public infrastructure? Toward the end of the 1990s, the vacancy rates in housing rose to a level that was no longer tolerable and in the long run would have led to a total collapse of the housing market and the bankruptcy of major housing companies. In 2002, the Federal Ministry of Transportation, Building and Urban Development initiated a subsidy program titled *Stadtumbau Ost* (urban restructuring in East Germany). In fact, most of the money goes into so-called *Rueckbau* (demolition measures). Today, the housing companies obtain a subsidy of between 50 and 60 euros per each square meter of ground floor that is demolished ($8 to $9 per square foot). Between 2002 and 2007, nearly 200,000 housing units were removed from the market in Eastern Germany by demolition. These activities are incorporated into regeneration schemes and accompanied by various measures to improve the conditions of the residual housing stock. Among other things, the restructuring of shrinking cities includes refurbishing public space, creating green spaces on derelict land, and adapting the existing technical and social infrastructures to changing demands.

HafenCity Hamburg—A former harbor area very close to the CBD is turned into a vibrant new urban area for 12,000 new inhabitants and 40,000 jobs, with signature architecture and high-quality design of public spaces.

PLANNING IN EASTERN EUROPE

Eastern Europe includes an amalgam of states with different histories, cultures, economies, and political structures—a fact that makes any attempt to generalize across the region difficult. The term *Eastern Europe,* as used in this section, applies primarily to the nations that were often referred to as the Satellite Nations or the Warsaw Bloc during the Cold War period and to the three Baltic nations. The former group was composed of Poland, East Germany (now reunited with the former West Germany), Czechoslovakia (now divided into the Czech Republic and Slovakia), Hungary, Bulgaria, and Romania. This group came under Soviet domination in 1944 and 1945 as the Soviet armies pushed the Germans back in the end stages of World War II. The three Baltic nations are Lithuania, Latvia, and Estonia, which had been forcibly incorporated into the Soviet Union in 1940 and did not emerge as independent nations until the collapse of the Soviet Union in 1991.

The Soviet Planning Style

The Soviet planning style was highly centralized. Public participation as we know it in the West was almost nonexistent for most of the Soviet period, though there was some citizen involvement in planning initiatives in the 1980s, when most communist regimes were weaker and, arguably, more liberal. Communist planners emphasized the needs of industry, which often came at the expense of the environment. Frequently, more land than necessary was reserved for industrial facilities. This was possible because communist economies functioned under command (rather than market) principles, and the state typically owned the majority of urban land. Thus there were no cost pressures or land-ownership conflicts to resolve when designating land for large industrial uses. On the positive side, the command economy and state ownership of land allowed communist governments to provide their citizens with vast amounts of public space, including parks. The grand scale—of both industrial enterprises and public facilities—was in itself a virtue for party ideologues eager to prove communism's triumph. The most telling example was perhaps in Romania, where the late dictator, Ceausescu, was so megalomaniacal that he built the People's Palace in Bucharest as the second largest public building in the world, smaller than only the U.S. Pentagon. This communist legacy of spatial generosity creates both problems and opportunities today. While many East European cities with postindustrial economies struggle with the liability of vast derelict industrial sites, their citizens often enjoy better access to parks and public spaces than do residents of Western cities.

The communist model of housing provision was also distinct. The state considered itself obliged to provide a decent minimum of housing to all. This commitment translated into innumerable massive, state-built apartment blocks, which today form the outskirts of most large East European cities, from Prague to St. Petersburg. While such spatial grandeur certainly seemed to fit the Soviet taste, some pragmatic reasons also made it more or less imperative. Specifically, the policy of rapid industrialization that marked the Soviet period demanded that extraordinary numbers of rural residents move to cities. To fulfill their commitment to the new workers and prevent mass housing crises, communist regimes had little choice but to construct new housing as efficiently, quickly, and cheaply as possible—which meant building large, uniform apartment blocks with prefabricated panels. The fact that the majority of new housing development occurred in such a manner—as opposed to the more scattered, private-sector-led fashion typical of free-market countries—led to one of the most fundamental differences between communist and many capitalist cities. While U.S. cities are typically surrounded by sprawling suburbs, communist cities were relatively compact and highly dense and

Massiveness was one hallmark of the Soviet planning style. This is a Soviet-era housing project in the former East Berlin.

had an urban contour clearly defined by the last towers of the communist housing districts.

Two other features distinguished communist from capitalist cities. First, because of the communist emphasis on industry, the production of commercial goods and service activities was neglected. As a result, communist cities had significantly fewer commercial spaces than capitalist cities—a difference that was strikingly visible to any visitor who compared East and West Berlin. Second, because of the lower purchasing power of communist citizens (which translated into lower car ownership, among other things), and because of the higher urban densities, communist cities functioned with very fully developed mass transit systems.

The Transition to a Market Economy

With the collapse of Soviet power, the nations of Eastern Europe necessarily had to make the transition from a command to a market economy. In the first years, this transition was often painful. Output and already low living standards declined, unemployment was sometimes widespread, and the spread between the highest and lowest incomes increased greatly.[25] Recovery started in the mid-1990s for some countries and post-2000 for others. Over the last few years, until the 2008 financial crisis, most East European states enjoyed GDP growth of 5 to 10 percent a year, which is much higher than the growth rates typical of Western economies.

Within a context of rapid social and political change, East European cities are undergoing substantial transformations. In short, they are gradually losing the typical features of communist spatial structure and acquiring those characteristic of capitalist structure. The increase in personal income has resulted in a major increase in automobile ownership. One result is that most large East European cities have by now developed suburban peripheries, comprising not only single-family homes but also Western-type commercial facilities like malls and hypermarkets. The proportion of commercial uses has skyrocketed, in both downtowns and the Soviet-style housing districts. While rapid commercial development has brought about economic benefits, it has also caused problems. Downtowns have lost significant portions of their residential populations. Few cities, aside from Prague, have managed to protect their historic centers from the pressure of market forces.

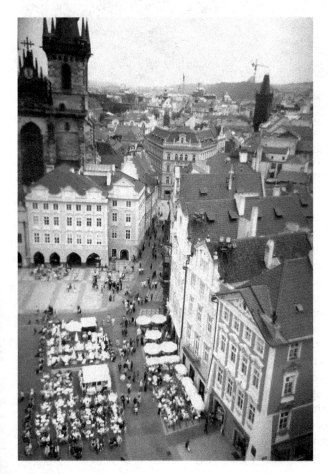

Part of the main square in the old center of Prague. Such areas need some protection from the free play of market forces to survive. Providing this may be a problem in parts of Eastern Europe, because half a century of Soviet domination gave all forms of planning a bad name.

With the collapse of communism and large increases in many people's incomes, there has been a wave of peripheral single-family construction in many Eastern European countries. Here, a development outside of Sofia, the capital of Bulgaria.

Since 1990, the role of the public sector in urban development has been greatly reduced. Most new development is now initiated by private investors, in large measure because it is private developers rather than municipal governments that have the necessary funds. Large amounts of urban land, which were previously under public ownership, have been privatized. Unfortunately, this has led to great losses in public space. In the Bulgarian capital of Sofia, for example, an estimated 15 percent of public green space was lost in 15 years. The trend of privatizing urban space is also evident in neighborhood design patterns. While Soviet-style apartment blocks are located amid free-flowing greenery accessible to all citizens, new housing developments are often walled and gated.

The planning response to these dramatic urban changes has been uncertain. Doubtless, the planning process has experienced several positive developments, such as increased citizen participation. However, shrinking public spaces, threatened historic landmarks, and Western-type sprawl hardly provide evidence of good planning. The 1990s were difficult for planners because of the unstable economic, political, and legal conditions, and because of the legitimacy crisis that plagued the profession. This legitimacy crisis came in part from the experience of half a century of Soviet domination. Most East European governments made a sharp turn to the political right and some viewed planning as a suspicious, quasi-communist activity. As a result, enthusiasm for the sanctity of private property overshadowed concerns for advancing the overall public interest—a concern at the very foundation of planning.

The Problem of Privatization

One major problem throughout Eastern Europe and the Baltics is that of *privatization*, the return to private ownership of vast amounts of land and buildings that became public property during the period of Soviet domination. Problems of unclear titles, incomplete records, of inflicting major gains and losses upon people who may be the children or grandchildren of the original owners, and the like are very substantial. The transfer of wealth that the process of privatization inevitably involves opens up major opportunities for corruption. For example, in Russia the so-called *oligarchs*, a very small number of individuals who have become billionaires since the collapse of the Soviet Union in 1991, to a substantial degree made their fortunes by receiving industrial, commercial, and other state assets at bargain basement prices.

In all countries, one difficult puzzle has been what to do with the land under and in between the apartment blocks built during communism. Typically, this was once private agricultural land. However, it cannot simply be returned to its precommunist owners, as this will lead to the loss of all green spaces between the apartment buildings. Thus in most countries this land continues to be municipal and various schemes have been devised to compensate its precommunist owners.

EU Membership and the Future of Planning in Eastern Europe

One factor favoring economic and political stabilization has been the incorporation of all of the East European and Baltic nations mentioned in the first paragraph of this section into the European Union (EU) beginning in 2004. This has integrated them into a group of nations with much more prosperous economies and older and more established political and economic institutions. As noted earlier in this section, planning in these newly admitted EU members faced a legitimacy crisis that was rooted in the bad experience that these nations had with the Soviet Union. In the EU there is much concern with egalitarianism and much willingness to restrict the market in the service of the public interest, but unlike the case in the former Soviet Union, there is also a high degree of political and personal freedom as well as a vastly higher standard of living.

An important indicator for the reestablishment of urban planning in Eastern Europe has been the increased attention to urban and regional sustainability issues. The new Central and East European members of the European Union have by now largely harmonized their national environmental legislation with European Union standards. Poland, for example, adopted its pioneering Concept on National Spatial Development in 1999. This document heavily emphasizes the principles of concentrated polycentricity and restraining development overspill into the metropolitan hinterlands—principles that are closely allied with the prescriptions of the European Spatial Development Perspective. However, depending on the perceived and real costs of adopting strict environmental standards and public support, implementation varies widely across the region.

PLANNING IN ASIA

Diverse as the planning scene is in Europe, it is much more so in Asia. One reason is the huge difference in income among the nations of Asia. Table 18–1 compares GDP (gross domestic product) per capita for a few Asian nations and the United States. Note that the wealthiest Asian country on the list, Japan, has approximately 20 times that of the poorest, Bangladesh.

The range of differences in national growth rates is also much greater than in Europe. Prosperous South Korea has a fertility rate of 1.2 (2.1 is replacement level). Its population has more or less topped out and will begin to decline shortly unless there is a major increase in fertility. In far less prosperous, albeit rapidly developing, India the fertility rate is 2.7. The country experiences roughly 25 million births per year, and grows at about 16 million people per year (Figure 18–2).[26]

TABLE 18–1 Per Capita GDP of Selected Nations, 2010

Bangladesh	$ 1,660
India	$ 3,400
Indonesia	$ 4,300
China	$ 7,400
South Korea	$ 30,200
Japan	$ 34,200
United States	$ 47,400

Source: CIA World Factbook, www.cia.gov/library/publications/the-worldfactbook/.

Note: Figures are based on purchasing power parity.

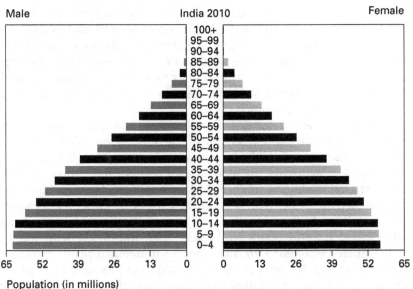

FIGURE 18-2 South Korea's population (top) now has a heavy concentration of people in middle age, a favorable situation for economic growth. But in another two decades or so it will be heavily weighted toward retirement age population, a much less favorable situation. Note that the population age 40–44 is almost twice the size of the population age 0–4. The present population stability will be replaced by one of substantial decline unless there is a large increase in fertility. In India (bottom) the youngest age cohorts are the largest, so population shrinkage, if it happens at all, is many decades away. The changing slope at the bottom of the pyramid indicates that India's still high fertility rate has been declining.

Source: U.S. Bureau of the Census International Data Base, www.census.gov/population/international/data/idb/.

The variety of political regimes in Asia is huge. A democratic and efficient regime in South Korea shares a border with North Korea, whose dysfunctional and impoverished regime is one of the most tyrannical on the planet. India's soft democracy contrasts sharply with the efficient, hard-edged democracy of places like Singapore. China's government—which is autocratic, repressive in the realm of ideas (Internet censorship, for example) and political disagreement, and yet accepting of a great deal of economic freedom—has been spectacularly successful as an engine of economic growth.[27]

For the previously mentioned reasons it is even harder to generalize about planning in Asia than in Europe. Consider, for example, South Korea. The nation enjoys a high living standard and is a powerful international competitor in manufacturing. Its 48 million people, who own perhaps 20 million automobiles, live on 38,000 square miles, somewhat less land area than the state of Virginia. Korean planners' concerns will all seem very familiar to European or U.S. planners. Given the high population density and the high rate of automobile ownership there is a great emphasis on both highway and public transportation planning. Seoul, the capital city, with a population of 10 million has the world's third largest subway system and an extensive network of bus and light-rail transport. The Seoul capital district contains almost half the population of the nation, and it continues to grow even as the nation as a whole has reached population stability. Thus new town planning is of major concern for Korean planners.

International economic competitiveness is also an issue with planners. The Songdo "intelligent city" developed on 1,500 acres of reclaimed land on the Incheon waterfront about 40 miles to the west of Seoul was expressly planned in part to help the nation compete in international trade and finance. Much of the city looks rather Western and, in fact, its master plan was done by the New York architectural and planning firm Kohn Pederson Fox. American planners and engineers who spend time in South Korea are often impressed with the speed with which the Koreans go from concept to detailed plans to completed project. In a parallel with the German situation (discussed earlier in this chapter) the huge uncertainty that hangs over the planning situation in South Korea is what will happen with North Korea. Just as Germany was divided between East and West at the end of World War II, Korea was divided between North and South. In the case of the Koreas the story is far from over.

Among other prosperous Asian states including Taiwan, Malaysia, and Singapore, many concerns are similar. In Japan, there has been an emphasis on public transportation and infrastructure development. There has also been much interest in urban growth boundaries (UGBs) and in

Songdo, South Korea.

channeling urban growth to preserve open spaces between places, much as in parts of the United States. Of course, at present Japan is primarily focused on recovery and rebuilding after the 2011 tsunami.

In faster-growing and less prosperous parts of Asia the planning concerns may be very different. Where rural areas are densely populated, the marginal or additional productivity of one more worker is necessarily very small and that leads to substantial migration to urban areas, even though economic opportunities for most rural migrants there are limited. That migration often shows up as large squatter settlements, both on the periphery and inside of cities.

Providing even the most minimal sort of housing is a tremendous problem in much of Asia. Some nations have tried public housing, but the scale of the problem has overwhelmed the funds available. A number of nations have taken a sites and services approach. Funding comes from the municipal government, sometimes the provincial or national government, and sometimes from international donor agencies. Typically the municipal government provides the site with

A sites and services project some years ago in Chennai (formerly Madras), India. The city government provides utilities and plots of land at nominal prices. Some of the construction is with indigenous materials such as reeds, sticks, and dried mud. Other construction is with modern materials such as concrete blocks.

utilities, often only a community tap, and with sewerage, or sometimes only with drainage and electricity. The prospective homeowner gets the site for a nominal fee and then builds his or her shelter on it. The shelter may be only indigenous materials like sticks, mud, and whatever scraps the owner can scavenge. In some cases more substantial materials are used. In time, larger and more substantial structures tend to replace the original ones. The house may serve as a store of wealth for the original occupant, perhaps being sold to obtain other housing or to start a small business venture. The sites and services approach has generally worked out better than direct provision of housing but it, too, often does not match the scale of the problem of housing large numbers of poor rural to urban migrants.

For a planner concerned with providing the residents of a squatter settlement with clean water so that they don't get waterborne diseases like cholera, concerns such as green spaces, sustainability, and walkability that engaged the interest of planners in Songdo may seem quite secondary.

In China and India huge middle classes have emerged along with modern economic sectors, the Chinese emphasizing manufacturing and the Indians emphasizing advanced services like information technology. These modern sectors and large and prosperous middle classes coexist with huge amounts of rural poverty and underdevelopment.

While some planners focus on the problems of poverty, others are involved with an entirely different set of problems. At this time more commercial and residential high-rise construction is going on in Shanghai than any other city in the world. Its planners will necessarily be preoccupied with questions of urban design, public transportation, and coming to terms with the nation's exploding automobile population. In China and to a lesser degree India, rapid industrialization has exacted a huge environmental price. Thus many planners will be concerned with environmental questions that will seem quite familiar to their Western colleagues. Conflict over priorities and the allocation of resources is inevitable.

This section started by discussing the great differences between Asian nations in income and demography. Perhaps the coming years will see some convergence. We noted India's high fertility rate, 2.7. But 15 years ago it was 3.4. Another drop like that and India will be down to replacement level, though it would take several more decades for population to stabilize. India and China are both still very poor by Western standards, but both are experiencing extremely rapid economic growth. Perhaps in several decades they will achieve the levels of prosperity that now prevail in South Korea or Japan. So too may that other very populous Asian nation, Indonesia.

Up to now the flow of planning ideas and technique has largely been from the West to Asia. The planner who travels to Indian cities cannot miss signs of the British town planning tradition in matters like parks, public spaces, and street layout. Some of Chandrigah in India was planned by the French planner Le Corbusier. Parts of Islamabad, once part of India and after the 1947 partition of India the capital of the newly created Pakistan, were planned by the Greek planner Constantine Doxiadis. A great many Asian planners have been trained in European and American planning schools. And American and European planning and architectural firms provide consulting services to numerous clients in Asia. But as Asian sophistication in planning continues to grow, the flow of ideas and expertise will almost certainly become more balanced.

SUMMARY _____

The chapter begins by noting some differences between the situation of planning in Western Europe and in the United States. Among these differences are the destruction of urban areas in Europe during World

War II, the unification of Europe, different attitudes about the role of government, the generally greater strength of the national government vis-à-vis provincial and local governments, and, generally, a greater willingness in Europe to regulate the uses of private property.

The chapter notes the building of new towns and the creation of greenbelts in Great Britain, and the French effort to reduce the dominance of Paris and the Ile de France by supporting the development of regional centers. We note the relatively centralized Dutch planning system and the creation of Randstad Holland. In the case of Sweden we note the use of public ownership of land and the dominant role of government in the housing market as the means by which Swedish municipal governments have shaped the pattern of development.

Throughout much of Western Europe in the 1980s and 1990s, there was an increase in property-led development so that the European planning scene came to resemble the American scene a bit more than had previously been the case. Among the reasons for this change were a general political shift to the right, an increase in economic competition between places, and fiscal pressures that made public monies less available.

In Eastern Europe we note the priority given the needs of industry, the construction of massive housing projects, and the relatively low emphasis on the needs of service activities during the period of Soviet domination. In the decade since the end of Soviet domination and the breakup of the Soviet Union, the planning situation has been uncertain. What sort of planning tradition will emerge is unclear. There has been some public suspicion of planning simply because the term is associated with the period of Soviet domination. Now that the nations of Eastern Europe are part of the European Union (EU), that attitude may begin to change.

In connection with planning in Asia, we note the great differences in income among nations, large differences in population growth, and the wide varieties of political structures. The chapter also notes the inevitability of conflicts over goals and resources where large modern sectors coexist with large numbers of rural and urban poor.

NOTES

1. The term *spent* in this usage also includes the term *transferred.* A great deal of the one-third of GNP "spent" by government in the United States is simply money like Social Security payments that are transferred to individuals and then spent by the individuals. In that sense the figures on government's share of the GNP may exaggerate the role of government in the economy.

2. J. Barry Cullingworth, *The Political Culture of Planning,* Routledge, London, 1993, p. 197.

3. Just before the start of World War II, Great Britain imported about four-fifths of all the food that it consumed. During the war,

the heavy dependence on food brought in by ship was a major problem, which focused attention on the desirability of preserving as much of the nation's agricultural potential as possible.

4. For a detailed account of the evolution of British planning in the post–World War II period, see Peter Hall, *Urban and Regional Planning*, 3rd ed., Routledge, London, 1992, chap. 4. See also J. Barry Cullingworth and Vincent Nadin, *Town and Country Planning in Britain*, Routledge, London, 11th ed., 1994, and earlier editions, chap. 1.

5. Hall, *Urban and Regional Planning*, p. 81.

6. Pierre Merlin, *New Towns, Regional Planning and Development*, Methuen & Co., Ltd., London, 1971.

7. This idea somewhat resembles the thinking of the late-nineteenth-century American writer on economic and social issues, Henry George. He argued that increases in land value generally occurred because of forces with which the property owner had little connection and that these increases in value, which were not earned by the property owner, should be taxed away. He thus argued for a tax system that relied entirely on the value of land.

8. The industrial revolution is generally considered to have been well under way in Great Britain by the last decades of the eighteenth century, about 1760 to 1800 or 1780 to 1800. Germany did not reach a comparable stage until at least the middle of the nineteenth century, and Scandinavia the end of the nineteenth century. For estimates of the dates of the so-called stage of economic takeoff in various countries, see W. W. Rostow, *The Stages of Economic Growth: A Non-Communist Manifesto*, Cambridge University Press, 1971.

9. That changed in subsequent years, and the British growth rate was higher than that on the continent, a fact the Conservatives were quick to attribute to the pro-market policies of Margaret Thatcher and John Major, policies generally continued under the Labour government of Tony Blair.

10. Anthony Bianco, "Faith and Fortune," *BusinessWeek*, January 20, 1997, pp. 55–69.

11. Hall, *Urban and Regional Planning*, p. 154.

12. Cullingworth and Nadin, *Town and Country*, pp. 205–213.

13. Hall, *Urban and Regional Planning*, p. 168.

14. The term *growth pole* originated with the French economic geographer François Perroux. Though he used it to describe an industrial sector that acted as the agent for promoting national industrial development (i.e., as the leading industrial sector, rather than a particular place), it quickly became used in the geographic sense. The term, in its geographic sense, was popularized in the United States by the regional economist Niles Hansen.

15. Hall, *Urban and Regional Planning*, p. 172.

16. France's high-speed passenger rail system, the *Train à Grande Vitesse* (TGV), literally "Train with Great Speed," is very heavily subsidized. It provides a level of passenger service that is unmatched in the United States; in fact, the French passenger rail system apart from the TGV is far superior to that of the United States. One reason is that the French are willing to subsidize passenger rail very heavily. The U.S. reluctance to sink large amounts of subsidy money into a modern, high-quality passenger rail system has been the object of much criticism. However, the defender of the U.S. reluctance might point out that it is not entirely capricious. U.S. population density is much lower than that of France, the land-use pattern is much more dispersed, and automobile ownership rates are higher. All those factors tend to stack the deck against public transportation and would make U.S. subsidy costs per passenger mile much higher.

17. Peter Newman and Andy Thornley, *Urban Planning in Europe*, Routledge, London and New York, 1996, chap. 7.

18. Ibid., p. 163.

19. Ibid., p. 48.

20. Hall, *Urban and Regional Planning*, pp. 197–202.

21. The idea that a small place may obtain some of the benefits or agglomeration economies of a nearby larger place has been termed "borrowed size" by the American planner William Alonso. See any standard text on urban economics, such as James Heilbrun, *Urban Economics and Public Policy*, 3rd ed., St. Martin's Press, New York, 1987.

22. Newman and Thornley, *Urban Planning*, p. 209.

23. Ibid., p. 208.

24. Author's interview with city of Helsinki Planning Dept., spring 1994.

25. In the Soviet Union and in many of the satellite nations, the extremes of wealth and poverty were much smaller than was later to become the case. Housing and

some other necessities of life were provided below cost and there was no unemployment. All workers were assigned to a workplace, even if there was very little for them to do there. In other words, unemployment was concealed, rather than explicit as in a capitalist society. A cynical expression for this at the time was "we pretend to work and they pretend to pay us." Though the total output of the economy was low and the society as a whole was very poor by Western standards, there was a minimal floor under everyone.

26. The fertility figures come from U.S. Bureau of the Census International Data Base, www. census.gov/population/international/data/idb/. The database provides current and past population figures, projections of future populations, and present and projected population pyramids for a large number of nations. Fertility and population figures for a number of nations can also be found in the International chapter of the *Statistical Abstract of the United States*, also published by the Bureau of the Census.

27. In 2010 China's GDP measured on a purchasing power parity basis was about 67 percent that of the United States. If the current difference in growth rates continues, China will catch the United States in GDP within less than a decade. The population of China is about 4.3 times that of the United States. Thus U.S. per capita GDP is about six and one-half times that of China. Purchasing power parity is used rather than the commonly used comparison based on official exchange rates because it avoids distortion caused by under or overvalued currencies. The calculations are based on figures from the *CIA World Factbook*, www.cia.gov/library/publications/the-world-factbook/.

SELECTED BIBLIOGRAPHY

BRENNER, NEIL, AND KEIL, ROGER, EDS., *The Global Cities Reader*, Routledge, New York, 2005.

CULLINGWORTH, J. BARRY, AND NADIN, VINCENT, *Town and Country Planning in Britain*, 11th ed., Routledge, London and New York, 1994.

HALL, PETER, *Urban and Regional Planning*, 3rd ed., Routledge, London and New York, 1992.

MERLIN, PIERRE (trans. Margaret Sparks), *New Towns, Regional Planning and Development*, Methuen and Co., Ltd., London, 1971.

NEWMAN, PETER, AND THORNLEY, ANDY, *Urban Planning in Europe*, Routledge, London and New York, 1996.

SILVER, CHRISTOPHER, *Planning the Megacity: Jakarta in the Twentieth Century*, Routledge, New York, 2008.

CHAPTER 19

Planning Theory

In this chapter we discuss planning theory from two perspectives: (1) theories of planning as a process, both how it ought to be done and how it is done, and (2) some ideological issues. But first, a legitimate question to ask is this: Is planning theory necessary? Cannot the planner simply apply his or her intelligence to a particular situation and proceed without theory?

IS THEORY NECESSARY?

The question of whether theory is not simply a waste of time is the question with which the "practical" person derides the philosopher. But theory cannot be avoided. We all possess theories that form the basis on which we act. Everyone has ideas about how things are and how the world works. One difference between the practical person and the theorist is that the former takes these ideas for granted, whereas the latter thinks about them consciously and makes them explicit. But when one acts, one inevitably acts on the basis of some theory about how things work. On what other basis can one act?

In 1936 John Maynard Keynes, whom some regard as the greatest economist of the twentieth century, wrote,

> Ideas of economists and political philosophers, both when they are right and when they are wrong, are more powerful than is commonly understood. Indeed, the world is ruled by little else. Practical men, who believe themselves to be quite exempt from intellectual influences, are usually the slave of some defunct economist. Madmen in authority, who hear voices in the air, are distilling their frenzy from some academic scribbler of a few years back.[1]

Keynes's reference to "madmen in authority" has particular reference to Europe of the 1930s—especially to Hitler, Stalin, and Mussolini. But the point that even the most powerful are themselves ruled by the ideas they hold is as valid today as it was then.

We noted in Chapter 6 several alternative roles the planner might play. How is a person to decide whether he or she favors an advocacy position, or a neutral civil servant position, without some theories of how society works, how decisions are made, and what constitutes right and wrong? At a more concrete level, assume the city is beset with housing problems. The planner is asked to comment on whether a rent control ordinance would be a good idea. How can he or she even begin to think about the issues without some theory of how housing markets work? To the extent that controls would deliver benefits to some individuals and losses to others, how can we decide whether these effects would be good or bad unless we have some theory of what constitutes social justice? If theory is inescapable, perhaps it is best to make it explicit.

It is common to make a distinction between theory and practice, and it is easy to exaggerate this difference. To a large extent, theory is developed and tested on the basis of the experience acquired in practice. As stated, every practitioner is, to some extent, a theoretician. Conversely, the experience of practice is likely to make the theoretician better at his or her chosen work. The theoretician who has had no contact with practice has not subjected his or her theorizing to the test and has little basis to assert its validity. Without the experience of practice, it is hard to separate good theory from bad theory and useful theory from useless theory.

A DISTINCTION BETWEEN PUBLIC AND PRIVATE PLANNING

It is true that public planning and nonpublic planning, such as that done by corporations, have much in common. However, there is at least one important difference: Public planning is often more difficult than private planning, and its results may sometimes appear to be less rational. The reason is very simple. Public planning must usually satisfy many different ends, some of which may be in conflict with one another. Private planning, very often, is directed toward satisfying a single or a very small number of ends. It thus often admits of more coherent solutions.

Consider the builder who is planning to build an apartment house. He or she is likely to have one major goal—profit.[2] No one reasonably expects a builder to consider the effect of one building on the city as a whole. Society has formulated a variety of rules regarding zoning, construction standards, taxation, and the like. Within these rules the builder is free to follow his or her own interests.

Now consider a public body that is building housing. It has cost and revenue estimates to make, as does the private builder. But it has numerous goals to consider that the private builder does not. How does the project affect community goals regarding integration? How will the project affect the process of gentrification? If the project involves demolition, where will the residents of the soon-to-be-demolished housing live? How does the rent structure of the project square with what is known about the income distribution of the city's population? And so on.

There is also the political imperative. The public body operates in the open and is accountable to the entire body politic of the city—voters, labor unions, neighborhood groups, civic groups, tenant organizations, landlord organizations, ad infinitum. The plan that the public body finally settles on must satisfy many of these groups. The plan does not have to have something for everybody, but it must have something for a number of parties if it is to have a chance of survival.

THE PROCESS OF PLANNING

Sometimes a distinction is made between "substantive" theory and "procedural" theory. Substantive theory in this usage is theory *in* planning, for example, the gravity model mentioned in connection with transportation planning. Procedural theory is theory *about* the act of planning. The various theories of planning to be discussed fall under the heading of procedural theory. Note, however, that the two types of theory are related. We have to have substantive ideas (ideas about how the world works) to form procedural theories.

Here, we address four approaches to the process of planning:

> The rational model
> Disjointed incrementalism
> Middle-range models
> Collaborative rationality

The Rational Model

The rational model has been prevalent for several decades and might be considered the orthodox view.[3] It is the philosophy reflected in the comprehensive plan. Though its proponents will readily admit that in the real world it cannot be carried out precisely as described, many would argue that it still constitutes a kind of holy grail to be approached as closely as possible. The idea behind the model, as its name suggests, is to make the planning process as rational and systematic as possible. A listing of steps in the model follows. Not every writer might list exactly this sequence, but the general idea would be the same.

1. *Define the problem.*   Obviously if more than one party is involved, then it is necessary to reach an agreement.

2. *Clarify values.*   Suppose the problem is stated as an inadequate housing stock. Before we can formulate policy, we have to agree on how highly we value certain conditions. How important is the physical condition of housing? Is physical condition more or less important than the cost of housing? How important is it that housing be racially integrated? How important is good traffic circulation in residential areas? How important is growth in the number of housing units? Often we will find that an action that takes us toward one goal takes us away from another. Tearing down substandard units will certainly improve housing quality. But by reducing the number of units on the market, demolition will push up rents. Should we do it? We cannot answer that question unless we have our values sorted out.

3. *Select goals.*   Having gone through steps 1 and 2, we are now presumably in a position to choose one or more goals relative to the problem.

4. *Formulate alternative plans or programs.*

5. *Forecast the consequences of the alternatives developed in the previous step.*

6. *Evaluate and select one or more courses of action (alternatives).*

7. *Develop detailed plans for implementing the alternatives selected.*

8. *Review and evaluate.*   Once implementation has begun, it is necessary periodically to review the process and results to date with a view to decide whether the original plan should still be followed or whether—as is usually the case—changes and adjustments are necessary.

Although the steps are presented in sequence, there is a great deal of going back and forth. For example, if step 4 suggests that a certain goal selected in step 3 cannot be reached or can be reached only at an exorbitant price, the planners may go back to step 3 to select an alternative goal. Obviously, defining the problem and clarifying values are closely intertwined. Very often, we do not know how much we value something until we learn its price and then have to decide whether to pay it. In that case, the insights that come out of the latter steps will often carry us back to the first three steps.

Criticisms of the Rational Model.   Although the rational model seems eminently sensible, it has been subject to a great deal of criticism. Some critics assert that the steps described are simply not how things are actually planned. If the model does not describe reality at least very roughly, what good is it?

Consider the first four steps. Few real problems can be approached as if there were a clean slate in front of the planner. Legal, political, and other constraints eliminate some possibilities and necessitate others. In fact, it has been argued that the mandatory requirements and limitations that legislative bodies impose on boards, commissions, local governments, and so on are intended precisely to constrain those organizations. They are there to prevent them from going back to square one and rethinking and hence resolving the problem from the beginning.

Critics also argue that value clarification sounds logical but often cannot be done. If agreement is necessary for action and the various parties have different values, making value clarification a requisite for the next step would make further progress impossible. During World War II the United States, Great Britain, and the USSR agreed on the necessity of cooperating to defeat Germany. But their values and goals were radically different. Cooperation was achieved only by suppressing, ignoring, or denying these very deep differences. Had honest value clarification been required as a first part of the planning process, no progress would have been made.

The critic of the model might also argue that the latter steps in the process do not describe reality very well. The laying out and studying of a number of alternatives is often simply not possible because of time or resources. In many cases the planner quickly arrives at a short list of alternatives and then focuses on implementation. The look-at-everything-to-make-the-optimum-choice approach is not possible.

A final point that critics make is that the goal of the rational model is optimization—making the best choice from a substantial array of possibilities. These possibilities have themselves been developed by a systematic and—as far as is possible—an all-inclusive process. It has been said that in most situations, organizations do not optimize but rather "satisfice," meaning that they strive for solutions that are satisfactory or adequate.[4] Optimization is simply too difficult.

So far the arguments against the rational model are essentially arguments from practicality. Charles Lindblom has suggested that even in the ideal, the rational model may not be best. He notes that it presumes that the participants in the planning process each consider the totality of goals and objectives and think of which courses of action produce the greatest good. But, he argues, this is just unrealistic. Let us admit that we live in a world of partisanship, constituencies, and special interests and therefore cannot expect the participants to act like candidates for sainthood. May we not, then, get a better result?

The argument Lindblom makes for a less highly structured and centralized approach is quite simple. Assume that the participants come into the planning process from various vantage points and that they, to some extent, represent special interests (as opposed to the public interest as a whole). Then it is doubtful that the interests of any major group in the public will be ignored.

The virtue of such hypothetical division of labor is that every important interest or value has its watchdog.... In a society like that of the United States in which individuals are free to combine to pursue almost any possible common interest they might have and in which government agencies are sensitive to the pressures of these groups, the system is approximated. Almost every interest has its watchdog. Without claiming that every interest has a sufficiently powerful watchdog, it can be argued that our system often can assure a more comprehensive regard for the values of the whole society than any attempt at intellectual comprehensiveness.[5]

In support of the "watchdog" argument, we note that it has been demonstrated beyond doubt that well-intentioned members of the majority often do not know what is important to members of minorities or how strongly members of minorities may feel. In the 1950s, how many whites knew quite how anguished blacks were about the constraints society placed on them? More recently, how many men understood how angry many women were about their limited job opportunities? How many heterosexuals perceived how frustrated gays felt about their second-class status? One can make a credible argument that no group's concerns can be completely understood by anyone other than members of that group itself. If this is true, an adversarial and a pluralistic planning process may give better results than a nonadversarial one, no matter how well intentioned. And, of course, the phrase *well intentioned* carries a heavy burden of assumption.

Lindblom's argument for an adversarial process is quite consistent with the Anglo-Saxon judicial and political tradition in the United States. Our courts function on an adversarial basis. We do not expect each party's attorney to present the facts objectively. Rather, within the constraints of the law, we expect an attorney to present the strongest possible case for his or her client. We assume that truth will best emerge from this clash of adversaries, and we are extremely suspicious of judicial systems in which the roles of judge, prosecution, and defense are combined in a single individual.

Party politics as practiced in the United States and other Western democracies are clearly adversarial. We are highly dubious of any political system in which there is no real clash of adversaries, for we suspect that the outward harmony is a mask for oppression.

In Defense of the Rational Model.   The defender of the rational model, of which there are many among practicing planners and planning educators, might answer some of these points as follows.

Of course values cannot always be clarified fully. But to the extent that they can be clarified, it is wise to do so. Not all parties will always be willing to reveal their real goals in the planning process, but again to the extent that goals can be clearly formulated, it is wise that this be done. We have no shortage of public programs with contradictory and unstated goals and purposes. Perhaps conscientious resort to the rational model might help.[6]

Perhaps the point about going back to square one is not such a damning criticism after all. In considering any problem, of course we must always take some things for granted. How far back we go depends on the importance of the problem, the time and resources available, and other practical considerations. The rational model suggests simply going as far back to square one *as is practical.*

The argument regarding the watchdog effect of an adversarial process is not easily countered. However, the defender of the rational process might argue that the need for representation of conflicting views can, in some measure, be accommodated by requiring adequate diversity of interests in the body that does the planning. Given that the planning body is ultimately selected and empowered by the political structure of the community, that responsibility lies with the executive and legislative branches.

Disjointed Incrementalism

Having expressed strong doubts about the rational model, in terms of both feasibility and underlying theory, its critics have suggested an alternative view of the planning process. The terms *incrementalism, disjointed incrementalism, muddling through,* and *successive limited comparisons* have been used for an alternative approach, of which Lindblom has been the most prominent advocate.[7]

Lindblom believes that value clarification at the outset, though it sounds attractive in principle, is usually not practical. Rather, what counts is achieving agreement on goals. Politics is, after all, "the art of compromise," not the art of optimization. He suggests that the range of possible courses of action not be the very comprehensive one suggested by the rational model. Rather, he argues, planners should quickly come down to a short list of serious possibilities and focus on these. He argues that planners and policy makers should be strongly influenced by precedent and by experience and that they should recognize the advantages of policy options that represent marginal or incremental changes from previous policies. The argument for an emphasis on marginal change is twofold. First, a policy that is simply an adjustment or fine-tuning of a previous policy is much more likely to gain acceptance than one that is a radical departure. Second, marginal or incremental adjustments require less knowledge and theory. Even if we do not really know why a policy or a program functions as it does, we can often see that if we adjusted it this way or that, it is likely to function better. In Lindblom's phrase, the rational model is "greedy for facts":

> It can be constructed only through a great collection of facts. . . . In contrast, the comparative [incremental] method both economizes on the need for facts and directs the analyst's attention to just those facts which are relevant to the fine choices faced by the decision-maker.[8]

The greed for facts is not a small point. Gathering facts takes time and costs money, and sometimes the facts cannot be had no matter how much effort is expended. Similar observations can be made regarding theory. Building theory takes time and money, and sometimes when all is said and done, alternate theories will prove equally plausible. What is one to rely on then? Perhaps it is best to rely on the fine-tuning of disjointed incrementalism. Piano tuning is an incremental process and it seems to work.

The arguments for the incremental, or muddling-through, approach are powerful, and most advocates of the rational model will admit that there are times when incrementalism is the most practical route. But it must be said that there is one important situation in which the incremental approach is not good—the situation in which a decision to move in a new direction must be made. If the problem is new, it is hard to see how an incremental approach can work. In the 1960s the United States began to confront the problem of nuclear waste disposal. There simply was no existing program that could be incrementally adjusted to deal with a problem that had not existed a decade earlier. Perhaps the reason we have hundreds of thousands of "hot" fuel rods in temporary storage at dozens of sites around the country is precisely because we took the incremental approach.

The critic of the incremental model might also argue that excessive reliance on the incremental approach can make one excessively dependent on precedent and past experience and thus blind to worthwhile new ideas. Thus heavy reliance on incrementalism can lead one into excessive caution and missed opportunities.

To some extent the choice between the rational model and the incremental model may be an expression of one's willingness to take risks. The rational model may hold out the hope of big gains because going back to the beginning may yield a new and much superior approach. But if one goes back to the beginning and gets things all wrong, there is the possibility of big losses. The incremental approach, by holding fast to the handrail of experience and precedent, reduces the chances of both big gains and big losses. Table 19–1 summarizes the circumstances in which one might favor one model or the other.

TABLE 19–1 Which Model to Use

Favors Rational Model	Favors Incremental Model
Adequate theory available	Adequate theory lacking
New question	Modification of old question
Resources generous	Resources limited
Substantial time for study	Limited time for study
Numerous relations to other policy issues	Few relations to other policy issues
Wide range of policies might be politically acceptable	Policy options highly limited by political realities

Middle-Range Models

The rational model and disjointed incrementalism represent opposite poles. Various intermediate approaches have also been proposed, perhaps the best known of which is "mixed scanning" by sociologist Amitai Etzioni.[9]

The idea is quite simple. Etzioni advocates a two-step process. First, a general scanning process is conducted to get the overall picture and to decide which elements merit more detailed examination. Etzioni uses the analogy of a weather monitoring system utilizing space satellites.

> The rationalistic approach [rational model] would seek an exhaustive survey of weather conditions . . . by scheduling reviews of the entire sky as often as possible. This would yield an avalanche of details, costly to analyze and likely to overwhelm our action capabilities.

He then goes on to contrast the rational model approach with his mixed scanning approach.

> A mixed scanning strategy would include elements of both approaches . . . a broad angle camera that would cover all parts of the sky but not in great detail and a second one which would zero in on those areas revealed by the first camera to require more examination. While mixed scanning might miss areas in which a detailed camera could reveal trouble, it is less likely than incrementalism to miss obvious trouble spots in unfamiliar areas.

Etzioni elaborates on his model by pointing out that the scanning process might actually have more than one stage. We might scan a large field quickly and then, depending on what we had learned, scan a smaller field somewhat more thoroughly. When we have located the area that deserves fine scrutiny, a systematic approach such as that of the rational model is appropriate.

Etzioni argues that his model avoids the excessive commitment to precedent and past experience inherent in the incremental model. At the same time, it is far more feasible than a doctrinaire rational model approach: "The strategy [mixed scanning] combines a detailed ('rationalistic') examination of some sectors—which, unlike the detailed examination of the entire area, is feasible—with a 'truncated' review of other sectors." Etzioni's advice resembles that given to strategic planners, sometimes summarized under the acronym SWOT, which stands for Strengths, Weaknesses, Opportunities, Threats. The advice is quickly to characterize the organization's overall position under those four general categories. When that general reconnaissance is done, then detailed planning following a structured, rational model-like approach can begin, with less fear of being blindsided by important factors that were overlooked in a rush to premature closure.

Mixed scanning has generally received a favorable response from planners interested in how-to-plan or what-is-planning questions. It seems to describe a fair amount of what planners actually do. The working planner is likely to spend a little time looking around very broadly, narrow his or her options quickly, and focus intently on a small range of possibilities. Etzioni's synthesis appears to allow the user the strengths of both models while minimizing their weaknesses.

Collaborative Rationality

Collaborative rationality is a more recent approach to complex and often multi-jurisdictional planning problems, which its advocates see as superior to the rational model discussed earlier. Booher and Innes, two of its most prominent academic proponents, characterize its basic requirements as diversity, interdependence, and authentic dialogue.[10]

Diversity means that a wide range of interests and viewpoints are represented in the process or, to say it another way, as many stakeholders as possible are represented in the process. If, after the planning process has started, other stakeholders emerge, the idea is to bring them in rather than close the process.

Interdependence means that the nature of the problem is such that the stakeholders understand that a mutually satisfying solution to the problem is in their own best interest. If they think they will be better off by getting their own way than with any likely compromise, they may conclude that it makes more sense to fight hard to be the winner rather than to seek a common solution.

The term *authentic dialogue* means that there must be an extensive and honest sharing of information, viewpoints, interests, and values. Where meetings have a facilitator, an important task of the facilitator is to bring about as compete a sharing as possible and not to close off exchange or push the process to a predetermined outcome. That is a very different stance than one sees in some hierarchical situations where control of knowledge and perhaps the limiting of the flow of information on a need-to-know basis is a technique by which an interested party pushes the decision toward a predetermined outcome.

The underlying philosophy behind collaborative rationality is somewhat different than that behind the rational model. The advocate of collaborative rationality might well deny that there is a single best plan toward which the stakeholders should strive. Rather, he or she might assert that there is no objective reality with regard to the "best plan" and that the goal should be to come to an understanding that is acceptable to a substantial majority of the various stakeholders. He or she might take a relativistic view of knowledge, arguing that it is "socially constructed" and therefore it is often not possible to say that one position is necessarily truer than another.

That is different from taking the position that "there is an objective truth out there; now let's try to come as close to it as possible." The proponent of collective rationality is likely to argue for placing relatively more weight on feelings, attitudes, and intuitions and less weight on scientific analysis than the proponent of the rational model. That may partly come from the view that knowledge is socially constructed and partly from the view that scientific analysis is often used to support or justify an already chosen position rather than to determine what position to take. Those who favor collaborative rationality tend toward a more horizontal rather than a hierarchical view of the planning process. They tend to favor extended dialogue and a great deal of cross-communication among many parties, rather than just communication between various parties and a small central group.

Collaborative planning can be a very slow process. In fact, given the need for authentic dialogue among a large number of stakeholders it cannot be rapid. Booher and Innes cite the Sacramento Area Water Forum as an example of a highly successful collaborative planning effort. For this complex, multi-jurisdictional situation the planning phase took six years and produced a 400-page document that served as the basis for subsequent implementation. They assert that the results on the gound were good, and the resolution of previously unresolvable conflicts was achieved because the process ultimately produced widely accepted understandings of the problems and widespread consensus about what should be done.

The philosophical roots of collaborative rationality are numerous. Booher and Innes cite Jurgen Habermas and various members of the "Frankfurt School" who clearly lend a relativistic and anti-establishment tone to it. They also cite chaos theory, which suggests that our capacity to predict is more limited than we once believed, which gets at the very roots of the rational model—that we can pick the best option and then head toward it with some degree of confidence. An exposition of underlying philosophy is beyond our purview here, but the interested reader can pursue it in their book. For the working planner the philosophic roots may be of little interest. The question is, does collaborative rationality work as a process for addressing complex multiparty, multi-stakeholder issues? It has worked in a number of cases, and a substantial number of planners take it quite seriously.

Of the four planning models presented the first three—the rational model, disjointed incrementalism, and the middle-range model (or mixed scanning)—clearly form a continuum. In fact, whether one views a planning effort as, say, an example of the rational model or of incrementalism may be partly a matter of scale. The decision to undertake a particular project might be made in an incremental way and then the details of doing that project—for example, using benefit–cost analysis to select which one of several possible ways to accomplish the project—might be approached using the rational model. Collaborative rationality is somewhat different in character, in part because of its different philosophical roots. But still, there are many similarities. For example, both the rational model and collaborative rationality may be time-consuming processes, and both may involve a huge amount of factual material and the examination of many different alternatives. Collaborative rationality and the incremental model espoused by Lindblom have big differences, but when Lindblom argues that every interest should have its own watchdog, that is not entirely different from the basic idea in collaborative rationality that it is important to include as many stakeholders as is feasible. The collaborative rationality position that there may not be one objectively best solution resembles an old notion expressed earlier in this book that because the public is composed of many parties with different interests, it may be difficult to define "the public interest." Different models are appropriate to different circumstances, and the thoughtful practitioner may draw from all of them as circumstances require.

ADVOCACY PLANNING: THE QUESTION OF FOR WHOM _____

The four approaches to planning just described do not specify for whom the planning shall be done. Absent any specific statement on that point, you would naturally assume that the object of the planning is to serve some general public interest. In the 1960s a rather different strand of planning theory appeared. Its focus was not on how to plan so much as for whom to plan and to whom the planner should give his or her loyalty.

The late Paul Davidoff is the founder of advocacy planning.[11] His career in planning began in a conventional way, and for a time he was a planner for a small town in Connecticut. But he soon decided that his real loyalties lay in a different direction from serving an affluent suburban population. Much of his subsequent career was devoted to attacking what was termed *exclusionary* zoning in the suburbs. He did this through a combination of speaking, writing, and litigation.

Beyond the specific issue of suburban zoning, he developed the much more general concept of advocacy planning. In this view the proper role for the planner is not to serve a general public interest but rather to serve the interests of the least fortunate or least-well-represented groups in society, which he identified as poor and minority groups.[12] He denied that planning could be value free or that it could be a primarily technical and objective process:

> The justice of the present social allocation of wealth, knowledge, skill and other social goods is clearly in debate. Solutions to questions about the share of wealth and other social commodities that should go to different classes cannot be technically derived; they must arise from social attitudes.

The Davidoffian view clearly comes from the left-hand side of the political spectrum. He was not willing to allow the distribution of wealth and privileges to be settled by the marketplace, as someone on the right would be. The view embodied in the language—that there are distinct classes and that which classes get what should be a matter of collective decision—is itself a distinctly left view. So, too, is the idea that knowledge and skills are socially allocated, rather than individually acquired.

The planner in the Davidoffian scheme would represent not a general public interest but a client, much as an attorney does. He or she would take the view that there should be a plurality of plans rather than a single plan:

> There is or should be a Republican and Democratic way of viewing city development; that there should be conservative and liberal plans, plans to support the private market and plans to support greater government control. There are many possible roads for a community to travel and many plans should show them.

Davidoff's view disturbed many planners. The notion that there was no central public interest to be served was hardly the way the profession had traditionally seen its role. What did a multiplicity of plans mean in practice? One cannot build a building or a machine from a welter of contrasting plans.

The idea of serving a client rather than the public at large also raises some issues of personal ethics. Suppose you are committed to the idea of advocacy planning but you are hired as a town planner. How much loyalty do you owe the group for whom you think you should be the advocate, and how much loyalty do you owe the taxpayers, who are paying your salary? If you work for a consultant hired by a town, the question is essentially the same. How much loyalty do you owe the political body that pays your consulting fee rather than some other group or cause? If you cannot give full loyalty to the client who pays your fee, is it right that you take the fee? These are not easily answered questions.

The advent of advocacy planning should be viewed in the context of the 1960s, a time when the Civil Rights movement was confronting America with the history of racism and the Vietnam War was splitting the nation in half. At present there are still a certain number of planners who see themselves as advocacy planners, but the movement passed its peak many years ago.

PLANNING FROM RIGHT AND LEFT

In this section we discuss ideologically based criticisms of planning—both the idea of planning and planning as actually practiced. The reader will note that there is a certain amount of national or systemwide material in this section. This larger focus is necessary because much of the ideological debate about planning, even as practiced in small jurisdictions, is based on different views of the nation's political and economic system.

The right-wing criticism that falls on city, town, or regional planning does so largely because planning in that particular sense happens to be in the general target area. Specifically, almost any sort of public planning requires some replacement of signals from the marketplace with the calculations of planners, technicians, bureaucrats, and others. For example, we noted earlier how zoning may interfere with the workings of the market by preventing those uses that, in a pure market situation, the property owner would choose on the basis of profitability. The person on the right, almost by definition, is one who is convinced of the wisdom of markets and of the efficacy of Adam Smith's "invisible hand." He or she is likely to see the inefficiency and loss of personal freedom in centrally planned economies not as accidents but as inevitable concomitants of excessive central control and of insufficient reliance on markets. With such a general worldview, one is likely to view specific instances of planning with a degree of suspicion.

The criticism from the left, in contrast, has not been directed at the idea of planning. The replacement of some market decision making by political decision making is part of the agenda of the left. A preference for planning and collective decision making as opposed to markets is one of the left's defining characteristics. Rather, the left's criticism has often been directed at municipal planning as currently practiced.

There is also another difference in the attacks from the right and the left. The criticism from the right, by and large, comes from people who are not trained as planners and who have not practiced as planners. This is hardly surprising, for if one disdains the idea of planning, one is not likely to become a planner. On the other hand, much of the criticism from the left comes from within the profession, not so much from practitioners but from planning educators—people who are trained in planning and who often have some experience as practitioners.

The View from the Right

The right-wing criticism makes two main points. First, it is argued that the marketplace does a better job of allocating resources than does planning. A modern economy involves thousands of different intermediate and final goods and, every day, millions of transactions. For this vast activity to be planned would require a degree of competence and foresight that it is unrealistic to expect from any organization. Then, too, it can be argued that performing this great task of planning would, beyond the issue of technical competence, make the virtually impossible demand that the planners know the preferences and interests of all those for whom they plan. The opponent of planning will argue that the market, because it is decentralized, requires no such knowledge of either objective facts or personal preferences. He or she would also argue that the decentralization of the marketplace permits more rapid adjustment to changes than does a centralized system.

Surpluses and shortages, price rises and falls send quick and unambiguous signals to suppliers of goods and services. Can anything unplanned provide both stability and easy adjustment to changed conditions? The free-market proponent would answer yes and might ask the doubter to consider an ecosystem such as a forest. No one planned it, yet it displays great stability over time, and should some external condition, say, the amount of rainfall, change, the ecosystem will change smoothly and quickly.

These arguments might be supplemented by comments on the administrative costs of central planning and the general slowness of bureaucratic decision making. Finally, the opponent of planning (the term here is used in its generic sense) might ask those who doubt his or her argument to consider the real world. Which economies seem to function smoothly, and which seem bedeviled with shortage and dislocations?

Perhaps more important to the proponent of the free market than efficiency is the view that economic and political freedom are inseparable. The conservative economist and Nobel Prize winner Milton Friedman argues,

> The kind of economic organization that provides economic freedom directly, namely, competitive capitalism, also promotes political freedom because it separates economic power from political power and in this way enables one to offset the other.
>
> Historical evidence speaks with a single voice on the relation between political freedom and a free market. I know of no example in time or place of a society that has been marked by a large measure of political freedom, and that has not also used something comparable to a free market to organize the bulk of economic activity.[13]

Note that Friedman's claim is a limited one. Although he states that the marketplace is necessary for political freedom, he does not state that it guarantees freedom—only that its absence guarantees the absence of freedom. Note, also, the phrase *bulk of economic activity*. He does not argue that all economic activity must be in the market sector for political freedom to prevail.

How might the planner of centrist political persuasion respond? One line of argument would be to grant the generality of the argument but point to two important caveats.

1. *Public goods.* Some goods and services must be provided outside the market because it is either impractical or impossible to create markets for them. National defense cannot be provided through market mechanisms because either everyone is defended or no one is defended. Therefore the nonpayer or "free rider" is as well served as the individual who pays. The lighthouse is often cited as a good that must be provided publicly because one is equally able to see the light whether one pays or does not pay. Since a market cannot be created, the good or service is either provided publicly or not at all. Other goods, such

as city streets, could, in principle, be provided through market mechanisms. But the difficulty of doing so renders the idea impractical.

2. *Externalities or spillovers.* If the good or service in question visits substantial effects on parties who are not represented in the transaction, the market, even though it produces optimal results when we consider only the interests of buyer and seller, will produce suboptimal results for society as a whole. As noted earlier, third-party effects related to land use are one of the principal justifications for zoning.

These ideas about public goods and externalities or spillovers are hardly radical and can be found in any standard economics text. They suggest that the market necessarily has its limits and thus that some degree of planning is inevitable. The issue, then, is not whether to plan or not to plan but rather how and how much to plan.

The planner might further argue that the conservative ought to favor timely public planning efforts on the grounds that dealing with problems early will alleviate the pressure for radical change later.[14] As we shall see, some radicals have castigated planners for performing exactly that function.

With regard to the issue of political freedom, the centrist might also grant the basic conservative argument but still raise an important caveat—that the sort of planning described in this book is hardly comparable to the sort of centralized planning that was practiced in the former Soviet Union. The difference in degree is so great as to constitute a real difference in kind. The word *planning* is applied to both, but we should not be misled by that semantic similarity.

In summary, the centrist could argue that he or she can agree with the right in its general view of central planning and the relationship between economic and political freedom. Yet he or she can still argue that in a capitalist democracy like the United States, planning is a necessary and useful activity.

The View from the Left

In the 1970s the planning profession and planning as practiced began to come under heavy criticism from the political far left. Much of the attack came from what might loosely be called neo-Marxism. Marxist theories made a comeback in academe during the 1970s and 1980s. The radical might argue that this was due to their inherent virtue. The skeptic might respond that the cause was historical, namely, the radicalizing effect of the Vietnam War.

The radical position was not a majority position among planning educators, but it was much more common among planning educators than among planning practitioners. One reason is that in a great many planning jobs, although not all, radicals would feel uncomfortable because they would be cooperating with a system that they did not respect and achieving ends to which they could not feel committed. That sort of psychological dissonance is not easy to live with.

What was the radical view? America's liberal capitalism, or welfare capitalism as it has been called, is regarded rather dimly (though many radicals will concede it to be more humane than the capitalism of earlier years). Radicals saw it as containing vast and inexcusable extremes of wealth and poverty and as largely dominated by and therefore run for the benefit of the capitalist class (bourgeoisie). They also believed that the working class, or the "masses," accept the system largely because they have been prevented from seeing the truth by those who control the flow of information and ideas. In this view the media and the educational system disguise reality and convey a picture that is favorable to the interests of the capitalists because they are owned or controlled by or in some way beholden to the capitalists. Planners, inadvertently or otherwise, cooperate in this process by *depoliticizing*—that is, converting what should be political issues into technical questions, thus *co-opting* those with serious grievances against the system.[15] It is therefore a view that is profoundly cynical about planning and about our society as it now exists.

How might the centrist respond? He or she might begin simply by questioning the most basic assumptions of the critique. For example, he or she might assert the basic goodness rather than badness of the system, perhaps by comparing it with other systems. He or she might argue that the amenability of the system to a long series of reforms and ameliorative measures, from the abolition of child labor to food stamps for the poor, says something very positive about the system. If one finds the system to be good, on balance, then one should have no overarching problems of conscience in cooperating with it. The centrist might attack the radical critique by asserting the pluralism of society. Although admitting that capitalists do indeed exercise much influence over the state, the centrist might note that other groups, including labor, academe, federal and local government workers, and so on, also exercise major influence over the actions of the state. He or she might thus deny the basic Marxist postulate that the state is the "executive committee" of the bourgeoisie. If it is true that the state, by virtue of this pluralism, does not confine its services in the main to a single small class, there is little reason to be troubled about serving it.

The centrist might argue that the radical critique regarding the planner as a co-opter or a disarmer of discontent is not a very strong argument. Rather, it is an obvious truth cast in a negative way. If one satisfies grievances, whether they be about poverty, housing, or some much smaller matter such as street noise or the need for a new stoplight at the corner, of course one is reducing discontent. But what is wrong with that? Should we deny food to the hungry lest when their stomachs are full, they will lose their righteous anger about being hungry?

The centrist might also agree with the radical that the planner does indeed depoliticize and cast what could be political issues in technical terms. But does not reducing the political heat and introducing some facts and numbers increase the chances of rational solutions? In short, is not depoliticizing a good thing to do?

Finally, the centrist might note that the radical academic who takes the planning profession to task for not waging the fight for radical change is asking the working planner to take risks that he or she is not required to take. As planning educator Michael Brooks has said,

> Certainly the progressive spirit thrives more readily in the halls of academe—where there is virtually no risk attached to its espousal—than it does in the nation's city halls.[16]

The radical critique unsettled many planners, for many people go into the profession out of idealism. Thus a critique that accuses the profession of allowing itself to be used as the tool of an unjust system tends to cause some soul-searching and psychic pain. To the extent that such pain causes productive introspection, it is useful. To the extent that it demoralizes, it is destructive. The critique just described never gained much ground with practitioners for reasons noted earlier. Its heyday among academicians is also past, though one still hears echoes of it. The tide of academic Marxism peaked sometime in the late 1970s or perhaps in the early 1980s and has receded since then. The overwhelming popular repudiation of the socialist dream in Eastern Europe during the 1980s, and then the collapse of the Soviet Union in 1991, drained much conviction out of Marxism in the West.

In the last two decades of the twentieth century and for much of the first decade of this century, the political pendulum in the United States swung to the right. At least some planners were happy simply not to lose ground, whether that was in court, in property rights-type referenda, or in the public anger after the *Kelo* decision. At this time the radical critique is more a matter of historical and theoretical interest than one of immediate practical concern.

SUMMARY

Approaches to the act of planning are (1) the rational model, (2) disjointed incrementalism, (3) a middle-range approach as exemplified by "mixed scanning," and (4) collaborative rationality.

The rational model prescribes a comprehensive approach, which begins with problem definition and proceeds through value clarification to selection of goals, formulation of alternative possible actions, forecasting the consequences of those actions, selection of a course of action, detailed plan formulation, and evaluation and modification. The model is comprehensive and systematic. It is designed to begin at square one and proceed to an optimum choice of actions. The model can be regarded as the orthodox view. It has been subjected to a variety of criticisms. Some have asserted that it is unrealistic and may ignore valid interests and considerations that would be taken into account in a planning process that placed less emphasis on system and optimization and more on reaching agreement among disparate and contending parties.

The incremental approach, of which Charles Lindblom is the best-known proponent, stresses reaching agreement, making incremental adjustments, and relying on precedent. For reasons discussed at length, he suggests that the use of the rational model is often neither possible nor wise.

The mixed scanning introduced by Amitai Etzioni is essentially a synthesis of these two approaches. It involves a less than complete scan of the situation followed by the application of a comprehensive approach to only parts of the total problem. It has been generally well received by planners, in part because it appears to describe a process that many planners actually follow.

Collaborative planning, the newest of the four approaches, emphasizes inclusion of as many stakeholders as possible and an extended period of "authentic dialogue." Its proponents see it as less hierarchical than the rational model process and as giving somewhat less weight to technical expertise and more to the interests, feelings, experience, and intuitions of stakeholders.

Criticism of planning from the right has generally been based on a view that market mechanisms are more efficient allocators of resources than are administrative decisions. Some antipathy on the right also stems from the view that political freedom is most likely to flourish in an environment in which decisions about the allocation of resources are made privately rather than collectively.

Criticism of planning from the left has not been directed at planning as an idea but rather at the manner in which planning is perceived to be done in the United States. Specifically, radicals have claimed that planning as practiced supports the interest of the capitalist class (which the left sees as the dominant class) and that it papers over major injustices and disparities in wealth and power with minor reforms and palliatives.

The chapter suggests the manner in which the planner of a more or less centrist ideological persuasion might respond to criticisms from right and left. How one views planning cannot be separated from one's overall political and ideological position.

NOTES

1. John Maynard Keynes, *The General Theory of Employment, Interest and Money,* first published in 1936. The quote is from the last page of the final chapter.

2. This example is taken, with some modification, from Edward C. Banfield, "Ends and Means in Planning," in *A Reader in Planning Theory*, Andreas Faludi, ed., Pergamon Press, New York, 1973.

3. For a description of the rational model, see Martin Meyerson and Edward C. Banfield, "Supplement: Note on Conceptual Scheme," *Politics, Planning and the Public Interest*, The Free Press, Glencoe, IL, 1955, pp. 314ff.

4. The term was invented by Herbert Simon. See his *Administrative Behavior*, Macmillan & Co., New York, 1955.

5. Charles E. Lindblom, "The Science of Muddling Through," *Public Administration Review*, Spring 1959. Reprinted in Faludi, *Planning Theory*, p. 163.

6. A commonly cited example of this sort of contradiction is federal housing policy. We have, over the years, spent many billions of federal funds through Urban Renewal, Community Development, Urban Development Action Grants, housing subsidies, and the like to restore the economic vitality of central cities. We also have a federal tax code that provides very powerful incentives to the construction of suburban housing. To some degree the contradictions may exist because we do not have a unified planning process for federal urban policy. The committees that write the tax law, for example, are not the same as the committees that write the housing and economic development legislation, nor is there any statutory requirement that they consult each other.

7. Lindblom, "Muddling Through."

8. Ibid.

9. Amitai Etzioni, "Mixed Scanning: A 'Third' Approach to Decision Making," in Faludi, *Planning Theory*, pp. 217–230.

10. Judith E. Innes and David E. Booher, *Planning with Complexity: An Introduction to Collaborative Rationality for Public Policy,*

Routledge, Taylor and Francis Group, London and New York, 2010, chap. 3. See also Judith E. Innes, David E. Booher, and Sarah DiVittorio, "Strategies for Megaregion Governance: Collaborative Dialogue, Networks and Self-Organization," *Journal of the American Planning Association*, Vol. 77, no. 1, Winter 2011, pp. 55–68; and Reid Ewing, "Research You Can Use." *Planning*, February 2011, p. 35.

11. Paul Davidoff, "Advocacy and Pluralism in Planning," *Journal of the American Planning Association*, vol. 31, no. 4, November 1965.

12. This view is similar to that expressed by the widely cited philosopher John Rawls, that how just a society is should be judged by how it treats the least fortunate of its members. See his *A Theory of Justice*, Belknap Press of Harvard University, Cambridge, MA, 1971.

13. Milton Friedman, *Capitalism and Freedom*, University of Chicago Press, Chicago, 1962.

14. For example, it has often been suggested that the reformist initiatives such as unemployment insurance, the right to collective bargaining, and the Social Security system during the Great Depression of the 1930s may well have prevented radical social change in the United States.

15. For a statement of this view at the time it was widely expressed see Norman I. Fainstein and Susan S. Fainstein, "New Debates in Urban Planning: The Impact of Marxist Theory Within the U.S.," *International Journal of Urban and Regional Research*, vol. 3, no. 3, 1979, pp. 381–402. Reprinted in *Critical Readings in Planning Theory*, Chris Paris, ed., Pergamon Press, New York, 1982, pp. 147–174.

16. Michael Brooks, "Four Critical Junctures in the History of the Urban Planning Profession," *Journal of the American Planning Association*, Spring 1988, pp. 241–248.

SELECTED BIBLIOGRAPHY

BIRCH, EUGENIE L., ED., *The Urban and Regional Planning Reader*, Routledge, New York, 2008.

BROOKS, MICHAEL P., *Planning Theory for Practitioners*, Planners Press, American Planning Association, Chicago, 2002.

FALUDI, ANDREAS, ED., *A Reader in Planning Theory*, Pergamon Press, New York, 1973.

FRIEDMAN, JOHN, *Planning in the Public Domain*, Princeton University Press, Princeton, NJ, 1987.

MEYERSON, MARTIN, and BANFIELD, EDWARD C., *Politics, Planning and the Public Interest*, The Free Press, Glencoe, IL, 1955.

STEIN, JAY M., ED., *Classic Readings in Urban Planning: An Introduction*, McGraw-Hill, Inc., New York, 1995.

INDEX

Abrams, Charles, 216
Acid rain, 314
Advocacy planning, 99
Affordable housing issues, 80–82, 222–224, 286–87
Agriculture, 22, 362, 309, 366–367
Air quality, 88, 254, 311–315
All-American Canal, 363
Amendment 37 (Colorado), 316
American Institute of Certified Planners, 6
American League for Civic Improvement, 35
American Planning Association (APA), 5, 78
American Recovery and Reinvestment Act, 318
Americans with Disabilities Act, 95
AmTrak, 239–40
Appalachian region, 265
Architectural review, 164
Arcosanti, AZ, 201
Asia, fertility rates 4–14
Arizona 207, 84
Atlanta Region Metropolitan Planning Commission, 354
Authorities (organizations), 344
See also Port Authority of New York and New Jersey
Automobiles/automobile ownership: boomburg phenomenon and, 24; in Eastern Europe, 402; emission standards, 312; fuel economy, 258; suburbanization and, 17, 18; technology of, 257–9; urban design and, 204–5

Baby boom, 18, 118
Baltimore, MD, 217, 222
Bartholomew, Keith, 262
Bassett, Edward M., 42, 74
Battery Park City, 173–175
Beltline, Atlanta, 243
Beltways, 242, 371
Benefit/cost analysis, 262–263
Berman v. Parker, 83
Blakely, Edward, 112
Booher, David E., 432
Bonds, 136–38
Boomburgs, 23–25
Bosselman, Fred, 167, 283
Boston, MA, 229
Boulder, CO, 286

Boulder Dam, 363
Broad Acre City, 191, 199, 204
Bronx River Parkway, 17, 370
Brooks, Michael, 440
Brownfields, 324–325
Brundtland Commission, 298
Bureau of Public Roads.
See Federal Highway Administration
Bureau of Reclamation, 362
Burnham, Daniel, 39, 40, 42
Bush, George W., 316–317
Bus Rapid Transit, 252–253

Calgary, Alberta, 182
California High-Speed Rail Authority, 239
Callies, David, 167
Calthorpe, Peter, 190
Canary Wharf, 389
Cap and trade system, 319
Capital improvements, 136–38
Carbon dioxide sequestration, 333
Carson, Rachel, 59
Carter, Jimmy, 266
Case-Shiller index, 226
Central-city shrinkage, 19–21
Central Park (New York), 33
China, 416, 419
Chicago, IL: Columbian Exposition of 1893, 37, 39; Plan of Chicago, 38–40, 69, 93, 343
Chicago Area Transportation Study, 58, 244–245
Chlorofluorocarbons, 314
Chu, Steven, 318
City Beautiful movement, 37–38
City Realty Corporation, 211
Civic art, 36
Civil Rights movement, 105
Clean Air Act, 59, 88, 314–15
Clean Water Act, 88, 314
Climate change, 308–311
Clinton, William J., 316
The Closing Circle (Commoner), 59
Cluster zoning, 157–158
Coal technologies, 316, future of, 333
Coastal Area Facility Review Act, 293
Coastal Zone Management Act, 323
Cohort survival population forecast, 126
Collateralized Debt Obligations, 227
Collaborative Rationality, 432–34

Colleges, land-grant, 360
Colorado River Compact, 363
Columbian Exposition of 1893, 37, 39
Commoner, Barry, 59
Community development, 218–221
Community Development Block Grants, 218, 225
Community Reinvestment Act, 228
Comprehensive plan/planning, 122–134; effectiveness of, 132–133; goals, 122–124; implementation, 129–130; plan formulation, 129; process, 124–132; rational model and, research, 125–128; review updating, 130–131, citizen participation, 131
Concurrency requirements, 291
Condemnation award, 70
Constitutional framework for planning, 68–70
Consultants, 101–102
Corporate Average Fuel Economy (CAFE) standards, 88, 318
Councils of Governments (COGs), 345–347
Credit Default Swaps, 227
Créteil, France, 392
Cul de sacs, 190

Dams, 363–364
Davidoff, Paul, 99, 434–35
Davis, CA, 327
Decentralization, 14–15
DeGrove, John M., 290
Demand response systems, 238
Development agreements, 159
Dillon's rule, 69–70
Disaster planning, 63–65, 115–16
Disjointed incrementalism, 429–30
Dolan v. City of Tigard (1994), 79
Doxiadis, Konstantinos, 419
Duany, Andres, 160, 187–89, 192
Dulles Toll Road, 256
Dust bowl, 363
Dynamic tolling, 257

Easement, 142
Eastern European planning, 408–414; EU membership and, 413–14; privatization and, 413; Soviet planning style, 408–9; transition to a market economy, 410–13

Economic development, 61, 262–79; assessment of consequences of, 276; cooperation and competition, 270; federal presence in, 264–67; historic roots, 263–64; infrastructure, 273; land-use controls, 274; sales and promotion efforts, 271; state efforts in, 267–68; subsidization, 271–72; systematic approach to, 277–78; Urban Renewal and, 213
Economic development administration, 265
Edge city, 193–200
Eisenhower, Dwight D., 370
Electric power, solar, 338
Electric vehicles, 258
Elliot, Donald L., 163
Embarcadero Freeway, 250
Eminent domain, 71, 82–84, 211
Employment: housing and, 343, 375
Energy Policy Act, 317
Energy production, consumption, U.S., 331
Energy planning, 59, 331–33
Energy security, 377
Environmental assessment, 321–23
Environmental impact statement, 59, 321–23
Environmental planning, 59–61, 307–40 See also Environmental policy; Sustainable development; analysis of physical environment, 327–330; environmental justice, 117; example, 327–330; global climate change and, 308–311; goals, 307; growth management and, 277; intergovernment context of, 321–22; national progress in, 311–12; NEPA process, 321
Environmental policy, 314–21; in Bush administration, 316–17; friendly criticism, 325–26; in Obama administration, 317–18; unfriendly criticism, 326–27
Environmental Protection Agency (EPA), 59, 314
Environmental racism, 117
Ethanol, 317
Erie Canal, 263
Etzioni, Amitai, 431–32
Euclid (Village of) *v. Ambler Realty Co.*, 75

Europe. *See* Eastern European planning; Western European planning; specific country
European Union (EU), 413–14
Ewing, Reid, 262, 295–96
Exactions, 159–60, 286
Exclusionary zoning, 80–82

Fairfax County, VA, 196, 287
Fannie Mae, 228, 372–73
Federal Aid Highway Act, 370
Federal Aid Road Act, 369
Federal government role, in local planning, 86–89
Federal grants, 54, 86–87, 138, 265, 370
Federal Highway Administration, 369
Federal Housing Administration (FHA), 55
Feminism and planning, 118
Financial Crisis of 2008, 226–29
Finland, 403
First Pacific Railway Act, 361
Fiscal impact analysis, 128, 146
Flood plain zoning, 64
Floor area ratio, 141,158
Florida growth management, 290–91
Foreclosures, 230–232
Form-based zoning. *See* Zoning
Fort Collins, CO, 157, 288
Foster, Norman, 203
France, planning in, 390–394
Freddie Mac, 228
Freedom Tower (NYC), 177–78
Fracking, 333, 373
Friedan, Betty, 118
Fuel cells, 258
Fukushima, 320
Fuller, R. Buckminster, 199

"Garden cities," 48–50
Garreau, Joel, 193–94
Gender issues in planning, 118
General plan. *See* Comprehensive plan/planning
Gentrification, 215
Geoengineering, 310
Geographic Information Systems, 126–27
George Washington Bridge, 350–52
Germany, planning in, 403–408
Glendenning, Parris, 295
Grants, 138–39
Gravier, Jean Français, 390
Gravity model, 246–47
Great Britain, planning in, 382–390
Great Depression, 54–56

Greenbelt concept, 384–86
Green building movement, 335–336
Greenfields, 325–26
Greenhouse effect, 308–311
Green Valley, NV, 112
Greenwich Village (NYC), 152
Greer, Guy, 211
"Gridiron" pattern, 30
Group homes, 107
Growth management, 60, 280–306; defined, 280; examples of, 285–89; origins of, 282–84; state level, 289–294

Hackensack Meadowlands Development Commission, 293–94
Hadacheck v. Sebastian, 72
HafenCity, Germany, 407–08
Hall, Peter, 385, 388, 396
Hansen, Alvin, 211
Haussmann, Baron, 97, 171–72
Hawaii, land-use controls, 289
Helsinki, Finland, 403
High Line (NYC), 154–56
High-occupancy toll lanes, 256–57
Highway Act of 1954, 244
Highways: expansion of, 18, 58; pattern of development and, 166; planning, 58; public expenditures and land development, 136
Highway Trust Fund, 241, 370
Historic preservation, 164
Holding-zones, 287
Home Affordable Modification Program (HAMP), 231
Homelessness, 113–15
Home rule legislation, 69
Homestead Act of 1862, 360
Homesteading (urban), 219
Hoover Dam, 363
HOT lanes, 257
Housing, 223–228; abandonment, 231–32; bubble, 226–30; federal government and, 55, 228, 372–75; group homes, 107; industrial revolution and, 10; low- and moderate-income, 223–25; planning for, 223–26; reform, 34–5; social issues, 106–7; in Third World, 417–19
Housing plans, 223–26
Housing Act of 1949, 211, 213
Housing and Community Development Act, 218
Housing and Urban Development (HUD), 225
Howard, Ebenezer, 48–51

Hubbert's peak, 332
Hurricane Katrina, 64, 369
Hybrid vehicles, 258
Hydroelectric power, 363–64

Ickes, Harold, 54
Immigration, 21
Inclusionary zoning, 156
Incremental planning, 429–30
Incubator buildings, 274
India, 418–19
Induced demand, traffic, 249
Industrial Revenue Bonds, 265
Industrial revolution, 10
Infill development, 291, 296
Infrastructure: economic development and, 274; studies, 126
Inner Harbor (Baltimore), 216
Innes, Judith E., 432
Intelligent vehicle technology, 257–58
Intercity rail transportation, 239–41
ISTEA, 253
Interstate Highway System, 55, 58
Irvine Spectrum (CA), 195

Jacobs, Jane, 150
Jepson, Edward J. Jr., 302

Kamen, Dean, 259
Kelo v. New London (2005), 84, 211
Kentlands (MD), 192
Keynes, John Maynard, 423
Kohn Pederson Fox, 416
Krumholz, Norman, 116

Labor markets, 264–65, 276
La Defense (Paris), 393
Laguna West, CA, 191
Land grant colleges, 360
Land grants to railroads, 361–62
Land-use controls. *See* Zoning
Land-use inventory, 126–27
Land-use planning, and energy, 334–35
Land value, accessibility and, 135, 36
Lang, Robert, 23
Largo, FL, 158
Leadership in Energy and Environmental Design (LEED), 335–36
Le Corbusier, 199–200
LEED program, 335–36
Lefurgy, Jennifer, 23
L'Enfant, Pierre Charles, 30
Letchworth, England, 49
Limited-access highway, 17
Lindblom, Charles, 427–29

Local energy production, 337
London, England, 383, 386
Los Angeles County, CA, 46, 315
Lucas v. South Carolina Coastal Council (1992), 78
Lynch, Kevin, 179

Mac Pherson v. DAS, 78
Mandated responsibilities, 90–91
Manufacturing, 10, 270
Maryland smart growth program, 293–98
Masdar, 203
Master plan. *See* Comprehensive plan/planning
"Master-planned" communities, 111
McCall, Thomas, 292
McMillan Commission, 38
Measure 37 (Oregon), 77
Metropolitan planning: Atlanta Regional Commission, 354–56; historical overview, 343–47; Minneapolis-St. Paul, 347–49; political elements, 341–43; Port Authority of NY and NJ, 349–54; post WWII, 345–47
Metropolitan Washington Council of Governments, 346
Middle-range models, 431–33
Milton Keynes, England, 387
Minneapolis, MN, 181–83, 347–49
Mixed scanning, 431–32
Morrill Land Grant Act, 360
Mortgage: defaults, 229–32; insurance, 53, 373–74
Mortgage Electronic Registration System (MERS), 230
Moses, Robert, 97, 351
Mt. Laurel II and III, 81–2
Mugler v. Kansas (1887), 72
Mumford, Lewis, 49
Municipal art movement, 36
Municipal improvement, 35–37
Municipal planning, expansion of, 57

National Ambient Air Quality Standards, 315
National Association of Regional Councils, 346
National Defense Highway Act of 1956, 18, 58, 244
National Environmental Policy Act (NEPA), 59, 311, 314
National Forest designations, 368
National League of Improvement Associations, 35
National parks, 375

National planning (U.S.), 358–379; housing financing and taxation, 372–75; ideology, 358; Interstate Highway System, 369–72; land management, 375–76; land settlement pattern, 359–60; rail network, 361–63; systematic regional planning, 366–69; water use in West, 362–66
National Railroad Passenger Corp., 239
National Resources Planning Board, 56
Natural disasters, planning for, 63–65
Natural gas, 332, 377
Neighborhood concept, 184–87
Neotraditional design, 187–93
Netherlands, 395–99
New England Regional Commission, 56
New Jersey growth management, 292–94; Meadowlands, 293
Newman, Peter, 396
New Orleans and Hurricane Katrina, 64–5
New Source Review, 317
New towns, 55, 384–85
New urbanism, 50, 187–193
New York City, 24; Central Park, 33; High Line, 154–56; housing reform, 34; Landmarks Preservation Commission, 75; Manhattan as cultural center, 215; population growth, 11, 21; Port Authority and, 349–53; Robert Moses and, 97; zoning and, 72–4
Nixon, Richard, 314
Nolen, John, 45
Nollan v. California Coastal Commission (1987), 78
Nonresident rights, 80–82
Norris, George, 367
Nuclear power, 320

Obama, Barack, 317–320
Oglethorpe, James, 28, 29
Oil imports, prices, 59, 332
Olmsted, Frederick Law, 33, 34, 37
Ordinance of 1785, 359
Oregon growth management, 290
Oregonians in Action, 77
Outsourcing, 18

Pacific Northwest Regional Planning Commission, 56
Palazzolo v. Rhode Island (2001), 79

Palm Desert, CA, 338
Paratransit, 238
Paris, France, 97, 391; Haussmann boulevard designs, 171–72; Voisin plan, 199–200
Parks, 33, 342
Peak oil, 332
Penn, William, 29, 31
Penn Central Transportation Company v. New York City, 75
Perry, Clarence, 184
Philadelphia, PA, 29–31
Pinelands Commission, 294
Planned communities, 110–13
Planned unit development (PUD), 157
Planners: backgrounds, 4; government-employed, 5; salaries, 6; job satisfaction/ discontents, 6–7; power and, 93–94; professional roles, 98–99; useful abilities, 7
Planning. *See also* Planning, history of: advocacy, 434–35; agencies, 100–101; citizen participation in, 95–97; consultants, 101–102; land-use (*see* Land-use controls; Zoning); legal basis of (*see* Legal framework); national (*see* National planning (U.S.)); political nature of, 91–104; process, 425; styles, 98–99; theory. (*see* Chapter 19)
Planning, history of: birth of modern city planning, 38–40; City Beautiful movement, 36–38; colonial America, 28–30; disaster planning, 63–65; economic development planning, 61; environmental planning, 58–60; Great Depression, 53–56; growth control and growth management, 60; highway planning, 58, Chapter 12; housing reform, 33–34; postwar period, 58–64; public safety, 65–66; regional and state planning, 44–46; smart growth, 61–2; statewide planning, 60; Urban Renewal, 57
Planning commissions, 42
Planning District Commissions (Virginia), 346
Plan of Chicago, 38–40
Platinum Mile (Westchester County, NY), 165

Plus 15, 182
Pod and collector system, 189–90
Police power, in land-use control, 71
Pollution. *See also* Environmental issues and planning: air, 313–14; expenditures for control of, 312
Population: growth control and management, 60; 19th century density of, 11–14; redistribution of, in 20th century, 15–17; regional, 19, 20; in Asia, 414–15
Population forecast, 126
Population pyramids, Asia, 415
Port Authority of New York and New Jersey, 47, 349–54
Port Newark-Elizabeth Marine Terminal, 351–52
Poverty: economic development planning and, 61; housing reform and, 34; urbanization of, 21–22
Prague, 411
Priority Funding Areas (Maryland), 297
Prisons, 275
Private communities, 110–13
Private property: public control issues, 40–44, 72–79 zoning, 41–42
Professional organizations, 5–6
Proffers, 283
"Property led" development, 389
Property rights, tradition of, 95
Property taxes, 148–49; land-use planning and, 348; local economic development and, 269; tax treatment of 374
Proposition 13, 61, 92
Pruitt-Igoe public housing (St. Louis), 106
Public authority, 334–35
Public Choice Theory, 87
Public goods, 437
Public health, and urban congestion, 12, 14
Public housing, 34, 106 Pruitt-Igoe, 106; Yonkers, NY, 107–110
Public safety, 62–63, 123
Public transportation, planning, 237–240. *See also* Transportation

Radburn, NJ, 43
Rail transportation: intercity, 239–40; urbanization and, 11–12; U.S. development and, 361–62

Ramapo, NY, 283
Randstad Holland, 398
Rational model, 425–429
Reagan, Ronald, 61
Reclamation Act of 1902, 362
Reed, Thomas, 354
Reform: housing, 32–34; sanitary, 31–3; urban congestion and, 12–14; urban open space, 33–34
Regional Contribution Agreement, 81
Regional Plan Association, 45
Regional planning, 45–47; agencies, 343–47; in Depression era, 59; in Germany, 406; New York City region, 45–47
Regulation (mandated responsibilities), 88
Reisner, Marc, 364
Renewable energy, 333
Rent controls, 224
Resettlement Administration, 55
Reston, VA, 111, 186
Restrictive zoning, 80–82
Retirement communities, 111
Riverside, IL, 34
Revolving loan funds, 274
Roanoke, VA, 220
Robosigning, 230
Roosevelt, Franklin D., 56, 367
Roosevelt, Theodore, 364
Rural Heritage program (Maryland), 298

SAFETEA-LU Act, 254, 256
"Sagebrush Rebellion," 326
Sand, Leonard B., 109
San Francisco, CA, 160
Sanitary reform, 31–33
Sarasota-Bradenton, Florida, 24
Savannah, GA, 28, 29
Scandinavia, 399–403
Schumacher, Ernest F., 283
Securitization, 277
Segway, 259
Separation of powers, 94
September 11 terrorist attacks, 62
Sewers, 31, 127, 342
Shell buildings, 273
Silent Spring (Carson), 59
Site-plan review, 163
"Sites and services" housing approach, 417
Skyscrapers, 12, 73, 199–202
Skyways, 182, 183
Smart growth, 61, 295–98
Smart highway, 257

Smith, Alfred E., 349
Social housing, 381
Social issues, 105–21; aging, 118–19; with economic development, 116; environmental policy, 117; feminism, 118; gender, 118; homelessness, 115–16; housing, 106–10; planning for catastrophe, 115; private communities, 110–14; social planners, 119; transportation planning, 116
Sofia, Bulgaria, 412
Soil studies, 127
Solar energy, 333, 335, 338
Soleri, Paolo, 202
Solid waste disposal, 327–331
Solyndra, 320
Songdo, S. Korea, 417
South Coast Air Quality Management District, 315
South Korea, 414–17
Southern Burlington NAACP vs. Mt. Laurel (NJ) (1975), 81–82
Spillovers, 438
St. Paul, MN, 347–49
Stamford, CT, 217
Standard Enabling Act, 42
State constitutions, 69
State implementation plans, 88, 322
State planning, 47
Stockholm, Sweden, 400, 401
Structural unemployment, 61, 264–65
Subdivision regulations, 140
Suburbanization, 14, 15, 16–18; feminist views on, 118; growth management and, 281; neotraditional planning, 187–88, 191–192; pod and collector plan, 189–90; postwar, 58; suburban sprawl, 295–96; tax policy, 373–75
Suffolk County, NY, 142
Sulfur dioxide, 319
Superfund, 325
Supreme Court of the U.S., 54, 75, 78–9
Sustainable development, 298–303; goals, 299; local implementation, 301–02; planning techniques, 302–03; social equity and, 299–300
Sweden, 400–02

Tahoe-Sierra case (2002), 79
"Takings," 72–73, 77–81
Tallahassee, FL, 159

Tapiola, Finland, 403
Taxes: low-income housing incentives, 222; property, 148–49; special tax treatment, 142; suburbanization and tax policy, 372–75
Tax-exempt bonds, 138, 265
Tax increment financing, 272
Taxpayer Relief Act, 374
Tax Reform Act of 1986, 374
Tenement House Act (1901), 34
Tennessee Valley Authority (TVA), 56, 366–69
Terrorism, 62-3
Thatcher, Margaret, 382
Theory, 423–42; advocacy planning, 434–35; disjointed incrementalism, 429–30; middle-range models, 431–32; rational model, 425–29
Thornley, Andy, 396
Toll roads, 255–57
Toxic Substances Control Act, 59
Traffic: congestion, 295; flow, 187–88; metering techniques, 257
Transfer of development rights, 153–56
Transit-oriented development (TOD), 190–91
Transportation: federal role in, 253–54; financing, 237–38; Gravity model, 247; inter-city rail, 239–40; Interstate Highway System, 369–72; land-use planning and, 127, 241–43; planning process, 243–51; policy decision, 248–51; public transportation planning, 251–53; recent trends, 238; reduction of energy consumption in, 258, 334; regional planning approach, 342; smart highway and intelligent vehicles, 257–58; social issues and planning of, 116; tolls and privatization, 255–59; traffic congestion and suburban sprawl, 296; transportation system management, 254–55; travel demand management, 255–56; urbanization and, 10, 11
Transportation Concurrency Exemption Areas, 291
Transportation Equity Act for the Twenty First Century, 254
Triborough Bridge and Tunnel Authority, 351

Tucker, William, 114
Tugwell, Rexford, 54
Tyson's Corner, VA, 196–99

United States Green Building Council, 335
Urban design: automobiles and, 204–05; city of future, 200–04; defined, 172–73; edge city, 193–96; goals, 184; neighborhood concept, 184–87; neotraditional, 187–193; pod and collector plan, 188–90
Urban Development Corporation (UDC), 389
Urban Growth Boundaries, 292
Urban homesteading, 219
Urbanization: boomburg phenomenon, 23–25; central-city shrinkage, 19–21; decentralization, 14–15; in 19th century, 9–15; poverty and, 22–23; recent population growth, 23–24; regional trends, 19, 20; suburbia, 18–19; trends since 2000, 21, 23
Urban Mass Transit Act, 345
Urban Renewal, 57, 173, 209–17; *versus* community development approach, 219–21; conceptual basis for, 57; economic development and, 214; eminent domain and, 211; funding, 211; homelessness and, 114; loss of low-income housing during, 213; origins of, 208–9; in retrospect, 210–12, 214–17; transportation planning and, 116
U.S. Constitution, 68–70

Vaux, Calvin, 33
Veiller, Lawrence, 35
Verchick, Robert R.M., 64, 115–16
Verrazano Bridge (NY), 351
Veterans Administration, 373
Vietnam War, 105
Village of Euclid v. Ambler Realty Co., 75
Ville Radieuse, 199
Virginia planning commissions, 85–86
Voisin plan, Paris, 200

Wallace, Henry, 54
Washington, D.C.: City Beautiful movement, 38; L'Enfant plan for, 31–32

Water: irrigation, 362; planning, 87, 350; "prior appropriation," 365; shortages in western U.S., 362–66; supply, 127

Water Resources Development Act, 365

Water supply and Western United States, 362–66

Waxman-Markey bill, 319

Weber, Adna, 10

Wells, H. G., 14–15

Welwyn Garden City, England, 49

Westchester County, NY, 45

Western European planning, 380–403

Westway highway project (NYC), 250

White Plains, NY, 165, 215

Whyte, William, 182

"Wise Use" movement, 327

World Trade Center reconstruction, 177–78

Wright, Frank Lloyd, 191, 199, 204

Yonkers, NY, 107–110, 150

Zero population growth, 60

Zoning, 141–63; bonus or incentive, 151; cluster, 157–58; density bonuses, 151; economic development and, 274; effectiveness of, 143, 144–45; Euclidean, 75; flexibility, 149–59; form-based, 160–63; inclusionary, 156; limitations of, 145–47; ordinances, 41–42, 143–45, performance zoning, 158–59; popularity of, 141–42; property taxes and, 147–48; "saturation studies," 150; suburban, 188; transfer of development rights, 152–56